Treaty Series

Treaties and international agreements registered or filed and recorded with the Secretariat of the United Nations

VOLUME 3208

Recueil des Traités

Traités et accords internationaux enregistrés ou classés et inscrits au répertoire au Secrétariat de l'Organisation des Nations Unies

United Nations • Nations Unies
New York, 2026

Print ISBN: 978-92-1-003307-7
e-ISBN: 978-92-1-106851-1
ISSN: 0379-8267
e-ISSN: 2412-1495

TABLE OF CONTENTS

I

Treaties and international agreements registered in November 2017 Nos. 54750 to 54762

TABLE DES MATIÈRES

I

Traités et accords internationaux
enregistrés en novembre 2017
Nos 54750 à 54762

NOTE BY THE SECRETARIAT

Under Article 102 of the Charter of the United Nations, every treaty and every international agreement entered into by any Member of the United Nations after the coming into force of the Charter shall, as soon as possible, be registered with the Secretariat and published by it. Furthermore, no party to a treaty or international agreement subject to registration which has not been registered may invoke that treaty or agreement before any organ of the United Nations. The General Assembly, by resolution 97 (I), established regulations to give effect to Article 102 of the Charter (see text of the regulations, vol. 859, p. VIII; https://treaties.un.org/Pages/Resource.aspx?path=Publication/Regulation/Page1_en.xml).

The terms "treaty" and "international agreement" have not been defined either in the Charter or in the regulations, and the Secretariat follows the principle that it acts in accordance with the position of the Member State submitting an instrument for registration that, so far as that party is concerned, the instrument is a treaty or an international agreement within the meaning of Article 102. Registration of an instrument submitted by a Member State, therefore, does not imply a judgement by the Secretariat on the nature of the instrument, the status of a party or any similar question. It is the understanding of the Secretariat that its acceptance for registration of an instrument does not confer on the instrument the status of a treaty or an international agreement if it does not already have that status, and does not confer upon a party a status which it would not otherwise have.

*

* *

NOTE DU SECRÉTARIAT

Aux termes de l'Article 102 de la Charte des Nations Unies, tout traité ou accord international conclu par un Membre des Nations Unies après l'entrée en vigueur de la Charte sera, le plus tôt possible, enregistré au Secrétariat et publié par lui. De plus, aucune partie à un traité ou accord international qui aurait dû être enregistré mais ne l'a pas été ne pourra invoquer ledit traité ou accord devant un organe de l'Organisation des Nations Unies. Par sa résolution 97 (I), l'Assemblée générale a adopté un règlement destiné à mettre en application l'Article 102 de la Charte (voir texte du règlement, vol. 859, p. IX; https://treaties.un.org/Pages/Resource.aspx?path=Publication/Regulation/Page1_fr.xml).

Les termes « traité » et « accord international » n'ont été définis ni dans la Charte ni dans le règlement, et le Secrétariat a pris comme principe de s'en tenir à la position adoptée à cet égard par l'État Membre qui a présenté l'instrument à l'enregistrement, à savoir que, en ce qui concerne cette partie, l'instrument constitue un traité ou un accord international au sens de l'Article 102. Il s'ensuit que l'enregistrement d'un instrument présenté par un État Membre n'implique, de la part du Secrétariat, aucun jugement sur la nature de l'instrument, le statut d'une partie ou toute autre question similaire. Le Secrétariat considère donc que son acceptation pour enregistrement d'un instrument ne confère pas audit instrument la qualité de traité ou d'accord international si ce dernier ne l'a pas déjà, et qu'il ne confère pas à une partie un statut que, par ailleurs, elle ne posséderait pas.

*

* *

I

Treaties and international agreements registered in November 2017 Nos. 54750 to 54762

Traités et accords internationaux enregistrés en novembre 2017 Nos 54750 à 54762

No. 54750

Cyprus and Kuwait

Convention between the Government of the Republic of Cyprus and the Government of the State of Kuwait for the avoidance of double taxation and the prevention of fiscal evasion with respect to taxes on income and on capital. Kuwait City, 15 December 1984

Entry into force: *25 September 1986 by notification, in accordance with article 29*

Authentic text: *English*

Registration with the Secretariat of the United Nations: *Cyprus, 1 November 2017*

Chypre et Koweït

Convention entre le Gouvernement de la République de Chypre et le Gouvernement de l'État du Koweït tendant à éviter les doubles impositions et à prévenir la fraude fiscale en matière d'impôts sur le revenu et sur la fortune. Koweït, 15 décembre 1984

Entrée en vigueur : *25 septembre 1986 par notification, conformément à l'article 29*

Texte authentique : *anglais*

Enregistrement au Secrétariat de l'Organisation des Nations Unies : *Chypre, 1er novembre 2017*

[TEXT IN ENGLISH – TEXTE EN ANGLAIS]

C O N V E N T I O N

BETWEEN THE GOVERNMENT OF THE REPUBLIC OF CYPRUS AND THE GOVERNMENT OF THE STATE OF KUWAIT FOR THE AVOIDANCE OF DOUBLE TAXATION AND THE PREVENTION OF FISCAL EVASION WITH RESPECT TO TAXES ON INCOME AND ON CAPITAL.

The Government of the Republic of Cyprus and the Government of the State of Kuwait desiring to conclude a Convention for the Avoidance of Double Taxation and the Prevention of Fiscal Evasion with Respect to Taxes on Income and on Capital, have agreed as follows:

Article 1

PERSONAL SCOPE

This Convention shall apply to persons who are residents of one or both of the Contracting States.

Article 2

TAXES COVERED

1. This Convention shall apply to taxes on income and on capital imposed on behalf of each Contracting State or of its political subdivisions or local authorities, irrespective of the manner in which they are levied.

2. There shall be regarded as taxes on income and on capital all taxes imposed on total income, or on total capital, or on elements of income or of capital including taxes on gains from the alienation of movable or immovable property as well as taxes on the total amounts of wages or salaries paid by enterprises.

3. The existing taxes to which the Convention shall apply are:

(a) in Cyprus:
the income tax,
the special contribution, and
the capital gains tax
(hereinafter referred to as "Cyprus tax");

(b) in Kuwait:
corporate tax
(hereinafter referred to as "Kuwait tax").

4. This Convention shall also apply to any identical or substantially similar taxes which are imposed after the date of signature of this Convention in addition to, or in place of, the existing taxes. The competent authorities of the Contracting States shall notify to each other any significant changes which have been made in their respective taxation laws.

Article 3

GENERAL DEFINITIONS

1. In this Convention, unless the context otherwise requires:

(a) the term "Cyprus" means the Republic of Cyprus, and includes any area adjacent to the territorial waters of Cyprus which in accordance with international law has been or may hereafter be designated, under the laws of Cyprus concerning the Continental Shelf, as an area within which the rights of Cyprus with respect to the sea bed and sub-soil and their natural resources may be exercised;

(b) the term "Kuwait" means the State of Kuwait;

(c) the terms "a Contracting State" and "the other Contracting State" mean Cyprus and Kuwait as the context requires;

(d) the term "person" comprises an individual, a company and any other body;

(e) the term "company" means any body corporate or any entity which is treated as a body corporate for tax purposes;

(f) the terms "enterprise of a Contracting State" and "enterprise of the other Contracting State" mean, respectively, an enterprise carried on by a resident of a Contracting State and an enterprise carried on by a resident of the other Contracting State;

(g) the term "national" means:

(i) any individual possessing the nationality of a Contracting State;

(ii) any legal person, partnership and association deriving its status as such from the law in force in a Contracting State;

(h) the term "international traffic" means any transport by a ship or aircraft operated by an enterprise which has its place of effective management in a Contracting State, except when the ship or aircraft is operated solely between places in the other Contracting State;

(i) the term "competent authority" means:

(i) in the case of Cyprus, the Minister of Finance or his authorised representative;

(ii) in the case of Kuwait, the Minister of Finance or his authorised representative.

2. In the application of this Convention by a Contracting State, any term not otherwise defined shall, unless the context otherwise requires, have the meaning which it has under the laws of that Contracting State relating to the taxes which are the subject of this Convention.

Article 4

FISCAL DOMICILE

1. For the purposes of this Convention, the term "resident of a Contracting State" means any person who, under the law of that State, is liable to taxation therein by reason of his domicile, residence, place of management or any other criterion of a similar nature.

2. Where by reason of the provisions of paragraph 1 an individual is a resident of both Contracting States, then this case shall be determined in accordance with the following rules:

(a) he shall be deemed to be a resident of the Contracting State in which he has a permanent home available to him. If he has a permanent home available to him in both Contracting States, he shall be deemed to be a resident of the Contracting State with which his personal and economic relations are closest (centre of vital interests);

(b) if the Contracting State in which he has his centre of vital interests cannot be determined, or if he has no permanent home available to him in either Contracting State, he shall be deemed to be a resident of the Contracting State in which he has a habitual abode;

(c) if he has a habitual abode in both Contracting States or in neither of them, he shall be deemed to be a resident of the Contracting State of which he is a national;

(d) if he is a national of both Contracting States or of neither of them, the competent authorities of the Contracting States shall settle the question by mutual agreement.

3. Where by reason of the provisions of paragraph 1 a person other than an individual is a resident of both Contracting States, then it shall be deemed to be a resident of the Contracting State in which its place of effective management is situated.

Article 5

PERMANENT ESTABLISHMENT AND PERMANENT BASE

A. PERMANENT ESTABLISHMENT:

1. For the purpose of this Convention the term "permanent establishment" means a fixed place of business in which the business of the enterprise is wholly or partly carried on.

2. The term "permanent establishment" shall include especially:

(a) a place of management;

(b) a branch;

(c) an office;

(d) a factory;

(e) a workshop;

(f) a mine, oil well, quarry or other place of extraction of natural resources;

(g) a building site or construction or installation or assembly project, which exists for more than twelve months. The competent authorities of the Contracting States may, however, by mutual agreement extend the twelve-month period in case where they deem necessary;

(h) a farm or plantation.

3. The term "permanent establishment" shall not be deemed to include:

(a) the use of facilities solely for the purpose of storage, display or delivery of goods or merchandise belonging to the enterprise;

(b) the maintenance of a stock of goods or merchandise belonging to the enterprise solely for the purpose of storage, display or delivery;

(c) the maintenance of a stock of goods or merchandise belonging to the enterprise solely for the purpose of processing by another enterprise;

(d) the maintenance of a fixed place of business solely for the purpose of purchasing goods or merchandise, or for collecting information, for the enterprise;

(e) the maintenance of a fixed place of business solely for the purpose of advertising, for the supply of information, for scientific research or for similar activities which have a preparatory or auxiliary character for the enterprise.

4. An enterprise of one of the Contracting States shall be deemed to have a permanent establishment in the other Contracting State if:

(a) it carries on supervisory activities in that other Contracting State for more than twelve months in connection with a construction, installation or assembly project which is being undertaken in that other Contracting State;

(b) it carries on a business which consists of providing the services of public entertainers of the kind referred to in Article 17 in that other Contracting State.

5. Subject to the provisions of paragraph 6 of this Article, a person acting in one of the Contracting States on behalf of an enterprise of the other Contracting State shall be deemed to be a permanent establishment in the first-mentioned Contracting State if:

(a) he has, and habitually exercises in that first-mentioned Contracting State, an authority to conclude contracts in the name of the enterprise, unless his activities are limited to the purchase of goods or merchandise for the enterprise; or

(b) he maintains in the first-mentioned Contracting State a stock of goods or merchandise belonging to the enterprise from which he regularly fills orders on behalf of the enterprise.

6. An enterprise of a Contracting State shall not be deemed to have a permanent establishment in the other Contracting State merely because it carries on business in the other State through a broker, general commission agent or any other agent of an independent status, where such persons are acting in the ordinary course of their business.

7. The fact that a company which is a resident of a Contracting State controls or is controlled by a company which is a resident of the other Contracting State, or which carries on business in that other State (whether through a permanent establishment or otherwise), shall not of itself make either company a permanent establishment of the other.

B. PERMANENT BASE

For the purpose of this Convention the term "fixed base" means a fixed place through which the activities of a person rendering independent personal services are wholly or partly carried on.

Article 6

INCOME FROM IMMOVABLE PROPERTY

1. Income from immovable property including income from agriculture or forestry may be taxed in the Contracting State in which such property is situated.

2. (a) The term "immovable property" shall, subject to the provisions of sub-paragraphs (b) and (c), be defined in accordance with the law of the Contracting State in which the property in question is situated;

(b) the term "immovable property" shall in any case include property accessory to immovable property, livestock and equipment used in agriculture and forestry, rights to which the provisions of general law respecting immovable property apply, usufruct of immovable property and rights to variable or fixed payments as consideration for the working of, or the right to work, mineral deposits, sources and other natural resources;

(c) ships and aircraft shall not be regarded as immovable property.

3. The provisions of paragraph 1 shall apply to income derived from the direct use, letting or use in any other form of immovable property.

4. The provisions of paragraphs 1 and 3 shall also apply to the income from immovable property of an enterprise and to income from immovable property used for the performance of professional services.

Article 7

BUSINESS PROFITS

1. The profits of an enterprise of a Contracting State shall be taxable only in that State unless the enterprise carries on business in the other Contracting State through a permanent establishment situated therein. If the enterprise carries on business as aforesaid, the profits of the enterprise may be taxed in the other State but only so much of them as is attributable to that permanent establishment.

2. Where an enterprise of a Contracting State carries on business in the other Contracting State through a permanent establishment situated therein, there shall in each Contracting State be attributed to that permanent establishment the profits which it might be expected to make if it were a distinct and separate enterprise engaged in the same or similar activities under the same or similar conditions and dealing wholly independently with the enterprise of which is a permanent establishment.

3. In the determination of the profits of a permanent establishment, there shall be allowed as deductions expenses which are incurred for the purposes of the permanent establishment including executive and general administrative expenses so incurred, whether in the State in which the permanent establishment is situated or elsewhere.

4. In so far as it has been customary in a Contracting State to determine the profits to be attributed to a permanent establishment on the basis of an apportionment of the total profits of the enterprise to its various parts, nothing in paragraph 2 shall preclude that Contracting State from determining the profits to be taxed by such an apportionment as may be customary. The method of apportionment adopted shall, however, be such that the result shall be in accordance with the principles laid down in this Article.

5. No profits shall be attributed to a permanent establishment by reason of the mere purchase by that permanent establishment of goods or merchandise for the enterprise.

6. For the purposes of the preceding paragraphs, the profits to be attributed to the permanent establishment, shall be determined by the same method year by year unless there is good and sufficient reason to the contrary.

7. Where profits include items of income which are dealt with separately in other Articles of this Convention, then the provisions of those Articles shall not be affected by the provisions of this Article.

Article 8

SHIPPING AND AIR TRANSPORT

1. Profit from the operation of ships or aircraft in international traffic shall be taxable only in the Contracting State in which the place of effective management of the enterprise is situated, irrespective of the assistance of a permanent establishment in the other Contracting State.

2. If the place of effective management of a shipping enterprise is aboard a ship, then it shall be deemed to be situated in the Contracting State in which the home harbour of the ship is situated, or, if there is no such home harbour, in the Contracting State of which the operator of the ship is a resident.

3. The provisions of paragraph 1 shall also apply to profits derived from the participation in a pool, in a joint business or in an international operations agency.

Article 9

ASSOCIATED ENTERPRISES

Where -

(a) an enterprise of a Contracting State participates directly or indirectly in the management, control or capital of an enterprise of the other Contracting State, or

(b) the same persons participate directly or indirectly in the management, control or capital of an enterprise of a Contracting State and an enterprise of the other Contracting State,

and in either case conditions are made or imposed between the two enterprises in their commercial or financial relations which differ from those which would be made between independent enterprises, then any profits which would, but for those conditions, have accrued to one of the enterprises, but, by reason of those conditions, have not so accrued, may be included in the profits of that enterprise and taxed accordingly.

Article 10

DIVIDENDS

1. Dividends paid by a company which is a resident of a Contracting State to a resident of the other Contracting State may be taxed in that other State.

2. However, such dividends may be taxed in the Contracting State of which the company paying the dividends is a resident, and according to the law of that State, but the tax so charged shall not exceed 10 per cent of the gross amount of the dividends.

3. Notwithstanding the provisions of paragraph 2, as long as Cyprus does not impose a tax on dividends in addition to the tax chargeable on the profits or income of a company, dividends paid by a company which is a resident of Cyprus to a resident of Kuwait shall be exempt from any tax in Cyprus which may be chargeable on dividends in addition to the tax chargeable on the profits or income of the company.

4. The competent authorities of the Contracting States shall by mutual agreement settle the mode of application of paragraphs 2 and 3.

5. The provisions of paragraphs 2 and 3 shall not affect the taxation of the company in respect of the profits out of which the dividends are paid.

6. The term "dividends" as used in this Article means income from shares, as well as income from other corporate rights which is subject to the same taxation treatment as income from shares by the taxation law of the State of which the company making the distribution is a resident.

7. The provisions of paragraphs 1, 2 and 3 shall not apply if the recipient of the dividends, being a resident of a Contracting State, carries on business in the other

Contracting State of which the company paying the dividends is a resident through a permanent establishment situated therein, or performs in that other State professional services from a fixed base situated therein and the holding in respect of which the dividends are paid is effectively connected with such permanent establishment or fixed base. In such a case, the provisions of Article 7 or Article 14, as the case may be, shall apply.

8. Where a company which is a resident of a Contracting State derives profits or income from the other Contracting State, that other State may not impose any tax on dividends paid by the company to residents of the first-mentioned State, or subject the company's undistributed profits to a tax on undistributed profits, even if the dividends paid, or the undistributed profits consist wholly or partly of profits or income arising in that other State.

Article 11

INTEREST

1. Interest arising in a Contracting State and paid to a resident of the other Contracting State may be taxed in that other State.

2. However, interest derived from one of the Contracting States by a resident of the other Contracting State who is the beneficial owner thereof, may also be taxed in the first-mentioned Contracting State at a rate not exceeding 10 per cent of the gross amount thereof.

3. Notwithstanding the provision of paragraph 2 of this Article interest arising from credits or loans accorded by the Government of a Contracting State or by a Bank or other institution in the name or on behalf of that Government shall be taxable only in that State.

4. The term "interest" as used in this Article means income from debt-claims of every kind, whether or not secured by mortgage, and whether or not carrying a right to participate in the debtor's profits, and in particular, income from government securities and income from bonds or debentures, including premiums and prizes attaching to bonds or debentures.

5. Interest shall be deemed to be derived from a Contracting State when the payer is that State itself, a political sub-division or a local authority thereof or a resident of that State. Where, however, the person paying the interest, whether he is resident of a Contracting State or not, has in a Contracting State a permanent establishment in connection with which indebtedness on which the interest is paid was incurred, and such interest is borne by such permanent establishment, then such interest shall be deemed to be derived from the Contracting State in which the permanent establishment is situated.

6. The provisions of paragraph 1 shall not apply if the recipient of the interest, being a resident of a Contracting

State carries on in the other Contracting State, in which the interest arises, a business through a permanent establishment situated therein, or performs in that other State professional services from a fixed base situated therein, and the debt-claim in respect of which the interest is paid is effectively connected with such permanent establishment or fixed base. In such a case, the provisions of Article 7 or Article 14, as the case may be, shall apply.

7. Where, owing to a special relationship between the payer and the recipient or between both of them and some other person, the amount of the interest paid, having regard to the debt-claim for which it is paid, exceeds the amount which would have been agreed upon by the payer and the recipient in the absence of such relationship, the provisions of this Article shall apply only to the last-mentioned amount. In that case the excess part of the payments shall remain taxable according to the law of each Contracting State, due regard had to the other provisions of this Convention.

Article 12

ROYALTIES

1. Royalties arising in a Contracting State and paid to a resident of the other Contracting State may be taxed in that other State.

2. However, royalties of the kind referred to in sub-paragraph (a) of paragraph 3 may be taxed in the Contracting State in which they arise, and according to the law of that State, but the tax so charged shall not exceed 5 per cent of the gross amount of the royalties. The competent authorities of the Contracting States shall by mutual agreement settle the mode of application of this limitation.

3. The term "royalties" as used in this article means payments of any kind received as a consideration for the use of, or the right to use,

(a) any patent, trade mark, design or model, plan, secret formula or process, or any industrial, commercial, or scientific equipment, or for information concerning industrial, commercial or scientific experience;

(b) any copyright of literary, artistic or scientific work including cinematograph films, and films or tapes for television or radio broadcasting.

4. The provisions of paragraphs 1 and 2 shall not apply if the recipient of the royalties, being a resident of a Contracting State, carries on in the other Contracting State in which the royalties arise a business through a permanent establishment situated therein, or performs in that other State professional services from a fixed base situated therein, and the right or property in respect of which the royalties are paid is effectively connected with such permanent establishment or fixed base. In such a case, the provisions of Article 7 or Article 14, as the case may be, shall apply.

5. Royalties shall be deemed to arise in a Contracting State when the payer is that Contracting State itself, a political subdivision, a local authority or a resident of that Contracting State. Where, however, the person paying the royalties, whether he is a resident of a Contracting State or not, has in a Contracting State a permanent establishment in connection with which the liability to pay the royalties was incurred, and such royalties are borne by such permanent establishment, then such royalties shall be deemed to arise in the Contracting State in which the permanent establishment is situated.

6. Where, owing to a special relationship between the payer and recipient or both or them and some other person, the amount of the royalties paid, having regard to the use right or information for which they are paid, exceeds the amount which would have been agreed upon by the payer and the recipient in the absence of such relationship, the provisions of this Article shall apply only to the last-mentioned amount. In that case, the excess part of the payments shall remain taxable according to the law of each Contracting State, due regard being had to the other provisions of this Convention

Article 13

CAPITAL GAINS

1. Gains from alienation of immovable property, as defined in paragraph 2 of Article 6, may be taxed in the Contracting State in which such immovable property is situated.

2. Gains from the alienation of movable property forming part of the business property of a permanent establishment which an enterprise of a Contracting State has in the other Contracting State or of movable property pertaining to a fixed base available to a resident of a Contracting State in the other Contracting State for the purpose of performing professional services, including such gains from the alienation of such a permanent establishment (alone or together with the whole enterprise) or of such a fixed base, may be taxed in the other State. However, gains from the alienation of movable property of the kind referred to in paragraph 3 of Article 22 shall be taxable only in the Contracting State in which such movable property is taxable according to the said Article.

3. Gains from the alienation of any property other than those mentioned in paragraphs 1 and 2, shall be taxable only in the Contracting State of which the alienator is a resident.

Article 14

INDEPENDENT PERSONAL SERVICES

1. Income derived by a resident of a Contracting State in respect of professional services or other independent activities of a similar character shall be taxable only in that State unless he has a fixed base regularly available to him in the other Contracting State for the purpose of performing his activities. If he has such a fixed base, the income may be taxed in the other Contracting State but only so much of it as attributable to that fixed base.

2. The term "professional services" includes, especially independent scientific, literary, artistic, educational or teaching activities as well as the independent activities of physicians, lawyers, engineers, architects, dentists and accountants.

Article 15

DEPENDENT PERSONAL SERVICES

1. Subject to the provisions of Articles 16, 18 and 19, salaries, wages and other similar remuneration derived by a resident of a Contracting State in respect of an employment shall be taxable only in that State unless the employment is exercised in the other Contracting State. If the employment is so exercised, such remuneration as is derived therefrom may be taxed in that other State.

2. Notwithstanding the provisions of paragraph 1, remuneration derived by a resident of a Contracting State in respect of an employment exercised in the other Contracting State shall be taxable only in the first-mentioned State if:

(a) the recipient is present in the other State for a period or periods not exceeding in the aggregate 183 days in the calendar year concerned, and

(b) the remuneration is paid by, or on behalf of, an employer who is not a resident of the other State, and

(c) the remuneration is not borne by a permanent establishment or a fixed base which the employer has in the other State.

3. Notwithstanding the preceding provisions of this Article, remuneration in respect of an employment exercised aboard a ship or aircraft in international traffic, may be taxed in the Contracting State in which the place of effective management of the enterprise is situated.

Article 16

DIRECTORS' FEES

Directors' fees and similar payments derived by a resident of a Contracting State in his capacity as a member of the board of directors or another similar organ of a company which is a resident of the other Contracting State may be taxed in that other State.

Article 17

ARTISTES AND ATHLETES

1. Notwithstanding the provisions of Articles 14 and 15, income derived by public entertainers, such as theatre, motion picture, radio or television artistes, and musicians, and by athletes from their personal activities as such may be taxed in the Contracting State in which these activities are exercised.

2. Where the services mentioned in paragraph (1) of this Article are provided in one of the Contracting States by an enterprise of the other Contracting State, then the income derived from providing those services by such enterprise shall be exempt from tax in the first-mentioned Contracting State, if the enterprise is directly or indirectly supported, wholly or substantially, from the public funds of the Government of that other Contracting State in connection with the provision of such services.

Article 18

GOVERNMENTAL FUNCTIONS

1. Remuneration, other than a pension, paid by a Contracting State or a political subdivision or a local authority thereof to an individual in respect of services rendered to that State or subdivision or authority shall be taxable only in that State.

2. However, remuneration referred to in paragraph 1 shall be taxable only in the other Contracting State if the services are rendered in that State and the individual is a resident of that State who:

(a) is a national of that State; or

(b) did not become a resident of that State solely for the purpose of rendering the services.

3. The provisions of paragraphs 1 and 2 shall not apply to remuneration in respect of services rendered in connection with a business carried on by a Contracting State or a political subdivision or a local authority thereof.

Article 19

Pensions

Pensions, annuities and other similar remuneration paid to a resident of a Contracting State shall be taxable only in that State.

Article 20

STUDENTS

1. Payments which a student or business apprentice who is present in a Contracting State solely for the purpose of his education or training and who is or was immediately before such visit a resident of the other Contracting State received for the purpose of his maintenance, education or training shall not be taxed in the first-mentioned Contracting State, provided that such payments are made to him from sources outside that State.

2. A student at a university or other institution for higher education in a Contracting State, or a business apprentice who is present in the other Contracting State and who is or was immediately before such visit a resident of the first-mentioned State, shall not be taxed in the other Contracting State in respect of remuneration for services rendered in that other State, provided that the services are in connection with his studies or training and the remuneration constitutes earnings necessary for his maintenance.

Article 21

INCOME NOT EXPRESSLY MENTIONED

Items of income of a resident of a Contracting State which are not expressly mentioned in the foregoing Articles of this Convention shall be taxable only in that State.

Article 22

CAPITAL

1. Capital represented by immovable property, as defined in paragraph 2 of Article 6, may be taxed in the Contracting State in which such immovable property is situated.

2. Capital represented by movable property forming part of the business property of a permanent establishment of an enterprise, or by movable property pertaining to a fixed base used for the performance of professional services, may be taxed in the Contracting State in which the permanent establishment or fixed base is situated.

3. Ships and aircraft operated in international traffic and movable property pertaining to the operation of such ships and aircraft, shall be taxable only in the Contracting State in which the place of effective management of the enterprise is situated.

4. All other elements of capital of a resident of a Contracting State shall be taxable only in that State.

Article 23

ELIMINATION OF DOUBLE TAXATION

1. The laws of each of the Contracting States shall continue to govern the taxation of income whether derived from the Contracting State or elsewhere except where express provisions to the contrary are made in this Convention. Where income derived from one of the Contracting States, is subject to tax in both Contracting States, relief from tax chargeable on such income shall be given in accordance with the provisions of paragraphs (2) and (3) of this Article.

2. In the case of Kuwait, tax payable in Cyprus on profits,income or gains arising in Cyprus shall be deducted from any Kuwait tax payable in respect of such profits, income or gains.

3. In the case of Cyprus, subject to the existing provisions of the law of Cyprus regarding the deduction from tax payable in Cyprus of tax paid in a territory outside Cyprus and to any subsequent modification of those provisions - which shall not affect the general principle hereof - and unless a greater deduction or relief is provided under the laws of Cyprus, tax payable in Kuwait on profits, income or gains arising in Kuwait shall be deducted from any Cyprus tax payable in respect of such profits, income or gains.

Article 24

LIMITATION OF RELIEF

Where under any provision of this Convention income is releived from tax in one of the Contracting States and, under the law in force in the other Contracting State, a person in respect of the said income, is subject to tax by reference to the amount thereof which is remitted to or received in that other Contracting State and not by reference to the full amount thereof then the relief to be allowed under this Convention in the first-mentioned Contracting State shall apply only to so much of the income as is remitted to or received in the other Contracting State.

Article 25

NON-DISCRIMINATION

1. The nationals of a Contracting State shall not be subjected in the other Contracting State to any taxation or any requirement connected therewith which is other or more burdensome than the taxation and connected requirements to which nationals of that other State in the same circumstances are or may be subjected.

2. The taxation on a permanent establishment which an enterprise of a Contracting State has in the other Contracting State shall not be less favourably levied in that other State than the taxation levied on enterprises of that other State carrying on the same activities.

This provision shall not be construed as obliging a Contracting State to grant to residents of the other Contracting State any personal allowances, reliefs and reductions for tax purposes on account of civil status or family responsibilities which it grants to its own residents.

3. Enterprises of a Contracting State, the capital of which is wholly or partly owned or controlled, directly or indirectly, by one or more residents of the other Contracting State, shall not be subjected in the first-mentioned Contracting State to any taxation or any requirement connected therewith which is other or more burdensome than the taxation and connected requirements to which other similar enterprises of that first-mentioned State are or may be subjected.

4. In this Article the term "taxation" means taxes of every kind and description.

Article 26

MUTUAL AGREEMENT PROCEDURE

1. Where a resident of a Contracting State considers that the actions of one or both of the Contracting States result or will result for him in taxation not in accordance with this Convention, he may, present his case to the competent authority of the Contracting State of which he is a resident. The claim for case must be lodged within a period of six months from the date of the assessment. The competent authorities of the Contracting States shall resolve the matter within one year from the date of a claim.

2. The competent authority shall endeavour, if the objection appears to it to be justified and if it is not itself able to arrive at an appropriate solution, to resolve the case by mutual agreement with the competent authority of the other Contracting State, with a view to the avoidance of taxation not in accordance with the Convention.

3. The competent authorities of the Contracting States shall endeavour to resolve by mutual agreement any difficulties or doubts arising as to the interpretation or application of the Convention. They may also consult together for the elimination of double taxation in cases not provided for in the Convention.

4. The competent authorities of the Contracting States may communicate with each other directly for the purpose of reaching an agreement in the sense of the preceding paragraphs. When it seems advisable in order to reach agreement to have an oral exchange of opinions, such exchange may take place through a Commission consisting of representatives of the competent authorities of the Contracting States.

Article 27

EXCHANGE OF INFORMATION

1. The competent authorities of the Contracting States shall exchange such information as is necessary for the carrying out of this Convention and of the domestic laws of the Contracting States concerning taxes covered by this Convention in so far as the taxation thereunder is in accordance with this Convention. Any information so exchanged shall be treated as secret and shall not be disclosed to any persons or authorities, including courts, other than those concerned with the assessment, collection, enforcement or prosecution in respect of taxes which are the subject of the Convention.

2. In no case shall the provisions of paragraph 1 be construed so as to impose on one of the Contracting States the obligation:

(a) to carry out administrative measures at variance with the laws or the administrative practice of that or of the other Contracting State;

(b) to supply particulars which are not obtainable under the laws or in the normal course of the administration of that or of the other Contracting State;

(c) to supply information which would disclose any trade, business, industrial, commercial or professional secret or trade process or information, the disclosure of which would be contrary to public policy (ordre public).

Article 28

DIPLOMATIC AND CONSULAR OFFICIALS

Nothing in this Convention shall affect the fiscal privileges of diplomatic or consular officials under the general rules of international law or under the provisions of special agreements.

Article 29

ENTRY INTO FORCE

1. The Governments of the Contracting States shall notify to each other that the constitutional requirements for the entry into force of this Convention have been complied with.

2. The Convention shall enter into force on the date of the later of the notifications referred to in paragraph 1 and its provisions shall have effect, in respect of taxes which are levied for any taxable year beginning on or after 1st January in the calendar year in which the Convention enters into force.

Article 30

TERMINATION AND AMENDMENT

This Convention shall remain in force until denounced by one of the Contracting States. Either Contracting State may denounce the Convention through diplomatic channels, by giving notice of termination at least six months before the end of any calendar year following after the period of five years from the date on which the Convention enters into force. In such event, the Convention shall cease to have effect in respect of taxes which are levied for any taxable year beginning on or after 1st January in the calendar year next following that in which the notice is given. This Convention may, however, be amended at any time by a subsequent agreement between the Contracting States.

In witness whereof the undersigned, duly authorised thereto, have signed this Convention.

Done in Kuwait City on the 15th December 1984 in two originals in the English language.

For the Government of the Republic of Cyprus:

For the Government of the State of Kuwait:

[TRANSLATION IN FRENCH – TRADUCTION EN FRANÇAIS]

CONVENTION ENTRE LE GOUVERNEMENT DE LA RÉPUBLIQUE DE CHYPRE ET LE GOUVERNEMENT DE L'ÉTAT DU KOWEÏT TENDANT À ÉVITER LES DOUBLES IMPOSITIONS ET À PRÉVENIR LA FRAUDE FISCALE EN MATIÈRE D'IMPÔTS SUR LE REVENU ET SUR LA FORTUNE

Le Gouvernement de la République de Chypre et le Gouvernement de l'État du Koweït, désireux de conclure une convention tendant à éviter les doubles impositions et à prévenir la fraude fiscale en matière d'impôts sur le revenu et sur la fortune, sont convenus de ce qui suit :

Article premier. Personnes visées

La présente Convention s'applique aux personnes qui sont des résidents d'un État contractant ou des deux États contractants.

Article 2. Impôts visés

1. La présente Convention s'applique aux impôts sur le revenu et sur la fortune prélevés pour le compte de chaque État contractant ou de ses subdivisions politiques ou de ses collectivités locales, quel que soit le système de perception.

2. Sont considérés comme impôts sur le revenu et sur la fortune les impôts perçus sur le revenu total, sur la fortune totale, ou sur des éléments du revenu ou de la fortune, y compris les impôts sur les gains provenant de l'aliénation de biens mobiliers ou immobiliers, ainsi que les impôts sur le montant global des salaires payés par les entreprises.

3. Les impôts actuels auxquels s'applique la présente Convention sont les suivants :

a) À Chypre :

L'impôt sur le revenu ;

La contribution spéciale ; et

L'impôt sur les gains en capital ;

(ci-après dénommés « impôt chypriote ») ;

b) Au Koweït :

L'impôt sur les sociétés ;

(ci-après dénommé « impôt koweïtien »).

4. La présente Convention s'applique aussi aux impôts de nature identique ou analogue qui seraient établis après la date de signature de la Convention et qui s'ajouteraient aux impôts actuels ou qui les remplaceraient. Les autorités compétentes des États contractants se communiquent les modifications importantes apportées à leurs législations fiscales respectives.

Article 3. Définitions générales

1. Au sens de la présente Convention, à moins que le contexte n'exige une interprétation différente :

a) Le terme « Chypre » désigne la République de Chypre, y compris toute zone adjacente aux eaux territoriales de Chypre qui, conformément au droit international, a été ou peut ultérieurement être désignée, aux termes de la législation chypriote relative au plateau continental, comme étant une zone au sein de laquelle Chypre peut exercer ses droits à l'égard du fond de la mer et du sous-sol, ainsi que des ressources naturelles qui s'y trouvent ;

b) Le terme « Koweït » désigne l'État du Koweït ;

c) Les expressions « un État contractant » et « l'autre État contractant » désignent, suivant le contexte, Chypre ou le Koweït ;

d) Le terme « personne » inclut les personnes physiques, les sociétés et tout autre organe ;

e) Le terme « société » s'entend de toute personne morale ou de toute entité qui est considérée comme une personne morale aux fins d'imposition ;

f) Les expressions « entreprise d'un État contractant » et « entreprise de l'autre État contractant » désignent respectivement une entreprise exploitée par un résident d'un État contractant et d'une entreprise exploitée par un résident de l'autre État contractant ;

g) Le terme « ressortissant » désigne :

   i) Toute personne physique qui possède la nationalité d'un État contractant ;

   ii) Toute personne morale, société de personnes et association qui est constituée conformément à la législation en vigueur dans un État contractant ;

h) L'expression « trafic international » désigne tout transport effectué par un navire ou un aéronef exploité par une entreprise dont le siège de direction effective est situé dans un État contractant, sauf lorsque le navire ou l'aéronef n'est exploité qu'entre des points situés dans l'autre État contractant ;

i) L'expression « autorité compétente » désigne :

   i) Dans le cas de Chypre, le Ministre des finances ou son représentant autorisé ;

   ii) Dans le cas du Koweït, le Ministre des finances ou son représentant autorisé.

2. Pour l'application de la présente Convention par un État contractant, toute expression ou tout terme qui n'y est pas autrement défini a, à moins que le contexte n'exige une interprétation différente, le sens que lui attribue la législation de cet État régissant les impôts visés par la présente Convention.

Article 4. Domicile fiscal

1. Aux fins de la présente Convention, l'expression « résident d'un État contractant » désigne toute personne qui, en vertu de la législation de cet État, y est assujettie à l'impôt en raison de son domicile, de sa résidence, de son siège de direction ou de tout autre critère de nature analogue.

2. Lorsque, selon les dispositions du paragraphe 1, une personne physique est un résident des deux États contractants, sa situation est déterminée de la manière suivante :

a) Cette personne est considérée comme un résident de l'État contractant où elle dispose d'un foyer d'habitation permanent. Si elle dispose d'un foyer d'habitation permanent dans les deux États contractants, elle est considérée comme un résident de l'État contractant avec lequel ses liens personnels et économiques sont les plus étroits (centre des intérêts vitaux) ;

b) Si l'État contractant où cette personne a ses intérêts vitaux ne peut pas être déterminé, ou si elle ne dispose d'un foyer d'habitation permanent dans aucun des États contractants, elle est considérée comme un résident de l'État contractant où elle séjourne de façon habituelle ;

c) Si cette personne séjourne de façon habituelle dans les deux États contractants ou si elle ne séjourne de façon habituelle dans aucun d'eux, elle est considérée comme un résident de l'État contractant dont elle est un ressortissant ;

d) Si cette personne possède la nationalité des deux États contractants ou si elle ne possède la nationalité d'aucun d'eux, les autorités compétentes des États contractants tranchent la question d'un commun accord.

3. Lorsque, selon les dispositions du paragraphe 1, une personne autre qu'une personne physique est un résident des deux États contractants, elle est considérée comme un résident de l'État contractant où son siège de direction effective est situé.

Article 5. Établissement stable et base fixe

A. Établissement stable :

1. Aux fins de la présente Convention, l'expression « établissement stable » désigne une installation fixe d'affaires dans laquelle une entreprise exerce tout ou partie de son activité.

2. L'expression « établissement stable » comprend notamment :

a) Un siège de direction ;

b) Une succursale ;

c) Un bureau ;

d) Une usine ;

e) Un atelier ;

f) Une mine, un puits de pétrole, une carrière ou tout autre lieu d'extraction de ressources naturelles ;

g) Un chantier de construction, un projet d'installation ou de montage qui existe pendant plus de 12 mois. Les autorités compétentes des États contractants peuvent toutefois, d'un commun accord, prolonger la période de 12 mois dans les cas où elles le jugent nécessaire ;

h) Une ferme ou une plantation.

3. Il est considéré que l'expression « établissement stable » ne comprend pas :

a) L'utilisation d'installations aux seules fins de stockage, d'exposition ou de livraison de biens ou de marchandises appartenant à l'entreprise ;

b) L'exploitation d'un stock de biens ou de marchandises appartenant à l'entreprise aux seules fins de stockage, d'exposition ou de livraison ;

c) L'exploitation d'un stock de biens ou de marchandises appartenant à l'entreprise aux seules fins de transformation par une autre entreprise ;

d) L'exploitation d'une installation fixe d'affaires aux seules fins d'acheter des biens ou des marchandises ou de réunir des informations pour l'entreprise ;

e) L'exploitation d'une installation fixe d'affaires aux seules fins de publicité, de fourniture d'informations, de recherche scientifique ou d'activités analogues qui ont un caractère préparatoire ou auxiliaire pour l'entreprise.

4. Une entreprise d'un État contractant est considérée comme ayant un établissement stable dans l'autre État contractant si :

a) Elle y exerce des activités de supervision pendant plus de 12 mois, dans le cadre d'un projet de construction, d'installation ou de montage entrepris dans cet autre État contractant ;

b) Elle exerce une activité qui consiste à fournir les services de professionnels du spectacle du type visé à l'article 17 dans cet autre État contractant.

5. Sous réserve des dispositions du paragraphe 6 du présent article, une personne agissant dans l'un des États contractants pour le compte d'une entreprise de l'autre État contractant est considérée comme un établissement stable dans le premier État contractant si :

a) Elle dispose dans ce premier État contractant de pouvoirs qu'elle y exerce habituellement lui permettant de conclure des contrats au nom de l'entreprise, à moins que l'activité de cette personne ne soit limitée à l'achat de biens ou de marchandises pour l'entreprise ; ou

b) Elle maintient dans ce premier État contractant un stock de biens ou de marchandises, appartenant à l'entreprise, au moyen duquel elle exécute régulièrement des commandes au nom de cette entreprise.

6. Une entreprise d'un État contractant n'est pas considérée comme ayant un établissement stable dans l'autre État contractant du seul fait qu'elle y exerce son activité par l'entremise d'un courtier, d'un commissionnaire général ou de tout autre agent jouissant d'un statut indépendant, à condition que ces personnes agissent dans le cadre ordinaire de leur activité.

7. Le fait qu'une société qui est un résident d'un État contractant contrôle ou est contrôlée par une société qui est un résident de l'autre État contractant ou qui y exerce son activité (que ce soit par l'intermédiaire d'un établissement stable ou non) ne suffit pas, en soi, à faire de l'une quelconque de ces sociétés un établissement stable de l'autre.

B. Base fixe

Aux fins de la présente Convention, l'expression « base fixe » désigne une installation fixe par l'intermédiaire de laquelle sont menées, en tout ou en partie, les activités d'une personne exerçant une profession indépendante.

Article 6. Revenus immobiliers

1. Les revenus qu'un résident d'un État contractant tire de biens immobiliers, y compris les revenus des exploitations agricoles ou forestières, sont imposables dans l'État contractant où ces biens sont situés.

2. a) L'expression « biens immobiliers », sous réserve des dispositions des alinéas b) et c), est définie conformément au droit de l'État contractant où les biens considérés sont situés ;

b) L'expression « biens immobiliers » comprend en tous cas les biens accessoires aux biens immobiliers, le cheptel et le matériel utilisé dans les exploitations agricoles et forestières, auxquels s'appliquent les dispositions du droit privé concernant la propriété foncière, l'usufruit des biens immobiliers et le droit à des paiements variables ou fixes pour l'exploitation ou la concession de l'exploitation de gisements minéraux, sources et autres ressources naturelles ;

c) Les navires et les aéronefs ne sont pas considérés comme des biens immobiliers.

3. Les dispositions du paragraphe 1 s'appliquent aux revenus provenant de l'exploitation directe, de la location ou de toute autre forme d'exploitation de biens immobiliers.

4. Les dispositions des paragraphes 1 et 3 s'appliquent également aux revenus provenant des biens immobiliers d'une entreprise ainsi qu'aux revenus de biens immobiliers servant à l'exercice d'une profession indépendante.

Article 7. Bénéfices des entreprises

1. Les bénéfices d'une entreprise d'un État contractant ne sont imposables que dans cet État, à moins que l'entreprise n'exerce son activité dans l'autre État contractant par l'intermédiaire d'un établissement stable qui y est situé. Si l'entreprise exerce son activité d'une telle façon, les bénéfices de cette entreprise sont imposables dans l'autre État, mais uniquement dans la mesure où ils sont imputables à cet établissement stable.

2. Lorsqu'une entreprise d'un État contractant exerce son activité dans l'autre État contractant par l'intermédiaire d'un établissement stable qui y est situé, il est imputé, dans chaque État contractant, à cet établissement stable les bénéfices qu'il aurait pu réaliser s'il avait constitué une entreprise distincte exerçant des activités identiques ou analogues dans des conditions identiques ou analogues et traitant en toute indépendance avec l'entreprise dont il constitue un établissement stable.

3. Pour déterminer les bénéfices d'un établissement stable, sont admises en déduction les dépenses relatives aux fins poursuivies par cet établissement stable, y compris les dépenses de direction et les frais généraux d'administration ainsi enregistrés, soit dans l'État où est situé l'établissement stable, soit ailleurs.

4. S'il est d'usage, dans un État contractant, de déterminer les bénéfices imputables à un établissement stable sur la base d'une répartition des bénéfices totaux de l'entreprise entre ses diverses composantes, aucune disposition du paragraphe 2 n'empêche cet État contractant de déterminer les bénéfices imposables selon la répartition en usage. La méthode de répartition adoptée doit cependant être telle que le résultat obtenu soit conforme aux principes énoncés dans le présent article.

5. Aucun bénéfice n'est imputé à un établissement stable du seul fait qu'il a acheté des biens ou des marchandises pour l'entreprise.

6. Aux fins des paragraphes précédents, les bénéfices à imputer à l'établissement stable sont déterminés chaque année selon la même méthode, à moins qu'il n'existe des motifs valables et suffisants de procéder autrement.

7. Lorsque les bénéfices comprennent des éléments de revenu traités séparément dans d'autres articles de la présente Convention, les dispositions de ces articles ne sont pas affectées par les dispositions du présent article.

Article 8. Transport maritime et aérien

1. Les bénéfices provenant de l'exploitation de navires ou d'aéronefs, en trafic international, ne sont imposables que dans l'État contractant où est situé le siège de direction effective de l'entreprise, indépendamment de l'assistance fournie par un établissement stable situé dans l'autre État contractant.

2. Si le siège de direction effective d'une compagnie maritime se trouve à bord d'un navire, il est considéré comme situé dans l'État contractant où se trouve le port d'attache de ce navire ou, à défaut de port d'attache, dans l'État contractant dont l'exploitant du navire est un résident.

3. Les dispositions du paragraphe 1 s'appliquent également aux bénéfices provenant de la participation à un consortium, à une coentreprise ou à un organisme international d'exploitation.

Article 9. Entreprises associées

Lorsque :

a) Une entreprise d'un État contractant participe directement ou indirectement à la direction, au contrôle ou au capital d'une entreprise de l'autre État ; ou que

b) Les mêmes personnes participent directement ou indirectement à la direction, au contrôle ou au capital d'une entreprise d'un État contractant et d'une entreprise de l'autre État contractant ;

et que, dans l'un et l'autre cas, les deux entreprises sont, dans leurs relations commerciales ou financières, liées par des conditions convenues ou imposées qui diffèrent de celles qui seraient convenues entre des entreprises indépendantes, les bénéfices qui, sans ces conditions, auraient été réalisés par l'une des entreprises, mais n'ont pu l'être en fait à cause de ces conditions, peuvent être inclus dans les bénéfices de cette entreprise et imposés en conséquence.

Article 10. Dividendes

1. Les dividendes payés par une société qui est un résident d'un État contractant à un résident de l'autre État contractant sont imposables dans cet autre État.

2. Toutefois, ces dividendes sont imposables dans l'État contractant dont la société qui paie les dividendes est un résident, et selon la législation de cet État, mais l'impôt ainsi établi ne peut excéder 10 % du montant brut des dividendes.

3. Nonobstant les dispositions du paragraphe 2, tant que Chypre ne prélève pas d'impôt sur les dividendes en sus de l'impôt frappant les bénéfices ou les revenus d'une société, les dividendes versés par une société résidente de Chypre à un résident du Koweït sont exonérés à Chypre de tout impôt sur les dividendes qui pourrait s'ajouter à l'impôt sur les bénéfices ou les revenus de la société.

4. Les autorités compétentes des États contractants règlent, d'un commun accord, les modalités d'application des paragraphes 2 et 3.

5. Les dispositions des paragraphes 2 et 3 n'affectent pas l'imposition de la société au titre des bénéfices qui servent au paiement des dividendes.

6. Le terme « dividendes » employé dans le présent article désigne les revenus provenant d'actions, ainsi que les revenus d'autres parts sociales soumis au même régime fiscal que les revenus d'actions par la législation fiscale de l'État contractant dont la société distributrice est un résident.

7. Les dispositions des paragraphes 1, 2 et 3 ne s'appliquent pas lorsque le bénéficiaire des dividendes, résident d'un État contractant, exerce dans l'autre État contractant dont la société qui paie les dividendes est un résident, soit une activité industrielle ou commerciale par l'intermédiaire d'un établissement stable qui y est situé, soit une profession indépendante au moyen d'une base fixe qui y est située, et que la participation génératrice des dividendes se rattache effectivement à cet établissement stable ou à cette base fixe. Dans ce cas, les dispositions de l'article 7 ou de l'article 14, suivant le cas, sont applicables.

8. Lorsqu'une société qui est un résident d'un État contractant tire des bénéfices ou des revenus de l'autre État contractant, cet autre État ne peut percevoir aucun impôt sur les dividendes payés par la société aux résidents du premier État ni prélever aucun impôt, au titre de l'imposition des bénéfices non distribués, sur les bénéfices non distribués de la société, même si les dividendes payés ou les bénéfices non distribués consistent en tout ou en partie en bénéfices ou revenus provenant de cet autre État.

Article 11. Intérêts

1. Les intérêts provenant d'un État contractant et payés à un résident de l'autre État contractant sont imposables dans cet autre État.

2. Toutefois, les intérêts provenant de l'un des États contractants et perçus par un résident de l'autre État contractant qui en est le bénéficiaire effectif sont également imposables dans le premier État contractant à un taux n'excédant pas 10 % de leur montant brut.

3. Nonobstant les dispositions du paragraphe 2 du présent article, les intérêts provenant de crédits ou de prêts accordés par le Gouvernement d'un État contractant ou par une banque ou une autre institution au nom ou pour le compte de ce Gouvernement ne sont imposables que dans cet État.

4. Le terme « intérêts » employé dans le présent article désigne les revenus des créances de toute nature, assorties ou non de garanties hypothécaires ou d'une clause de participation aux bénéfices du débiteur, et notamment les revenus des fonds publics et des obligations d'emprunts, y compris les primes et lots attachés à ces titres.

5. Les intérêts sont considérés comme provenant d'un État contractant lorsque le débiteur est cet État lui-même, l'une de ses subdivisions politiques ou collectivités locales ou un résident de cet État. Toutefois, lorsque le débiteur des intérêts, qu'il soit ou non un résident d'un État contractant, a dans un État contractant un établissement stable pour lequel la dette donnant lieu au paiement des intérêts a été contractée et qui supporte la charge de ces intérêts, ceux-ci sont considérés comme provenant de l'État contractant où l'établissement stable est situé.

6. Les dispositions du paragraphe 1 ne s'appliquent pas lorsque le bénéficiaire des intérêts, résident d'un État contractant, exerce dans l'autre État contractant d'où proviennent les intérêts, soit une activité industrielle ou commerciale par l'intermédiaire d'un établissement stable qui y est situé,

soit une profession indépendante à partir d'une base fixe qui y est située, et que la créance génératrice des intérêts se rattache effectivement à cet établissement stable ou à cette base fixe. Dans ce cas, les dispositions de l'article 7 ou de l'article 14, suivant le cas, sont applicables.

7. Si, en raison de relations particulières existant entre le débiteur et le bénéficiaire, ou entre eux et une tierce personne, le montant des intérêts versés, compte tenu de la créance au titre de laquelle ils sont versés, excède le montant dont le débiteur et le bénéficiaire seraient convenus en l'absence de pareilles relations, les dispositions du présent article ne s'appliquent qu'à ce dernier montant. Dans ce cas, la partie excédentaire des paiements reste imposable selon la législation de chaque État contractant et compte tenu des autres dispositions de la présente Convention.

Article 12. Redevances

1. Les redevances générées dans un État contractant et payées à un résident de l'autre État contractant sont imposables dans cet autre État.

2. Toutefois, les redevances du type visé à l'alinéa a) du paragraphe 3 sont imposables dans l'État contractant de la source, conformément à la législation de cet État, mais l'impôt ainsi établi ne peut excéder 5 % du montant brut des redevances. Les autorités compétentes des États contractants règlent d'un commun accord les modalités d'application de cette limitation.

3. Le terme « redevances » employé dans le présent article désigne les paiements de toute nature perçus en contrepartie de l'usage ou de la concession de l'usage :

a) D'un brevet, d'une marque de fabrique ou commerciale, d'un concept ou d'un modèle, d'un plan, d'une formule ou d'un procédé secrets, ou d'un équipement industriel, commercial ou scientifique, ou d'informations ayant trait à une expérience acquise dans le domaine industriel, commercial ou scientifique ;

b) D'un droit d'auteur sur une œuvre littéraire, artistique ou scientifique, y compris les films cinématographiques et les films ou les enregistrements destinés à la radiodiffusion ou à la télévision.

4. Les dispositions des paragraphes 1 et 2 ne s'appliquent pas lorsque le bénéficiaire des redevances, résident d'un État contractant, exerce dans l'autre État contractant source des redevances, soit une activité industrielle ou commerciale par l'intermédiaire d'un établissement stable qui y est situé, soit une profession indépendante au moyen d'une base fixe qui y est située, et que le droit ou le bien générateur des redevances se rattache effectivement à cet établissement stable ou à cette base fixe. Dans ce cas, les dispositions de l'article 7 ou de l'article 14, suivant le cas, sont applicables.

5. Les redevances sont considérées comme provenant d'un État contractant lorsque le débiteur est cet État contractant lui-même, l'une de ses subdivisions politiques ou collectivités locales ou un résident de cet État contractant. Toutefois, lorsque le débiteur des redevances, qu'il soit ou non un résident d'un État contractant, a dans un État contractant un établissement stable pour lequel l'engagement donnant lieu aux redevances a été contracté et qui supporte la charge de ces redevances, celles-ci sont considérées comme provenant de l'État contractant où l'établissement stable est situé.

6. Si, en raison de relations particulières existant entre le débiteur et le bénéficiaire, ou que l'un et l'autre entretiennent avec de tierces personnes, le montant des redevances payées, compte tenu de l'usage, de la concession de l'usage ou des informations pour lesquels elles sont versées, excède celui dont seraient convenus le débiteur et le bénéficiaire en l'absence de pareilles relations,

les dispositions du présent article ne s'appliquent qu'à ce dernier montant. Dans ce cas, la partie excédentaire des paiements reste imposable selon la législation de chaque État contractant et compte tenu des autres dispositions de la présente Convention.

Article 13. Gains en capital

1. Les gains provenant de l'aliénation de biens immobiliers, tels qu'ils sont définis au paragraphe 2 de l'article 6, sont imposables dans l'État contractant où ces biens sont situés.

2. Les gains provenant de l'aliénation de biens mobiliers qui font partie de l'actif d'un établissement stable qu'une entreprise d'un État contractant a dans l'autre État contractant, ou de biens mobiliers qui appartiennent à une base fixe dont un résident d'un État contractant dispose dans l'autre État contractant pour l'exercice d'une profession indépendante, y compris de tels gains provenant de l'aliénation de cet établissement stable (seul ou avec l'ensemble de l'entreprise) ou de cette base fixe, sont imposables dans l'autre État. Toutefois, les gains provenant de l'aliénation des biens mobiliers visés au paragraphe 3 de l'article 22 ne sont imposables que dans l'État contractant où les biens mobiliers considérés sont eux-mêmes imposables en vertu dudit article.

3. Les gains provenant de l'aliénation de tous biens autres que ceux qui sont mentionnés aux paragraphes 1 et 2 ne sont imposables que dans l'État contractant dont le cédant est un résident.

Article 14. Professions indépendantes

1. Les revenus qu'un résident d'un État contractant tire d'une profession indépendante ou d'autres activités de caractère indépendant de nature analogue ne sont imposables que dans cet État, à moins que ce résident ne dispose de façon habituelle dans l'autre État contractant d'une base fixe pour l'exercice de ses activités. S'il dispose d'une telle base fixe, les revenus sont imposables dans l'autre État contractant, mais uniquement dans la mesure où ils sont imputables à ladite base fixe.

2. L'expression « profession indépendante » se rapporte notamment aux activités indépendantes d'ordre scientifique, littéraire, artistique, éducatif ou pédagogique, ainsi qu'aux activités indépendantes des médecins, avocats, ingénieurs, architectes, dentistes et comptables.

Article 15. Professions dépendantes

1. Sous réserve des dispositions des articles 16, 18 et 19, les salaires, traitements et autres rémunérations similaires qu'un résident d'un État contractant reçoit au titre d'un emploi salarié ne sont imposables que dans cet État, à moins que l'emploi ne soit exercé dans l'autre État contractant. Si l'emploi y est exercé, les rémunérations reçues à ce titre sont imposables dans cet autre État.

2. Nonobstant les dispositions du paragraphe 1, les rémunérations qu'un résident d'un État contractant reçoit au titre d'un emploi salarié exercé dans l'autre État contractant ne sont imposables que dans le premier État si :

a) Le bénéficiaire séjourne dans l'autre État pendant une période ou des périodes n'excédant pas au total 183 jours au cours de l'année civile concernée ; et

b) Les rémunérations sont payées par un employeur ou pour le compte d'un employeur qui n'est pas un résident de l'autre État ; et

c) La charge des rémunérations n'est pas supportée par un établissement stable ou une base fixe que l'employeur a dans l'autre État.

3. Nonobstant les dispositions précédentes du présent article, les rémunérations perçues au titre d'un emploi exercé à bord d'un navire ou d'un aéronef exploité en trafic international sont imposables dans l'État contractant où le siège de direction effective de l'entreprise est situé.

Article 16. Tantièmes

Les tantièmes, jetons de présence et autres rémunérations similaires qu'un résident d'un État contractant reçoit en sa qualité de membre du conseil d'administration ou d'un autre organe similaire d'une société qui est résidente de l'autre État contractant sont imposables dans cet autre État.

Article 17. Artistes et athlètes

1. Nonobstant les dispositions des articles 14 et 15, les revenus que les artistes du spectacle, tels les artistes de théâtre, de cinéma, de la radio ou de la télévision et les musiciens, ainsi que les athlètes tirent de leurs activités personnelles sont imposables dans l'État contractant où ces activités sont exercées.

2. Lorsque les services mentionnés au paragraphe 1 du présent article sont fournis dans l'un des États contractants par une entreprise de l'autre État contractant, les revenus provenant de la prestation de ces services par cette entreprise sont exonérés d'impôt dans le premier État contractant, si l'entreprise est financée directement ou indirectement, en totalité ou en grande partie, par les fonds publics du Gouvernement de cet autre État contractant dans le cadre de la prestation de ces services.

Article 18. Fonction publique

1. Les rémunérations, autres que les pensions, payées par un État contractant ou l'une de ses subdivisions politiques ou collectivités locales à une personne physique au titre de services fournis à cet État ou à cette subdivision ou collectivité ne sont imposables que dans cet État.

2. Toutefois, les rémunérations visées au paragraphe 1 ne sont imposables que dans l'autre État contractant si les services sont fournis dans cet État et si la personne physique est un résident de cet État qui :

a) Est un ressortissant de cet État ; ou

b) N'est pas devenu un résident de cet État à la seule fin d'exécuter les services en question.

3. Les dispositions des paragraphes 1 et 2 ne s'appliquent pas aux rémunérations payées au titre de services fournis dans le cadre d'une activité industrielle ou commerciale exercée par un État contractant ou l'une de ses subdivisions politiques ou collectivités locales.

Article 19. Pensions

Les pensions, les rentes et autres rémunérations similaires versées à un résident d'un État contractant ne sont imposables que dans cet État.

Article 20. Étudiants

1. Les sommes qu'un étudiant ou un stagiaire qui séjourne dans un État contractant à seule fin d'y poursuivre ses études ou sa formation et qui est, ou qui était immédiatement avant de se

rendre dans cet État, un résident de l'autre État contractant, a reçues pour couvrir ses frais d'entretien, d'études et de formation ne sont pas imposables dans le premier État, à condition qu'elles proviennent de sources situées en dehors de cet État.

2. Un étudiant dans une université ou dans un autre établissement d'enseignement supérieur dans un État contractant ou un stagiaire, qui séjourne dans l'autre État contractant et qui est, ou qui était immédiatement avant de se rendre dans cet État, un résident du premier État contractant n'est pas imposable dans l'autre État contractant pour la rémunération reçue au titre des services fournis dans cet autre État, à condition que ces services soient liés à ses études ou à sa formation et que la rémunération constitue des gains nécessaires à son entretien.

Article 21. Revenus non expressément mentionnés

Les éléments du revenu d'un résident d'un État contractant qui ne sont pas expressément mentionnés dans les articles précédents de la présente Convention ne sont imposables que dans cet État.

Article 22. Fortune

1. La fortune constituée par des biens immobiliers au sens du paragraphe 2 de l'article 6 est imposable dans l'État contractant où ces biens sont situés.

2. La fortune constituée par des biens meubles faisant partie de l'actif d'un établissement stable d'une entreprise ou par des biens meubles qui appartiennent à une base fixe servant à l'exercice d'une profession indépendante, est imposable dans l'État contractant où l'établissement stable ou la base fixe sont situés.

3. Les navires et aéronefs exploités en trafic international, ainsi que les biens meubles affectés à leur exploitation, ne sont imposables que dans l'État contractant où se trouve le siège de direction effective de l'entreprise.

4. Les autres éléments de la fortune d'un résident d'un État contractant ne sont imposables que dans cet État.

Article 23. Élimination des doubles impositions

1. Sauf dispositions expresses contraires de la présente Convention, les législations de chaque État contractant continuent de régir l'imposition des revenus provenant de l'État contractant ou d'ailleurs. Lorsque les revenus provenant de l'un des États contractants sont soumis à l'impôt dans les deux États contractants, l'exonération de l'impôt exigible sur ces revenus est accordée conformément aux dispositions des paragraphes 2 et 3 du présent article.

2. Dans le cas du Koweït, l'impôt dû à Chypre sur les bénéfices, revenus ou gains provenant de Chypre est déduit de l'impôt koweïtien dû au titre de ces bénéfices, revenus ou gains.

3. Dans le cas de Chypre, sous réserve des dispositions existantes de la législation chypriote concernant l'imputation de l'impôt payé dans un territoire en dehors de Chypre sur l'impôt chypriote payable et de toute modification ultérieure de ces dispositions qui n'en affecterait pas le principe général, et sans préjudice d'une déduction ou d'un dégrèvement plus important prévu par la législation chypriote, l'impôt dû au Koweït au titre des bénéfices, revenus ou gains provenant du Koweït est porté en déduction de tout impôt chypriote dû au titre des mêmes bénéfices, revenus ou gains.

Article 24. Limitation des dégrèvements

Lorsque, en application d'une quelconque disposition de la présente Convention, un revenu est exonéré d'impôt dans l'un des États contractants et lorsque, en vertu de la législation en vigueur dans l'autre État contractant, une personne est assujettie à l'impôt en ce qui concerne ledit revenu, non à raison de son montant intégral, mais à raison du montant qui y est transféré ou perçu, l'exonération à accorder dans le premier État contractant en application de la présente Convention ne s'applique qu'au montant ainsi transféré ou perçu dans l'autre État contractant.

Article 25. Non-discrimination

1. Les ressortissants d'un État contractant ne sont soumis dans l'autre État contractant à aucune imposition ou obligation correspondante, qui est autre ou plus lourde que celles auxquelles sont ou pourraient être soumis les ressortissants de cet autre État qui se trouvent dans la même situation.

2. L'imposition d'un établissement stable qu'une entreprise d'un État contractant a dans l'autre État contractant n'est pas établie dans cet autre État d'une façon moins favorable que l'imposition des entreprises de cet autre État qui exercent la même activité.

La présente disposition ne peut être interprétée comme obligeant un État contractant à accorder aux résidents de l'autre État contractant les déductions personnelles, abattements et réductions d'impôts en fonction de la situation ou des charges de famille qu'il accorde à ses propres résidents.

3. Les entreprises d'un État contractant dont le capital est, en totalité ou en partie, directement ou indirectement, détenu ou contrôlé par un ou plusieurs résidents de l'autre État contractant ne sont soumises dans le premier État contractant à aucune imposition ou obligation correspondante qui est autre ou plus lourde que celles auxquelles sont ou pourraient être soumises les autres entreprises similaires du premier État.

4. Dans le présent article, le terme « imposition » désigne les impôts de toute nature ou dénomination.

Article 26. Procédure amiable

1. Lorsqu'un résident d'un État contractant estime que les mesures prises par l'un des États contractants ou par les deux États contractants entraînent ou entraîneront pour lui une imposition non conforme aux dispositions de la présente Convention, il peut soumettre son cas à l'autorité compétente de l'État contractant dont il est un résident. La réclamation correspondante doit être introduite dans un délai de six mois à compter de la date de l'établissement de l'impôt. Les autorités compétentes des États contractants règlent la question dans un délai d'un an à compter de la date de la réclamation.

2. L'autorité compétente s'efforce, si la réclamation lui paraît fondée et si elle n'est pas elle-même en mesure d'y apporter une solution satisfaisante, de résoudre le cas par voie d'accord amiable avec l'autorité compétente de l'autre État contractant, en vue d'éviter une imposition non conforme à la Convention.

3. Les autorités compétentes des États contractants s'efforcent, par voie d'accord amiable, de résoudre les difficultés ou de dissiper les doutes auxquels peuvent donner lieu l'interprétation ou l'application de la Convention. Elles peuvent aussi se concerter en vue d'éliminer les doubles impositions dans les cas non prévus par la Convention.

4. Les autorités compétentes des États contractants peuvent communiquer directement entre elles en vue de parvenir à un accord au sens des paragraphes précédents. Si, pour parvenir à un tel accord, il est jugé souhaitable d'avoir un échange verbal d'opinions, il peut avoir lieu dans le cadre d'une commission composée des représentants des autorités compétentes des États contractants.

Article 27. Échange de renseignements

1. Les autorités compétentes des États contractants échangent les renseignements nécessaires pour appliquer les dispositions de la présente Convention et celles de la législation interne des États contractants relative aux impôts visés par la présente Convention, dans la mesure où l'imposition qu'elle prévoit est conforme à la Convention. Les renseignements ainsi échangés sont tenus secrets et ne peuvent être communiqués qu'aux personnes ou autorités, y compris les tribunaux, qui sont concernées par l'établissement ou le recouvrement des impôts visés par la Convention ou par les procédures et poursuites concernant ces impôts.

2. Les dispositions du paragraphe 1 ne peuvent en aucun cas être interprétées comme imposant à un État contractant l'obligation :

a) De prendre des mesures administratives dérogeant à sa législation et à sa pratique administrative ou à celles de l'autre État contractant ;

b) De fournir des renseignements qui ne pourraient être obtenus sur la base de sa législation ou dans le cadre de sa pratique administrative normale ou de celles de l'autre État contractant ;

c) De fournir des renseignements qui révéleraient un secret commercial, industriel, professionnel ou un procédé commercial ou des renseignements dont la communication serait contraire à l'ordre public.

Article 28. Membres de missions diplomatiques et de postes consulaires

Les dispositions de la présente Convention ne portent pas atteinte aux privilèges fiscaux dont bénéficient les fonctionnaires diplomatiques ou consulaires en vertu soit des règles générales du droit international, soit des dispositions d'accords particuliers.

Article 29. Entrée en vigueur

1. Les Gouvernements des États contractants se notifient mutuellement l'accomplissement de leurs formalités constitutionnelles requises pour l'entrée en vigueur de la présente Convention.

2. La Convention entre en vigueur à la date de la dernière des notifications visées au paragraphe 1 et ses dispositions prennent effet à l'égard des impôts perçus pour toute année d'imposition commençant le 1er janvier de l'année civile au cours de laquelle la Convention entre en vigueur, ou après cette date.

Article 30. Dénonciation et amendement

La présente Convention demeure en vigueur jusqu'à sa dénonciation par l'un des États contractants. L'un ou l'autre État contractant peut dénoncer la Convention, par la voie diplomatique, moyennant une notification écrite faite au moins six mois avant la fin de toute année civile suivant l'expiration d'un délai de cinq ans à compter de la date à laquelle la Convention entre en vigueur.

Dans ce cas, la Convention cesse d'être applicable à l'égard des impôts perçus pour tout exercice fiscal commençant le 1er janvier de l'année civile suivant celle au cours de laquelle la notification a été faite, ou après cette date. La présente Convention peut toutefois être amendée à tout moment par un accord subséquent entre les États contractants.

EN FOI DE QUOI, les soussignés, à ce dûment autorisés, ont signé la présente Convention.

FAIT à Koweït, le 15 décembre 1984, en deux exemplaires originaux en langue anglaise.

Pour le Gouvernement de la République de Chypre :
[SIGNÉ]

Pour le Gouvernement de l'État du Koweït :
[SIGNÉ]

No. 54751

Ireland
and
Botswana

Agreement between the Government of the Republic of Botswana and the Government of Ireland for the avoidance of double taxation and the prevention of fiscal evasion with respect to taxes on income (with protocol). Gaborone, 10 June 2014

Entry into force: *3 February 2016 by notification, in accordance with article 29*

Authentic text: *English*

Registration with the Secretariat of the United Nations: *Ireland, 1 November 2017*

Irlande
et
Botswana

Accord entre le Gouvernement de la République du Botswana et le Gouvernement de l'Irlande tendant à éviter les doubles impositions et à prévenir la fraude fiscale en matière d'impôts sur le revenu (avec protocole). Gaborone, 10 juin 2014

Entrée en vigueur : *3 février 2016 par notification, conformément à l'article 29*

Texte authentique : *anglais*

Enregistrement au Secrétariat de l'Organisation des Nations Unies : *Irlande, 1er novembre 2017*

[TEXT IN ENGLISH – TEXTE EN ANGLAIS]

AGREEMENT

BETWEEN

THE GOVERNMENT OF THE REPUBLIC OF BOTSWANA

AND

THE GOVERNMENT OF IRELAND

FOR

THE AVOIDANCE OF DOUBLE TAXATION

AND

THE PREVENTION OF FISCAL EVASION WITH RESPECT

TO

TAXES ON INCOME

Preamble

The Government of the Republic of Botswana and the Government of Ireland, desiring to conclude an Agreement for the avoidance of double taxation and the prevention of fiscal evasion with respect to taxes on income, have agreed as follows:

Article 1

PERSONS COVERED

This Agreement shall apply to persons who are residents of one or both of the Contracting States.

Article 2

TAXES COVERED

1. This Agreement shall apply to taxes on income imposed by each Contracting State, irrespective of the manner in which they are levied.

2. There shall be regarded as taxes on income all taxes imposed on total income or on elements of income, including taxes on gains from the alienation of movable or immovable property.

3. The existing taxes to which this Agreement shall apply are in particular:

(a) in Botswana:

(i) the income tax; and

(ii) the capital gains tax;

(hereinafter referred to as "Botswana tax"); and

(b) in Ireland:

(i) the income tax;

(ii) the universal social charge;

(iii) the corporation tax; and

(iv) the capital gains tax;

(hereinafter referred to as " Irish tax").

4. The Agreement shall apply also to any identical or substantially similar taxes which are imposed by either Contracting State after the date of signature of the Agreement in addition to, or in place of, the existing taxes. The competent authorities of the Contracting States shall notify each other of any significant changes which have been made in their respective taxation laws.

Article 3

GENERAL DEFINITIONS

1. For the purposes of this Agreement, unless the context otherwise requires:

(a) the term "Botswana" means the Republic of Botswana;

(b) the term "Ireland" includes any area outside the territorial waters of Ireland which has been or may hereafter be designated, under the laws of Ireland concerning the Exclusive Economic Zone and the Continental Shelf, as an area within which Ireland may exercise such sovereign rights and jurisdiction as are in conformity with international law;

(c) the terms "a Contracting State" and "the other Contracting State" mean Botswana or Ireland, as the context requires; and the term "Contracting States" means Botswana and Ireland;

(d) the term "company" means any body corporate or any entity which is treated as a body corporate for tax purposes;

(e) the term "competent authority" means:

(i) in Botswana, the Minister of Finance and Development Planning, represented by the Commissioner General of the Botswana Unified Revenue Service or his authorised representative; and

(ii) in Ireland, the Revenue Commissioners or their authorised representative;

(f) the term "enterprise" applies to the carrying on of any business;

(g) the terms "enterprise of a Contracting State" and "enterprise of the other Contracting State" mean respectively an enterprise carried on by a resident of a Contracting State and an enterprise carried on by a resident of the other Contracting State;

(h) the term "international traffic" means any transport by a ship or aircraft operated by an enterprise of a Contracting State, except when the ship or aircraft is operated solely between places in the other Contracting State;

(i) the term "national", in relation to a Contracting State, means:
  (i) any individual possessing the nationality or citizenship of that Contracting State; and
  (ii) any legal person or association deriving its status as such from the laws in force in that Contracting State;

(j) the term "person" includes an individual, a trust, a company and any other body of persons;

(k) the term "business" includes the performance of professional services and of other activities of an independent character.

2. As regards the application of the provisions of this Agreement at any time by a Contracting State, any term not defined therein shall, unless the context otherwise requires, have the meaning that it has at that time under the law of that State for the purposes of the taxes to which this Agreement applies, any meaning under the applicable tax laws of that State prevailing over a meaning given to the term under other laws of that State.

Article 4

RESIDENT

1. For the purposes of this Agreement, the term "resident of a Contracting State" means any person who, under the laws of that State, is liable to tax therein by reason of his domicile,

residence, place of management or any other criterion of a similar nature, and also includes that State and any local authority thereof. This term, however, does not include any person who is liable to tax in that State in respect only of income from sources in that State.

2. Where by reason of the provisions of paragraph 1 an individual is a resident of both Contracting States, then his status shall be determined as follows:

(a) he shall be deemed to be a resident only of the State in which he has a permanent home available to him; if he has a permanent home available to him in both States, he shall be deemed to be a resident only of the State with which his personal and economic relations are closer (centre of vital interests);

(b) if the State in which he has his centre of vital interests cannot be determined, or if he has not a permanent home available to him in either State, he shall be deemed to be a resident only of the State in which he has an habitual abode;

(c) if he has an habitual abode in both States or in neither of them, he shall be deemed to be a resident only of the State of which he is a national;

(d) if he is a national of both States or of neither of them, the competent authorities of the Contracting States shall settle the question by mutual agreement.

3. Where by reason of the provisions of paragraph 1 a person other than an individual is a resident of both Contracting States, then it shall be deemed to be a resident only of the State in which its place of effective management is situated. If the place in which its place of effective management is situated cannot be determined, then the competent authorities of the Contracting States shall endeavour to settle the question by mutual agreement.

Article 5

PERMANENT ESTABLISHMENT

1. For the purposes of this Agreement, the term "permanent establishment" means a fixed place of business through which the business of an enterprise is wholly or partly carried on.

2. The term "permanent establishment" includes especially:

   (a) a place of management;

   (b) a branch;

   (c) an office;

   (d) a factory;

   (e) a workshop;

   (f) a mine, an oil or gas well, a quarry or any other place of extraction or exploitation of natural resources; and

   (g) an installation or structure used for the exploration of natural resources provided that the installation or structure continues for a period of more than six months within any twelve-month period.

3. The term "permanent establishment" likewise encompasses:

   (a) a building site, a construction, assembly or installation project, but only where such site or project continues for a period of more than six months within any twelve-month period;

   (b) the furnishing of services, including consultancy services, by an enterprise through employees or other personnel engaged by an enterprise for such purpose, but only where activities of that nature continue (for the same or a connected project) within the Contracting State for a period or periods aggregating more than six months within any twelve-month period; and

   (c) the performance of professional services or other activities of an independent character by an individual, but only where those services or activities continue within a Contracting State for a period or periods exceeding in the aggregate 183 days in any twelve-month period commencing or ending in the fiscal year concerned.

4. Notwithstanding the preceding provisions of this Article, the term "permanent establishment" shall be deemed not to include:

(a) the use of facilities solely for the purpose of storage, display or delivery of goods or merchandise belonging to the enterprise;

(b) the maintenance of a stock of goods or merchandise belonging to the enterprise solely for the purpose of processing by another enterprise;

(c) the maintenance of a stock of goods or merchandise belonging to the enterprise solely for the purpose of storage, display or delivery;

(d) the maintenance of a fixed place of business solely for the purpose of purchasing goods or merchandise, or for collecting information, for the enterprise;

(e) the maintenance of a fixed place of business solely for the purpose of carrying on, for the enterprise, any other activity of a preparatory or auxiliary character; and

(f) the maintenance of a fixed place of business solely for any combination of activities mentioned in subparagraphs (a) to (e), provided that the overall activity of the fixed place of business resulting from this combination is of a preparatory or auxiliary character.

5. Notwithstanding the provisions of paragraphs 1 and 2, where a person – other than an agent of an independent status to whom paragraph 6 applies – is acting in a Contracting State on behalf of an enterprise of the other Contracting State, that enterprise shall be deemed to have a permanent establishment in the first-mentioned Contracting State in respect of any activities which that person undertakes for the enterprise, if such person has, and habitually exercises, in that State an authority to conclude contracts in the name of the enterprise, unless the activities of such person are limited to those mentioned in paragraph 4 which, if exercised through a fixed place of business, would not make this fixed place of business a permanent establishment under the provisions of that paragraph.

6. An enterprise of a Contracting State shall not be deemed to have a permanent establishment in the other Contracting State merely because it carries on business in that other State through a broker, general commission agent or any other agent of an independent status, provided that such persons are acting in the ordinary course of their business.

7. The fact that a company which is a resident of a Contracting State controls or is controlled by a company which is a resident of the other Contracting State, or which carries on business in that other State (whether through a permanent establishment or otherwise), shall not of itself constitute either company a permanent establishment of the other.

Article 6

INCOME FROM IMMOVABLE PROPERTY

1. Income derived by a resident of a Contracting State from immovable property, including income from agriculture or forestry, situated in the other Contracting State may be taxed in that other State.

2. The term "immovable property" shall have the meaning which it has under the law of the Contracting State in which the property in question is situated. The term shall in any case include property accessory to immovable property, livestock and equipment used in agriculture and forestry, rights to which the provisions of general law respecting landed property apply, usufruct of immovable property and rights to variable or fixed payments as consideration for the working of, or the right to work, mineral deposits, sources and other natural resources; ships, boats and aircraft shall not be regarded as immovable property.

3. The provisions of paragraph 1 shall apply to income derived from the direct use, letting or use in any other form of immovable property.

4. The provisions of paragraphs 1 and 3 shall also apply to the income from immovable property of an enterprise.

Article 7
BUSINESS PROFITS

1. The profits of an enterprise of a Contracting State shall be taxable only in that State unless the enterprise carries on business in the other Contracting State through a permanent establishment situated therein. If the enterprise carries on business as aforesaid, the profits of the enterprise may be taxed in the other State but only so much of them as is attributable to that permanent establishment.

2. Subject to the provisions of paragraph 3, where an enterprise of a Contracting State carries on business in the other Contracting State through a permanent establishment situated therein, there shall in each Contracting State be attributed to that permanent establishment the profits which it might be expected to make if it were a distinct and separate enterprise engaged in the same or similar activities under the same or similar conditions and dealing wholly independently with the enterprise of which it is a permanent establishment.

3. In determining the profits of a permanent establishment, there shall be allowed as deductions expenses which are incurred for the purposes of the permanent establishment, including executive and general administrative expenses so incurred, whether in the State in which the permanent establishment is situated or elsewhere. However, no such deduction shall be allowed in respect of amounts, if any, paid (otherwise than towards reimbursement of actual expenses) by the permanent establishment to the head office of the enterprise or any of its other offices, by way of royalties, fees or other similar payments in return for the use of patents or other rights, or by way of commission, for specific services performed or for management, or, except in the case of a banking enterprise, by way of interest on moneys lent to the permanent establishment. Likewise, no account shall be taken, in the determination of the profits of a permanent establishment, for amounts charged (otherwise than towards reimbursement of actual expenses) by the permanent establishment to the head office of the enterprise or any of its other offices, by way of royalties, fees or other similar payments in return for use of patents or other rights, or by way of commission for specific services performed or for management, or except in the case of a banking enterprise, by way of interest on moneys lent to the head office of the enterprise or any of its other offices.

4. Insofar as it has been customary in a Contracting State to determine the profits to be attributed to a permanent establishment on the basis of an apportionment of the total profits of the enterprise to its various parts, nothing in paragraph 2 shall preclude that Contracting State from determining the profits to be taxed by such an apportionment as may be customary; the method of apportionment adopted shall, however, be such that the result shall be in accordance with the principles contained in this Article.

5. No profits shall be attributed to a permanent establishment by reason of the mere purchase by that permanent establishment of goods or merchandise for the enterprise.

6. For the purposes of the preceding paragraphs, the profits to be attributed to the permanent establishment shall be determined by the same method year by year unless there is good and sufficient reason to the contrary.

7. Where profits include items of income or gains which are dealt with separately in other Articles of this Agreement, then the provisions of those Articles shall not be affected by the provisions of this Article.

Article 8

INTERNATIONAL TRANSPORT

1. Profits of an enterprise of a Contracting State from the operation of ships or aircraft in international traffic shall be taxable only in that State.

2. For the purposes of this Article, profits derived from the operation of ships or aircraft in international traffic include profits derived from the rental of ships or aircraft if such ships or aircraft are operated in international traffic or if such rental profits are incidental to other profits described in paragraph 1.

3. Profits of an enterprise of a Contracting State from the use or rental of containers (including trailers, barges, and related equipment for the transport of containers) used for the transport in international traffic of goods or merchandise shall be taxable only in that State.

4. The provisions of paragraph 1 shall also apply to profits from the participation in a pool, a joint business or an international operating agency.

Article 9

ASSOCIATED ENTERPRISES

1. Where:

   (a) an enterprise of a Contracting State participates directly or indirectly in the management, control or capital of an enterprise of the other Contracting State, or

   (b) the same persons participate directly or indirectly in the management, control or capital of an enterprise of a Contracting State and an enterprise of the other Contracting State,

and in either case conditions are made or imposed between the two enterprises in their commercial or financial relations which differ from those which would be made between independent enterprises, then any profits which would, but for those conditions, have accrued to one of the enterprises, but, by reason of those conditions, have not so accrued, may be included in the profits of that enterprise and taxed accordingly.

2. Where a Contracting State includes in the profits of an enterprise of that State – and taxes accordingly – profits on which an enterprise of the other Contracting State has been charged to tax in that other State and the profits so included are profits which would have accrued to the enterprise of the first-mentioned State if the conditions made between the two enterprises had been those which would have been made between independent enterprises, then that other State shall make an appropriate adjustment to the amount of the tax charged therein on those profits. In determining such adjustment, due regard shall be had to the other provisions of this Agreement and the competent authorities of the Contracting States shall if necessary consult each other.

Article 10
DIVIDENDS

1. Dividends paid by a company which is a resident of a Contracting State to a resident of the other Contracting State may be taxed in that other State.

2. However, such dividends may also be taxed in the Contracting State of which the company paying the dividends is a resident and according to the laws of that State, but if the beneficial owner of the dividends is a resident of the other Contracting State, the tax so charged shall not exceed 5 per cent of the gross amount of the dividends in all cases.

This paragraph shall not affect taxation of the company in respect of the profits out of which the dividends are paid.

3. Notwithstanding the provisions of paragraph 2, dividends arising in a Contracting State and paid to, and beneficially owned by, the Government of the other Contracting State shall be exempt from tax in the first-mentioned State.

4. The term "dividends" as used in this Article means income from shares, "jouissance" shares or "jouissance" rights, mining shares, founders' shares or other rights (not being debt-claims) participating in profits, as well as income from other corporate rights which is subjected to the same taxation treatment as income from shares by the laws of the Contracting State of which the company making the distribution is a resident.

5. The provisions of paragraphs 1 and 2 shall not apply if the beneficial owner of the dividends, being a resident of a Contracting State, carries on business in the other Contracting State of which the company paying the dividends is a resident through a permanent establishment situated therein and the holding in respect of which the dividends are paid is effectively connected with such permanent establishment. In such case, the provisions of Article 7 shall apply.

6. Where a company which is a resident of a Contracting State derives profits or income from the other Contracting State, that other State may not impose any tax on the dividends paid by the company, except insofar as such dividends are paid to a resident of that other State or insofar as the holding in respect of which the dividends are paid is effectively connected with a permanent establishment situated in that other State, nor subject the company's undistributed profits to a tax on undistributed profits, even if the dividends paid or the undistributed profits consist wholly or partly of profits or income arising in such other State.

Article 11
INTEREST

1. Interest arising in a Contracting State and paid to a resident of the other Contracting State may be taxed in that other State.

2. However, such interest may also be taxed in the State in which it arises and according to the laws of that State, but if the recipient is the beneficial owner of the interest, the tax so charged shall not exceed 7.5 per cent of the gross amount of the interest.

3. Notwithstanding the provisions of paragraph 2, interest arising in a Contracting State shall be exempt from tax in that State if it is paid to, and beneficially owned by, the Government of the other Contracting State or a local authority thereof.

4. The term "interest" as used in this Article means income from debt-claims of every kind, whether or not secured by mortgage and whether or not carrying a right to participate in the debtor's profits, and in particular, income from government securities and income from bonds or debentures, including premiums and prizes attaching to such securities, bonds or debentures. Penalty charges for late payment shall not be regarded as interest for the purposes of this Article.

5. The provisions of paragraphs 1 and 2 shall not apply if the beneficial owner of the interest, being a resident of a Contracting State, carries on business in the other Contracting State in which the interest arises through a permanent establishment situated therein and the debt-claim

in respect of which the interest is paid is effectively connected with such permanent establishment. In such case, the provisions of Article 7 shall apply.

6. Interest shall be deemed to arise in a Contracting State when the payer is a resident of that State. Where, however, the person paying the interest, whether he is a resident of a Contracting State or not, has in a Contracting State a permanent establishment in connection with which the indebtedness on which the interest is paid was incurred, and such interest is borne by such permanent establishment, then such interest shall be deemed to arise in the State in which the permanent establishment is situated.

7. Where, by reason of a special relationship between the payer and the beneficial owner or between both of them and some other person, the amount of the interest, having regard to the debt-claim for which it is paid, exceeds the amount which would have been agreed upon by the payer and the beneficial owner in the absence of such relationship, the provisions of this Article shall apply only to the last-mentioned amount. In such case, the excess part of the payments shall remain taxable according to the laws of each Contracting State, due regard being had to the other provisions of this Agreement.

Article 12

ROYALTIES

1. Royalties arising in a Contracting State and paid to a resident of the other Contracting State may be taxed in that other State.

2. However, such royalties may also be taxed in the Contracting State in which they arise, and according to the laws of that State, but if the recipient is the beneficial owner of the royalties, the tax so charged shall not exceed:

(a) 5 per cent of the gross amount of the royalties in respect of the use of or the right to use industrial, commercial or scientific equipment; and

(b) 7.5 per cent of the gross amount of the royalties in all other cases.

3. The term "royalties" as used in this Article means payments of any kind received as a consideration for the use of, or the right to use, any copyright of literary, artistic or scientific work (including cinematographic films and recordings on tape or other media used for radio or television broadcasting or other means of reproduction or transmission), any patent, trade mark, design or model, plan, secret formula or process, or the use of or the right to use industrial, commercial or scientific equipment or for information concerning industrial, commercial or scientific experience.

4. The provisions of paragraphs 1 and 2 shall not apply if the beneficial owner of the royalties, being a resident of a Contracting State, carries on business in the other Contracting State in which the royalties arise through a permanent establishment situated therein and the right or property in respect of which the royalties are paid is effectively connected with such permanent establishment. In such case, the provisions of Article 7 shall apply.

5. Royalties shall be deemed to arise in a Contracting State when the payer is a resident of that State. Where, however, the person paying the royalties, whether he is a resident of a Contracting State or not, has in a Contracting State a permanent establishment in connection with which the liability to pay the royalties was incurred, and such royalties are borne by such permanent establishment, then such royalties shall be deemed to arise in the State in which the permanent establishment is situated.

6. Where, by reason of a special relationship between the payer and the beneficial owner or between both of them and some other person, the amount of the royalties, having regard to the use, right or information for which they are paid, exceeds the amount which would have been agreed upon by the payer and the beneficial owner in the absence of such relationship, the provisions of this Article shall apply only to the last-mentioned amount. In such case, the excess part of the payments shall remain taxable according to the laws of each Contracting State, due regard being had to the other provisions of this Agreement.

Article 13

CAPITAL GAINS

1. Gains derived by a resident of a Contracting State from the alienation of immovable property referred to in Article 6 and situated in the other Contracting State may be taxed in that other State.

2. Gains from the alienation of movable property forming part of the business property of a permanent establishment which an enterprise of a Contracting State has in the other Contracting State, including such gains from the alienation of such a permanent establishment (alone or with the whole enterprise), may be taxed in that other State.

3. Gains of an enterprise of a Contracting State from the alienation of ships or aircraft operated in international traffic, or movable property pertaining to the operation of such ships or aircraft, shall be taxable only in that State.

4. Gains derived by a resident of a Contracting State from the alienation of:

(a) shares, other than shares quoted on a recognised stock exchange, deriving more than 50 per cent of their value directly or indirectly from immovable property situated in the other Contracting State; or

(b) an interest in a partnership or trust deriving more than 50 per cent of its value directly or indirectly from immovable property situated in the other Contracting State,

may be taxed in that other State.

5. Gains from the alienation of any property, other than that referred to in paragraphs 1, 2, 3 and 4, shall be taxable only in the Contracting State of which the alienator is a resident.

6. The provisions of paragraph 5 shall not affect the right of a Contracting State to levy, according to its law, a tax on gains from the alienation of any property derived by an individual

who is a resident of the other Contracting State and has been a resident of the first-mentioned State at any time during the five years immediately preceding the alienation of the property.

Article 14

INCOME FROM EMPLOYMENT

1. Subject to the provisions of Articles 15, 17 and 18, salaries, wages and other similar remuneration derived by a resident of a Contracting State in respect of an employment shall be taxable only in that State unless the employment is exercised in the other Contracting State. If the employment is so exercised, such remuneration as is derived therefrom may be taxed in that other State.

2. Notwithstanding the provisions of paragraph 1, remuneration derived by a resident of a Contracting State in respect of an employment exercised in the other Contracting State shall be taxable only in the first-mentioned State if:

(a) the recipient is present in the other Contracting State for a period or periods not exceeding in the aggregate 183 days in any twelve-month period commencing or ending in the fiscal year concerned; and

(b) the remuneration is paid by, or on behalf of, an employer who is not a resident of the other State; and

(c) the remuneration is not borne by a permanent establishment which the employer has in the other State.

3. Notwithstanding the preceding provisions of this Article, remuneration derived in respect of an employment exercised aboard a ship or aircraft operated in international traffic by an enterprise of a Contracting State may be taxed in that Contracting State.

Article 15

DIRECTORS' FEES

Directors' fees and other similar payments derived by a resident of a Contracting State in his capacity as a member of the board of directors of a company which is a resident of the other Contracting State may be taxed in that other State.

Article 16

ENTERTAINERS AND SPORTSPERSONS

1. Notwithstanding the provisions of Articles 7 and 14, income derived by a resident of a Contracting State as an entertainer, such as a theatre, motion picture, radio or television artiste, or a musician, or as a sportsperson, from his personal activities as such exercised in the other Contracting State, may be taxed in that other State.

2. Where income in respect of personal activities exercised by an entertainer or a sportsperson is his capacity as such accrues not to the entertainer or sportsperson himself but to another person, that income may, notwithstanding the provisions of Articles 7 and 14, be taxed in the Contracting State in which the activities of the entertainer or sportsperson are exercised.

3. The provisions of paragraphs 1 and 2 shall not apply to income derived by entertainers or sportspersons who are residents of a Contracting State from their personal activities as entertainers or sportspersons exercised in the other Contracting State if their visit to that other State is supported wholly or mainly by public funds of the first-mentioned Contracting State, or a local authority thereof, or takes place under a cultural agreement or arrangement between the Governments of the Contracting States. In such a case, the income shall be taxable only in the Contracting State of which the entertainer or sportsperson, as the case may be, is a resident.

Article 17

PENSIONS AND ANNUITIES

1. Subject to the provisions of paragraph 2 of Article 18, pensions and other similar remuneration in consideration of past employment and any annuity arising in a Contracting State

and paid to a resident of the other Contracting State may be taxed in the first-mentioned Contracting State.

2. The term "annuity" means a stated sum payable periodically at stated times during life or during a specified or ascertainable period of time under an obligation to make the payments in return for adequate and full consideration in money or money's worth.

Article 18

GOVERNMENT SERVICE

1. (a) Salaries, wages and other similar remuneration paid by a Contracting State or a local authority thereof to an individual in respect of services rendered to that State or authority shall be taxable only in that State.

(b) However, such salaries, wages and other similar remuneration shall be taxable only in the other Contracting State if the services are rendered in that State and the individual is a resident of that State who:

(i) is a national of that State; or

(ii) did not become a resident of that State solely for the purpose of rendering the services.

2. (a) Notwithstanding the provisions of paragraph 1, pensions and other similar remuneration paid by, or out of funds created by, a Contracting State or a local authority thereof to an individual in respect of services rendered to that State or authority shall be taxable only in that State.

(b) However, such pensions and other similar remuneration shall be taxable only in the other Contracting State if the individual is a resident of, and a national of, that State.

3. The provisions of Articles 14, 15, 16 and 17 shall apply to salaries, wages, pensions and other similar remuneration in respect of services rendered in connection with a business carried on by a Contracting State or a local authority thereof.

Article 19

STUDENTS, APPRENTICES AND BUSINESS TRAINEES

A student, apprentice or business trainee who is present in a Contracting State solely for the purpose of his education or training and who is, or immediately before being so present was, a resident of the other Contracting State shall be exempt from tax in the first-mentioned State on payments received from outside that first-mentioned State for the purposes of his maintenance, education or training.

Article 20

TECHNICAL FEES

1. Technical fees arising in a Contracting State which are paid to a resident of the other Contracting State may be taxed in that other State.

2. However, such technical fees may also be taxed in the Contracting State in which they arise, and according to the law of that State, but where such technical fees are paid to a resident of the other Contracting State who is subject to tax in that State in respect thereof, the tax charged in the Contracting State in which the technical fees arise shall not exceed 7.5 per cent of the gross amount of such fees.

3. The term "technical fees" as used in this Article means payments of any kind to any person, other than to an employee of the person making the payments, in consideration for any services of an administrative, technical, managerial or consultancy nature.

4. The provisions of paragraphs 1 and 2 of this Article shall not apply if the recipient of the technical fees, being a resident of a Contracting State, carries on business in the other Contracting State in which the technical fees arise, through a permanent establishment situated therein and the technical fees are effectively connected with such permanent establishment. In such case, the provisions of Article 7 shall apply.

5. Technical fees shall be deemed to arise in a Contracting State when the payer is that State, or a local authority thereof or a resident of that State. Where, however, the person paying the technical fees, whether he is a resident of a Contracting State or not, has in a Contracting State a permanent establishment in connection with which the obligation to pay the technical fees was incurred, and such technical fees are borne by that permanent establishment, then such technical fees shall be deemed to arise in the State in which the permanent establishment is situated.

6. Where, by reason of a special relationship between the payer and the recipient or between both of them and some other person, the amount of the technical fees paid exceeds, for whatever reason, the amount which would have been agreed upon by the payer and the recipient in the absence of such relationship, the provisions of this Article shall apply only to the last-mentioned amount. In such case, the excess part of the payments shall remain taxable according to the law of each Contracting State, due regard being had to the other provisions of this Agreement.

7. Notwithstanding paragraph 2, where, in any Agreement for the avoidance of double taxation and the prevention of fiscal evasion entered into by Botswana with any State other than Ireland after the signing of this Agreement, the rate of tax specified in the Article relating to technical fees is a rate less than 7.5 per cent, such lower rate shall apply as if it had been the rate specified in this Article.

Article 21

OTHER INCOME

1. Items of income of a resident of a Contracting State, wherever arising, not dealt with in the foregoing Articles of this Agreement shall be taxable only in that State.

2. The provisions of paragraph 1 shall not apply to income, other than income from immovable property as defined in paragraph 2 of Article 6, if the beneficial owner of such income, being a resident of a Contracting State, carries on business in the other Contracting State through a permanent establishment situated therein and the right or property in respect of which the income is paid is effectively connected with such permanent establishment. In such case, the provisions of Article 7 shall apply.

Article 22

MISCELLANEOUS RULES APPLICABLE TO CERTAIN OFFSHORE ACTIVITIES

1. The provisions of this Article shall apply notwithstanding any other provision of this Agreement where activities (in this Article called "relevant activities") are carried on offshore in connection with the exploration or exploitation of the seabed and subsoil and their natural resources situated in a Contracting State.

2. An enterprise of a Contracting State which carries on relevant activities in the other Contracting State shall, subject to paragraph 3 of this Article, be deemed to be carrying on business in that other State through a permanent establishment situated therein.

3. Relevant activities which are carried on by an enterprise of a Contracting State in the other Contracting State for a period or periods not exceeding in the aggregate 30 days within any period of twelve months shall not constitute the carrying on of business through a permanent establishment situated therein. For the purposes of this paragraph:

(a) where an enterprise of a Contracting State carrying on relevant activities in the other Contracting State is associated with another enterprise carrying on substantially similar relevant activities there, the former enterprise shall be deemed to be carrying on all such activities of the latter enterprise, except to the extent that those activities are carried on at the same time as its own activities;

(b) an enterprise shall be regarded as associated with another enterprise if one participates directly or indirectly in the management, control or capital of the other or if the same persons participate directly or indirectly in the management, control or capital of both enterprises.

4. Salaries, wages and similar remuneration derived by a resident of a Contracting State in respect of an employment connected with relevant activities in the other Contracting State may,

to the extent that the duties are performed offshore in that other State, be taxed in that other State.

5. Gains derived by a resident of a Contracting State from the alienation of:

(a) exploration or exploitation rights; or

(b) shares (or comparable instruments) deriving their value or the greater part of their value directly or indirectly from such rights,

may be taxed in that other State.

In this paragraph "exploration or exploitation rights" mean rights to assets to be produced by the exploration or exploitation of the seabed or subsoil or their natural resources in the other Contracting State, including rights to interests in or to the benefit of such assets.

Article 23

ELIMINATION OF DOUBLE TAXATION

1. Double taxation shall be eliminated as follows:

(a) in Botswana, subject to the provisions of the laws of Botswana regarding the allowance of a credit against Botswana tax of tax payable under the laws of a country outside Botswana, Irish tax payable under the laws of Ireland and in accordance with this Agreement, whether directly or by deduction, on profits or income liable to tax in Ireland shall be allowed as a credit against any Botswana tax payable in respect of the same profits or income by reference to which the Irish tax is computed. However, the amount of such credit shall not exceed the amount of the Botswana tax payable on that income in accordance with the laws of Botswana;

(b) in Ireland, subject to the provisions of the laws of Ireland regarding the allowance as a credit against Irish tax of tax payable in a territory outside Ireland (which shall not affect the general principle thereof) -

(i) Botswana tax payable under the laws of Botswana and in accordance with this Agreement, whether directly or by deduction, on profits, income or gains from sources within Botswana (excluding in the case of a dividend tax payable in respect of the profits out of which the dividend is paid) shall be allowed as a credit against any Irish tax computed by reference to the same profits, income or gains by reference to which Botswana tax is computed;

(ii) in the case of a dividend paid by a company which is a resident of Botswana to a company which is a resident of Ireland and which controls directly or indirectly 5 per cent or more of the voting power in the company paying the dividend, the credit shall take into account (in addition to any Botswana tax creditable under the provisions of subparagraph (b)(i)) Botswana tax payable by the company in respect of the profits out of which such dividend is paid;

(iii) for the purposes of subparagraph (i), profits, income and capital gains owned by a resident of Ireland which may be taxed in Botswana in accordance with this Agreement shall be deemed to be derived from sources in Botswana.

2. Where in accordance with any provision of the Agreement income derived by a resident of a Contracting State is exempt from tax in that State, such State may nevertheless, in calculating the amount of tax on the remaining income of such resident, take into account the exempted income.

3. Where under any provision of this Agreement, income or gains is or are wholly or partly relieved from tax in a Contracting State and, under the laws in force in the other Contracting State, an individual, in respect of the said income or gains, is subject to tax by reference to the amount thereof which is remitted to or received in that other State, and not by reference to the full amount thereof, then the relief to be allowed under this Agreement in the first-mentioned State shall apply only to so much of the income or gains as is remitted to or received in that other State.

Article 24

NON-DISCRIMINATION

1. Nationals of a Contracting State shall not be subjected in the other Contracting State to any taxation or any requirement connected therewith, which is other or more burdensome than the taxation and connected requirements to which nationals of that other State in the same circumstances, in particular with respect to residence, are or may be subjected. This provision shall, notwithstanding the provisions of Article 1, also apply to persons who are not residents of one or both of the Contracting States.

2. The taxation on a permanent establishment which an enterprise of a Contracting State has in the other Contracting State shall not be less favourably levied in that other State than the taxation levied on enterprises of that other State carrying on the same activities. This provision shall not be construed as obliging a Contracting State to grant to residents of the other Contracting State any personal allowances, reliefs and reductions for taxation purposes on account of civil status or family responsibilities which it grants to its own residents.

3. Enterprises of a Contracting State, the capital of which is wholly or partly owned or controlled, directly or indirectly, by one or more residents of the other Contracting State, shall not be subjected in the first-mentioned State to any taxation or any requirement connected therewith which is other or more burdensome than the taxation and connected requirements to which other similar enterprises of that first-mentioned State are or may be subjected.

4. Except where the provisions of paragraph 1 of Article 9, paragraph 7 of Article 11, paragraph 6 of Article 12 and paragraph 6 of Article 20 apply, interest, royalties, technical fees and other disbursements paid by an enterprise of a Contracting State to a resident of the other Contracting State shall, for the purpose of determining the taxable profits of such enterprise, be deductible under the same conditions as if they had been paid to a resident of the first-mentioned State.

Article 25

MUTUAL AGREEMENT PROCEDURE

1. Where a person considers that the actions of one or both of the Contracting States result or will result for him in taxation not in accordance with the provisions of this Agreement, he may, irrespective of the remedies provided by the domestic law of those States, present his case to the competent authority of the Contracting State of which he is a resident or, if his case comes under paragraph 1 of Article 24, to that of the Contracting State of which he is a national. The case must be presented within three years from the first notification of the action resulting in taxation not in accordance with the provisions of this Agreement.

2. The competent authority shall endeavour, if the objection appears to it to be justified and if it is not itself able to arrive at a satisfactory solution, to resolve the case by mutual agreement with the competent authority of the other Contracting State, with a view to the avoidance of taxation which is not in accordance with the Agreement. Any agreement reached shall be implemented notwithstanding any time limits in the domestic law of the Contracting States.

3. The competent authorities of the Contracting States shall endeavour to resolve by mutual agreement any difficulties or doubts arising as to the interpretation or application of the Agreement. They may also consult together for the elimination of double taxation in cases not provided for in the Agreement.

4. The competent authorities of the Contracting States may communicate with each other directly for the purpose of reaching an agreement in the sense of the preceding paragraphs.

Article 26

EXCHANGE OF INFORMATION

1. The competent authorities of the Contracting States shall exchange such information as is foreseeably relevant for carrying out the provisions of this Agreement or to the administration or enforcement of the domestic laws concerning taxes of every kind and description imposed on behalf of the Contracting States, or of their political subdivisions or local authorities, insofar as

the taxation thereunder is not contrary to the Agreement. The exchange of information is not restricted by Articles 1 and 2.

2. Any information received under paragraph 1 by a Contracting State shall be treated as secret in the same manner as information obtained under the domestic laws of that State and shall be disclosed only to persons or authorities (including courts and administrative bodies) concerned with the assessment or collection of, the enforcement or prosecution in respect of, the determination of appeals in relation to the taxes referred to in paragraph 1, or the oversight of the above. Such persons or authorities shall use the information only for such purposes. They may disclose the information in public court proceedings or in judicial decisions.

3. In no case shall the provisions of paragraphs 1 and 2 be construed so as to impose on a Contracting State the obligation:

(a) to carry out administrative measures at variance with the laws and administrative practice of that or of the other Contracting State;

(b) to supply information which is not obtainable under the laws or in the normal course of the administration of that or of the other Contracting State;

(c) to supply information which would disclose any trade, business, industrial, commercial or professional secret or trade process, or information the disclosure of which would be contrary to public policy (*ordre public*).

4. If information is requested by a Contracting State in accordance with this Article, the other Contracting State shall use its information gathering measures to obtain the requested information, even though that other State may not need such information for its own tax purposes. The obligation contained in the preceding sentence is subject to the limitations of paragraph 3 but in no case shall such limitations be construed to permit a Contracting State to decline to supply information solely because it has no domestic interest in such information.

5. In no case shall the provisions of paragraph 3 be construed to permit a Contracting State to decline to supply information solely because the information is held by a bank, other financial institution, nominee or person acting in an agency or a fiduciary capacity or because it relates to ownership interests in a person.

Article 27

ASSISTANCE IN COLLECTION

1. The Contracting States shall to the extent permitted by their respective domestic law, lend assistance to each other in order to collect the taxes referred to in Article 2 as well as interest and penalties with regard to such taxes, provided that reasonable steps to recover such taxes have been taken by the Contracting State requesting such assistance.

2. Claims which are the subject of requests for assistance shall not have priority over taxes owing in the Contracting State rendering assistance and the provisions of paragraph 1 of Article 26 shall also apply to any information which, by virtue of this Article, is supplied to the competent authority of a Contracting State.

3. The competent authorities of the Contracting States shall by mutual agreement settle the mode of application of the provisions of this Article.

Article 28

MEMBERS OF DIPLOMATIC MISSIONS AND CONSULAR POSTS

Nothing in this Agreement shall affect the fiscal privileges of members of diplomatic missions or consular posts under the general rules of international law or under the provisions of special agreements.

Article 29

ENTRY INTO FORCE

1. Each of the Contracting States shall notify to the other the completion of the procedures required by its law for the bringing into force of this Agreement. This Agreement shall enter into force on the date of receipt of the later of these notifications.

2. The provisions of the Agreement shall thereupon have effect:

(a) in Botswana:

(i) as respects taxes withheld at source, for any amounts paid or credited on or after the thirtieth day following the date upon which the Agreement enters into force; and

(ii) as respects other taxes, for any year of assessment beginning on or after the first day of July next following the year in which the Agreement enters into force;

(b) in Ireland:

(i) as respects income tax, the universal social charge and capital gains tax, for any year of assessment beginning on or after the first day of January next following the year in which this Agreement enters into force;

(ii) as respects corporation tax, for any financial year beginning on or after the first day of January next following the year in which this Agreement enters into force.

Article 30

TERMINATION

1. This Agreement shall remain in force until terminated by a Contracting State. Either Contracting State may terminate the Agreement after five years from the date on which the Agreement enters into force provided that at least six months prior written notice of termination has been given through diplomatic channels.

2. In such event this Agreement shall cease to have effect:

(a) in Botswana:

(i) as respects taxes withheld at source, for any amounts credited on or after the thirtieth day following the date on which the notice of termination is given;

(ii) as respects other taxes, for taxable income derived on or after the first day of July of the year next following that in which the notice of termination is given;

(b) in Ireland:

(i) as respects income tax, the universal social charge and capital gains tax, for any year of assessment beginning on or after the first day of January in the calendar year next following that in which the notice of termination is given;

(ii) as respects corporation tax, for any financial year beginning on or after the first day of January in the calendar year next following that in which the notice of termination is given.

IN WITNESS WHEREOF the undersigned, being duly authorised thereto, have signed this Agreement.

DONE at Gaborone, this 10 day of June 2014 in duplicate, in the English language.

[signature]

FOR THE GOVERNMENT OF THE REPUBLIC OF BOTSWANA

[signature]

FOR THE GOVERNMENT OF IRELAND

PROTOCOL

On signing the Agreement between the Government of the Republic of Botswana and the Government of Ireland for the avoidance of double taxation and the prevention of fiscal evasion with respect to taxes on income, the signatories, being duly authorised thereto, have in addition agreed on the following provisions which shall form an integral part of the said Agreement:

(1) With reference to Article 4:

It is understood that a Common Contractual Fund (CCF) established in Ireland shall not be regarded as a resident of Ireland and shall be treated as fiscally transparent for the purposes of granting treaty benefits.

(2) With reference to Articles 10 and 11:

For the purpose of paragraph 3 of Article 10 and paragraph 3 of Article 11, the term "Government" shall include:

(i) in the case of Botswana, the Bank of Botswana;

(ii) in the case of Ireland, the Central Bank of Ireland and the National Treasury Management Agency and bodies under its aegis;

and

(iii)in either case, a statutory body or any institution wholly or mainly owned by the Government of Botswana or the Government of Ireland as may be agreed from time to time between the competent authorities of the Contracting States.

IN WITNESS WHEREOF the undersigned, being duly authorised thereto, have signed this Protocol.

DONE at Gaborone, this 12 day of June 2014 in duplicate, in the English language.

FOR THE GOVERNMENT OF THE REPUBLIC OF BOTSWANA

FOR THE GOVERNMENT OF IRELAND

[TRANSLATION IN FRENCH – TRADUCTION EN FRANÇAIS]

ACCORD ENTRE LE GOUVERNEMENT DE LA RÉPUBLIQUE DU BOTSWANA ET LE GOUVERNEMENT DE L'IRLANDE TENDANT À ÉVITER LES DOUBLES IMPOSITIONS ET À PRÉVENIR LA FRAUDE FISCALE EN MATIÈRE D'IMPÔTS SUR LE REVENU

Préambule

Le Gouvernement de la République du Botswana et le Gouvernement de l'Irlande, désireux de conclure un accord tendant à éviter les doubles impositions et à prévenir la fraude fiscale en matière d'impôts sur le revenu, sont convenus de ce qui suit :

Article premier. Personnes visées

Le présent Accord s'applique aux personnes qui sont des résidents d'un État contractant ou des deux États contractants.

Article 2. Impôts visés

1. Le présent Accord s'applique aux impôts sur le revenu perçus par chacun des États contractants, quel que soit le système de perception.

2. Sont considérés comme impôts sur le revenu tous les impôts perçus sur le revenu total ou sur des éléments du revenu, y compris les impôts sur les gains provenant de l'aliénation de biens mobiliers ou immobiliers.

3. Les impôts actuels auxquels s'applique le présent Accord sont notamment :

a) Au Botswana :

i) L'impôt sur le revenu ; et

ii) L'impôt sur les gains en capital ;

(ci-après dénommés « impôt botswanais ») ; et

b) En Irlande :

i) L'impôt sur le revenu ;

ii) La charge sociale universelle ;

iii) L'impôt sur les sociétés ; et

iv) L'impôt sur les gains en capital ;

(ci-après dénommés « impôt irlandais »).

4. L'Accord s'applique aussi aux impôts de nature identique ou analogue qui seraient établis par l'un ou l'autre État contractant après la date de signature de l'Accord et qui s'ajouteraient aux impôts actuels ou qui les remplaceraient. Les autorités compétentes des États contractants se communiquent les modifications notables apportées à leurs législations fiscales respectives.

Article 3. Définitions générales

1. Aux fins du présent Accord, à moins que le contexte n'exige une interprétation différente :

a) Le terme « Botswana » désigne la République du Botswana ;

b) Le terme « Irlande » comprend toute zone située en dehors des eaux territoriales de l'Irlande qui a été ou peut ultérieurement être désignée, conformément à la législation irlandaise relative à la zone économique exclusive et au plateau continental, comme une zone à l'intérieur de laquelle l'Irlande peut exercer ses droits souverains et sa juridiction conformément au droit international ;

c) Les expressions « un État contractant » et « l'autre État contractant » désignent, suivant le contexte, le Botswana ou l'Irlande ; et l'expression « États contractants » désigne le Botswana et l'Irlande ;

d) Le terme « société » désigne toute personne morale ou toute entité considérée comme une personne morale aux fins d'imposition ;

e) L'expression « autorité compétente » désigne :

i) Au Botswana, le Ministre des finances et de la planification du développement, représenté par le Commissaire général du Service unifié des recettes du Botswana (Botswana Unified Revenue Service) ou par son représentant autorisé ; et

ii) En Irlande, l'administration fiscale (Revenue Commissioners) ou son représentant autorisé ;

f) Le terme « entreprise » désigne l'exercice de toute activité ;

g) Les expressions « entreprise d'un État contractant » et « entreprise de l'autre État contractant » désignent respectivement une entreprise exploitée par un résident d'un État contractant et une entreprise exploitée par un résident de l'autre État contractant ;

h) L'expression « trafic international » désigne tout transport effectué par un navire ou un aéronef exploité par une entreprise d'un État contractant, sauf lorsque le navire ou l'aéronef n'est exploité qu'entre des points situés dans l'autre État contractant ;

i) Le terme « ressortissant », en ce qui concerne un État contractant, désigne :

i) Toute personne physique possédant la nationalité ou la citoyenneté de cet État contractant ; et

ii) Toute personne morale ou association constituée en vertu de la législation en vigueur dans cet État contractant ;

j) Le terme « personne » comprend les personnes physiques, les fiducies, les sociétés et tous autres groupements de personnes ;

k) Le terme « activité » comprend l'exercice d'une profession indépendante et d'autres activités de caractère indépendant.

2. Pour l'application des dispositions du présent Accord à un moment donné par un État contractant, toute expression ou tout terme qui n'y est pas défini a, à moins que le contexte n'exige une interprétation différente, le sens que lui attribue, au moment considéré, la législation de cet État en ce qui concerne les impôts auxquels s'applique le présent Accord, le sens que lui attribue la législation fiscale applicable dans cet État prévalant sur le sens qui lui est attribué par d'autres branches du droit de cet État.

Article 4. Résident

1. Aux fins du présent Accord, l'expression « résident d'un État contractant » désigne toute personne qui, en vertu de la législation de cet État, est assujettie à l'impôt dans cet État, en raison de son domicile, de sa résidence, de son siège de direction ou de tout autre critère analogue, et elle s'applique également à cet État et à ses collectivités locales. Cette expression n'inclut toutefois pas les personnes qui ne sont assujetties à l'impôt dans cet État uniquement que pour les revenus de sources situées dans cet État.

2. Lorsque, selon les dispositions du paragraphe 1, une personne physique est un résident des deux États contractants, sa situation est déterminée comme suit :

a) Elle est réputée être un résident seulement de l'État où elle dispose d'un foyer d'habitation permanent ; si elle dispose d'un foyer d'habitation permanent dans les deux États, elle est réputée être un résident seulement de l'État avec lequel ses liens personnels et économiques sont les plus étroits (centre des intérêts vitaux) ;

b) Si l'État où cette personne a le centre de ses intérêts vitaux ne peut pas être déterminé, ou si elle ne dispose d'un foyer d'habitation permanent dans aucun des deux États, elle est réputée être un résident seulement de l'État où elle séjourne habituellement ;

c) Si elle séjourne habituellement dans les deux États, ou si elle ne séjourne habituellement dans aucun des deux, elle est réputée être un résident seulement de l'État dont elle est un ressortissant ;

d) Si elle est ressortissante des deux États, ou si elle n'est ressortissante d'aucun des deux, les autorités compétentes des États contractants règlent la question d'un commun accord.

3. Lorsque, selon les dispositions du paragraphe 1, une personne autre qu'une personne physique est un résident des deux États contractants, elle est réputée être un résident seulement de l'État où se situe son siège de direction effective. Si le lieu où se situe son siège de direction effective ne peut pas être déterminé, les autorités compétentes des États contractants s'efforcent de régler la question d'un commun accord.

Article 5. Établissement stable

1. Aux fins du présent Accord, l'expression « établissement stable » désigne une installation fixe d'affaires par l'intermédiaire de laquelle une entreprise exerce tout ou partie de son activité.

2. L'expression « établissement stable » désigne notamment :

a) Un siège de direction ;

b) Une succursale ;

c) Un bureau ;

d) Une usine ;

e) Un atelier ;

f) Une mine, un puit de pétrole ou de gaz, une carrière ou tout autre lieu d'extraction ou d'exploitation de ressources naturelles ; et

g) Une installation ou une structure utilisée pour l'exploration de ressources naturelles, à condition que cette installation ou structure soit maintenue pendant plus de six mois au cours de toute période de 12 mois.

3. L'expression « établissement stable » comprend également :

a) Un chantier, un projet de construction, de montage ou d'installation, mais uniquement lorsque ce chantier ou ce projet se poursuivent pendant plus de six mois au cours de toute période de 12 mois ;

b) La fourniture, par une entreprise, de services, y compris les services de consultants, par l'intermédiaire de salariés ou autre personnel engagés par l'entreprise à cette fin, mais seulement lorsque des activités de cette nature se poursuivent (pour le même projet ou un projet connexe) dans l'État contractant pendant une ou plusieurs périodes totalisant plus de six mois au cours de toute période de 12 mois ; et

c) L'exercice d'une profession indépendante ou d'autres activités de caractère indépendant par une personne physique, mais seulement lorsque lesdits services ou activités se poursuivent dans un État contractant pendant une période ou plusieurs périodes totalisant plus de 183 jours au cours de toute période de 12 mois commençant ou se terminant au cours de l'exercice fiscal considéré.

4. Nonobstant les dispositions précédentes du présent article, il est considéré qu'un « établissement stable » ne comprend pas :

a) L'utilisation d'installations aux seules fins de stockage, d'exposition ou de livraison de biens ou de marchandises appartenant à l'entreprise ;

b) L'exploitation d'un stock de biens ou de marchandises appartenant à l'entreprise aux seules fins de transformation par une autre entreprise ;

c) L'exploitation d'un stock de biens ou de marchandises appartenant à l'entreprise aux seules fins de stockage, d'exposition ou de livraison ;

d) L'exploitation d'une installation fixe d'affaires aux seules fins d'acheter des biens ou des marchandises ou de recueillir des renseignements pour l'entreprise ;

e) L'exploitation d'une installation fixe d'affaires aux seules fins d'exercer, pour l'entreprise, toute autre activité de caractère préparatoire ou auxiliaire ;

f) L'exploitation d'une installation fixe d'affaires aux seules fins de l'exercice cumulé d'activités visées aux alinéas a) à e), à condition que l'activité d'ensemble de l'installation fixe d'affaires résultant de ce cumul ait un caractère préparatoire ou auxiliaire.

5. Nonobstant les dispositions des paragraphes 1 et 2, si une personne, autre qu'un agent jouissant d'un statut indépendant auquel s'applique le paragraphe 6, agit dans un État contractant pour le compte d'une entreprise de l'autre État contractant, cette entreprise est réputée avoir un établissement stable dans le premier État pour toute activité que cette personne exerce pour l'entreprise si cette personne dispose dans cet État de pouvoirs qu'elle y exerce habituellement, lui permettant de conclure des contrats au nom de l'entreprise, à moins que les activités de cette personne ne soient limitées à celles qui sont énumérées au paragraphe 4 et qui, si elles étaient exercées par l'intermédiaire d'une installation fixe d'affaires, ne permettraient pas de considérer cette installation fixe d'affaires comme un établissement stable selon les dispositions de ce paragraphe.

6. Une entreprise d'un État contractant n'est pas réputée avoir un établissement stable dans l'autre État contractant du seul fait qu'elle y exerce son activité par l'entremise d'un courtier, d'un commissionnaire général ou de tout autre agent jouissant d'un statut indépendant, à condition que ces personnes agissent dans le cadre ordinaire de leurs activités.

7. Le fait qu'une société qui est un résident d'un État contractant contrôle ou est contrôlée par une société qui est un résident de l'autre État contractant ou qui y exerce son activité (que ce soit par l'intermédiaire d'un établissement stable ou non) ne suffit pas, en soi, à faire de l'une quelconque de ces sociétés un établissement stable de l'autre.

Article 6. Revenus de biens immobiliers

1. Les revenus qu'un résident d'un État contractant tire de biens immobiliers, y compris les revenus provenant des exploitations agricoles ou forestières, situés dans l'autre État contractant, sont imposables dans cet autre État.

2. L'expression « biens immobiliers » a le sens que lui attribue le droit de l'État contractant dans lequel les biens considérés sont situés. Cette expression comprend dans tous les cas les biens accessoires aux biens immobiliers, le cheptel et le matériel utilisé dans les exploitations agricoles et forestières, les droits auxquels s'appliquent les dispositions du droit privé concernant la propriété foncière, l'usufruit des biens immobiliers et les droits à des paiements variables ou fixes pour l'exploitation ou la concession de l'exploitation de gisements minéraux, sources ou autres ressources naturelles. Les navires, bateaux, et aéronefs ne sont pas considérés comme des biens immobiliers.

3. Les dispositions du paragraphe 1 s'appliquent aux revenus provenant de l'exploitation directe, de la location ou de toute autre forme d'exploitation de biens immobiliers.

4. Les dispositions des paragraphes 1 et 3 s'appliquent également aux revenus provenant des biens immobiliers d'une entreprise.

Article 7. Bénéfices des entreprises

1. Les bénéfices d'une entreprise d'un État contractant ne sont imposables que dans cet État, à moins que l'entreprise n'exerce une activité dans l'autre État contractant par l'intermédiaire d'un établissement stable qui y est situé. Si l'entreprise exerce son activité d'une telle façon, les bénéfices de cette entreprise sont imposables dans l'autre État, mais uniquement dans la mesure où ils sont imputables audit établissement stable.

2. Sous réserve des dispositions du paragraphe 3, lorsqu'une entreprise d'un État contractant exerce une activité dans l'autre État contractant par l'intermédiaire d'un établissement stable qui y est situé, il est imputé à cet établissement stable, dans chacun des États contractants, les bénéfices qu'il aurait pu réaliser s'il avait constitué une entreprise distincte exerçant des activités identiques ou analogues dans des conditions identiques ou analogues et traitant en toute indépendance avec l'entreprise dont il constitue un établissement stable.

3. Pour déterminer les bénéfices d'un établissement stable, sont admises en déduction les dépenses relatives aux fins poursuivies par cet établissement stable, y compris les dépenses de direction et les frais généraux d'administration ainsi enregistrés, soit dans l'État où est situé l'établissement stable, soit ailleurs. Toutefois, aucune déduction n'est admise pour les sommes qui seraient, le cas échéant, versées (à d'autres titres que le remboursement des frais) par l'établissement stable au siège de l'entreprise ou à l'un quelconque de ses bureaux, comme redevances, honoraires ou autres paiements similaires, pour l'usage de brevets ou d'autres droits, ou comme commission, pour des services précis fournis ou pour une activité de direction ou, sauf dans le cas d'une entreprise bancaire, comme intérêts sur des sommes prêtées à l'établissement stable. De même, il n'est pas tenu compte, dans le calcul des bénéfices d'un établissement stable, des sommes (autres que le

remboursement des frais) portées par l'établissement stable au débit du siège de l'entreprise ou de l'un quelconque de ses autres bureaux, comme redevances, honoraires ou autres paiements similaires, pour l'usage de brevets ou d'autres droits, ou comme commission pour des services précis fournis ou pour une activité de direction ou, sauf dans le cas d'une entreprise bancaire, comme intérêts sur des sommes prêtées au siège de l'entreprise ou à l'un quelconque de ses autres bureaux.

4. S'il est d'usage, dans un État contractant, de déterminer les bénéfices imputables à un établissement stable sur la base d'une répartition des bénéfices totaux de l'entreprise entre ses diverses composantes, aucune disposition du paragraphe 2 n'empêche cet État contractant de déterminer les bénéfices imposables selon la répartition en usage. Cependant, la méthode de répartition adoptée doit être telle que le résultat obtenu soit conforme aux principes énoncés au présent article.

5. Aucun bénéfice n'est imputé à un établissement stable au seul motif qu'il a acquis des biens ou des marchandises pour l'entreprise.

6. Aux fins des paragraphes précédents, les bénéfices à imputer à l'établissement stable sont déterminés chaque année selon la même méthode, à moins qu'il n'existe des motifs valables et suffisants de procéder autrement.

7. Lorsque les bénéfices comprennent des éléments de revenu ou des gains traités séparément dans d'autres articles du présent Accord, les dispositions de ces articles n'affectent pas les dispositions du présent article.

Article 8. Transport international

1. Les bénéfices d'une entreprise d'un État contractant qui proviennent de l'exploitation en trafic international de navires ou d'aéronefs ne sont imposables que dans cet État.

2. Aux fins du présent article, les bénéfices tirés de l'exploitation en trafic international de navires ou d'aéronefs comprennent les bénéfices provenant de la location de navires ou d'aéronefs lorsque lesdits navires ou aéronefs sont exploités en trafic international ou lorsque les bénéfices provenant de la location sont accessoires à d'autres bénéfices visés au paragraphe 1.

3. Les bénéfices d'une entreprise d'un État contractant qui proviennent de l'utilisation ou de la location de conteneurs (y compris les remorques, les barges et les équipements connexes pour le transport de conteneurs) utilisés pour le transport des biens ou des marchandises ne sont imposables que dans cet État.

4. Les dispositions du paragraphe 1 s'appliquent aussi aux bénéfices provenant de la participation à un consortium, à une coentreprise ou à un organisme international d'exploitation.

Article 9. Entreprises associées

1. Lorsque :

   a) Une entreprise d'un État contractant participe directement ou indirectement à la direction, au contrôle ou au capital d'une entreprise de l'autre État contractant ; ou que

   b) Les mêmes personnes participent, directement ou indirectement, à la direction, au contrôle ou au capital d'une entreprise d'un État contractant et d'une entreprise de l'autre État contractant ;

et que, dans l'un et l'autre cas, les deux entreprises sont, dans leurs relations commerciales ou financières, liées par des conditions convenues ou imposées qui diffèrent de celles qui seraient convenues entre des entreprises indépendantes, les bénéfices qui auraient été réalisés par l'une des entreprises, mais n'ont pas pu l'être à cause de ces conditions peuvent être inclus dans les bénéfices de cette entreprise et imposés en conséquence.

2. Lorsqu'un État contractant inclut dans les bénéfices d'une de ses entreprises, et impose en conséquence, des bénéfices sur lesquels une entreprise de l'autre État contractant a été imposée dans cet autre État, et que les bénéfices ainsi inclus sont des bénéfices qui auraient été réalisés par l'entreprise du premier État si les conditions convenues entre les deux entreprises avaient été celles qui auraient été convenues entre des entreprises indépendantes, alors l'autre État procède à un ajustement approprié du montant de l'impôt qui a été perçu sur ces bénéfices. L'ajustement est déterminé compte dûment tenu des autres dispositions du présent Accord et, si nécessaire, les autorités compétentes des États contractants se consultent.

Article 10. Dividendes

1. Les dividendes payés par une société qui est un résident d'un État contractant à un résident de l'autre État contractant sont imposables dans cet autre État.

2. Toutefois, ces dividendes sont également imposables dans l'État contractant dont la société qui paie les dividendes est un résident et selon la législation de cet État, mais si le bénéficiaire effectif des dividendes est un résident de l'autre État contractant, l'impôt ainsi établi ne peut excéder, dans tous les cas, 5 % du montant brut des dividendes.

Le présent paragraphe est sans incidence sur l'imposition de la société au titre des bénéfices qui servent au paiement des dividendes.

3. Nonobstant les dispositions du paragraphe 2, les dividendes provenant d'un État contractant et versés au Gouvernement de l'autre État contractant, qui en est le bénéficiaire effectif, sont exonérés d'impôt dans le premier État.

4. Le terme « dividendes » employé dans le présent article désigne les revenus provenant d'actions, d'actions ou de bons de jouissance, de parts de mine, d'actions de fondateur ou d'autres parts bénéficiaires (à l'exception des créances) ainsi que les revenus d'autres parts sociales soumis au même régime fiscal que les revenus d'actions par la législation de l'État contractant dont la société distributrice est un résident.

5. Les dispositions des paragraphes 1 et 2 ne s'appliquent pas lorsque le bénéficiaire effectif des dividendes, résident d'un État contractant, exerce dans l'autre État contractant dont la société qui paie les dividendes est un résident, une activité industrielle ou commerciale par l'intermédiaire d'un établissement stable qui y est situé, et que la participation génératrice des dividendes se rattache effectivement audit établissement stable. Dans ce cas, les dispositions de l'article 7 s'appliquent.

6. Lorsqu'une société qui est un résident d'un État contractant tire des bénéfices ou des revenus de l'autre État contractant, cet autre État ne peut percevoir aucun impôt sur les dividendes payés par la société, sauf dans la mesure où ces dividendes sont payés à un résident de cet autre État ou dans la mesure où la participation génératrice des dividendes se rattache effectivement à un établissement stable situé dans cet autre État, ni prélever aucun impôt, au titre de l'imposition sur les bénéfices non distribués, sur les bénéfices non distribués de la société, même si les dividendes payés ou les bénéfices non distribués consistent en tout ou en partie en bénéfices ou revenus provenant de cet autre État.

Article 11. Intérêts

1. Les intérêts provenant d'un État contractant et payés à un résident de l'autre État contractant sont imposables dans cet autre État.

2. Toutefois, ces intérêts sont aussi imposables dans l'État contractant d'où ils proviennent et selon la législation de cet État, mais si le bénéficiaire est le bénéficiaire effectif des intérêts, l'impôt ainsi établi ne peut excéder 7,5 % du montant brut des intérêts.

3. Nonobstant les dispositions du paragraphe 2, les intérêts produits dans un État contractant sont exonérés d'impôt dans cet État s'ils sont payés au Gouvernement de l'autre État contractant ou à l'une de ses collectivités locales, qui est en le bénéficiaire effectif.

4. Le terme « intérêts » employé dans le présent article désigne les revenus des créances des toute nature, assorties ou non de garanties hypothécaires ou d'une clause de participation aux bénéfices du débiteur, et notamment les revenus des fonds publics et des obligations d'emprunt, y compris les primes et lots rattachés à ces titres. Les pénalités pour paiement tardif ne sont pas considérées comme des intérêts au sens du présent article.

5. Les dispositions des paragraphes 1 et 2 ne s'appliquent pas lorsque le bénéficiaire effectif des intérêts, résident d'un État contractant, exerce dans l'autre État contractant d'où proviennent les intérêts une activité industrielle ou commerciale par l'intermédiaire d'un établissement stable qui y est situé, et que la créance génératrice des intérêts se rattache effectivement audit établissement stable. Dans ce cas, les dispositions de l'article 7 s'appliquent.

6. Les intérêts sont considérés comme provenant d'un État contractant lorsque le débiteur est un résident de cet État. Toutefois, lorsque le débiteur des intérêts, qu'il soit ou non résident d'un État contractant, a dans un État contractant un établissement stable pour lequel la dette donnant lieu au paiement des intérêts a été contractée et qui supporte la charge de ces intérêts, ceux-ci sont considérés comme provenant de l'État contractant où l'établissement stable est situé.

7. Lorsque, en raison de relations spéciales qui existent entre le débiteur et le bénéficiaire effectif ou que l'un et l'autre entretiennent avec une tierce personne, le montant des intérêts, compte tenu de la créance pour laquelle ils sont payés, excède celui dont seraient convenus le débiteur et le bénéficiaire effectif en l'absence de pareilles relations, les dispositions du présent article ne s'appliquent qu'à ce dernier montant. Dans ce cas, la partie excédentaire des paiements reste imposable conformément à la législation de chaque État contractant et compte dûment tenu des autres dispositions du présent Accord.

Article 12. Redevances

1. Les redevances générées dans un État contractant et payées à un résident de l'autre État contractant sont imposables dans cet autre État.

2. Toutefois, ces redevances sont également imposables dans l'État contractant de la source et selon la législation de cet État, mais si le bénéficiaire effectif des redevances est un résident de l'autre État contractant, l'impôt ainsi établi ne peut excéder :

a) 5 % du montant brut des redevances en ce qui concerne l'usage ou la concession de l'usage d'un équipement industriel, commercial ou scientifique ; et

b) 7,5 % du montant brut des redevances dans tous les autres cas.

3. Le terme « redevances » employé dans le présent article désigne les rémunérations de toute nature payées pour l'usage ou la concession de l'usage d'un droit d'auteur sur une œuvre littéraire,

artistique ou scientifique (y compris les films cinématographiques, les enregistrements sur des bandes ou d'autres supports utilisés pour les émissions radiophoniques ou télévisées, ou d'autres moyens de reproduction ou de transmission), d'un brevet, d'une marque commerciale, d'un dessin ou d'un modèle, d'un plan, d'une formule ou d'un procédé secrets et pour des informations ayant trait à une expérience acquise dans le domaine industriel, commercial ou scientifique.

4. Les dispositions des paragraphes 1 et 2 ne s'appliquent pas lorsque le bénéficiaire effectif des redevances, résident d'un État contractant, exerce dans l'autre État contractant source des redevances une activité industrielle ou commerciale par l'intermédiaire d'un établissement stable qui y est situé, et que le droit ou le bien générateur des redevances se rattache effectivement audit établissement stable. Dans ce cas, les dispositions de l'article 7 s'appliquent.

5. Les redevances sont considérées comme provenant d'un État contractant lorsque le débiteur est un résident de cet État. Toutefois, lorsque le débiteur des redevances, résident ou non d'un État contractant, a dans un État contractant un établissement stable pour lequel l'engagement donnant lieu au paiement des redevances et qui supporte la charge de ces redevances, celles-ci sont considérées comme provenant de l'État où l'établissement stable est situé.

6. Lorsque, en raison de relations spéciales qui existent entre le débiteur et le bénéficiaire effectif ou que l'un et l'autre entretiennent avec une tierce personne, le montant des redevances, compte tenu de l'usage, du droit ou des informations pour lesquels elles sont payées, excède celui dont seraient convenus le débiteur et le bénéficiaire effectif en l'absence de pareilles relations, les dispositions du présent article ne s'appliquent qu'à ce dernier montant. Dans ce cas, la partie excédentaire des paiements reste imposable selon la législation de chaque État contractant et compte dûment tenu des autres dispositions du présent Accord.

Article 13. Gains en capital

1. Les gains qu'un résident d'un État contractant tire de l'aliénation de biens immobiliers visés à l'article 6 et situés dans l'autre État contractant sont imposables dans cet autre État.

2. Les gains provenant de l'aliénation de biens mobiliers qui font partie de l'actif d'un établissement stable qu'une entreprise d'un État contractant a dans l'autre État contractant, y compris les gains provenant de l'alinéation de cet établissement stable (seul ou avec l'ensemble de l'entreprise), sont imposables dans cet autre État.

3. Les gains qu'une entreprise d'un État contractant tire de l'aliénation de navires ou d'aéronefs exploités en trafic international, ou de biens mobiliers affectés à l'exploitation de ces navires ou aéronefs, ne sont imposables que dans cet État.

4. Les gains qu'un résident d'un État contractant tire de l'aliénation :

a) D'actions autres que des actions cotées sur une bourse reconnue, qui tirent directement ou indirectement plus de 50 % de leur valeur de biens immobiliers situés dans l'autre État contractant ; ou

b) D'une participation dans une société de personnes ou une fiducie, qui tire directement ou indirectement plus de 50 % de sa valeur de biens immobiliers situés dans l'autre État contractant ;

sont imposables dans cet autre État.

5. Les gains provenant de l'aliénation de biens autres que ceux visés aux paragraphes 1, 2, 3 et 4 ne sont imposables que dans l'État contractant dont le cédant est un résident.

6. Les dispositions du paragraphe 5 n'affectent pas le droit d'un État contractant de percevoir, conformément à sa législation, un impôt sur les gains provenant de l'aliénation d'un bien et réalisés par une personne physique qui est un résident de l'autre État contractant et qui a été un résident du premier État à un moment quelconque au cours des cinq années précédant immédiatement l'alinéation du bien.

Article 14. Revenus provenant d'un emploi

1. Sous réserve des dispositions des articles 15, 17 et 18, les salaires, traitements et autres rémunérations similaires qu'un résident d'un État contractant perçoit au titre d'un emploi salarié ne sont imposables que dans cet État, à moins que l'emploi ne soit exercé dans l'autre État contractant. Si l'emploi y est exercé, les rémunérations perçues à ce titre sont imposables dans cet autre État.

2. Nonobstant les dispositions du paragraphe 1, les rémunérations qu'un résident d'un État contractant perçoit au titre d'un emploi salarié exercé dans l'autre État contractant n'est imposable que dans le premier État si :

a) Le bénéficiaire séjourne dans l'autre État contractant pendant une période ou plusieurs périodes d'une durée totale ne dépassant pas 183 jours au cours de toute période de 12 mois commençant ou se terminant au cours de l'exercice considéré ; et

b) La rémunération est payée par un employeur ou pour le compte d'un employeur qui n'est pas un résident de l'autre État ; et

c) La charge des rémunérations n'est pas supportée par un établissement stable que l'employeur a dans l'autre État.

3. Nonobstant les dispositions précédentes du présent article, les rémunérations perçues au titre d'un emploi salarié exercé à bord d'un navire ou d'un aéronef exploité en trafic international par une entreprise d'un État contractant sont imposables dans cet État contractant.

Article 15. Tantièmes

Les tantièmes et autres rémunérations similaires qu'un résident d'un État contractant perçoit en sa qualité de membre du conseil d'administration d'une société qui est un résident de l'autre État contractant sont imposables dans cet autre État.

Article 16. Artistes du spectacle et sportifs

1. Nonobstant les dispositions des articles 7 et 14, les revenus qu'un résident d'un État contractant tire de ses activités personnelles exercées dans l'autre État contractant en tant qu'artiste du spectacle, notamment artiste de théâtre, de cinéma, de radio ou de télévision, ou musicien ou en tant que sportif, sont imposables dans cet autre État.

2. Lorsque les revenus d'activités qu'un artiste du spectacle ou un sportif exerce personnellement et en cette qualité sont attribués, non pas à l'artiste du spectacle ou au sportif lui-même, mais à une autre personne, ces revenus sont, nonobstant les dispositions des articles 7 et 14, imposables dans l'État contractant où sont exercées les activités de l'artiste du spectacle ou du sportif.

3. Les dispositions des paragraphes 1 et 2 ne s'appliquent pas aux revenus qu'un artiste du spectacle ou un sportif, résident d'un État contractant, tire d'activités exercées personnellement et

en cette qualité dans l'autre État contractant, si son séjour dans cet autre État est entièrement ou principalement financé par des fonds publics du premier État contractant ou de l'une de ses collectivités locales, ou se déroule dans le cadre d'un accord culturel ou d'un accord conclu entre les Gouvernements des États contractants. Dans ce cas, les revenus ne sont imposables que dans l'État contractant dont l'artiste du spectacle ou le sportif, selon le cas, est un résident.

Article 17. Pensions et rentes

1. Sous réserve des dispositions du paragraphe 2 de l'article 18, les pensions et autres rémunérations similaires au titre d'un emploi antérieur, ainsi que les rentes, qui proviennent d'un État contractant et qui sont payées à un résident de l'autre État contractant sont imposables dans le premier État contractant.

2. Le terme « rente » désigne une somme déterminée payable périodiquement à échéances fixes, à titre viager ou pendant une période déterminée ou pouvant l'être, en vertu d'une obligation d'effectuer des paiements en contrepartie d'un capital suffisant versé intégralement ou en une valeur appréciable en espèces.

Article 18. Fonction publique

1. a) Les salaires, traitements et autres rémunérations similaires payés par un État contractant ou une de ses collectivités locales à une personne physique, au titre de services fournis à cet État ou à cette collectivité, ne sont imposables que dans cet État.
   b) Toutefois, ces traitements, salaires et autres rémunérations similaires ne sont imposables que dans l'autre État contractant si les services sont fournis dans cet État et si la personne physique est un résident de cet État qui :
      i) Est un ressortissant de cet État ; ou
      ii) N'est pas devenu un résident de cet État à seule fin d'exécuter les services en question.
2. a) Nonobstant les dispositions du paragraphe 1, les pensions et autres rémunérations similaires payées par un État contractant ou une de ses collectivités locales, soit directement soit par prélèvement sur des fonds qu'ils ont constitués, à une personne physique au titre de services fournis à cet État ou à cette collectivité ne sont imposables que dans cet État.
   b) Toutefois, ces pensions ou autres rémunérations similaires ne sont imposables que dans l'autre État contractant si la personne physique est un résident et un ressortissant de cet État.

3. Les dispositions des articles 14, 15, 16 et 17 s'appliquent aux salaires, traitements, pensions et aux autres rémunérations similaires au titre de services fournis dans le cadre d'une activité industrielle ou commerciale exercée par un État contractant ou une de ses collectivités locales.

Article 19. Étudiants, apprentis et stagiaires

Les sommes qu'un étudiant, un apprenti ou un stagiaire qui séjourne dans un État contractant à seule fin d'y poursuivre ses études ou sa formation et qui est, ou qui était immédiatement avant de se rendre dans cet État, un résident de l'autre État contractant, reçoit de sources situées en dehors de ce premier État pour couvrir ses frais d'entretien, d'études ou de formation ne sont pas imposables dans le premier État.

Article 20. Honoraires techniques

1. Les honoraires techniques provenant d'un État contractant et payés à un résident de l'autre État contractant sont imposables dans cet autre État.

2. Toutefois, ces honoraires techniques sont également imposables dans l'État contractant d'où ils proviennent et selon la législation de cet État, mais lorsque ces honoraires techniques sont payés à un résident de l'autre État contractant qui est assujetti à l'impôt concernant lesdits honoraires dans cet État, l'impôt ainsi établi dans l'État contractant où les honoraires techniques ont leur source ne peut excéder 7,5 % du montant brut de ces honoraires.

3. L'expression « honoraires techniques » employée dans le présent article désigne les paiements de toute nature versés à une personne, autre qu'un salarié de la personne effectuant les paiements, en contrepartie de services de caractère administratif, technique, consultatif ou de gestion.

4. Les dispositions des paragraphes 1 et 2 du présent article ne s'appliquent pas lorsque la personne qui perçoit les honoraires techniques, résident d'un État contractant, exerce dans l'autre État contractant d'où proviennent les honoraires techniques une activité par l'intermédiaire d'un établissement stable qui y est situé, et que les honoraires techniques se rattachent effectivement à cet établissement stable. Dans ce cas, les dispositions de l'article 7 s'appliquent.

5. Les honoraires techniques sont réputés provenir d'un État contractant lorsque le débiteur est cet État lui-même, l'une de ses collectivités locales ou l'un de ses résidents. Toutefois, lorsque la personne versant les honoraires techniques, qu'elle soit ou non résidente d'un État contractant, a dans un État contractant un établissement stable pour lequel l'obligation de verser les honoraires techniques a été contractée et qui supporte la charge de ces honoraires techniques, ceux-ci sont réputés provenir de l'État contractant où l'établissement stable est situé.

6. Lorsque, en raison de relations spéciales existant entre le débiteur et le bénéficiaire ou que l'un et l'autre entretiennent avec une tierce personne, le montant des honoraires techniques versés excède, pour quelque raison que ce soit, celui dont seraient convenus le débiteur et le bénéficiaire en l'absence de pareilles relations, les dispositions du présent article ne s'appliquent qu'à ce dernier montant. Dans ce cas, la partie excédentaire des paiements reste imposable selon la législation de chaque État contractant et compte dûment tenu des autres dispositions du présent Accord.

7. Nonobstant les dispositions du paragraphe 2, lorsque, dans un accord tendant à éviter les doubles impositions et à prévenir la fraude fiscale conclu entre le Botswana et un État autre que l'Irlande après la signature du présent Accord, le taux d'imposition prévu à l'article relatif aux honoraires techniques est inférieur à 7,5 %, ce taux s'applique comme s'il avait été celui énoncé au présent article.

Article 21. Autres revenus

1. Les éléments de revenu d'un résident d'un État contractant, d'où qu'ils proviennent, qui ne sont pas traités dans les articles précédents du présent Accord, ne sont imposables que dans cet État.

2. Les dispositions du paragraphe 1 ne s'appliquent pas aux revenus autres que ceux provenant de biens immobiliers, tels qu'ils sont décrits au paragraphe 2 de l'article 6, lorsque le

bénéficiaire effectif de tels revenus, résident d'un État contractant, exerce dans l'autre État contractant une activité industrielle ou commerciale par l'intermédiaire d'un établissement stable qui y est situé, et que le droit ou le bien générateur des revenus se rattache effectivement audit établissement stable. Dans ce cas, les dispositions de l'article 7 s'appliquent.

Article 22. Règles diverses applicables à certaines activités en mer

1. Les dispositions du présent article s'appliquent nonobstant toute autre disposition du présent Accord lorsque des activités (dénommées dans le présent article « activités pertinentes ») sont exercées au large dans le cadre de l'exploration ou de l'exploitation des fonds et du sous-sol marins et de leurs ressources naturelles situés dans un État contractant.

2. Une entreprise d'un État contractant qui exerce des activités pertinentes dans l'autre État contractant est, sous réserve du paragraphe 3 du présent article, considérée comme exerçant une activité dans cet autre État par l'intermédiaire d'un établissement stable qui y est situé.

3. Les activités pertinentes exercées par une entreprise d'un État contractant dans l'autre État contractant, pendant une période ou plusieurs périodes d'une durée totale ne dépassant pas 30 jours au cours de toute période de 12 mois, ne sont pas considérées comme des activités exercées par l'intermédiaire d'un établissement stable qui y est situé. Aux fins du présent paragraphe :

a) Lorsqu'une entreprise d'un État contractant qui exerce des activités pertinentes dans l'autre État contractant est associée à une autre entreprise y exerçant des activités essentiellement similaires, la première entreprise est considérée comme exerçant toutes les activités de la deuxième, sauf si ces activités sont exercées en même temps que ses propres activités ;

b) Une entreprise est considérée comme associée à une autre entreprise si l'une participe directement ou indirectement à la direction, au contrôle ou au capital de l'autre ou si les mêmes personnes participent directement ou indirectement à la direction, au contrôle ou au capital des deux entreprises.

4. Les salaires, traitements et autres rémunérations similaires qu'un résident d'un État contractant perçoit au titre d'un emploi exercé dans le cadre d'activités pertinentes dans l'autre État contractant sont, dans la mesure où les fonctions sont exercées au large dans cet autre État, imposables dans ce dernier.

5. Les gains qu'un résident d'un État contractant tire de l'aliénation :

a) De droits d'exploration ou d'exploitation ; ou

b) D'actions (ou d'instruments comparables) tirant leur valeur ou la plus grande partie de leur valeur, directement ou indirectement, de ces droits ;

sont imposables dans cet autre État.

Dans le présent paragraphe, l'expression « droits d'exploration ou d'exploitation » désigne les droits afférents à des actifs qui seront produits par l'exploration ou l'exploitation des fonds ou du sous-sol marins ou de leurs ressources naturelles situés dans l'autre État, y compris les droits afférents à la participation dans de tels actifs ou au bénéfice de ceux-ci.

Article 23. Élimination des doubles impositions

1. Les doubles impositions sont éliminées comme suit :

   a) Au Botswana, sous réserve des dispositions de la législation botswanaise concernant les crédits pouvant être déduits de l'impôt botswanais au titre de l'impôt dû en vertu de la législation d'un pays autre que le Botswana, l'impôt irlandais dû en vertu de la législation irlandaise et conformément au présent Accord, directement ou par voie de retenue, sur les bénéfices ou les revenus soumis à l'impôt en Irlande est déduit de l'impôt botswanais exigible au titre des mêmes bénéfices ou revenus que ceux sur lesquels est calculé l'impôt irlandais. Toutefois, cette déduction ne peut excéder la fraction de l'impôt botswanais exigible au titre de ces revenus conformément à la législation botswanaise ;

   b) En Irlande, sous réserve des dispositions de la législation irlandaise concernant les crédits pouvant être déduits de l'impôt irlandais au titre de l'impôt payable dans un territoire situé en dehors d'Irlande (qui n'affectent pas le principe général ici posé) :

      i) L'impôt botswanais dû en vertu de la législation botswanaise et conformément au présent Accord, directement ou par voie de retenue, sur les bénéfices, les revenus ou les gains provenant de sources situées au Botswana (à l'exclusion, dans le cas des dividendes, de l'impôt exigible au titre des bénéfices servant au paiement des dividendes) est déduit de l'impôt irlandais calculé sur les mêmes bénéfices, revenus ou gains imposables que ceux sur lesquels est calculé l'impôt botswanais ;

      ii) Dans le cas de dividendes versés par une société qui est un résident du Botswana à une société qui est un résident d'Irlande et qui contrôle, directement ou indirectement, au moins 5 % des titres avec droit de vote de la société distributrice des dividendes, il est tenu compte dans le calcul du crédit (en plus de l'impôt botswanais pouvant être déduit en application du sous-alinéa i) de l'alinéa b)) de l'impôt botswanais que la société doit payer sur les bénéfices servant au paiement de ces dividendes ;

      iii) Aux fins du sous-alinéa i), les bénéfices, revenus et gains en capital d'un résident d'Irlande qui sont imposables au Botswana conformément au présent Accord sont considérés comme provenant de sources situées au Botswana.

2. Lorsque, conformément à toute disposition du présent Accord, les revenus perçus par un résident d'un État contractant sont exonérés d'impôt dans cet État, ledit État peut néanmoins, pour calculer le montant de l'impôt sur le reste des revenus de ce résident, tenir compte des revenus ainsi exonérés.

3. Lorsque, en vertu d'une disposition quelconque du présent Accord, une personne physique a droit dans un État contractant à un allégement d'impôt sur tout ou partie de ses revenus ou gains et que, en vertu de la législation en vigueur dans l'autre État contractant, cette personne, à l'égard de ces revenus ou gains, est assujettie à l'impôt à raison du montant de ces revenus ou gains qui est transféré ou perçu dans cet autre État et non à raison de leur montant total, l'allégement qui doit être accordé en vertu du présent Accord dans le premier État ne s'applique qu'au montant de ces revenus ou gains qui est transféré ou perçu dans cet autre État.

Article 24. Non-discrimination

1. Les ressortissants d'un État contractant ne sont soumis, dans l'autre État contractant, à aucune imposition ni à aucune obligation correspondante, qui est autre ou plus lourde que celles auxquelles sont ou peuvent être assujettis les ressortissants de cet autre État qui se trouvent dans une situation analogue, notamment au regard de la résidence. Nonobstant les dispositions de l'article premier, la présente disposition s'applique aussi aux personnes qui ne sont pas des résidents d'un État contractant ou des deux États contractants.

2. L'imposition d'un établissement stable qu'une entreprise d'un État contractant a dans l'autre État contractant n'est pas établie dans cet autre État contractant d'une façon moins favorable que l'imposition des entreprises de cet autre État qui exercent les mêmes activités. La présente disposition ne peut être interprétée comme obligeant un État contractant à accorder aux résidents de l'autre État contractant les déductions personnelles, abattements et réductions d'impôt qu'il accorde à ses propres résidents en fonction de leur état civil ou de leurs charges de famille.

3. Les entreprises d'un État contractant dont le capital est en tout ou en partie détenu ou contrôlé, directement ou indirectement, par un ou plusieurs résidents de l'autre État contractant ne sont assujettis dans le premier État à aucune imposition ni à aucune obligation correspondante qui est autre ou plus lourde que celles auxquelles sont ou peuvent être assujetties d'autres entreprises similaires du premier État.

4. À moins que les dispositions du paragraphe 1 de l'article 9, du paragraphe 7 de l'article 11, du paragraphe 6 de l'article 12 ou du paragraphe 6 de l'article 20 ne s'appliquent, les intérêts, redevances, honoraires techniques et autres montants payés par une entreprise d'un État contractant à un résident de l'autre État contractant sont, aux fins du calcul des bénéfices imposables de cette entreprise, déductibles dans les mêmes conditions que s'ils avaient été payés à un résident du premier État.

Article 25. Procédure amiable

1. Lorsqu'une personne estime que les mesures prises par un État contractant ou par les deux États contractants entraînent ou entraîneront pour elle une imposition non conforme aux dispositions du présent Accord, elle peut, indépendamment des recours prévus par le droit interne de ces États, présenter son cas à l'autorité compétente de l'État contractant dont elle est un résident ou, si sa situation relève du paragraphe 1 de l'article 24, à celle de l'État contractant dont elle est ressortissante. Le cas doit être présenté dans un délai de trois ans à compter de la première notification des mesures à l'origine d'une imposition non conforme aux dispositions du présent Accord.

2. L'autorité compétente s'efforce, si la réclamation lui paraît fondée et si elle n'est pas elle-même en mesure d'y apporter une solution satisfaisante, de résoudre le cas par voie amiable avec l'autorité compétente de l'autre État contractant, en vue d'éviter une imposition non conforme aux dispositions du présent Accord. Tout accord conclu est appliqué nonobstant les délais prévus par le droit interne des États contractants.

3. Les autorités compétentes des États contractants s'efforcent, par voie d'accord amiable, de résoudre les difficultés ou de dissiper les doutes auxquels peuvent donner lieu l'interprétation ou l'application du présent Accord. Elles peuvent aussi se concerter en vue d'éliminer les doubles impositions dans les cas non prévus par le présent Accord.

4. Les autorités compétentes des États contractants peuvent communiquer directement entre elles en vue de parvenir à un accord au sens des paragraphes précédents.

Article 26. Échange de renseignements

1. Les autorités compétentes des États contractants échangent les renseignements vraisemblablement pertinents pour appliquer des dispositions du présent Accord ou celles du droit interne relatif aux impôts de toute nature et de toute dénomination perçus pour le compte des États contractants ou de leurs subdivisions politiques ou collectivités locales, dans la mesure où l'imposition prévue n'est pas contraire au présent Accord. L'échange de renseignements n'est pas limité par les articles premier et 2.

2. Tous les renseignements reçus par un État contractant au titre du paragraphe 1 sont tenus secrets de la même manière que les renseignements obtenus en application du droit interne de cet État et ne sont communiqués qu'aux personnes ou autorités (y compris les tribunaux et organes administratifs) concernées par l'établissement ou le recouvrement des impôts visés au paragraphe 1, par les poursuites ou procédures concernant lesdits impôts, par les décisions sur les recours relatifs à ces impôts, ou par le contrôle de ce qui précède. Ces personnes ou autorités n'utilisent ces renseignements qu'à ces fins. Elles peuvent faire état de ces renseignements au cours d'audiences publiques de tribunaux ou dans des jugements.

3. Les dispositions des paragraphes 1 et 2 ne peuvent en aucun cas être interprétées comme imposant à un État contractant l'obligation :

a) De prendre des mesures administratives dérogeant à sa législation et à ses pratiques administratives ou à celles de l'autre État contractant ;

b) De fournir des renseignements qui ne pourraient être obtenus sur la base de sa législation ou de celle de l'autre État contractant ou dans le cadre de ses pratiques administratives normales ou de celles de l'autre État contractant ;

c) De fournir des renseignements qui révéleraient un secret commercial, industriel ou professionnel ou un procédé commercial ou des renseignements dont la communication serait contraire à l'ordre public.

4. Si des renseignements sont demandés par un État contractant conformément au présent article, l'autre État contractant utilise ses mesures de collecte de renseignements pour obtenir les renseignements demandés, quand bien même cet autre État n'aurait pas besoin de ces renseignements à ses propres fins fiscales. L'obligation énoncée dans la phrase précédente est soumise aux restrictions prévues au paragraphe 3, lesquelles ne sauraient toutefois en aucun cas être interprétées comme autorisant un État contractant à refuser de fournir des renseignements pour la seule raison qu'il ne détient aucun intérêt national dans de tels renseignements.

5. Les dispositions du paragraphe 3 ne peuvent en aucun cas être interprétées comme autorisant un État contractant à refuser de communiquer des renseignements uniquement parce que ceux-ci sont détenus par une banque, une autre institution financière, un mandataire ou une personne agissant en qualité d'agent ou à titre fiduciaire ou parce que ces renseignements se rapportent aux droits de propriété d'une personne.

Article 27. Assistance en matière de recouvrement

1. Les États contractants, dans la mesure autorisée par leurs législations respectives, se prêtent mutuellement assistance pour recouvrer les impôts visés à l'article 2 ainsi que les intérêts et les amendes relatifs à ces impôts, à condition que l'État contractant qui demande l'assistance ait pris des mesures raisonnables pour recouvrer lesdits impôts.

2. Les créances qui font l'objet de demandes d'assistance n'ont pas la priorité sur les impôts dus dans l'État contractant qui prête assistance et les dispositions du paragraphe 1 de l'article 26 s'appliquent aussi à tout renseignement qui, en vertu du présent article, est fourni à l'autorité compétente d'un État contractant.

3. Les autorités compétentes des États contractants fixent d'un commun accord les modalités d'application des dispositions du présent article.

Article 28. Membres des missions diplomatiques et des postes consulaires

Les dispositions du présent Accord sont sans préjudice des privilèges fiscaux dont bénéficient les membres des missions diplomatiques ou des postes consulaires en vertu des règles générales du droit international ou des dispositions d'accords particuliers.

Article 29. Entrée en vigueur

1. Chacun des États contractants notifie à l'autre l'accomplissement des procédures requises par sa législation pour l'entrée en vigueur du présent Accord. Le présent Accord entre en vigueur à la date de réception de la dernière de ces notifications.

2. Les dispositions du présent Accord s'appliquent alors :

a) Au Botswana :

i) En ce qui concerne les impôts retenus à la source, aux montants payés ou crédités à partir du trentième jour suivant la date d'entrée en vigueur du présent Accord ; et

ii) En ce qui concerne les autres impôts, pour toute année d'imposition commençant à partir du 1er juillet suivant l'année au cours de laquelle le présent Accord entre en vigueur ;

b) En Irlande :

i) En ce qui concerne l'impôt sur le revenu, la charge sociale universelle et l'impôt sur les gains en capital, pour toute année d'imposition commençant à partir du 1er janvier suivant l'année au cours de laquelle le présent Accord entre en vigueur ;

ii) En ce qui concerne l'impôt sur les sociétés, pour toute année financière commençant à partir du 1er janvier suivant l'année au cours de laquelle le présent Accord entre en vigueur.

Article 30. Dénonciation

1. Le présent Accord reste en vigueur tant qu'il n'est pas dénoncé par un État contractant. L'un ou l'autre État contractant peut dénoncer l'Accord après l'expiration d'une période de cinq ans à compter de la date de son entrée en vigueur, moyennant une notification écrite au moins six mois plus tôt adressée par la voie diplomatique.

2. Dans ce cas, l'Accord cesse de produire ses effets :

a) Au Botswana :

i) En ce qui concerne les impôts retenus à la source, sur les montants payés ou crédités à partir du trentième jour suivant la date à laquelle la notification de dénonciation est donnée ;

ii) En ce qui concerne les autres impôts, pour les revenus imposables perçus à partir du 1er juillet de l'année suivant celle au cours de laquelle la notification de dénonciation est donnée ;

b) En Irlande :

i) En ce qui concerne l'impôt sur le revenu, la charge sociale universelle et l'impôt sur les gains en capital, pour toute année d'imposition commençant à partir du 1er janvier de l'année civile suivant celle au cours de laquelle la notification de dénonciation est donnée ;

ii) En ce qui concerne les autres impôts, pour toute année financière commençant à partir du 1er janvier de l'année civile suivant celle au cours de laquelle la notification de dénonciation est donnée.

EN FOI DE QUOI, les soussignés, à ce dûment autorisés, ont signé le présent Accord.

FAIT à Gaborone, le 10 juin 2014, en deux exemplaires en langue anglaise.

Pour le Gouvernement de la République du Botswana :

[O. K. MATAMBO]

Pour le Gouvernement de l'Irlande :

[JOE COSTELLO]

PROTOCOLE

À la signature de l'Accord entre le Gouvernement de la République du Botswana et le Gouvernement de l'Irlande tendant à éviter les doubles impositions et à prévenir la fraude fiscale en matière d'impôts sur le revenu, les signataires, à ce dûment autorisés, sont en outre convenus des dispositions ci-après, qui font partie intégrante dudit Accord :

1) En ce qui concerne l'article 4 :

Il est entendu qu'un Fonds commun contractuel (Common Contractual Fund) établi en Irlande ne peut être considéré comme un résident de l'Irlande et doit être traité comme fiscalement transparent aux fins de l'octroi des avantages découlant d'un traité ;

2) En ce qui concerne les article 10 et 11 :

Aux fins du paragraphe 3 de l'article 10 et du paragraphe 3 de l'article 11, le terme « Gouvernement » comprend :

i) Dans le cas du Botswana, la Banque du Botswana ;

ii) Dans le cas de l'Irlande, la Banque centrale d'Irlande, l'Agence nationale de gestion du Trésor ainsi que les organismes sous son égide ; et

iii) Dans l'un ou l'autre cas, un organisme public ou toute institution entièrement ou principalement détenue par le Gouvernement du Botswana ou par le Gouvernement de l'Irlande, comme il peut être convenu de temps à autre par les autorités compétentes des États contractants.

EN FOI DE QUOI, les soussignés, à ce dûment autorisés, ont signé le présent Protocole.

FAIT à Gaborone, le 10 juin 2014, en deux exemplaires en langue anglaise.

Pour le Gouvernement de la République du Botswana :

[O. K. MATAMBO]

Pour le Gouvernement de l'Irlande :

[JOE COSTELLO]

No. 54752

Ireland and Ethiopia

Convention between Ireland and the Federal Democratic Republic of Ethiopia for the avoidance of double taxation and the prevention of fiscal evasion with respect to taxes on income (with protocol). Addis Ababa, 3 November 2014

Entry into force: *12 August 2016 by notification, in accordance with article 29*

Authentic text: *English*

Registration with the Secretariat of the United Nations: *Ireland, 1 November 2017*

Irlande et Éthiopie

Convention entre l'Irlande et la République fédérale démocratique d'Éthiopie tendant à éviter les doubles impositions et à prévenir la fraude fiscale en matière d'impôts sur le revenu (avec protocole). Addis-Abeba, 3 novembre 2014

Entrée en vigueur : *12 août 2016 par notification, conformément à l'article 29*

Texte authentique : *anglais*

Enregistrement au Secrétariat de l'Organisation des Nations Unies : *Irlande, 1er novembre 2017*

[TEXT IN ENGLISH – TEXTE EN ANGLAIS]

CONVENTION BETWEEN IRELAND AND THE FEDERAL DEMOCRATIC REPUBLIC OF ETHIOPIA FOR THE AVOIDANCE OF DOUBLE TAXATION AND THE PREVENTION OF FISCAL EVASION WITH RESPECT TO TAXES ON INCOME

The Government of Ireland and the Government of the Federal Democratic Republic of Ethiopia, desiring to conclude a Convention for the avoidance of double taxation and the prevention of fiscal evasion with respect to taxes on income, have agreed as follows:

Article 1

PERSONS COVERED

This Convention shall apply to persons who are residents of one or both of the Contracting States.

Article 2

TAXES COVERED

1. This Convention shall apply to taxes on income imposed on behalf of a Contracting State or of its political subdivisions or local authorities, irrespective of the manner in which they are levied.

2. There shall be regarded as taxes on income all taxes imposed on total income or on elements of income, including taxes on gains from the alienation of movable or immovable property.

3. The existing taxes to which this Convention shall apply are in particular:

(a) in the case of Ethiopia:

(i) the tax on income and profit; and

(ii) the tax on income from mining, petroleum and agricultural activities;

(hereinafter referred to as "Ethiopian tax");

(b) in the case of Ireland:

(i) the income tax;

(ii) the universal social charge;

(iii) the corporation tax; and

(iv) the capital gains tax;

(hereinafter referred to as "Irish tax").

4. This Convention shall apply also to any identical or substantially similar taxes that are imposed after the date of signature of this Convention in addition to, or in place of, the existing taxes. The competent authorities of the Contracting States shall notify each other of any significant changes that have been made in their respective taxation laws.

Article 3

GENERAL DEFINITIONS

1. For the purposes of this Convention, unless the context otherwise requires:

(a) the terms "a Contracting State" and "the other Contracting State" mean Ethiopia or Ireland, as the context requires; and the term "Contracting States" means Ethiopia and Ireland;

(b) the term "Ethiopia" means the Federal Democratic Republic of Ethiopia, when used in a geographical sense, it means the national territory and any other area which in accordance with the laws of Ethiopia and international law is or may be designated as an area in which Ethiopia exercises sovereign rights or its jurisdiction;

(c) the term "Ireland" includes any area outside the territorial waters of Ireland which has been or may hereafter be designated, under the laws of Ireland concerning the Exclusive Economic Zone and the Continental Shelf, as an area within which Ireland may exercise such sovereign rights and jurisdiction as are in conformity with international law;

(d) the term "person" includes an individual, a company and any other body of persons;

(e) the term "company" means any body corporate or any entity that is treated as a body corporate for tax purposes;

(f) the terms "enterprise of a Contracting State" and "enterprise of the other Contracting State" mean respectively an enterprise carried on by a resident of a Contracting State and an enterprise carried on by a resident of the other Contracting State;

(g) the term "international traffic" means any transport by a ship or aircraft operated by an enterprise which has its place of effective management in a Contracting State, except when the ship or aircraft is operated solely between places in the other Contracting State;

(h) the term "national", in relation to a Contracting State, means:

(i) any individual possessing the nationality or citizenship of that Contracting State; and

(ii) any legal person, partnership or association deriving its status as such from the laws in force in that Contracting State;

(i) the term "competent authority" means:

(i) in the case of Ethiopia, the Minister of Finance and Economic Development or his authorised representative;

(ii) in the case of Ireland, the Revenue Commissioners or their authorised representative.

2. As regards the application of this Convention at any time by a Contracting State, any term not defined therein shall, unless the context otherwise requires, have the meaning that it has at that time under the law of that State for the purposes of the taxes to which the Convention applies, any meaning under the applicable tax laws of that State prevailing over a meaning given to the term under other laws of that State.

Article 4
RESIDENT

1. For the purposes of this Convention, the term "resident of a Contracting State" means any person who, under the laws of that State, is liable to tax therein by reason of his domicile, residence, place of incorporation, place of management or any other criterion of a similar nature, and also includes that State and any political subdivision or local authority thereof. This term, however, does not include any person who is liable to tax in that State in respect only of income from sources in that State.

2. Where by reason of the provisions of paragraph 1 an individual is a resident of both Contracting States, then his status shall be determined as follows:

(a) he shall be deemed to be a resident only of the State in which he has a permanent home available to him; if he has a permanent home available to him in both States, he shall be deemed to be a resident only of the State with which his personal and economic relations are closer (centre of vital interests);

(b) if the State in which he has his centre of vital interests cannot be determined, or if he has not a permanent home available to him in either State, he shall be deemed to be a resident only of the State in which he has an habitual abode;

(c) if he has an habitual abode in both States or in neither of them, he shall be deemed to be a resident only of the State of which he is a national;

(d) if he is a national of both States or of neither of them, the competent authorities of the Contracting States shall settle the question by mutual agreement.

3. Where by reason of the provisions of paragraph 1 a person other than an individual is a resident of both Contracting States, then it shall be deemed to be a resident only of the State in which its place of effective management is situated.

Article 5
PERMANENT ESTABLISHMENT

1. For the purposes of this Convention, the term "permanent establishment" means a fixed place of business through which the business of an enterprise is wholly or partly carried on.

2. The term "permanent establishment" includes especially:

(a) a place of management;
(b) a branch;
(c) an office;
(d) a factory;
(e) a workshop;
(f) a commercial warehouse;

(g) a farm, plantation or other place where agricultural, forestry, plantation or related activities are carried on; and

(h) a mine, an oil or gas well, a quarry or any other place of extraction of natural resources.

3. A building site or construction or installation project constitutes a permanent establishment only if it lasts more than six months.

4. Notwithstanding the preceding provisions of this Article, the term "permanent establishment" shall be deemed not to include:

(a) the use of facilities solely for the purpose of storage, display or delivery of goods or merchandise belonging to the enterprise;

(b) the maintenance of a stock of goods or merchandise belonging to the enterprise solely for the purpose of storage, display or delivery;

(c) the maintenance of a stock of goods or merchandise belonging to the enterprise solely for the purpose of processing by another enterprise;

(d) the maintenance of a fixed place of business solely for the purpose of purchasing goods or merchandise or of collecting information, for the enterprise;

(e) the maintenance of a fixed place of business solely for the purpose of carrying on, for the enterprise, any other activity of a preparatory or auxiliary character;

(f) the maintenance of a fixed place of business solely for any combination of activities mentioned in subparagraphs (a) to (e), provided that the overall activity of the fixed place of business resulting from this combination is of a preparatory or auxiliary character.

5. Notwithstanding the provisions of paragraphs 1 and 2, where a person - other than an agent of an independent status to whom paragraph 6 applies - is

acting on behalf of an enterprise and has, and habitually exercises, in a Contracting State an authority to conclude contracts in the name of the enterprise, that enterprise shall be deemed to have a permanent establishment in that State in respect of any activities which that person undertakes for the enterprise, unless the activities of such person are limited to those mentioned in paragraph 4 which, if exercised through a fixed place of business, would not make this fixed place of business a permanent establishment under the provisions of that paragraph.

6. An enterprise shall not be deemed to have a permanent establishment in a Contracting State merely because it carries on business in that State through a broker, general commission agent or any other agent of an independent status, provided that such persons are acting in the ordinary course of their business. However, where the activities of such an agent are devoted wholly or mainly to that enterprise and conditions are made or imposed between that enterprise and the agent in their commercial and financial relations which differ from those which would have been made between independent enterprises, he would not be considered an agent of an independent status within the meaning of this paragraph.

7. The fact that a company which is a resident of a Contracting State controls or is controlled by a company which is a resident of the other Contracting State, or which carries on business in that other State (whether through a permanent establishment or otherwise), shall not of itself constitute either company a permanent establishment of the other.

Article 6

INCOME FROM IMMOVABLE PROPERTY

1. Income derived by a resident of a Contracting State from immovable property (including income from agriculture or forestry) situated in the other Contracting State may be taxed in that other State.

2. The term "immovable property" shall have the meaning which it has under the law of the Contracting State in which the property in question is situated. The term shall in any case include property accessory to immovable property, livestock and equipment used in agriculture and forestry, rights to which the provisions of general law respecting landed property apply, usufruct of immovable property and rights to variable or fixed payments as consideration for the working of, or the right to work, mineral deposits, sources and other natural resources; ships and aircraft shall not be regarded as immovable property.

3. The provisions of paragraph 1 shall apply to income derived from the direct use, letting, or use in any other form of immovable property.

4. The provisions of paragraphs 1 and 3 shall also apply to the income from immovable property of an enterprise and to income from immovable property used for the performance of independent personal services.

Article 7

BUSINESS PROFITS

1. The profits of an enterprise of a Contracting State shall be taxable only in that State unless the enterprise carries on business in the other Contracting State through a permanent establishment situated therein. If the enterprise

carries on business as aforesaid, the profits of the enterprise may be taxed in the other State but only so much of them as is attributable to that permanent establishment.

2. Subject to the provisions of paragraph 3, where an enterprise of a Contracting State carries on business in the other Contracting State through a permanent establishment situated therein, there shall in each Contracting State be attributed to that permanent establishment the profits which it might be expected to make if it were a distinct and separate enterprise engaged in the same or similar activities under the same or similar conditions and dealing wholly independently with the enterprise of which it is a permanent establishment.

3. In determining the profits of a permanent establishment, there shall be allowed as deductions expenses which are incurred for the purposes of the permanent establishment, including executive and general administrative expenses so incurred, whether in the State in which the permanent establishment is situated or elsewhere.

4. Insofar as it has been customary in a Contracting State to determine the profits to be attributed to a permanent establishment on the basis of an apportionment of the total profits of the enterprise to its various parts, nothing in paragraph 2 shall preclude that Contracting State from determining the profits to be taxed by such an apportionment as may be customary; the method of apportionment adopted shall, however, be such that the result shall be in accordance with the principles contained in this Article.

5. No profits shall be attributed to a permanent establishment by reason of the mere purchase by that permanent establishment of goods or merchandise for the enterprise.

6. For the purposes of the preceding paragraphs, the profits to be attributed to the permanent establishment shall be determined by the same method year by year unless there is good and sufficient reason to the contrary.

7. Where profits include items of income or gains which are dealt with separately in other Articles of this Convention, then the provisions of those Articles shall not be affected by the provisions of this Article.

Article 8

INTERNATIONAL TRAFFIC

1. Profits from the operation of ships or aircraft in international traffic shall be taxable only in the Contracting State in which the place of effective management of the enterprise is situated.

2. If the place of effective management of a shipping enterprise is aboard a ship, then it shall be deemed to be situated in the Contracting State in which the home harbour of the ship is situated, or, if there is no such home harbour, in the Contracting State of which the operator of the ship is a resident.

3. For the purposes of this Article, profits derived from the operation of ships or aircraft in international traffic include:

(a) profits derived from the rental of ships or aircraft if such ships or aircraft are operated in international traffic or if such rental profits are incidental to other profits described in paragraph 1;

(b) profits from the use, maintenance or rental of containers (including trailers and related equipment for the transport of containers) used for the transport of goods or merchandise, where such rental, use or maintenance, as the case may be, is incidental to the operation of ships or aircraft in international traffic; and

(c) profits from the sale of tickets for the service of transportation by sea or air on behalf of other enterprises.

4. For the purposes of this Article, interest on funds directly connected with the operation of ships or aircraft in international traffic shall be regarded as profits derived from the operation of such ships or aircraft, and the provisions of Article 11 shall not apply in relation to such interest.

5. The provisions of paragraph 1 of this Article shall also apply to profits from the participation in a pool, a joint business or an international operating agency.

Article 9

ASSOCIATED ENTERPRISES

1. Where

(a) an enterprise of a Contracting State participates directly or indirectly in the management, control or capital of an enterprise of the other Contracting State, or

(b) the same persons participate directly or indirectly in the management, control or capital of an enterprise of a Contracting State and an enterprise of the other Contracting State,

and in either case conditions are made or imposed between the two enterprises in their commercial or financial relations which differ from those which would be made between independent enterprises, then any profits which would, but for those conditions, have accrued to one of the enterprises, but, by reason of those conditions have not so accrued, may be included in the profits of that enterprise and taxed accordingly.

2. Where a Contracting State includes in the profits of an enterprise of that State - and taxes accordingly - profits on which an enterprise of the other Contracting State has been charged to tax in that other State and the profits so included are profits which would have accrued to the enterprise of the first-mentioned State if the conditions made between the two enterprises had been those which would have been made between independent enterprises, then that other State shall make an appropriate adjustment to the amount of the tax charged therein on those profits. In determining such adjustment, due regard shall be had to the other provisions of this Convention and the competent authorities of the Contracting States shall if necessary consult each other.

Article 10

DIVIDENDS

1. Dividends paid by a company which is a resident of a Contracting State to a resident of the other Contracting State may be taxed in that other State.

2. However, such dividends may also be taxed in the Contracting State of which the company paying the dividends is a resident and according to the laws of that State, but if the beneficial owner of the dividends is a resident of the other Contracting State, the tax so charged shall not exceed 5 per cent of the gross amount of the dividends.

This paragraph shall not affect the taxation of the company in respect of the profits out of which the dividends are paid.

3. The term "dividends" as used in this Article means income from shares, including mining shares, founders' shares or other rights, not being debt-claims, participating in profits, as well as income from other corporate rights which is subjected to the same taxation treatment as income from shares by the laws of the State of which the company making the distribution is a resident.

4. The provisions of paragraphs 1 and 2 shall not apply if the beneficial owner of the dividends, being a resident of a Contracting State, carries on business in the other Contracting State of which the company paying the dividends is a resident through a permanent establishment situated therein, or performs in that other State independent personal services from a fixed base situated therein, and the holding in respect of which the dividends are paid is effectively connected with such permanent establishment or fixed base. In such case the provisions of Article 7 or Article 14, as the case may be, shall apply.

5. Where a company which is a resident of a Contracting State derives profits or income from the other Contracting State, that other State may not impose any tax on the dividends paid by the company, except insofar as such dividends are paid to a resident of that other State or insofar as the holding in respect of which the dividends are paid is effectively connected with a permanent establishment or a fixed base situated in that other State, nor subject the company's undistributed profits to a tax on the company's undistributed profits, even if the dividends paid or the undistributed profits consist wholly or partly of profits or income arising in such other State.

Article 11

INTEREST

1. Interest arising in a Contracting State and paid to a resident of the other Contracting State may be taxed in that other State.

2. However, such interest may also be taxed in the Contracting State in which it arises and according to the laws of that State, but if the beneficial owner of the interest is a resident of the other Contracting State, the tax so charged shall not exceed 5 per cent of the gross amount of the interest.

The competent authorities of the Contracting States shall consult each other regarding the mode of application of the provisions of this paragraph.

3. Notwithstanding the provisions of paragraph 2, interest arising in a Contracting State shall be exempt from tax in that State, provided that it is derived and beneficially owned by:

(a) the Government, a political subdivision or local authority of the other Contracting State; or

(b) (i) in the case of Ethiopia, the National Bank of Ethiopia;
(ii) in the case of Ireland, the Central Bank of Ireland or the National Treasury Management Agency.

4. The term "interest" as used in this Article means income from debt-claims of every kind, whether or not secured by mortgage, and whether or not carrying a right to participate in the debtor's profits, and in particular, income from government securities and income from bonds or debentures, including premiums and prizes attaching to such securities, bonds or debentures as well as all other income treated as income from money lent by the laws of the State in which the income arises but does not include any income which is treated as

a dividend under Article 10. Penalty charges for late payment shall not be regarded as interest for the purpose of this Article.

5. The provisions of paragraphs 1 and 2 shall not apply if the beneficial owner of the interest, being a resident of a Contracting State, carries on business in the other Contracting State in which the interest arises through a permanent establishment situated therein, or performs in that other State independent personal services from a fixed base situated therein, and the debt-claim in respect of which the interest is paid is effectively connected with such permanent establishment or fixed base. In such case the provisions of Article 7 or Article 14, as the case may be, shall apply.

6. Interest shall be deemed to arise in a Contracting State when the payer is a resident of that State. Where, however, the person paying the interest, whether he is a resident of a Contracting State or not, has in a Contracting State a permanent establishment or a fixed base in connection with which the indebtedness on which the interest is paid was incurred, and such interest is borne by such permanent establishment or fixed base, then such interest shall be deemed to arise in the Contracting State in which the permanent establishment or fixed base is situated.

7. Where, by reason of a special relationship between the payer and the beneficial owner or between both of them and some other person, the amount of the interest, having regard to the debt- claim for which it is paid, exceeds the amount which would have been agreed upon by the payer and the beneficial owner in the absence of such relationship, the provisions of this Article shall apply only to the last-mentioned amount. In such case, the excess part of the payments shall remain taxable according to the laws of each Contracting State, due regard being had to the other provisions of this Convention.

Article 12

ROYALTIES

1. Royalties arising in a Contracting State and paid to a resident of the other Contracting State may be taxed in that other State.

2. However, such royalties may also be taxed in the Contracting State in which they arise and according to the laws of that State, but if the beneficial owner of the royalties is a resident of the other Contracting State, the tax so charged shall not exceed 5 per cent of the gross amount of the royalties.

3. The term "royalties" as used in this Article means payments of any kind received as a consideration for the use of, or the right to use, any copyright of literary, artistic or scientific work including computer software, cinematographic films and recordings on tape or other media used for radio or television broadcasting or other means of reproduction or transmission, any patent, trade mark, design or model, plan, secret formula or process, or for information concerning industrial, commercial or scientific experience.

4. The provisions of paragraphs 1 and 2 shall not apply if the beneficial owner of the royalties, being a resident of a Contracting State, carries on business in the other Contracting State in which the royalties arise through a permanent establishment situated therein, or performs in that other State independent personal services from a fixed base situated therein, and the right or property in respect of which the royalties are paid is effectively connected with such permanent establishment or fixed base. In such case the provisions of Article 7 or Article 14, as the case may be, shall apply.

5. Royalties shall be deemed to arise in a Contracting State when the payer is a resident of that State. Where, however, the person paying the royalties, whether he is a resident of a Contracting State or not, has in a Contracting State

a permanent establishment or a fixed base in connection with which the liability to pay the royalties was incurred, and such royalties are borne by such permanent establishment or fixed base, then such royalties shall be deemed to arise in the Contracting State in which the permanent establishment or fixed base is situated.

6. Where, by reason of a special relationship between the payer and the beneficial owner or between both of them and some other person, the amount of the royalties, having regard to the use, right or information for which they are paid, exceeds the amount which would have been agreed upon by the payer and the beneficial owner in the absence of such relationship, the provisions of this Article shall apply only to the last-mentioned amount. In such case, the excess part of the payments shall remain taxable according to the laws of each Contracting State, due regard being had to the other provisions of this Convention.

Article 13
CAPITAL GAINS

1. Gains derived by a resident of a Contracting State from the alienation of immovable property referred to in Article 6 and situated in the other Contracting State may be taxed in that other State.

2. Gains from the alienation of movable property forming part of the business property of a permanent establishment which an enterprise of a Contracting State has in the other Contracting State or of movable property pertaining to a fixed base available to a resident of a Contracting State in the other Contracting State for the purpose of performing independent personal services, including such gains from the alienation of such a permanent

establishment (alone or with the whole enterprise) or of such fixed base, may be taxed in that other State.

3. Gains from the alienation of ships or aircraft operated in international traffic or movable property pertaining to the operation of such ships or aircraft shall be taxable only in the Contracting State in which the place of effective management of the enterprise is situated.

4. Gains derived by a resident of a Contracting State from the alienation of:

(a) shares, other than shares quoted on a recognised stock exchange, deriving more than 50 per cent of their value directly or indirectly from immovable property situated in the other Contracting State; or

(b) an interest in a partnership or trust deriving more than 50 per cent of its value directly or indirectly from immovable property situated in the other Contracting State,

may be taxed in that other State.

5. Gains from the alienation of any property, other than that referred to in paragraphs 1, 2, 3 and 4, shall be taxable only in the Contracting State of which the alienator is a resident.

6. The provisions of paragraph 5 shall not affect the right of a Contracting State to levy, according to its law, a tax on gains from the alienation of any property derived by an individual who is a resident of the other Contracting State and has been a resident of the first-mentioned State at any time during the five years immediately preceding the alienation of the property.

Article 14

INDEPENDENT PERSONAL SERVICES

1. Income derived by a resident of a Contracting State in respect of professional services or other activities of an independent character shall be taxable only in that State unless he has a fixed base regularly available to him in the other Contracting State for the purpose of performing his activities. If he has such a fixed base, the income may be taxed in the other State but only so much of it as is attributable to that fixed base.

2. The term "professional services" includes especially independent scientific, literary, artistic, educational or teaching activities as well as the independent activities of physicians, lawyers, engineers, architects, dentists and accountants.

Article 15

DEPENDENT PERSONAL SERVICES

1. Subject to the provisions of Articles 16, 18, 19 and 21, salaries, wages and other similar remuneration derived by a resident of a Contracting State in respect of an employment shall be taxable only in that State unless the employment is exercised in the other Contracting State. If the employment is so exercised, such remuneration as is derived therefrom may be taxed in that other State.

2. Notwithstanding the provisions of paragraph 1, remuneration derived by a resident of a Contracting State in respect of an employment exercised in the other Contracting State shall be taxable only in the first- mentioned State if:

(a) the recipient is present in the other State for a period or periods not exceeding in the aggregate 183 days in any twelve month period commencing or ending in the calendar year concerned, and

(b) the remuneration is paid by, or on behalf of, an employer who is not a resident of the other State, and

(c) the remuneration is not borne by a permanent establishment or a fixed base which the employer has in the other State.

3. Notwithstanding the preceding provisions of this Article, remuneration derived by a resident of a Contracting State in respect of an employment exercised aboard a ship or aircraft operated in international traffic may be taxed in the Contracting State in which the place of effective management of the enterprise is situated.

Article 16
DIRECTORS' FEES

Directors' fees and other similar payments derived by a resident of a Contracting State in his capacity as a member of the board of directors of a company which is a resident of the other Contracting State may be taxed in that other State.

Article 17
ARTISTES AND SPORTSPERSONS

1. Notwithstanding the provisions of Articles 14 and 15, income derived by a resident of a Contracting State as an entertainer, such as a theatre, motion picture, radio or television artiste, or a musician, or as a sportsperson, from his

personal activities as such exercised in the other Contracting State, may be taxed in that other State.

2. Where income in respect of personal activities exercised by an entertainer or a sportsperson in his capacity as such accrues not to the entertainer or sportsperson himself but to another person, that income may, notwithstanding the provisions of Articles 7, 14 and 15, be taxed in the Contracting State in which the activities of the entertainer or sportsperson are exercised.

3. Notwithstanding the provisions of paragraphs 1 and 2, income derived from the activities referred to in paragraph 1 within the framework of cultural or sports exchanges agreed to by the Governments of the Contracting States and carried out other than for the purpose of profit, shall be exempt from tax in the Contracting State in which these activities are exercised.

Article 18

PENSIONS AND ANNUITIES

1. Subject to the provisions of paragraph 2 of Article 19, pensions and other similar remuneration paid to a resident of a Contracting State in consideration of past employment and any annuity paid to such a resident shall be taxable only in that State.

2. Notwithstanding the provisions of paragraph 1, such pension, similar remuneration or annuity may be taxed in the Contracting State in which it arises if it is not subject to tax in the other Contracting State.

3. The term "annuity" means a stated sum payable periodically at stated times during life or during a specified or ascertainable period of time under an

obligation to make the payments in return for adequate and full consideration in money or money's worth.

Article 19

GOVERNMENT SERVICE

1. (a) Salaries, wages and other similar remuneration paid by a Contracting State or a political subdivision or a local authority thereof to an individual in respect of services rendered to that State or subdivision or authority shall be taxable only in that State.

(b) However, such salaries, wages and other similar remuneration shall be taxable only in the other Contracting State if the services are rendered in that State and the individual is a resident of that State who:

(i) is a national of that State; or

(ii) did not become a resident of that State solely for the purpose of rendering the services.

2. (a) Notwithstanding the provisions of paragraph 1, pensions and other similar remuneration paid by, or out of funds created by, a Contracting State or a political subdivision or a local authority thereof to an individual in respect of services rendered to that State or subdivision or authority shall be taxable only in that State.

(b) However, such pensions and other similar remuneration shall be taxable only in the other Contracting State if the individual is a resident of, and a national of, that State.

3. The provisions of Articles 15, 16, 17 and 18 shall apply to salaries, wages, pensions and other similar remuneration in respect of services rendered in connection with a business carried on by a Contracting State or a political subdivision or a local authority thereof.

Article 20

STUDENTS AND BUSINESS APPRENTICES

1. Payments which a student or business apprentice who is or was immediately before visiting a Contracting State a resident of the other Contracting State and who is present in the first-mentioned State solely for the purpose of his education or training receives for the purpose of his maintenance, education or training shall not be taxed in that State, provided that such payments arise from sources outside that State.

2. In respect of grants, scholarships and remuneration from employment not covered by paragraph 1, a student or business apprentice referred to in that paragraph shall, in addition, be entitled during such education or training to the same exemptions, reliefs, or reductions in respect of taxes available to residents of the Contracting State which he is visiting.

Article 21

PROFESSORS AND RESEARCHERS

1. An individual who is or was a resident of a Contracting State immediately before making a visit to the other Contracting State and who, at the invitation of any university, college, school or other similar non-profitable educational institution, which is recognised by the Government of that other Contracting State, is present in that other State for a period not exceeding two

years from the date of his first arrival in that other Contracting State, solely for the purpose of teaching or research or both, at such educational institution shall be exempt from tax in that other Contracting State on his remuneration for teaching or research. An individual shall be entitled to the benefits of this Article only once.

2. The provisions of paragraph 1 of this Article shall not apply to income from research if such research is undertaken not in the public interest but for the private benefit of a specific person or persons.

Article 22

OTHER INCOME

1. Items of income of a resident of a Contracting State, wherever arising, not dealt with in the foregoing Articles of this Convention shall be taxable only in that State.

2. The provisions of paragraph 1 shall not apply to income, other than income from immovable property as defined in paragraph 2 of Article 6, if the beneficial owner of such income , being a resident of a Contracting State, carries on business in the other Contracting State through a permanent establishment situated therein, or performs in that other State independent personal services from a fixed base situated therein, and the right or property in respect of which the income is paid is effectively connected with such permanent establishment or fixed base. In such case the provisions of Article 7 or Article 14, as the case may be, shall apply.

3. Notwithstanding the provisions of paragraphs 1 and 2, items of income of a resident of a Contracting State not dealt with in the foregoing Articles of

this Convention and arising in the other Contracting State may also be taxed in that other State.

Article 23

MISCELLANEOUS RULES APPLICABLE TO CERTAIN OFFSHORE ACTIVITIES

1. The provisions of this Article shall apply notwithstanding any other provision of this Convention where activities (in this Article called "relevant activities") are carried on offshore in connection with the exploration or exploitation of the sea bed and subsoil and their natural resources situated in a Contracting State.

2. An enterprise of a Contracting State which carries on relevant activities in the other Contracting State shall, subject to paragraph 3 of this Article, be deemed to be carrying on business in that other State through a permanent establishment situated therein.

3. Relevant activities which are carried on by an enterprise of a Contracting State in the other Contracting State for a period or periods not exceeding in the aggregate 30 days within any period of twelve months shall not constitute the carrying on of business through a permanent establishment situated therein. For the purposes of this paragraph:

(a) where an enterprise of a Contracting State carrying on relevant activities in the other Contracting State is associated with another enterprise carrying on substantially similar relevant activities there, the former enterprise shall be deemed to be carrying on all such activities of the latter enterprise, except to the extent that those activities are carried on at the same time as its own activities;

(b) an enterprise shall be regarded as associated with another enterprise if one participates directly or indirectly in the management, control or capital of the other or if the same persons participate directly or indirectly in the management, control or capital of both enterprises.

4. Salaries, wages and similar remuneration derived by a resident of a Contracting State in respect of an employment connected with relevant activities in the other Contracting State may, to the extent that the duties are performed offshore in that other State, be taxed in that other State.

5. Gains derived by a resident of a Contracting State from the alienation of:

(a) exploration or exploitation rights; or

(b) shares (or comparable instruments) deriving their value or the greater part of their value directly or indirectly from such rights,

may be taxed in that other State.

In this paragraph "exploration or exploitation rights" mean rights to assets to be produced by the exploration or exploitation of the seabed or subsoil or their natural resources in the other Contracting State, including rights to interests in or to the benefit of such assets.

Article 24
ELIMINATION OF DOUBLE TAXATION

1. Where a resident of Ethiopia derives income or gains which, in accordance with the provisions of this Convention, may be taxed in Ireland, Ethiopia shall allow as a deduction from the tax on the income or gains of that resident an amount equal to the tax paid in Ireland. Such deduction shall not, however, exceed that part of the income tax, as computed before the deduction

is given, which is attributable to the income or gains which may be taxed in Ireland.

2. Subject to the provisions of the laws of Ireland regarding the allowance as a credit against Irish tax of tax payable in a territory outside Ireland (which shall not affect the general principle hereof) -

(a) Ethiopian tax payable under the laws of Ethiopia and in accordance with this Convention, whether directly or by deduction, on profits, income or gains from sources within Ethiopia (excluding in the case of a dividend tax payable in respect of the profits out of which the dividend is paid) shall be allowed as a credit against any Irish tax computed by reference to the same profits, income or gains by reference to which Ethiopian tax is computed;

(b) in the case of a dividend paid by a company which is a resident of Ethiopia to a company which is a resident of Ireland and which controls directly or indirectly 5 per cent or more of the voting power in the company paying the dividend, the credit shall take into account (in addition to any Ethiopian tax creditable under the provisions of subparagraph (a)) Ethiopian tax payable by the company in respect of the profits out of which such dividend is paid.

3. For the purposes of paragraphs 1 and 2 profits, income or capital gains owned by a resident of a Contracting State which may be taxed in the other Contracting State in accordance with this Convention shall be deemed to be derived from sources in that other Contracting State.

4. Where in accordance with any provision of the Convention income derived by a resident of a Contracting State is exempt from tax in that State,

such State may nevertheless, in calculating the amount of tax on the remaining income of such resident, take into account the exempted income.

5. Where, under any provision of this Convention, income or gains is or are wholly or partly relieved from tax in a Contracting State and, under the laws in force in the other Contracting State, an individual, in respect of the said income or gains, is subject to tax by reference to the amount thereof which is remitted to or received in that other State, and not by reference to the full amount thereof, then the relief to be allowed under this Convention in the first-mentioned State shall apply only to so much of the income or gains as is remitted to or received in that other State.

6. For the purpose of paragraph 2, the term "Ethiopian tax payable" shall be deemed to include any amount which would have been payable as Ethiopian tax but for any exemption or reduction of tax granted to promote economic development in Ethiopia under the provisions of Council of Ministers Regulation No. 270/2012 on Investment Incentives and Investment Areas Reserved for Domestic Investors, as they may be updated or amended from time to time, provided that the scope of activities covered by such provisions is not materially changed up to the date of signature of this Convention. The competent authorities of the Contracting States may consult with each other to resolve any matter that may arise concerning the proper application and administration of this paragraph.

This paragraph shall apply with respect to profits of the company during the period of five years immediately following the date of entry into force of this Convention. This period may be extended by agreement between the competent authorities of the Contracting States.

Article 25

NON-DISCRIMINATION

1. Nationals of a Contracting State shall not be subjected in the other Contracting State to any taxation or any requirement connected therewith, which is other or more burdensome than the taxation and connected requirements to which nationals of that other State in the same circumstances, in particular with respect to residence, are or may be subjected. This provision shall, notwithstanding the provisions of Article 1, also apply to persons who are not residents of one or both of the Contracting States.

2. The taxation on a permanent establishment which an enterprise of a Contracting State has in the other Contracting State shall not be less favourably levied in that other State than the taxation levied on enterprises of that other State carrying on the same activities. This provision shall not be construed as obliging a Contracting State to grant to residents of the other Contracting State any personal allowances, reliefs and reductions for taxation purposes on account of civil status or family responsibilities which it grants to its own residents.

3. Except where the provisions of paragraph 1 of Article 9, paragraph 7 of Article 11, or paragraph 6 of Article 12, apply, interest, royalties and other disbursements paid by an enterprise of a Contracting State to a resident of the other Contracting State shall, for the purpose of determining the taxable profits of such enterprise, be deductible under the same conditions as if they had been paid to a resident of the first- mentioned State.

4. Enterprises of a Contracting State, the capital of which is wholly or partly owned or controlled, directly or indirectly, by one or more residents of the other Contracting State, shall not be subjected in the first- mentioned State to any taxation or any requirement connected therewith which is other or more

burdensome than the taxation and connected requirements to which other similar enterprises of the first- mentioned State are or may be subjected.

5. The provisions of this Article shall apply only to taxes which are covered by this Convention.

Article 26

MUTUAL AGREEMENT PROCEDURE

1. Where a person considers that the actions of one or both of the Contracting States result or will result for him in taxation not in accordance with the provisions of this Convention, he may, irrespective of the remedies provided by the domestic law of those States, present his case to the competent authority of the Contracting State of which he is a resident or, if his case comes under paragraph 1 of Article 25, to that of the Contracting State of which he is a national. The case must be presented within three years from the first notification of the action resulting in taxation not in accordance with the provisions of this Convention.

2. The competent authority shall endeavour, if the objection appears to it to be justified and if it is not itself able to arrive at a satisfactory solution, to resolve the case by mutual agreement with the competent authority of the other Contracting State, with a view to the avoidance of taxation which is not in accordance with this Convention. Any agreement reached shall be implemented notwithstanding any time limits in the domestic law of the Contracting States.

3. The competent authorities of the Contracting States shall endeavour to resolve by mutual agreement any difficulties or doubts arising as to the interpretation or application of this Convention. They may also consult together for the elimination of double taxation in cases not provided for in this Convention.

4. The competent authorities of the Contracting States may communicate with each other directly, including through a joint commission consisting of themselves or their representatives, for the purpose of reaching an agreement in the sense of the preceding paragraphs.

Article 27
EXCHANGE OF INFORMATION

1. The competent authorities of the Contracting States shall exchange such information as is foreseeably relevant for carrying out the provisions of this Convention or to the administration or enforcement of the domestic laws concerning taxes of every kind and description imposed on behalf of the Contracting States, or of their political subdivisions or local authorities, insofar as the taxation thereunder is not contrary to this Convention. The exchange of information is not restricted by Articles 1 and 2.

2. Any information received under paragraph 1 by a Contracting State shall be treated as secret in the same manner as information obtained under the domestic laws of that State and shall be disclosed only to persons or authorities (including courts and administrative bodies) concerned with the assessment or collection of, the enforcement or prosecution in respect of, the determination of appeals in relation to the taxes referred to in paragraph 1, or the oversight of the above. Such persons or authorities shall use the information only for such purposes. They may disclose the information in public court proceedings or in judicial decisions.

3. In no case shall the provisions of paragraphs 1 and 2 be construed so as to impose on a Contracting State the obligation:

(a) to carry out administrative measures at variance with the laws and administrative practice of that or of the other Contracting State;

(b) to supply information which is not obtainable under the laws or in the normal course of the administration of that or of the other Contracting State;

(c) to supply information which would disclose any trade, business, industrial, commercial or professional secret or trade process, or information the disclosure of which would be contrary to public policy (ordre public).

4. If information is requested by a Contracting State in accordance with this Article, the other Contracting State shall use its information gathering measures to obtain the requested information, even though that other State may not need such information for its own tax purposes. The obligation contained in the preceding sentence is subject to the limitations of paragraph 3 but in no case shall such limitations be construed to permit a Contracting State to decline to supply information solely because it has no domestic interest in such information.

5. In no case shall the provisions of paragraph 3 be construed to permit a Contracting State to decline to supply information solely because the information is held by a bank, other financial institution, nominee or person acting in an agency or a fiduciary capacity or because it relates to ownership interests in a person.

Article 28

MEMBERS OF DIPLOMATIC MISSIONS AND CONSULAR POSTS

Nothing in this Convention shall affect the fiscal privileges of members of diplomatic missions or consular posts under the general rules of international law or under the provisions of special agreements.

Article 29

ENTRY INTO FORCE

1. The Contracting States shall notify each other in writing through diplomatic channels that their constitutional requirements for entry into force of this Convention have been fulfilled.

2. This Convention shall enter into force on the date of receipt of the later of these notifications and shall thereupon have effect:

(a) In the case of Ethiopia:

(i) with regard to taxes withheld at source, in respect of amounts paid on or after the eighth day of July next following the date on which this Convention enters into force; and

(ii) with regard to other taxes, in respect of tax year beginning on or after the eighth day of July next following the date on which this Convention enters into force.

(b) In the case of Ireland:

(i) with regard to income tax, the universal social charge and capital gains tax, for any year of assessment beginning on or after the first day of January next following the date on which this Convention enters into force; and

(ii) with regard to corporation tax, for any financial year beginning on or after the first day of January next following the date on which this Convention enters into force.

Article 30

TERMINATION

This Convention shall remain in force until terminated by a Contracting State. Either Contracting State may terminate the Convention at any time after five years from the date on which the Convention enters into force provided that at least six months prior written notice of termination has been given through diplomatic channels.

In such event, the Convention shall cease to have effect:

(a) In the case of Ethiopia:

(i) with regard to taxes withheld at source, in respect of amounts paid on or after the eighth day of July next following the date on which the period specified in the said notice of termination expires; and

(ii) with regard to other taxes, in respect of tax year beginning on or after the eighth day of July next following the date on which the period specified in the said notice of termination expires.

(b) In the case of Ireland:

(i) with regard to income tax, the universal social charge and capital gains tax, for any year of assessment beginning on or after the first day of January next following the date on which the period specified in the said notice of termination expires; and

(ii) with regard to corporation tax, for any financial year beginning on or after the first day of January next following the date on which the period specified in the said notice of termination expires.

IN WITNESS WHEREOF the undersigned, duly authorised thereto, have signed this Convention.

Done in duplicate at Addis Ababa this 3rd day of Nov, 2014, in the English language.

FOR THE GOVERNMENT OF IRELAND:

L SHERLOCK

FOR THE GOVERNMENT OF THE FEDERAL DEMOCRATIC REPUBLIC OF ETHIOPIA

ATO AHMED SHIDE

PROTOCOL TO THE CONVENTION BETWEEN IRELAND AND THE FEDERAL DEMOCRATIC REPUBLIC OF ETHIOPIA FOR THE AVOIDANCE OF DOUBLE TAXATION AND THE PREVENTION OF FISCAL EVASION WITH RESPECT TO TAXES ON INCOME

At the moment of signing the Convention between Ireland and the Federal Democratic Republic of Ethiopia for the Avoidance of Double Taxation and the Prevention of Fiscal Evasion with respect to Taxes on Income, the undersigned have agreed that the following provisions shall form an integral part of the Convention.

It is understood that:

1. A Common Contractual Fund (CCF) established in Ireland shall not be regarded as a resident of Ireland and shall be treated as fiscally transparent for the purposes of granting treaty benefits.
2. With respect to paragraph 2(f) of Article 5, a "commercial warehouse" refers to facilities maintained by an enterprise of a Contracting State for storage of goods or merchandise for other enterprises for profit purposes.
3. With respect to paragraph 2(a) of Article 15, the reference to "in the calendar year concerned" means the Gregorian calendar.

IN WITNESS WHEREOF the undersigned, duly authorised thereto, have signed this Protocol.

FOR THE GOVERNMENT OF IRELAND:	FOR THE GOVERNMENT OF THE FEDERAL DEMOCRATIC REPUBLIC OF ETHIOPIA

[TRANSLATION IN FRENCH – TRADUCTION EN FRANÇAIS]

CONVENTION ENTRE L'IRLANDE ET LA RÉPUBLIQUE FÉDÉRALE DÉMOCRATIQUE D'ÉTHIOPIE TENDANT À ÉVITER LES DOUBLES IMPOSITIONS ET À PRÉVENIR LA FRAUDE FISCALE EN MATIÈRE D'IMPÔTS SUR LE REVENU

Le Gouvernement de l'Irlande et le Gouvernement de la République fédérale démocratique d'Éthiopie, désireux de conclure une convention tendant à éviter les doubles impositions et à prévenir la fraude fiscale en matière d'impôts sur le revenu, sont convenus de ce qui suit :

Article premier. Personnes visées

La présente Convention s'applique aux personnes qui sont des résidents d'un État contractant ou des deux États contractants.

Article 2. Impôts visés

1. La présente Convention s'applique aux impôts sur le revenu perçus pour le compte d'un État contractant ou de l'une de ses subdivisions politiques ou collectivités locales, quel que soit le système de perception.

2. Sont considérés comme impôts sur le revenu les impôts perçus sur le revenu total ou sur des éléments du revenu, y compris les impôts sur les gains provenant de l'aliénation de biens mobiliers ou immobiliers.

3. Les impôts actuels auxquels s'applique la présente Convention sont notamment :

a) Dans le cas de l'Éthiopie :

i) L'impôt sur le revenu et les bénéfices ; et

ii) L'impôt sur les revenus tirés d'activités minières, pétrolières et agricoles ;

(ci-après dénommés « impôt éthiopien ») ;

b) Dans le cas de l'Irlande :

i) L'impôt sur le revenu ;

ii) La charge sociale universelle ;

iii) L'impôt sur les sociétés ; et

iv) L'impôt sur les gains en capital ;

(ci-après dénommés « impôt irlandais »).

4. La présente Convention s'applique aussi aux impôts de nature identique ou analogue qui seraient établis après la date de signature de la présente Convention et qui s'ajouteraient aux impôts actuels ou qui les remplaceraient. Les autorités compétentes des États contractants se communiquent les modifications substantielles apportées à leurs législations fiscales respectives.

Article 3. Définitions générales

1. Aux fins de la présente Convention, à moins que le contexte n'exige une interprétation différente :

a) Les expressions « un État contractant » et « l'autre État contractant » désignent, selon le contexte, l'Éthiopie ou l'Irlande ; et l'expression « États contractants » désigne l'Éthiopie et l'Irlande ;

b) Le terme « Éthiopie » désigne la République fédérale démocratique d'Éthiopie et, lorsqu'il est employé dans un sens géographique, le territoire national et toute autre zone qui, conformément à la législation éthiopienne et au droit international, est ou peut être désignée comme une zone dans laquelle l'Éthiopie exerce des droits souverains ou sa juridiction ;

c) Le terme « Irlande » comprend toute zone située en dehors des eaux territoriales de l'Irlande qui a été ou peut ultérieurement être désignée, conformément à la législation irlandaise relative à la zone économique exclusive et au plateau continental, comme une zone à l'intérieur de laquelle l'Irlande peut exercer des droits souverains et sa juridiction conformément au droit international ;

d) Le terme « personne » comprend les personnes physiques, les sociétés et tous autres groupements de personnes ;

e) Le terme « société » désigne toute personne morale ou toute entité considérée comme une personne morale aux fins d'imposition ;

f) Les expressions « entreprise d'un État contractant » et « entreprise de l'autre État contractant » désignent respectivement une entreprise exploitée par un résident d'un État contractant et une entreprise exploitée par un résident de l'autre État contractant ;

g) L'expression « trafic international » désigne tout transport effectué par un navire ou un aéronef exploité par une entreprise dont le siège de direction effective est situé dans un État contractant, sauf lorsque le navire ou l'aéronef n'est exploité qu'entre des points situés dans l'autre État contractant ;

h) Le terme « ressortissant », en ce qui concerne un État contractant, désigne :

   i) Toute personne physique possédant la nationalité ou jouissant de la citoyenneté de cet État contractant ; et

   ii) Toute personne morale, société de personnes ou association constituée en vertu de la législation de cet État contractant ;

i) L'expression « autorité compétente » désigne :

   i) Dans le cas de l'Éthiopie, le Ministre des finances et du développement économique ou son représentant autorisé ;

   ii) Dans le cas de l'Irlande, l'administration des impôts (Revenue Commissioners) ou son représentant autorisé ;

2. Pour l'application de la présente Convention à un moment donné par un État contractant, toute expression ou tout terme qui n'y est pas défini a, à moins que le contexte n'exige une interprétation différente, le sens que lui attribue, au moment considéré, la législation de cet État concernant les impôts auxquels s'applique la Convention, le sens attribué à cette expression ou à ce terme par la législation fiscale de cet État prévalant sur le sens que lui attribuent les autres branches du droit de cet État.

Article 4. Résident

1. Aux fins de la présente Convention, l'expression « résident d'un État contractant » désigne toute personne qui, en vertu de la législation de cet État, est assujettie à l'impôt dans cet État en raison de son domicile, de sa résidence, de son lieu d'enregistrement, de son siège de direction ou de tout autre critère de nature analogue, et s'applique également à cet État et à ses subdivisions politiques et collectivités locales. Cette expression ne comprend cependant pas les personnes qui ne sont assujetties à l'impôt dans cet État que pour les revenus de sources situées dans cet État.

2. Lorsque, selon les dispositions du paragraphe 1, une personne physique est un résident des deux États contractants, sa situation est réglée comme suit :

a) Elle est réputée être un résident seulement de l'État où elle dispose d'un foyer d'habitation permanent ; si elle dispose d'un foyer d'habitation permanent dans les deux États, elle est réputée être un résident seulement de l'État avec lequel ses liens personnels et économiques sont les plus étroits (centre des intérêts vitaux) ;

b) Si l'État où se trouve le centre de ses intérêts vitaux ne peut pas être déterminé, ou si elle ne dispose d'un foyer d'habitation permanent dans aucun des deux États, elle est réputée être un résident seulement de l'État où elle séjourne de façon habituelle ;

c) Si elle séjourne de façon habituelle dans les deux États, ou si elle ne séjourne de façon habituelle dans aucun d'eux, elle est réputée être un résident seulement de l'État dont elle est ressortissante ;

d) Si elle est ressortissante des deux États, ou si elle n'est ressortissante d'aucun d'eux, les autorités compétentes des États contractants règlent la question d'un commun accord.

3. Lorsque, selon les dispositions du paragraphe 1, une personne autre qu'une personne physique est un résident des deux États contractants, elle est réputée être un résident seulement de l'État où se situe son siège de direction effective.

Article 5. Établissement stable

1. Aux fins de la présente Convention, l'expression « établissement stable » désigne une installation fixe d'affaires par l'intermédiaire de laquelle une entreprise exerce tout ou partie de son activité.

2. L'expression « établissement stable » désigne notamment :

a) Un siège de direction ;

b) Une succursale ;

c) Un bureau ;

d) Une usine ;

e) Un atelier ;

f) Un entrepôt commercial ;

g) Une ferme, une plantation ou tout autre lieu où sont réalisées des activités agricoles, forestières ou de plantation ou des activités connexes ; et

h) Une mine, un puits de pétrole ou de gaz, une carrière ou tout autre lieu d'extraction de ressources naturelles.

3. Un chantier ou un projet de construction ou d'installation constitue un établissement stable, mais uniquement s'il dure plus de six mois.

4. Nonobstant les dispositions précédentes du présent article, il est considéré qu'un « établissement stable » ne comprend pas :

a) L'utilisation d'installations aux seules fins de stockage, d'exposition ou de livraison de biens ou de marchandises appartenant à l'entreprise ;

b) L'exploitation d'un stock de biens ou de marchandises appartenant à l'entreprise aux seules fins de stockage, d'exposition ou de livraison ;

c) L'exploitation d'un stock de biens ou de marchandises appartenant à l'entreprise aux seules fins de transformation par une autre entreprise ;

d) L'exploitation d'une installation fixe d'affaires aux seules fins d'acheter des biens ou des marchandises ou de recueillir des renseignements, pour l'entreprise ;

e) L'exploitation d'une installation fixe d'affaires aux seules fins d'exercer pour l'entreprise toute autre activité de caractère préparatoire ou auxiliaire ;

f) L'exploitation d'une installation fixe d'affaires aux seules fins de l'exercice cumulé d'activités visées aux alinéas a) à e), sous réserve que l'activité globale de l'installation fixe d'affaires résultant de ce cumul ait un caractère préparatoire ou auxiliaire.

5. Nonobstant les dispositions des paragraphes 1 et 2, lorsqu'une personne, autre qu'un agent jouissant d'un statut indépendant auquel s'applique le paragraphe 6, agit pour le compte d'une entreprise et dispose dans un État contractant de pouvoirs qu'elle y exerce habituellement lui permettant de conclure des contrats au nom de l'entreprise, cette entreprise est considérée comme ayant un établissement stable dans cet État pour toutes les activités que cette personne exerce pour l'entreprise, à moins que les activités de cette personne ne soient limitées à celles qui sont mentionnées au paragraphe 4 et qui, si elles étaient exercées par l'intermédiaire d'une installation fixe d'affaires, ne permettraient pas de considérer cette installation comme un établissement stable selon les dispositions de ce paragraphe.

6. Une entreprise n'est pas considérée comme ayant un établissement stable dans un État contractant du seul fait qu'elle y exerce son activité par l'entremise d'un courtier, d'un commissionnaire général ou de tout autre agent jouissant d'un statut indépendant, à condition que ces personnes agissent dans le cadre ordinaire de leurs activités. Toutefois, lorsqu'il agit totalement ou presque totalement pour le compte de cette entreprise et que cette dernière et l'agent sont, dans leurs relations commerciales ou financières, liées par des conditions établies ou imposées qui diffèrent de celles qui auraient été établies entre des entreprises indépendantes, celui-ci n'est pas considéré comme un agent jouissant d'un statut indépendant au sens du présent paragraphe.

7. Le fait qu'une société qui est un résident d'un État contractant contrôle ou est contrôlée par une société qui est un résident de l'autre État contractant ou qui exerce une activité dans cet autre État (que ce soit par l'intermédiaire d'un établissement stable ou non) ne suffit pas, en lui-même, à faire de l'une quelconque de ces sociétés un établissement stable de l'autre.

Article 6. Revenus de biens immobiliers

1. Les revenus qu'un résident d'un État contractant tire de biens immobiliers (y compris ceux provenant d'exploitations agricoles ou forestières) situés dans l'autre État contractant sont imposables dans cet autre État.

2. L'expression « biens immobiliers » a le sens que lui attribue la législation de l'État contractant dans lequel les biens considérés sont situés. Cette expression comprend dans tous les cas les accessoires aux biens immobiliers, le cheptel et le matériel utilisé dans les exploitations agricoles et forestières, les droits auxquels s'appliquent les dispositions du droit privé concernant la propriété foncière, l'usufruit des biens immobiliers et les droits à des paiements variables ou fixes pour l'exploitation ou la concession de l'exploitation de gisements minéraux, sources ou autres ressources naturelles. Les navires et les aéronefs ne sont pas considérés comme des biens immobiliers.

3. Les dispositions du paragraphe 1 s'appliquent aux revenus provenant de l'exploitation directe, de la location et de toute autre forme d'exploitation de biens immobiliers.

4. Les dispositions des paragraphes 1 et 3 s'appliquent également aux revenus provenant des biens immobiliers d'une entreprise ainsi qu'aux revenus provenant des biens immobiliers servant à l'exercice d'une profession indépendante.

Article 7. Bénéfices des entreprises

1. Les bénéfices d'une entreprise d'un État contractant ne sont imposables que dans cet État, à moins que l'entreprise n'exerce son activité dans l'autre État contractant par l'intermédiaire d'un établissement stable qui y est situé. Si l'entreprise exerce son activité d'une telle façon, les bénéfices de cette entreprise sont imposables dans l'autre État, mais uniquement dans la mesure où ils sont imputables audit établissement stable.

2. Sous réserve des dispositions du paragraphe 3, lorsqu'une entreprise d'un État contractant exerce une activité dans l'autre État contractant par l'intermédiaire d'un établissement stable qui y est situé, il est imputé dans chacun des États contractants audit établissement stable les bénéfices qu'il aurait pu réaliser s'il avait constitué une entreprise distincte exerçant des activités identiques ou analogues dans des conditions identiques ou analogues et traitant en toute indépendance avec l'entreprise dont il est un établissement stable.

3. Pour déterminer les bénéfices d'un établissement stable, sont admises en déduction les dépenses relatives aux fins poursuivies par cet établissement stable, y compris les dépenses de direction et les frais généraux d'administration ainsi enregistrés, soit dans l'État où est situé cet établissement stable soit ailleurs.

4. S'il est d'usage, dans un État contractant, de déterminer les bénéfices imputables à un établissement stable sur la base d'une répartition des bénéfices totaux de l'entreprise entre ses diverses composantes, aucune disposition du paragraphe 2 n'empêche cet État contractant de déterminer les bénéfices imposables selon la répartition en usage ; la méthode de répartition adoptée doit cependant être telle que le résultat obtenu soit conforme aux principes énoncés au présent article.

5. Aucun bénéfice n'est imputé à un établissement stable au seul motif qu'il a acheté des biens ou des marchandises pour l'entreprise.

6. Aux fins des paragraphes précédents, les bénéfices à imputer à l'établissement stable sont déterminés chaque année selon la même méthode, à moins qu'il n'existe des motifs valables et suffisants de procéder autrement.

7. Lorsque les bénéfices comprennent des éléments de revenu ou des gains traités séparément dans d'autres articles de la présente Convention, les dispositions de ces articles ne sont pas affectées par les dispositions du présent article.

Article 8. Trafic international

1. Les bénéfices provenant de l'exploitation, en trafic international, de navire ou d'aéronefs ne sont imposables que dans l'État contractant où le siège de direction effective de l'entreprise est situé.

2. Si le siège de direction effective d'une entreprise de transport maritime est situé à bord d'un navire, le siège est considéré comme étant situé dans l'État contractant où se trouve le port d'attache de ce navire ou, à défaut de port d'attache, dans l'État contractant dont l'exploitant du navire est un résident.

3. Aux fins du présent article, les bénéfices provenant de l'exploitation, en trafic international, de navires ou d'aéronefs, comprennent :

a) Les bénéfices provenant de la location de navires ou d'aéronefs lorsque lesdits navires ou aéronefs sont exploités en trafic international ou lorsque lesdits bénéfices provenant de la location sont accessoires à d'autres bénéfices visés au paragraphe 1 ;

b) Les bénéfices provenant de l'utilisation, de l'entretien ou de la location de conteneurs (y compris les remorques et les équipements connexes pour le transport de tels conteneurs) utilisés pour le transport de biens ou de marchandises, si cette location, cette utilisation ou cet entretien, selon le cas, est accessoire à l'exploitation des navires ou des aéronefs en trafic international ; et

c) Les bénéfices provenant de la vente de billets pour les services de transport maritime ou aérien pour le compte d'autres entreprises.

4. Aux fins du présent article, les intérêts des fonds directement liés à l'exploitation des navires ou des aéronefs en trafic international sont considérés comme des bénéfices tirés de l'exploitation de tels navires ou aéronefs, et les dispositions de l'article 11 ne s'appliquent pas à ces intérêts.

5. Les dispositions du paragraphe 1 du présent article s'appliquent aussi aux bénéfices provenant de la participation à un consortium, une coentreprise ou un organisme international d'exploitation.

Article 9. Entreprises associées

1. Lorsque :

a) Une entreprise d'un État contractant participe, directement ou indirectement, à la direction, au contrôle ou au capital d'une entreprise de l'autre État contractant ; ou que

b) Les mêmes personnes participent, directement ou indirectement, à la direction, au contrôle ou au capital d'une entreprise d'un État contractant et d'une entreprise de l'autre État contractant ;

et que, dans l'un et l'autre cas, les deux entreprises sont, dans leurs relations commerciales ou financières, liées par des conditions convenues ou imposées, qui diffèrent de celles qui seraient convenues entre des entreprises indépendantes, les bénéfices qui auraient été réalisés par l'une des entreprises, mais n'ont pu l'être à cause de ces conditions peuvent être inclus dans les bénéfices de cette entreprise et imposés en conséquence.

2. Lorsqu'un État contractant inclut dans les bénéfices d'une entreprise de cet État, et impose en conséquence, des bénéfices sur lesquels une entreprise de l'autre État contractant a été imposée

dans cet autre État et que les bénéfices ainsi inclus sont des bénéfices qui auraient été réalisés par l'entreprise du premier État si les conditions convenues entre les deux entreprises avaient été celles qui auraient été convenues entre des entreprises indépendantes, alors cet autre État procède à un ajustement approprié du montant de l'impôt qui a été perçu sur ces bénéfices. L'ajustement est déterminé compte dûment tenu des autres dispositions de la présente Convention et, si nécessaire, les autorités compétentes des États contractants se consultent.

Article 10. Dividendes

1. Les dividendes payés par une société qui est résidente d'un État contractant à un résident de l'autre État contractant sont imposables dans cet autre État.

2. Toutefois, ces dividendes sont également imposables dans l'État contractant dont la société qui paie les dividendes est un résident et selon la législation de cet État, mais si le bénéficiaire effectif des dividendes est un résident de l'autre État contractant, l'impôt ainsi établi ne peut excéder 5 % du montant brut des dividendes.

Le présent paragraphe est sans incidence sur l'imposition de la société au titre des bénéfices qui servent au paiement des dividendes.

3. Le terme « dividendes » employé dans le présent article désigne les revenus provenant d'actions, de parts de mine, de parts de fondateur ou d'autres parts bénéficiaires, à l'exception des créances, ainsi que les revenus d'autres parts sociales soumis au même régime fiscal que les revenus d'actions par la législation de l'État dont la société distributrice est un résident.

4. Les dispositions des paragraphes 1 et 2 ne s'appliquent pas lorsque le bénéficiaire effectif des dividendes, résident d'un État contractant, exerce dans l'autre État contractant, dont la société distributrice des dividendes est un résident, soit une activité industrielle ou commerciale par l'intermédiaire d'un établissement stable qui y est situé, soit une profession indépendante au moyen d'une base fixe qui y est située, et que la participation génératrice des dividendes se rattache effectivement audit établissement stable ou à ladite base fixe. En pareil cas, les dispositions de l'article 7 ou de l'article 14, suivant le cas, sont applicables.

5. Lorsqu'une société qui est un résident d'un État contractant tire des bénéfices ou des revenus de l'autre État contractant, cet autre État ne peut percevoir aucun impôt sur les dividendes payés par la société, sauf dans la mesure où ces dividendes sont payés à un résident de cet autre État ou dans la mesure où la participation génératrice des dividendes se rattache effectivement à un établissement stable ou à une base fixe situés dans cet autre État, ni prélever aucun impôt, au titre de l'imposition des bénéfices non distribués, sur les bénéfices non distribués de la société, même si les dividendes payés ou les bénéfices non distribués consistent en tout ou partie de bénéfices ou de revenus provenant de cet autre État.

Article 11. Intérêts

1. Les intérêts provenant d'un État contractant et payés à un résident de l'autre État contractant sont imposables dans cet autre État.

2. Toutefois, ces intérêts sont également imposables dans l'État contractant d'où ils proviennent et selon la législation de cet État, mais si le bénéficiaire effectif des intérêts est un résident de l'autre État contractant, l'impôt ainsi établi ne peut dépasser 5 % du montant brut des intérêts.

Les autorités compétentes des États contractants se consultent sur les modalités d'application des dispositions du présent paragraphe.

3. Nonobstant les dispositions du paragraphe 2, les intérêts provenant d'un État contractant sont exonérés d'impôt dans cet État, s'ils ont pour bénéficiaire effectif :

a) Le Gouvernement d'un État contractant ou l'une de ses subdivisions politiques ou collectivités locales ; ou

b) i) Dans le cas de l'Éthiopie, la Banque nationale d'Éthiopie ;

ii) Dans le cas de l'Irlande, la Banque centrale d'Irlande ou l'Agence nationale de gestion du Trésor.

4. Le terme « intérêts » employé dans le présent article désigne les revenus des créances de toute nature, assorties ou non de garanties hypothécaires ou d'une clause de participation aux bénéfices du débiteur, et notamment les revenus des fonds publics et des obligations d'emprunt, y compris les primes et lots rattachés à ces titres, ainsi que tous autres revenus assimilés aux revenus de sommes prêtées par la législation de l'État d'où proviennent les revenus, mais il ne comprend pas les revenus considérés comme des dividendes au titre de l'article 10. Les pénalités pour paiement tardif ne sont pas considérées comme des intérêts au sens du présent article.

5. Les dispositions des paragraphes 1 et 2 ne s'appliquent pas lorsque le bénéficiaire effectif des intérêts, résident d'un État contractant, exerce dans l'autre État contractant d'où proviennent les intérêts, soit une activité industrielle ou commerciale par l'intermédiaire d'un établissement stable qui y est situé, soit une profession indépendante au moyen d'une base fixe qui y est située, et que la créance génératrice des intérêts se rattache effectivement audit établissement stable ou à ladite base fixe. En pareil cas, les dispositions de l'article 7 ou de l'article 14, suivant le cas, sont applicables.

6. Les intérêts sont réputés provenir d'un État contractant lorsque le débiteur est un résident de cet État. Toutefois, lorsque le débiteur des intérêts, résident ou non d'un État contractant, a dans un État contractant un établissement stable ou une base fixe pour lesquels la dette donnant lieu au paiement des intérêts a été contractée et qui supportent la charge de ces intérêts, ceux-ci sont considérés comme provenant de l'État contractant où l'établissement stable, ou la base fixe, est situé.

7. Lorsque, en raison de relations spéciales existant entre le débiteur et le bénéficiaire effectif ou que l'un et l'autre entretiennent avec de tierces personnes, le montant des intérêts, compte tenu de la créance pour laquelle ils sont payés, excède celui dont seraient convenus le débiteur et le bénéficiaire effectif en l'absence de pareilles relations, les dispositions du présent article ne s'appliquent qu'à ce dernier montant. Dans ce cas, la partie excédentaire des paiements reste imposable conformément à la législation de chaque État contractant et compte dûment tenu des autres dispositions de la présente Convention.

Article 12. Redevances

1. Les redevances générées dans un État contractant et payées à un résident de l'autre État contractant sont imposables dans cet autre État.

2. Toutefois, ces redevances sont également imposables dans l'État contractant de la source et selon la législation de cet État, mais si le bénéficiaire effectif des redevances est un résident de l'autre État contractant, l'impôt ainsi exigé ne peut excéder 5 % du montant brut des redevances.

3. Le terme « redevances » employé dans le présent article désigne les rémunérations de toute nature payées pour l'usage ou la concession de l'usage d'un droit d'auteur sur une œuvre littéraire,

artistique ou scientifique, y compris les logiciels informatiques, les films cinématographiques, les enregistrements sur des bandes ou d'autres supports utilisés pour les émissions radiophoniques ou télévisées, ou d'autres moyens de reproduction ou de transmission, d'un brevet, d'une marque de fabrique ou de commerce, d'un dessin ou d'un modèle, d'un plan, d'une formule ou d'un procédé secrets et pour des informations ayant trait à une expérience acquise dans le domaine industriel, commercial ou scientifique.

4. Les dispositions des paragraphes 1 et 2 du présent article ne s'appliquent pas lorsque le bénéficiaire effectif des redevances, résident d'un État contractant, exerce dans l'autre État contractant source des redevances, soit une activité industrielle ou commerciale par l'intermédiaire d'un établissement stable qui y est situé, soit une profession indépendante au moyen d'une base fixe qui y est située, et que le droit ou le bien générateur des redevances se rattache effectivement audit établissement stable ou à ladite base fixe. En pareil cas, les dispositions de l'article 7 ou de l'article 14, suivant le cas, sont applicables.

5. Les redevances sont réputées provenir d'un État contractant lorsque le débiteur est un résident de cet État. Toutefois, lorsque le débiteur des redevances, résident ou non d'un État contractant, a dans un État contractant un établissement stable ou une base fixe, pour lesquels l'engagement donnant lieu au paiement des redevances a été contracté et qui supportent la charge de ces redevances, celles-ci sont réputées provenir de l'État contractant où l'établissement stable, ou la base fixe, est situé.

6. Lorsque, en raison de relations spéciales existant entre le débiteur et le bénéficiaire effectif, ou que l'un et l'autre entretiennent avec une tierce personne, le montant des redevances, compte tenu de l'usage, du droit ou des informations pour lesquels elles sont payées, excède celui dont seraient convenus le débiteur et le bénéficiaire effectif en l'absence de pareilles relations, les dispositions du présent article ne s'appliquent qu'à ce dernier montant. Dans ce cas, la partie excédentaire des paiements reste imposable conformément à la législation de chaque État contractant et compte dûment tenu des autres dispositions de la présente Convention.

Article 13. Gains en capital

1. Les gains qu'un résident d'un État contractant tire de l'aliénation de biens immobiliers visés à l'article 6 et situés dans l'autre État contractant sont imposables dans cet autre État.

2. Les gains provenant de l'aliénation de biens mobiliers qui font partie de l'actif d'un établissement stable qu'une entreprise d'un État contractant a dans l'autre État contractant, ou de biens mobiliers qui appartiennent à une base fixe dont un résident d'un État contractant dispose dans l'autre État contractant pour l'exercice d'une profession indépendante, y compris les gains provenant de l'aliénation de cet établissement stable (seul ou avec l'ensemble de l'entreprise) ou de cette base fixe, sont imposables dans cet autre État.

3. Les gains provenant de l'aliénation de navires ou d'aéronefs exploités en trafic international ou de biens immobiliers affectés à l'exploitation de ces navires ou aéronefs ne sont imposables que dans l'État contractant où le siège de direction effective de l'entreprise est situé.

4. Les gains qu'un résident d'un État contractant tire de l'aliénation :

a) D'actions, autres que des actions cotées dans une bourse reconnue, qui tirent directement ou indirectement plus de 50 % de leur valeur de biens immobiliers situés dans l'autre État contractant ; ou

b) De la participation dans une société de personnes ou une fiducie qui tire directement ou indirectement plus de 50 % de sa valeur de biens immobiliers situés dans l'autre État contractant ;

sont imposables dans cet autre État.

5. Les gains provenant de l'aliénation de biens autres que ceux visés aux paragraphes 1, 2, 3 et 4 ne sont imposables que dans l'État contractant dont le cédant est un résident.

6. Les dispositions du paragraphe 5 n'affectent pas le droit d'un État contractant de percevoir, conformément à sa législation, un impôt sur les gains provenant de l'aliénation d'un bien et réalisés par une personne physique qui est un résident de l'autre État contractant et qui a été un résident du premier État à un moment quelconque au cours des cinq années précédant immédiatement l'aliénation du bien.

Article 14. Professions indépendantes

1. Les revenus qu'un résident d'un État contractant tire d'une profession libérale ou d'autres activités de caractère indépendant ne sont imposables que dans cet État, sauf si ce résident dispose de manière régulière d'une base fixe dans l'autre État contractant aux fins de l'exercice de ses activités. Dans ce cas, n'est imputable dans cet État que la fraction des revenus imputable à cette base fixe.

2. L'expression « profession indépendante » comprend notamment les activités indépendantes d'ordre scientifique, littéraire, artistique, éducatif ou pédagogique, ainsi que les activités indépendantes des médecins, avocats, ingénieurs, architectes, dentistes et comptables.

Article 15. Professions salariées

1. Sous réserve des dispositions des articles 16, 18, 19 et 21, les salaires, traitements et autres rémunérations similaires qu'un résident d'un État contractant perçoit au titre d'un emploi salarié ne sont imposables que dans cet État, sauf si l'emploi est exercé dans l'autre État contractant. Dans ce cas, les rémunérations perçues à ce titre sont imposables dans cet autre État.

2. Nonobstant les dispositions du paragraphe 1 du présent article, les rémunérations qu'un résident d'un État contractant reçoit au titre d'un emploi salarié exercé dans l'autre État contractant ne sont imposables que dans le premier État si :

a) Le bénéficiaire séjourne dans l'autre État pendant une période ou des périodes n'excédant pas au total 183 jours au cours de toute période de 12 mois commençant ou se terminant au cours de l'année civile considérée ; et

b) Les rémunérations sont payées par un employeur ou pour le compte d'un employeur qui n'est pas un résident de l'autre État ; et

c) La charge des rémunérations n'est pas supportée par un établissement stable ou une base fixe que l'employeur a dans l'autre État.

3. Nonobstant les dispositions précédentes du présent article, les rémunérations reçues par un résident d'un État contractant au titre d'un emploi salarié exercé à bord d'un navire ou d'un aéronef exploité en trafic international ne sont imposables que dans l'État contractant où le siège de direction effective de l'entreprise est situé.

Article 16. Tantièmes

Les tantièmes et autres rémunérations similaires qu'un résident d'un État contractant perçoit en sa qualité de membre du conseil d'administration d'une société qui est un résident de l'autre État contractant sont imposables dans cet autre État.

Article 17. Artistes et sportifs

1. Nonobstant les dispositions des articles 14 et 15, les revenus qu'un résident d'un État contractant tire de ses activités personnelles exercées dans l'autre État contractant en tant qu'artiste du spectacle, tel qu'un artiste de théâtre, de cinéma, de radio ou de télévision, ou musicien ou en tant que sportif, sont imposables dans cet autre État.

2. Lorsque les revenus d'activités qu'un artiste du spectacle ou un sportif exerce personnellement et en cette qualité, sont attribués non pas à l'artiste ou au sportif lui-même, mais à une autre personne, ces revenus sont, nonobstant les dispositions des articles 7, 14 et 15, imposables dans l'État contractant où les activités de l'artiste ou du sportif sont exercées.

3. Nonobstant les dispositions des paragraphes 1 et 2, les revenus tirés des activités visées au paragraphe 1, exercées dans un but non lucratif dans le cadre d'échanges culturels ou sportifs approuvés par les Gouvernements des États contractants, ne sont pas imposables dans l'État contractant dans lequel ces activités sont exercées.

Article 18. Pensions et rentes

1. Sous réserve des dispositions du paragraphe 2 de l'article 19, les pensions et autres rémunérations similaires qui sont payées à un résident d'un État contractant au titre d'un emploi antérieur et les rentes payées à ce résident ne sont imposables que dans cet État.

2. Nonobstant les dispositions du paragraphe 1 du présent article, les pensions, rémunérations similaires ou rentes sont imposables dans l'État contractant d'où elles proviennent si elles ne sont pas soumises à l'impôt dans l'autre État contractant.

3. Le terme « rente » désigne une somme déterminée payable périodiquement à échéances fixes, à titre viager ou pendant une période déterminée ou pouvant l'être, en vertu d'une obligation d'effectuer des paiements en contrepartie d'un capital suffisant versé intégralement ou en une valeur appréciable en espèces.

Article 19. Fonction publique

1. a) Les salaires, traitements et autres rémunérations similaires payés par un État contractant ou l'une de ses subdivisions politiques ou collectivités locales à une personne physique au titre de services fournis à cet État ou à cette subdivision ou collectivité ne sont imposables que dans cet État.

   b) Toutefois, ces traitements, salaires et autres rémunérations similaires ne sont imposables que dans l'autre État contractant si les services sont fournis dans cet État et si la personne physique est un résident de cet État qui :

      i) Est un ressortissant cet État ; ou

ii) N'est pas devenu un résident de cet État à seule fin de fournir les services en question.

2. a) Nonobstant les dispositions du paragraphe 1, les pensions et autres rémunérations similaires payées par un État contractant ou une de ses subdivisions politiques ou collectivités locales, soit directement soit par prélèvement sur des fonds qu'ils ont constitués, à une personne physique au titre de services fournis à cet État ou à cette subdivision ou collectivité ne sont imposables que dans cet État.

b) Toutefois, ces pensions et autres rémunérations similaires ne sont imposables que dans l'autre État contractant si la personne physique est un résident et un ressortissant de cet État.

3. Les dispositions des articles 15, 16, 17 et 18 s'appliquent aux traitements, salaires et autres rémunérations similaires, ainsi qu'aux pensions, payés au titre de services fournis dans le cadre d'une activité industrielle ou commerciale exercée par un État contractant ou l'une de ses subdivisions politiques ou collectivités locales.

Article 20. Étudiants et stagiaires

1. Les sommes qu'un étudiant ou un stagiaire qui est, ou qui était immédiatement avant de se rendre dans un État contractant, un résident de l'autre État contractant et qui séjourne dans le premier État à seule fin d'y poursuivre ses études ou sa formation, reçoit pour couvrir ses frais d'entretien, d'études ou de formation ne sont pas imposables dans cet État, à condition que ces sommes proviennent de sources situées en dehors de cet État.

2. En ce qui concerne les subventions, les bourses et les rémunérations tirées d'un emploi salarié non visé au paragraphe 1, l'étudiant ou le stagiaire mentionné audit paragraphe a, en outre, droit, pendant la durée de ces études ou de cette formation, aux mêmes exonérations, allégements ou réductions d'impôt que les résidents de l'État contractant dans lequel il séjourne.

Article 21. Professeurs et chercheurs

1. Une personne physique qui est, ou qui était un résident d'un État contractant immédiatement avant de se rendre dans l'autre État contractant, et qui, à l'invitation d'une université, d'une école ou d'un autre établissement d'enseignement à but non lucratif reconnu par le Gouvernement de cet autre État contractant, séjourne dans cet autre État contractant, pour une période n'excédant pas deux ans à compter de sa première arrivée dans cet État contractant, à seule fin d'y mener des activités d'enseignement, de recherche, ou les deux, dans un tel établissement d'enseignement est exonéré d'impôts dans cet autre État contractant à l'égard de toute rémunération qu'elle reçoit pour ses activités d'enseignement ou de recherche. Une personne physique ne peut bénéficier des dispositions du présent article qu'une seule fois.

2. Les dispositions du paragraphe 1 du présent article ne s'appliquent pas aux revenus des activités de recherche si celles-ci sont entreprises non pas dans l'intérêt public, mais au profit privé d'une ou de plusieurs personnes déterminées.

Article 22. Autres revenus

1. Les éléments de revenu d'un résident d'un État contractant, d'où qu'ils proviennent, qui ne sont pas traités dans les articles précédents de la présente Convention, ne sont imposables que dans cet État.

2. Les dispositions du paragraphe 1 du présent article ne s'appliquent pas aux revenus, autres que ceux provenant de biens immobiliers, tels qu'ils sont décrits au paragraphe 2 de l'article 6, lorsque le bénéficiaire effectif de ces revenus, résident d'un État contractant, exerce dans l'autre État contractant soit une activité industrielle ou commerciale par l'intermédiaire d'un établissement stable qui y est situé, soit une profession indépendante au moyen d'une base fixe qui y est située, et que le droit ou le bien générateur des revenus se rattache effectivement audit établissement stable ou à ladite base fixe. En pareil cas, les dispositions de l'article 7 ou de l'article 14, suivant le cas, sont applicables.

3. Nonobstant les dispositions des paragraphes 1 et 2, les éléments de revenu d'un résident d'un État contractant qui ne sont pas traités dans les articles précédents de la présente Convention et qui proviennent de l'autre État contractant sont également imposables dans cet autre État.

Article 23. Règles diverses applicables à certaines activités en mer

1. Les dispositions du présent article s'appliquent nonobstant toute autre disposition de la présente Convention lorsque des activités (dénommées dans le présent article « activités pertinentes ») sont exercées en mer dans le cadre de l'exploration ou de l'exploitation des fonds et du sous-sol marins et de leurs ressources naturelles situés dans un État contractant

2. Une entreprise d'un État contractant qui exerce des activités pertinentes dans l'autre État contractant est, sous réserve du paragraphe 3 du présent article, considérée comme exerçant une activité dans cet autre État par l'intermédiaire d'un établissement stable qui y est situé.

3. Les activités pertinentes exercées par une entreprise d'un État contractant dans l'autre État contractant, pour une période ou des périodes d'une durée totale ne dépassant pas 30 jours au cours de toute période de 12 mois, ne sont pas considérées comme des activités exercées par l'intermédiaire d'un établissement stable qui y est situé. Aux fins du présent paragraphe :

a) Lorsqu'une entreprise d'un État contractant qui exerce des activités pertinentes dans l'autre État contractant est associée à une autre entreprise y exerçant des activités pertinentes essentiellement similaires, la première entreprise est considérée comme exerçant toutes les activités de la deuxième, sauf si ces activités sont exercées en même temps que ses propres activités ;

b) Une entreprise est considérée comme associée à une autre entreprise si l'une participe, directement ou indirectement, à la direction, au contrôle ou au capital de l'autre ou si les mêmes personnes participent directement ou indirectement à la direction, au contrôle ou au capital des deux entreprises.

4. Les salaires, traitements et autres rémunérations similaires qu'un résident d'un État contractant perçoit au titre d'un emploi exercé dans le cadre d'activités pertinentes dans l'autre État contractant sont, dans la mesure où les fonctions sont exercées en mer dans cet autre État, imposables dans cet autre État.

5. Les gains qu'un résident d'un État contractant tire de l'aliénation :

a) De droits d'exploration ou d'exploitation ; ou

b) D'actions (ou d'instruments comparables) tirant leur valeur ou la plus grande partie de leur valeur, directement ou indirectement, de ces droits ;

sont imposables dans cet autre État.

Dans le présent paragraphe, l'expression « droits d'exploration ou d'exploitation » désigne les droits liés à des actifs qui seront produits par l'exploration ou l'exploitation des fonds marins, de leur sous-sol ou de leurs ressources naturelles, situés dans cet autre État contractant, y compris les droits liés à la participation dans de tels actifs ou au bénéfice de ceux-ci.

Article 24. Élimination des doubles impositions

1. Lorsqu'un résident de l'Éthiopie perçoit des revenus ou des gains qui, conformément aux dispositions de la présente Convention, sont imposables en Irlande, l'Éthiopie admet en déduction de l'impôt sur les revenus ou les gains de ce résident un montant égal à l'impôt payé en Irlande. Cette déduction ne peut toutefois dépasser la partie du montant de l'impôt sur les revenus, calculé avant que la déduction ne soit accordée, qui est imputable aux revenus ou aux gains imposables en Irlande.

2. Sous réserve des dispositions de la législation irlandaise concernant les crédits pouvant être déduits de l'impôt irlandais au titre de l'impôt dû dans un territoire situé en dehors de l'Irlande (qui n'affectent pas le principe général ici posé) :

a) L'impôt éthiopien payable en vertu de la législation éthiopienne et conformément à la présente Convention, directement ou par voie de retenue, sur les bénéfices, revenus ou gains provenant de sources situées en Éthiopie (à l'exclusion, dans le cas des dividendes, de l'impôt exigible au titre des bénéfices affectés aux dividendes) est déduit de l'impôt irlandais calculé sur les mêmes bénéfices, revenus ou gains imposables que ceux sur lesquels est calculé l'impôt éthiopien ;

b) Dans le cas de dividendes versés par une société qui est un résident de l'Éthiopie à une société qui est un résident de l'Irlande et qui contrôle, directement ou indirectement, au moins 5 % des titres avec droit de vote de la société distributrice des dividendes, il est tenu compte dans le calcul du crédit (en plus de l'impôt éthiopien pouvant être déduit en application de l'alinéa a)) de l'impôt éthiopien que la société doit payer sur les bénéfices servant au paiement des dividendes.

3. Aux fins des paragraphes 1 et 2, les bénéfices, revenus ou gains en capital d'un résident d'un État contractant qui sont imposables dans l'autre État contractant conformément à la présente Convention sont réputés provenir de sources situées dans cet autre État contractant.

4. Lorsque, conformément à une disposition quelconque de la présente Convention, les revenus perçus par un résident d'un État contractant sont exonérés d'impôts dans cet État, cet État peut néanmoins, pour calculer le montant de l'impôt à percevoir sur le reste des revenus de ce résident, tenir compte des revenus exonérés.

5. Lorsque, en vertu d'une disposition quelconque de la présente Convention, une personne physique a droit, dans un État contractant, à un allégement d'impôt sur tout ou partie de ses revenus ou gains et que, en vertu de la législation en vigueur dans l'autre État contractant, cette personne, à l'égard de ces revenus ou gains, est assujettie à l'impôt à raison du montant de ces revenus ou gains qui est transféré ou perçu dans cet autre État et non à raison de leur montant total, l'allégement qui

doit être accordé en vertu de la présente Convention dans le premier État ne s'applique qu'au montant de ces revenus ou gains qui est transféré ou perçu dans l'autre État.

6. Aux fins du paragraphe 2, l'expression « impôt éthiopien payable » est réputé inclure tout montant qui aurait été dû au titre de l'impôt éthiopien en l'absence de toute exonération ou allégement d'impôt accordé, dans le but de promouvoir le développement économique en Éthiopie, en application des dispositions du Règlement n° 270/2012 du Conseil des ministres relatif aux incitations aux investissements et zones d'investissement réservées aux investisseurs nationaux, et des mises à jour ou des modifications qui peuvent leur être apportées de temps à autre, à condition que les activités visées par lesdites dispositions n'aient pas été modifiées de façon substantielle avant la date de signature de la présente Convention. Les autorités compétentes des États contractants peuvent se consulter en vue de résoudre toute question ayant trait à la bonne application ou administration du présent paragraphe.

Le présent paragraphe s'applique aux bénéfices des sociétés pour une durée de cinq ans immédiatement après la date d'entrée en vigueur de la présente Convention. Cette période peut être prolongée d'un commun accord entre les autorités compétentes des États contractants.

Article 25. Non-discrimination

1. Les ressortissants d'un État contractant ne sont soumis, dans l'autre État contractant, à aucune imposition ni à aucune obligation correspondante qui est autre ou plus lourde que celles auxquelles sont ou peuvent être assujettis les ressortissants de cet autre État qui se trouvent dans la même situation, notamment au regard de la résidence. Nonobstant les dispositions de l'article premier, la présente disposition s'applique aussi aux personnes qui ne sont pas des résidents d'un des États contractants ou des deux États contractants.

2. L'imposition d'un établissement stable qu'une entreprise d'un État contractant a dans l'autre État contractant n'est pas établie dans cet autre État d'une façon moins favorable que l'imposition des entreprises de cet autre État qui exercent les mêmes activités. La présente disposition ne peut être interprétée comme obligeant un État contractant à accorder aux résidents de l'autre État contractant les déductions personnelles, abattements et réductions d'impôt qu'il accorde à ses propres résidents en raison de leur état civil ou de leurs charges de famille.

3. Sauf dans les cas où les dispositions du paragraphe 1 de l'article 9, du paragraphe 7 de l'article 11 ou du paragraphe 6 de l'article 12 s'appliquent, les intérêts, redevances et autres montants payés par une entreprise d'un État contractant à un résident de l'autre État contractant sont, pour la détermination des bénéfices imposables de cette entreprise, déductibles dans les mêmes conditions que s'ils avaient été payés à un résident du premier État.

4. Les entreprises d'un État contractant dont le capital est en tout ou en partie détenu ou contrôlé, directement ou indirectement, par un ou plusieurs résidents de l'autre État contractant, ne sont soumises, dans le premier État, à aucune imposition ni à aucune obligation correspondante qui est autre ou plus lourde que celles auxquelles sont ou pourront être assujetties d'autres entreprises similaires du premier État.

5. Les dispositions du présent article s'appliquent uniquement aux impôts qui font l'objet de la présente Convention.

Article 26. Procédure amiable

1. Lorsqu'une personne estime que les mesures prises par un État contractant ou par les deux États contractants entraînent ou entraîneront pour elle une imposition non conforme aux dispositions de la présente Convention, elle peut, indépendamment des recours prévus par le droit interne de ces États, présenter son cas à l'autorité compétente de l'État contractant dont elle est un résident ou, si sa situation relève du paragraphe 1 de l'article 25, à celle de l'État contractant dont elle est ressortissante. Le cas doit être soumis dans un délai de trois ans à compter de la première notification des mesures à l'origine d'une imposition non conforme aux dispositions de la présente Convention.

2. L'autorité compétente s'efforce, si la réclamation lui paraît fondée et si elle n'est pas elle-même en mesure d'y apporter une solution satisfaisante, de résoudre le cas par voie amiable avec l'autorité compétente de l'autre État contractant, en vue d'éviter une imposition non conforme aux dispositions de la présente Convention. Tout accord conclu est appliqué nonobstant les délais prévus par le droit interne des États contractants.

3. Les autorités compétentes des États contractants s'efforcent, par voie d'accord amiable, de résoudre les difficultés ou de dissiper les doutes auxquels peuvent donner lieu l'interprétation ou l'application de la présente Convention. Elles peuvent aussi se concerter en vue d'éliminer les doubles impositions dans les cas non prévus par la présente Convention.

4. Les autorités compétentes des États contractants peuvent communiquer directement entre elles, y compris par l'intermédiaire d'une commission mixte composée de ces autorités ou de leurs représentants, en vue de parvenir à un accord au sens des paragraphes précédents.

Article 27. Échange de renseignements

1. Les autorités compétentes des États contractants échangent les renseignements qui sont vraisemblablement pertinents pour appliquer les dispositions de la présente Convention ou celles de la législation interne relative aux impôts de toute nature et de toute dénomination perçus pour le compte des États contractants ou de leurs subdivisions politiques ou collectivités locales, dans la mesure où l'imposition prévue n'est pas contraire à la présente Convention. L'échange de renseignements n'est pas limité par les articles premier et 2.

2. Les renseignements reçus par un État contractant au titre du paragraphe 1 sont tenus secrets de la même manière que les renseignements obtenus en application du droit interne de cet État et ne sont communiqués qu'aux personnes ou autorités (y compris les tribunaux et organes administratifs) concernées par l'établissement ou le recouvrement des impôts visés au paragraphe 1, par les procédures ou poursuites concernant ces impôts, par les décisions sur les recours relatifs à ces impôts, ou par le contrôle de ce qui précède. Ces personnes ou autorités n'utilisent ces renseignements qu'à ces fins. Elles peuvent faire état de ces renseignements au cours d'audiences publiques de tribunaux ou dans des décisions judiciaires.

3. Les dispositions des paragraphes 1 et 2 du présent article ne peuvent en aucun cas être interprétées comme imposant à un État contractant l'obligation :

a) De prendre des mesures administratives dérogeant à sa législation et à sa pratique administrative ou à celles de l'autre État contractant ;

b) De fournir des renseignements qui ne pourraient être obtenus sur la base de sa législation ou dans le cadre de sa pratique administrative normale ou de celles de l'autre État contractant ;

c) De fournir des renseignements qui révéleraient un secret commercial, industriel, professionnel ou un procédé commercial, ou des renseignements dont la communication serait contraire à l'ordre public.

4. Si des renseignements sont demandés par un État contractant conformément au présent article, l'autre État contractant utilise ses mesures de collecte de renseignements pour obtenir les renseignements demandés, quand bien même s'il n'aurait pas besoin de ces renseignements à ses propres fins fiscales. L'obligation contenue dans la phrase précédente est soumise aux restrictions prévues au paragraphe 3, lesquelles ne sauraient toutefois en aucun cas être interprétées comme permettant à un État contractant de refuser de communiquer des renseignements uniquement parce qu'il ne détient aucun intérêt national dans de tels renseignements.

5. Les dispositions du paragraphe 3 ne peuvent en aucun cas être interprétées comme autorisant un État contractant à refuser de communiquer des renseignements uniquement parce que ceux-ci sont détenus par une banque, une autre institution financière, un mandataire ou une personne agissant en tant qu'agent ou à titre fiduciaire ou parce que ces renseignements se rapportent aux droits de propriété d'une personne.

Article 28. Membres de missions diplomatiques et de postes consulaires

Les dispositions de la présente Convention sont sans préjudice des privilèges fiscaux dont bénéficient les membres des missions diplomatiques ou des postes consulaires en vertu des règles générales du droit international ou des dispositions d'accords particuliers.

Article 29. Entrée en vigueur

1. Les États contractants se notifient, par écrit et par la voie diplomatique, l'accomplissement de leurs formalités constitutionnelles requises pour l'entrée en vigueur de la présente Convention.

2. La présente Convention entre en vigueur à la date de réception de la dernière de ces notifications et s'applique :

a) Dans le cas de l'Éthiopie :

i) En ce qui concerne les impôts retenus à la source, aux montants payés à partir du 8 juillet suivant la date d'entrée en vigueur de la présente Convention ; et

ii) En ce qui concerne les autres impôts, pour les années d'imposition commençant à partir du 8 juillet suivant la date d'entrée en vigueur de la présente Convention ;

b) Dans le cas de l'Irlande :

i) En ce qui concerne l'impôt sur le revenu, la charge sociale universelle et l'impôt sur les gains en capital, pour toute année d'imposition commençant à partir du 1er janvier suivant la date d'entrée en vigueur de la présente Convention ; et

ii) En ce qui concerne l'impôt sur les sociétés, pour toute année financière commençant à partir du 1er janvier suivant la date d'entrée en vigueur de la présente Convention.

Article 30. Dénonciation

La présente Convention reste en vigueur tant qu'elle n'est pas dénoncée par l'un des États contractants. L'un ou l'autre État contractant peut à tout moment dénoncer la Convention, après l'expiration d'un délai de cinq ans à compter de la date de son entrée en vigueur, moyennant une notification écrite au moins six mois avant adressée par la voie diplomatique.

En pareil cas, la Convention cesse de produire ses effets :

a) Dans le cas de l'Éthiopie :

   i) En ce qui concerne les impôts retenus à la source, sur les montants payés à partir du 8 juillet suivant la date d'expiration de la période indiquée dans la notification de dénonciation ; et

   ii) En ce qui concerne les autres impôts, pour les années d'imposition commençant à partir du 8 juillet suivant la date d'expiration de la période indiquée dans la notification de dénonciation ;

b) Dans le cas de l'Irlande :

   i) En ce qui concerne l'impôt sur le revenu, la charge sociale universelle et l'impôt sur les gains en capital, pour toute année d'imposition commençant à partir du 1er janvier suivant la date d'expiration de la période indiquée dans la notification de dénonciation ; et

   ii) En ce qui concerne l'impôt sur les sociétés, pour toute année financière commençant à partir du 1er janvier suivant la date d'expiration de la période indiquée dans la notification de dénonciation.

EN FOI DE QUOI, les soussignés, à ce dûment autorisés, ont signé la présente Convention.

FAIT à Addis-Abeba, le 3 novembre 2014, en deux exemplaires en langue anglaise.

Pour le Gouvernement de l'Irlande :
[SEÁN SHERLOCK]

Pour le Gouvernement de la République fédérale démocratique d'Éthiopie :
[ATO AHMED SHIDE]

PROTOCOLE À LA CONVENTION ENTRE L'IRLANDE ET LA RÉPUBLIQUE FÉDÉRALE DÉMOCRATIQUE D'ÉTHIOPIE TENDANT À ÉVITER LES DOUBLES IMPOSITIONS ET À PRÉVENIR LA FRAUDE FISCALE EN MATIÈRE D'IMPÔTS SUR LE REVENU

À la signature de la Convention entre l'Irlande et la République fédérale démocratique d'Éthiopie tendant à éviter les doubles impositions et à prévenir la fraude fiscale en matière d'impôts sur le revenu, les soussignés sont convenus des dispositions ci-après, qui font partie intégrante de la Convention.

Il est entendu que :

1. Un Fonds commun contractuel (Common Contractual Fund) créé en Irlande ne peut être considéré comme un résident de l'Irlande et doit être traité comme fiscalement transparent aux fins de l'octroi des avantages découlant d'un traité.

2. En ce qui concerne l'alinéa f) du paragraphe 2 de l'article 5, l'expression « entrepôt commercial » désigne des installations utilisées par une entreprise d'un État contractant pour entreposer, à des fins lucratives, des biens ou des marchandises pour d'autres entreprises.

3. En ce qui concerne l'alinéa a) du paragraphe 2 de l'article 15, l'expression « dans l'année civile considérée » fait référence au calendrier grégorien.

EN FOI DE QUOI, les soussignés, à ce dûment autorisés, ont signé le présent Protocole.

Pour le Gouvernement de l'Irlande :
[SEÁN SHERLOCK]

Pour le Gouvernement de la République fédérale démocratique d'Éthiopie :
[ATO AHMED SHIDE]

No. 54753

Ireland and Pakistan

Convention between the Government of Ireland and the Government of the Islamic Republic of Pakistan for the avoidance of double taxation and the prevention of fiscal evasion with respect to taxes on income (with protocol). Dublin, 16 April 2015

Entry into force: *11 October 2016 by notification, in accordance with article 28*

Authentic text: *English*

Registration with the Secretariat of the United Nations: *Ireland, 1 November 2017*

Irlande et Pakistan

Convention entre le Gouvernement de l'Irlande et le Gouvernement de la République islamique du Pakistan tendant à éviter les doubles impositions et à prévenir la fraude fiscale en matière d'impôts sur le revenu (avec protocole). Dublin, 16 avril 2015

Entrée en vigueur : *11 octobre 2016 par notification, conformément à l'article 28*

Texte authentique : *anglais*

Enregistrement au Secrétariat de l'Organisation des Nations Unies : *Irlande, 1er novembre 2017*

[TEXT IN ENGLISH – TEXTE EN ANGLAIS]

CONVENTION BETWEEN THE GOVERNMENT OF IRELAND AND THE GOVERNMENT OF THE ISLAMIC REPUBLIC OF PAKISTAN FOR THE AVOIDANCE OF DOUBLE TAXATION AND THE PREVENTION OF FISCAL EVASION WITH RESPECT TO TAXES ON INCOME

PREAMBLE

The Government of Ireland and the Government of the Islamic Republic of Pakistan, desiring to conclude a Convention for the avoidance of double taxation and the prevention of fiscal evasion with respect to taxes on income, and to promote and strengthen the economic relations between the two countries, have agreed as follows:

CHAPTER I
SCOPE OF THE CONVENTION

Article 1

PERSONS COVERED

This Convention shall apply to persons who are residents of one or both of the Contracting States.

Article 2

TAXES COVERED

1. This Convention shall apply to taxes on income imposed on behalf of a Contracting State or of its political subdivisions or local authorities, irrespective of the manner in which they are levied.

2. There shall be regarded as taxes on income all taxes imposed on total income or on elements of income, including taxes on gains from the alienation of movable or immovable property.

3. The existing taxes to which the Convention shall apply are in particular:

(a) in the case of Ireland:

(i) the income tax;
(ii) the universal social charge;
(iii) the corporation tax; and
(iv) the capital gains tax;

(hereinafter referred to as "Irish tax");

(b) in the case of Pakistan, the income tax;

(hereinafter referred to as "Pakistan tax").

4. The Convention shall apply also to any identical or substantially similar taxes that are imposed after the date of signature of the Convention in addition to, or in place of, the existing taxes. The competent authorities of the Contracting States shall notify each other of any significant changes that have been made in their respective taxation laws.

CHAPTER II
DEFINITIONS

Article 3

GENERAL DEFINITIONS

1. For the purposes of this Convention, unless the context otherwise requires:

(a) the term "Ireland" includes any area outside the territorial waters of Ireland which has been or may hereafter be designated, under the laws of Ireland concerning the Exclusive Economic Zone and the Continental Shelf, as an area within which Ireland may exercise such sovereign rights and jurisdiction as are in conformity with international law;

(b) the term "Pakistan" when used in a geographical sense means Pakistan as defined in the constitution of the Islamic Republic of Pakistan and includes any area outside the territorial waters of Pakistan which under the laws of Pakistan and international law is an area within which Pakistan exercises sovereign rights and exclusive jurisdiction with respect to the natural resources of the seabed and subsoil and superjacent waters;

(c) the term "Contracting State" and the "other Contracting State" mean Ireland or Pakistan as the context requires;

(d) the term "person" includes an individual, a company and any other body of persons;

(e) the term "company" means any body corporate or any entity that is treated as a body corporate for tax purposes;

(f) the terms "enterprise of a Contracting State" and "enterprise of the other Contracting State" mean respectively an enterprise carried on by a resident of a Contracting State and an enterprise carried on by a resident of the other Contracting State;

(g) the term "international traffic" means any transport by a ship or aircraft operated by an enterprise of a Contracting State, except when the ship or aircraft is operated solely between places in the other Contracting State;

(h) the term "national", in relation to a Contracting State, means:

(i) any individual possessing the nationality or citizenship of that Contracting State; and

(ii) any legal person, partnership or association deriving its status as such from the laws in force in that Contracting State;

(i) the term "competent authority" means:

(i) in the case of Ireland, the Revenue Commissioners or their authorised representative;

(ii) in the case of Pakistan, the Federal Board of Revenue or its authorised representative.

2. As regards the application of the Convention at any time by a Contracting State, any term not defined therein shall, unless the context otherwise requires, have the meaning that it has at that time under the law of that State for the purposes of the taxes to which the Convention applies, any meaning under the applicable tax laws of that State prevailing over a meaning given to the term under other laws of that State.

Article 4

RESIDENT

1. For the purposes of this Convention, the term "resident of a Contracting State" means any person who, under the laws of that State, is liable to tax therein by reason of his domicile, residence, place of management or any other criterion of a similar nature, and also includes that State and any political subdivision or local authority thereof. This term, however, does not include any person who is liable to tax in that State in respect only of income from sources in that State.

2. Where by reason of the provisions of paragraph 1 an individual is a resident of both Contracting States, then his status shall be determined as follows:

(a) he shall be deemed to be a resident only of the State in which he has a permanent home available to him; if he has a permanent home available to him in both States, he shall be deemed to be a resident only of the State with which his personal and economic relations are closer (centre of vital interests);

(b) if the State in which he has his centre of vital interests cannot be determined, or if he has not a permanent home available to him in either State, he shall be deemed to be a resident only of the State in which he has an habitual abode;

(c) if he has an habitual abode in both States or in neither of them, he shall be deemed to be a resident only of the State of which he is a national;

(d) if he is a national of both States or of neither of them, the competent authorities of the Contracting States shall settle the question by mutual agreement.

3. Where by reason of the provisions of paragraph 1 a person other than an individual is a resident of both Contracting States, then it shall be deemed to be a resident only of the State in which its place of effective management is situated.

Article 5

PERMANENT ESTABLISHMENT

1. For the purposes of this Convention, the term "permanent establishment" means a fixed place of business through which the business of an enterprise is wholly or partly carried on.

2. The term "permanent establishment" includes especially:

(a) a place of management;

(b) a branch;

(c) an office;

(d) a factory;

(e) a workshop;

(f) a sales outlet; and

(g) a mine, an oil or gas well, a quarry or any other place of extraction of natural resources.

3. The term "permanent establishment" also encompasses a building site, a construction, assembly or installation project or supervisory activities in connection therewith, but only if such site, project or activities last more than 6 months.

4. Notwithstanding the preceding provisions of this Article, the term "permanent establishment" shall be deemed not to include:

(a) the use of facilities solely for the purpose of storage, display or delivery of goods or merchandise belonging to the enterprise;

(b) the maintenance of a stock of goods or merchandise belonging to the enterprise solely for the purpose of storage, display or delivery;

(c) the maintenance of a stock of goods or merchandise belonging to the enterprise solely for the purpose of processing by another enterprise;

(d) the maintenance of a fixed place of business solely for the purpose of purchasing goods or merchandise or of collecting information, for the enterprise;

(e) the maintenance of a fixed place of business solely for the purpose of carrying on, for the enterprise, any other activity of a preparatory or auxiliary character;

(f) the maintenance of a fixed place of business solely for any combination of activities mentioned in subparagraphs (a) to (e), provided that the overall activity of the fixed place of business resulting from this combination is of a preparatory or auxiliary character.

5. Notwithstanding the provisions of paragraphs 1 and 2, where a person - other than an agent of an independent status to whom paragraph 7 applies - is acting in a Contracting State on behalf of an enterprise of the other Contracting State, that enterprise shall be deemed to have a permanent establishment in the first-mentioned Contracting State in respect of any activities which that person undertakes for the enterprise, if such a person has and habitually exercises in that State an authority to conclude contracts in the name of the enterprise, unless the activities of such person are limited to those mentioned in paragraph 4 which, if exercised through a fixed place of business, would not make this fixed place of business a permanent establishment under the provisions of that paragraph.

6. Notwithstanding the preceding provisions of this Article, an insurance enterprise of a Contracting State shall, except in regard to re-insurance, be deemed to have a permanent establishment in the other Contacting State if it insures risks situated in the territory of that other State through a person other than an agent of an independent status to whom paragraph 7 applies.

7. An enterprise of a Contracting State shall not be deemed to have a permanent establishment in the other Contracting State merely because it carries on business in that other State through a broker, general commission agent or any other agent of an independent status, provided that such persons are acting in the ordinary course of their business. However, when the activities of such an agent are devoted wholly or almost wholly on behalf of that enterprise, and conditions are made or imposed between that enterprise and the agent in their commercial and financial relations which differ from those which would have been made between independent enterprises, he will not be considered an agent of an independent status within the meaning of this paragraph.

8. The fact that a company which is a resident of a Contracting State controls or is controlled by a company which is a resident of the other Contracting State, or which carries on business in that other State (whether through a permanent establishment or otherwise), shall not of itself constitute either company a permanent establishment of the other.

CHAPTER III
TAXATION OF INCOME

Article 6

INCOME FROM IMMOVABLE PROPERTY

1. Income derived by a resident of a Contracting State from immovable property (including income from agriculture or forestry) situated in the other Contracting State may be taxed in that other State.

2. The term "immovable property" shall have the meaning which it has under the law of the Contracting State in which the property in question is situated. The term shall in any case include property accessory to immovable property, livestock and equipment used in agriculture and forestry, rights to which the provisions of general law respecting landed property apply, usufruct of immovable property and rights to variable or fixed payments as consideration for the working of, or the right to work, mineral deposits, sources and other natural resources; ships, boats and aircraft shall not be regarded as immovable property.

3. The provisions of paragraph 1 shall apply to income derived from the direct use, letting, or use in any other form of immovable property.

4. The provisions of paragraphs 1 and 3 shall also apply to the income from immovable property of an enterprise and to income from immovable property used for the performance of independent personal services.

Article 7

BUSINESS PROFITS

1. The profits of an enterprise of a Contracting State shall be taxable only in that State unless the enterprise carries on business in the other Contracting State through a permanent establishment situated therein. If the enterprise carries on business as aforesaid, the profits of the enterprise may be taxed in the other State but only so much of them as is attributable to that permanent establishment.

2. Subject to the provisions of paragraph 3, where an enterprise of a Contracting State carries on business in the other Contracting State through a permanent establishment situated therein, there shall in each Contracting State be attributed to that permanent establishment the profits which it might be expected to make if it were a distinct and separate enterprise engaged in the same or similar activities under the same or similar conditions and dealing wholly independently with the enterprise of which it is a permanent establishment.

3. (a) In the determination of the profits of a permanent establishment, there shall be allowed as deductions expenses which are incurred for the purposes of the business of the permanent establishment including only those executive and general administrative expenses so incurred, whether in the State in which the permanent establishment is situated or elsewhere.

(b) However, no such deduction shall be allowed in respect of amounts, if any, paid (otherwise than towards reimbursement of actual expenses) by the permanent establishment to the head office of the enterprise or any of its other offices, by way of royalties, fees or other similar payments in return for the use of patents or other rights, or by way of commission, for specific services performed or for management, or, except in the case of a banking enterprise, by way of interest on moneys lent to the permanent establishment. Likewise, no account shall be taken, in the determination of the profits of a permanent establishment, for amounts charged (otherwise than towards reimbursement of actual expenses), by the permanent establishment to the head office of the enterprise or any of its other offices, by way of royalties, fees or other similar payments in return for the use of patents or other rights, or by way of commission for specific services performed or for management, or, except in the case of a banking enterprise, by way of interest on moneys lent to the head office of the enterprise or any of its other offices.

4. In so far as it has been customary in a Contracting State to determine the profits to be attributed to a permanent establishment on the basis of an apportionment of the total profits of the enterprise to its various parts, nothing in paragraph 2 shall preclude that Contracting State from determining the profits to be taxed by such an apportionment as may be customary; the method of apportionment adopted shall, however, be such that the result shall be in accordance with the principles contained in this Article.

5. No profits shall be attributed to a permanent establishment by reason of the mere purchase by that permanent establishment of goods or merchandise for the enterprise.

6. For the purposes of the preceding paragraphs, the profits to be attributed to the permanent establishment shall be determined by the same method year by year unless there is good and sufficient reason to the contrary.

7. Where profits include items of income or gains which are dealt with separately in other Articles of this Convention, then the provisions of those Articles shall not be affected by the provisions of this Article.

Article 8

SHIPPING AND AIR TRANSPORT

1. Profits of an enterprise of a Contracting State from the operation or rental of ships or aircraft in international traffic shall be taxable only in that State.

2. If the place of effective management of a shipping enterprise is aboard a ship, then it shall be deemed to be situated in the Contracting State in which the home harbour of the ship is situated, or, if there is no such home harbour, in the Contracting State of which the operator of the ship is a resident.

3. The provisions of paragraph 1 shall also apply to profits from the participation in a pool, a joint business or an international operating agency.

Article 9

ASSOCIATED ENTERPRISES

1. Where

(a) an enterprise of a Contracting State participates directly or indirectly in the management, control or capital of an enterprise of the other Contracting State, or

(b) the same persons participate directly or indirectly in the management, control or capital of an enterprise of a Contracting State and an enterprise of the other Contracting State,

and in either case conditions are made or imposed between the two enterprises in their commercial or financial relations which differ from those which would be made between independent enterprises, then any profits which would, but for those conditions, have accrued to one of the enterprises, but, by reason of those conditions have not so accrued, may be included in the profits of that enterprise and taxed accordingly.

2. Where a Contracting State includes in the profits of an enterprise of that State - and taxes accordingly - profits on which an enterprise of the other Contracting State has been charged to tax in that other State and the profits so included are profits which would have accrued to the enterprise of the first-mentioned State if the conditions made between the two enterprises had been those which would have been made between independent enterprises, then that other State shall make an appropriate adjustment to the amount of the tax charged therein on those profits. In determining such adjustment, due regard shall be had to the other provisions of this Convention and the competent authorities of the Contracting States shall, if necessary, consult each other.

Article 10

DIVIDENDS

1. Dividends paid by a company which is a resident of a Contracting State to a resident of the other Contracting State may be taxed in that other State.

2. However, such dividends may also be taxed in the Contracting State of which the company paying the dividends is a resident and according to the laws of that State, but if the beneficial owner of the dividends is a resident of the other Contracting State, the tax so charged shall not exceed:

(a) 5 per cent of the gross amount of the dividends if the beneficial owner is a company (other than a partnership) which holds directly at least 25 per cent of the share capital of the company paying the dividends;

(b) 10 per cent of the gross amount of the dividends in all other cases.

This paragraph shall not affect the taxation of the company in respect of the profits out of which the dividends are paid.

3. The term "dividends" as used in this Article means income from shares, "jouissance" shares or "jouissance" rights, mining shares, founders' shares or other rights, not being debt-claims, participating in profits, as well as income from other corporate rights which is subjected to the same taxation treatment as income from shares by the laws of the State of which the company making the distribution is a resident.

4. The provisions of paragraphs 1 and 2 shall not apply if the beneficial owner of the dividends, being a resident of a Contracting State, carries on business in the other

Contracting State of which the company paying the dividends is a resident, through a permanent establishment situated therein, or performs in that other State independent personal services from a fixed base situated therein, and the holding in respect of which the dividends are paid is effectively connected with such permanent establishment or fixed base. In such case the provisions of Article 7 or Article 14, as the case may be, shall apply.

5. Where a company which is a resident of a Contracting State derives profits or income from the other Contracting State, that other State may not impose any tax on the dividends paid by the company, except insofar as such dividends are paid to a resident of that other State or insofar as the holding in respect of which the dividends are paid is effectively connected with a permanent establishment situated in that other State, nor subject the company's undistributed profits to a tax on the company's undistributed profits, even if the dividends paid or the undistributed profits consist wholly or partly of profits or income arising in such other State.

Article 11

INTEREST

1. Interest arising in a Contracting State and paid to a resident of the other Contracting State may be taxed in that other State.

2. However, such interest may also be taxed in the Contracting State in which it arises and according to the laws of that State, but if the beneficial owner of the interest is a resident of the other Contracting State, the tax so charged shall not exceed 10 per cent of the gross amount of the interest.

3. Notwithstanding the provisions of paragraph 2, interest arising in a Contracting State and paid to a resident of the other Contracting State shall be taxable only in the other Contracting State if such recipient is the beneficial owner of the interest and such interest is paid to:

(a) in the case of Ireland—

(i) the Central Bank of Ireland;

(ii) the National Treasury Management Agency;

(iii) the National Pension Reserve Fund; and

(iv) a statutory body or any institution wholly owned by the Government of Ireland as may be agreed from time to time between the competent authorities of the Contracting States; and

(b) in the case of Pakistan—

(i) the State Bank of Pakistan; and

(ii) a statutory body or any institution wholly owned by the Government of Pakistan as may be agreed from time to time between the competent authorities of the Contracting States.

4. The term "interest", as used in this Article, means income from debt-claims of every kind, whether or not secured by mortgage, and whether or not carrying a right to participate in the debtor's profits, and in particular, income from government securities and income from bonds or debentures, including premiums and prizes attaching to such securities, bonds or debentures. Penalty charges for late payment shall not be regarded as interest for the purpose of this Article.

5. The provisions of paragraph 1 and 2 shall not apply if the beneficial owner of the interest, being a resident of a Contracting State, carries on business in the other Contracting State in which the interest arises, through a permanent establishment situated therein, or performs in that other State independent personal services from a fixed base situated therein, and the debt-claim in respect of which the interest is paid is effectively connected with such permanent establishment or fixed base. In such cases the provisions of Article 7 or Article 14, as the case may be, shall apply.

6. Interest shall be deemed to arise in a Contracting State when the payer is a resident of that State. Where, however, the person paying the interest, whether he is a resident of a Contracting State or not, has in a Contracting State a permanent establishment or a fixed base in connection with which the indebtedness on which the interest is paid was incurred, and such interest is borne by such permanent establishment or fixed base, then such interest shall be deemed to arise in the State in which the permanent establishment or fixed base is situated.

7. Where, by reason of a special relationship between the payer and the beneficial owner or between both of them and some other person, the amount of the interest, having regard to the debt-claim for which it is paid, exceeds the amount which would have been agreed upon by the payer and the beneficial owner in the absence of such relationship, the provisions of this Article shall apply only to the last-mentioned amount. In such case, the excess part of the payments shall remain taxable according to the laws of each Contracting State, due regard being had to the other provisions of this Convention.

Article 12

ROYALTIES AND FEES FOR TECHNICAL SERVICES

1. Royalties or fees for technical services arising in a Contracting State and paid to a resident of the other Contracting State may be taxed in that other State.

2. However, such royalties or fees for technical services may also be taxed in the Contracting State in which they arise and according to the laws of that State, but if the beneficial owner of the royalties of fees for technical services is a resident of the other Contracting State, the tax so charged shall not exceed 10 per cent of the gross amount of the royalties or fees for technical services.

3. (a) The term "royalties" as used in this Article means payments of any kind received as a consideration for the use of, or the right to use, any copyright of literary, artistic or scientific work including cinematograph films, or films or tapes used for radio or television broadcasting, any patent, trade mark, design or model, plan, secret formula or process or for information concerning industrial, commercial or scientific experience.

(b) The term "fees for technical services" means payment of any kind in consideration for the rendering of any managerial, technical or consultancy services including the provision of services by technical or other personnel but does not include payments for services mentioned in Articles 14 and 15 of this Convention.

4. The provisions of paragraph 1 and 2 shall not apply if the beneficial owner of the royalties or fees for technical services, being a resident of a Contracting State, carries on business in the other Contracting State in which the royalties arise, through a permanent establishment situated therein, or performs in that other State

independent personal services from a fixed base situated therein, and the right or property in respect of which the royalties or fees for technical services are paid is effectively connected with such permanent establishment or fixed base. In such case the provisions of Article 7 or Article 14, as the case may be, shall apply.

5. Royalties or fees for technical services shall be deemed to arise in a Contracting State where the payer is a resident of that State. Where, however, the person paying the royalties or fees for technical services, whether he is a resident of a Contracting State or not, has in a Contracting State a permanent establishment or a fixed base in connection with which the liability to pay the royalties or fees for technical services was incurred, and such royalties or fees for technical services are borne by such permanent establishment or fixed base, then such royalties or fees for technical services shall be deemed to arise in the State in which the permanent establishment or fixed base is situated.

6. Where, by reason of a special relationship between the payer and the beneficial owner or between both of them and some other person, the amount of the royalties or fees for technical services, having regard to the use, right or information for which they are paid, exceeds the amount which would have been agreed upon by the payer and the beneficial owner in the absence of such relationship, the provisions of this Article shall apply only to the last-mentioned amount. In such case, the excess part of the payments shall remain taxable according to the laws of each Contracting State, due regard being had to the other provisions of this Convention.

Article 13

CAPITAL GAINS

1. Gains derived by a resident of a Contracting State from the alienation of immovable property referred to in Article 6 and situated in the other Contracting State may be taxed in that other State.

2. Gains from the alienation of shares, other than shares quoted on a stock exchange, of the capital stock of a company, or of an interest in a partnership, trust or estate, the property of which consists directly or indirectly principally of immovable property situated in a Contracting State may be taxed in that State. In particular:

(a) Nothing contained in this paragraph shall apply to a company, partnership, trust or estate, other than a company, partnership, trust or estate engaged in the business of management of immovable properties, the property of which consists directly or indirectly principally of immovable property used by such company, partnership, trust or estate in its business activities.

(b) For the purposes of this paragraph, "principally" in relation to ownership of immovable property means the value of such immovable property exceeding fifty per cent of the aggregate value of all assets owned by the company, partnership, trust or estate.

3. Gains, other than those dealt with in paragraph 2, from the alienation of movable property forming part of the business property of a permanent establishment which an enterprise of a Contracting State has in the other Contracting State or of movable property pertaining to a fixed base available to a resident of a Contracting State in the other Contracting State for the purpose of performing independent personal services, including such gains from the alienation of such a permanent

establishment (alone or with the whole enterprise) or of such fixed base, may be taxed in that other State.

4. Gains derived by an enterprise of a Contracting State from the alienation of ships or aircraft operated in international traffic, or movable property pertaining to the operation of such ships, or aircraft, shall be taxable only in that State.

5. Gains from the alienation of any property, other than that referred to in paragraphs 1 to 4, shall be taxable only in the Contracting State of which the alienator is a resident.

Article 14

INDEPENDENT PERSONAL SERVICES

1. Income derived by a resident of a Contracting State in respect of professional services or other activities of an independent character shall be taxable only in that State except in the following circumstances, when such income may also be taxed in the other Contracting State:

(a) If he has a fixed base regularly available to him in the other Contracting State for the purpose of performing his activities; in that case, only so much of the income as is attributable to that fixed base may be taxed in that other Contracting State; or

(b) If his stay in the other Contracting State is for a period or periods amounting to or exceeding in the aggregate 183 days in the fiscal year concerned; in that case, only so much of the income as is derived from his activities performed in that other State may be taxed in that other State.

2. The term "professional services" includes especially independent scientific, literary, artistic, educational or teaching activities as well as the independent activities of physicians, lawyers, engineers, architects, dentists and accountants.

Article 15

DEPENDENT PERSONAL SERVICES

1. Subject to the provisions of Articles 14, 16, 18 and 19,salaries, wages and other similar remuneration derived by a resident of a Contracting State in respect of an employment shall be taxable only in that State unless the employment is exercised in the other Contracting State. If the employment is so exercised, such remuneration as is derived there from may be taxed in that other State.

2. Notwithstanding the provisions of paragraph 1, remuneration derived by a resident of a Contracting State in respect of an employment exercised in the other Contracting State shall be taxable only in the first-mentioned State if:

(a) the recipient is present in the other State for a period or periods not exceeding in the aggregate 183 days in any twelve month period commencing or ending in the fiscal year concerned, and

(b) the remuneration is paid by, or on behalf of, an employer who is not a resident of the other State, and

(c) the remuneration is not borne by a permanent establishment or a fixed base which the employer has in the other State.

3. Notwithstanding the preceding provisions of this Article, remuneration derived in respect of an employment exercised aboard a ship or aircraft operated in international traffic by an enterprise of a Contracting State may be taxed in that Contracting State.

Article 16

DIRECTORS' FEES

Directors' fees and other similar payments derived by a resident of a Contracting State in his capacity as a member of the board of directors of a company which is a resident of the other Contracting State may be taxed in that other State.

Article 17

ARTISTES AND SPORTSPERSONS

1. Notwithstanding the provisions of Articles 7, 14 and 15, income derived by a resident of a Contracting State as an entertainer, such as a theatre, motion picture, radio or television artiste, or a musician, or as a sportsperson, from his personal activities as such exercised in the other Contracting State, may be taxed in that other State.

2. Where income in respect of personal activities exercised by an entertainer or a sportsperson in his capacity as such accrues not to the entertainer or sportsperson himself but to another person, that income may, notwithstanding the provisions of Articles 7, 14 and 15, be taxed in the Contracting State in which the activities of the entertainer or sportsperson are exercised.

Article 18

PENSIONS, ANNUITIES AND SOCIAL SECURITY PAYMENTS

1. Subject to the provisions of paragraph 2 of Article 19, pensions and other similar remuneration paid to a resident of a Contracting State in consideration of past employment and any annuity paid to such a resident in consideration of past employment shall be taxable only in that State.

2. The term "annuity" means a stated sum payable periodically at stated times during life or during a specified or ascertainable period of time under an obligation to make the payments in return for adequate and full consideration in money or money's worth.

3. Notwithstanding the provisions of paragraph 1, pensions paid and other payments made under a public scheme which is part of the social security system of a Contracting State or a political subdivision or a local authority thereof shall be taxable only in that State.

Article 19

GOVERNMENT SERVICE

1. (a) Salaries, wages and other similar remuneration paid by a Contracting State or a political subdivision or a local authority thereof to an individual in respect of services rendered to that State or subdivision or authority in the discharge of functions of a governmental nature shall be taxable only in that State.

(b) However, such salaries, wages and other similar remuneration shall be taxable only in the other Contracting State if the services are rendered in that State and the individual is a resident of that State who:

(i) is a national of that State; or

(ii) did not become a resident of that State solely for the purpose of rendering the services.

2. (a) Notwithstanding the provisions of paragraph 1, pensions and other similar remuneration paid by, or out of funds created by, a Contracting State or a political subdivision or a local authority thereof to an individual in respect of services rendered to that State or subdivision or authority in the discharge of functions of a governmental nature shall be taxable only in that State.

(b) However, such pensions and other similar remuneration shall be taxable only in the other Contracting State if the individual is a resident of, and a national of, that State.

3. The provisions of Articles 14, 15, 16, 17 and 18 shall apply to salaries, wages, pensions and other similar remuneration in respect of services rendered in connection with a business carried on by a Contracting State or a political subdivision or a local authority thereof.

Article 20
STUDENTS

1. Payments which a student or business trainee or apprentice who is or was immediately before visiting a Contracting State a resident of the other Contracting State and who is present in the first-mentioned State solely for the purpose of his education or training receives for the purpose of his maintenance, education or training shall not be taxed in that State, provided that such payments arise from sources outside that State.

2. In respect of remuneration from employment, a student or business trainee or apprentice referred to in paragraph 1 shall, in addition, be entitled during such education or training to the same exemptions, credits, reliefs or reductions in respect of taxes as are available to residents of the Contracting State which he is visiting, providing that such employment is directly related to that education or training or is undertaken for the purposes of his maintenance during that education or training.

Article 21

OTHER INCOME

1. Items of income of a resident of a Contracting State, wherever arising, not dealt with in the foregoing Articles of this Convention shall be taxable only in that State.

2. The provisions of paragraph 1 shall not apply to income, other than income from immovable property as defined in paragraph 2 of Article 6, if the recipient of such income, being a resident of a Contracting State, carries on business in the other Contracting State through a permanent establishment situated therein, or performs in that other State independent personal services from a fixed base situated therein, and the right or property in respect of which the income is paid is effectively connected with such permanent establishment or fixed base. In such case the provisions of Article 7 or Article 14, as the case may be, shall apply.

3. Notwithstanding the provisions of paragraphs 1 and 2, items of income of a resident of a Contracting State not dealt with in the foregoing Articles of this Convention and arising in the other Contracting State may also be taxed in that other State in accordance with domestic laws.

Article 22

OFFSHORE ACTIVITIES

1. The provisions of this Article shall apply notwithstanding any other provision of this Convention where activities (in this Article called "relevant activities") are carried on offshore in connection with the exploration or exploitation of the seabed and subsoil and their natural resources situated in a Contracting State.

2. A person who is a resident of a Contracting State which carries on relevant activities in the other Contracting State shall, subject to paragraph 3 of this Article, be deemed to be carrying on business in that other State through a permanent establishment or fixed base situated therein.

3. Relevant activities which are carried on by an enterprise of a Contracting State in the other Contracting State for a period or periods not exceeding in the aggregate 30 days within any period of twelve months shall not constitute the carrying on of business through a permanent establishment or a fixed base situated therein. For the purposes of this paragraph:

(a) where a resident of a Contracting State carrying on relevant activities in the other Contracting State is associated with another person carrying on substantially similar relevant activities there, the former person shall be deemed to be carrying on all such activities of the latter person, except to the extent that those activities are carried on at the same time as its own activities;

(b) a person shall be deemed to be associated with another person if one is controlled directly or indirectly by the other, or both are controlled directly or indirectly by a third person or third persons.

4. Salaries, wages and similar remuneration derived by a resident of a Contracting State in respect of an employment connected with relevant activities in the other Contracting State may, to the extent that the duties are performed offshore in that other State, be taxed in that other State.

CHAPTER IV
METHODS FOR THE ELIMINATION OF DOUBLE TAXATION

Article 23

ELIMINATION OF DOUBLE TAXATION

1. Subject to the provisions of the laws of Ireland regarding the allowance as a credit against Irish tax of tax payable in a territory outside Ireland (which shall not affect the general principle hereof):

(a) Pakistan tax payable under the laws of Pakistan and in accordance with this Convention, whether directly or by deduction, on profits, income or gains from sources within Pakistan (excluding in the case of a dividend tax payable in respect of the profits out of which the dividend is paid) shall be allowed as a credit against any Irish tax computed by reference to the same profits, income or gains by reference to which Pakistan tax is computed;

(b) in the case of a dividend paid by a company which is a resident of Pakistan to a company which is a resident of Ireland and which controls directly or indirectly 5 per cent or more of the voting power in the company paying the dividend, the credit shall take into account (in addition to any Pakistan tax creditable under the provisions of subparagraph (a) of this paragraph) Pakistan tax payable by the company in respect of the profits out of which such dividend is paid.

2. In Pakistan, double taxation shall be eliminated as follows:

Subject to the provisions of the laws of Pakistan, regarding the allowance as a credit against Pakistan tax, the amount of Irish tax payable, under the laws of Ireland and in accordance with the provisions of this Agreement, whether directly or by deduction, by a resident of Pakistan, in respect of income from sources within Ireland which has been subject to a tax both in Pakistan and in Ireland shall be allowed as a credit against the Pakistan tax payable in respect of such income but in an amount not exceeding that proportion of Pakistan tax which such income bears to the entire income chargeable to Pakistan tax.

3. For the purposes of paragraphs 1 and 2 profits, income and capital gains owned by a resident of a Contracting State which may be taxed in the other Contracting State in accordance with this Convention shall be deemed to be derived from sources in that other Contracting State.

4. Where in accordance with any provision of the Convention income derived by a resident of a Contracting State is exempt from tax in that State, such State may nevertheless, in calculating the amount of tax on the remaining income of such resident, take into account the exempted income.

CHAPTER V
SPECIAL PROVISIONS

Article 24

NON-DISCRIMINATION

1. Nationals of a Contracting State shall not be subjected in the other Contracting State to any taxation or any requirement connected therewith, which is other or more burdensome than the taxation and connected requirements to which nationals of that other State in the same circumstances, in particular with respect to residence, are or may be subjected. This provision shall, notwithstanding the provisions of Article 1, also apply to persons who are not residents of one or both of the Contracting States.

2.. Stateless persons who are residents of a Contracting State shall not be subjected in either Contracting State to any taxation or any requirement connected therewith which is other or more burdensome than the taxation and connected requirements to which nationals of the State concerned in the same circumstances, are or may be subjected.

3. The taxation on a permanent establishment which an enterprise of a Contracting State has in the other Contracting State shall not be less favourably levied in that other State than the taxation levied on enterprises of that other State carrying on the same activities. This provision shall not be construed as obliging a Contracting State to grant to residents of the other Contracting State any personal allowances, reliefs and reductions for taxation purposes on account of civil status or family responsibilities which it grants to its own residents.

4. Except where the provisions of paragraph 1 of Article 9, paragraph 7 of Article 11, or paragraph 6 of Article 12 apply, interest, royalties, fees for technical services and other disbursements paid by an enterprise of a Contracting State to a

resident of the other Contracting State shall, for the purpose of determining the taxable profits of such enterprise, be deductible under the same conditions as if they had been paid to a resident of the first-mentioned State.

5. Enterprises of a Contracting State, the capital of which is wholly or partly owned or controlled, directly or indirectly, by one or more residents of the other Contracting State, shall not be subjected in the first-mentioned State to any taxation or any requirement connected therewith which is other or more burdensome than the taxation and connected requirements to which other similar enterprises of the first-mentioned State are or may be subjected.

Article 25

MUTUAL AGREEMENT PROCEDURE

1. Where a person considers that the actions of one or both of the Contracting States result or will result for him in taxation not in accordance with the provisions of this Convention, he may, irrespective of the remedies provided by the domestic law of those States, present his case to the competent authority of the Contracting State of which he is a resident or, if his case comes under paragraph 1 of Article 24, to that of the Contracting State of which he is a national. The case must be presented within three years from the first notification of the action resulting in taxation not in accordance with the provisions of the Convention.

2. The competent authority shall endeavour, if the objection appears to it to be justified and if it is not itself able to arrive at a satisfactory solution, to resolve the case by mutual agreement with the competent authority of the other Contracting State, with a view to the avoidance of taxation which is not in accordance with the Convention. Any agreement reached shall be implemented notwithstanding any time limits in the domestic law of the Contracting State.

3. The competent authorities of the Contracting States shall endeavour to resolve by mutual agreement any difficulties or doubts arising as to the interpretation or application of the Convention. They may also consult together for the elimination of double taxation in cases not provided for in the Convention.

4. The competent authorities of the Contracting State may communicate with each other directly, including through a joint commission consisting of themselves or their representatives, for the purpose of reaching an agreement in the sense of the preceding paragraphs.

Article 26

EXCHANGE OF INFORMATION

1. The competent authorities of the Contracting States shall exchange such information as is foreseeably relevant for carrying out the provisions of this Convention or to the administration or enforcement of the domestic laws concerning taxes covered by this Convention imposed on behalf of the Contracting States, or of their political subdivisions or local authorities, insofar as the taxation thereunder is not contrary to the Convention. The exchange of information is not restricted by Article 1.

2. Any information received under paragraph 1by a Contracting State shall be treated as secret in the same manner as information obtained under the domestic laws of that State and shall be disclosed only to persons or authorities (including courts and administrative bodies) concerned with the assessment or collection of, the enforcement or prosecution in respect of, the determination of appeals in relation to the taxes referred to in paragraph 1,or the oversight of the above. Such persons or authorities shall use the information only for such purposes. They may disclose the information in public court proceedings or in judicial decisions.

3. In no case shall the provisions of paragraphs 1 and 2 be construed so as to impose on a Contracting State the obligation:

a) to carry out administrative measures at variance with the laws and administrative practice of that or of the other Contracting State;

b) to supply information which is not obtainable under the laws or in the normal course of the administration of that or of the other Contracting State;

c) to supply information which would disclose any trade, business, industrial, commercial or professional secret or trade process, or information, the disclosure of which would be contrary to public policy (ordre public).

4. If information is requested by a Contracting State in accordance with this Article, the other Contracting State shall use its information gathering measures to obtain the requested information, even though that other State may not need such information for its own tax purposes. The obligation contained in the preceding sentence is subject to the limitations of paragraph 3 but in no case shall such limitations be construed to permit a Contracting State to decline to supply information solely because it has no domestic interest in such information.

5. In no case shall the provisions of paragraph 3 be construed to permit a Contracting State to decline to supply information solely because the information is held by a bank, other financial institution, nominee or person acting in an agency or a fiduciary capacity or because it relates to ownership interests in a person.

Article 27

MEMBERS OF DIPLOMATIC MISSIONS AND CONSULAR POSTS

Nothing in this Convention shall affect the fiscal privileges of members of diplomatic missions or consular posts under the general rules of international law or under the provisions of special agreements.

CHAPTER VI
FINAL PROVISIONS

Article 28

ENTRY INTO FORCE

1. Each of the Contracting States shall notify to the other the completion of the procedure required by its law for the bringing into force of this Convention.

2. This Convention shall enter into force on the date of receipt of the later of these notifications and shall thereupon have effect:

(a) in the case of Ireland—

(i) with regard to income tax, universal social charge and capital gains tax, for any year of assessment beginning on or after the first day of January in the calendar year next following the date in which this Convention enters into force;

(ii) with regard to corporation tax, for any financial year beginning on or after the first day of January in the calendar year next following the date in which this Convention enters into force;

(b) in the case of Pakistan—

(i) with regard to taxes withheld at source, in respect of amounts paid or credited on or after the first day of July next following the date upon which the Convention enters into force; and

(ii) with regard to other taxes, in respect of taxable years beginning on or after the first day of July next following the date upon which the Convention enters into force.

3. The Convention between the Government of Ireland and the Government of the Islamic Republic of Pakistan for the Avoidance of Double Taxation with respect to Taxes on Income signed at Paris on 13 April 1973, (hereinafter referred to as "the 1973 Convention"), shall cease to have effect from the dates on which this Convention becomes effective in accordance with paragraph 2 of this Article.

4. Notwithstanding paragraph 3, where any provision of the 1973 Convention would have afforded any greater relief from tax than is due under this Convention, any such provision as aforesaid shall continue to have effect for

(a) a period of twelve months, and

(b) subject to paragraph 5, in the case of paragraphs 1 and 2 of Article XV of the 1973 Convention, for a period of 5 years

from the date on which the provisions of this Convention would otherwise have effect in accordance with the provisions of paragraph 2 of this Article.

5. For the purposes of the application of subparagraph (b)(i) of paragraph 2 of Article XV of the 1973 Convention, the provisions of clauses (126D), (126E) and (133) of Part 1 of the Second Schedule to the Income Tax Ordinance 2001 shall apply in place of the provisions listed in that subparagraph.

Article 29

TERMINATION

1. This Convention shall remain in force until terminated by a Contracting State. Either Contracting State may terminate the Convention, through diplomatic channels, by giving notice of termination at least six months before the end of any calendar year starting five year after the year in which the Convention entered into force.

In such event, the Convention shall cease to have effect:

(a) in the case of Ireland—

(i) with regard to income tax, universal social charge and capital gains tax, for any year of assessment beginning on or after the first day of January next following the date on which the period specified in the said notice of termination expires;

(ii) with regard to corporation tax, for any financial year beginning on or after the first day of January next following the date on which the period specified in the said notice of termination expires;

(b) in the case of Pakistan—

(i) with regard to taxes withheld at source, for amounts taxable on or after the first day of January of the calendar year next following that in which the notice is given; and

(ii) with regard to other taxes, for the tax year beginning on or after the first day of July of the calendar year next following that in which the notice is given.

IN WITNESS WHEREOF the undersigned, being duly authorised thereto, have signed this Convention.

Done in duplicate at Dublin this .16TH......day of APRIL 2015..., in the English language.

For the Government of Ireland

For the Government of the Islamic Republic of Pakistan

Protocol

At the time of signing this Convention between the Government of Ireland
and
the Government of the Islamic Republic of Pakistan
for the Avoidance of Double Taxation and the Prevention of Fiscal Evasion with respect to Taxes on Income, the undersigned have agreed that the following provisions shall form an integral part of this Convention:

1. **With respect to Approved Retirement Funds in Ireland:**

   It is understood that, taking account of tax-relief given for contributions or premiums paid in respect of retirement benefit schemes, retirement annuity contracts or other pension products, and the exemption from tax of income and gains accruing to a fund (referred to in this paragraph as a "pension fund") created by such contributions or premiums, the distributions from an approved retirement fund in Ireland that was created by the transfer of accrued rights or assets from a pension fund shall only be taxable in Ireland, notwithstanding any provision of this Convention.

2. **With reference to Article 4:**

   It is understood that a Common Contractual Fund (CCF) established in Ireland shall not be regarded as a resident of Ireland and shall be treated as fiscally transparent for the purposes of granting tax treaty benefits.

3. **With reference to Article 13, paragraph 5:**

Where

(a) an individual domiciled in Ireland ceases to be a resident in Ireland,

(b) disposes of property acquired prior to the first day of the calendar year in which he ceased to be resident in Ireland as mentioned in subparagraph (a) above, and

(c) then becomes resident again in Ireland within 5 years of ceasing to be so resident,

the provisions of paragraph 5 shall not affect the right of Ireland to tax the individual according to its law by reference to that disposal but the amount of the tax charged shall not exceed the amount of tax that would be charged on the amount of any gain arising on a deemed disposal by the individual of that property at market value on the day immediately before the first day of the calendar year in which he ceased to be resident in Ireland as mentioned in subparagraph (a) above.

Provided that if, after the date of signature of this Convention, the laws of Pakistan are changed to include a capital gains tax then Pakistan may inform the Irish competent authority of this development and, if Pakistan so requests, Ireland shall immediately enter into negotiations reviewing the relevance, in the light of such development, of the provisions of the preceding paragraph with a view to amending or repealing those provisions where appropriate.

Done in duplicate at DUBLIN this 16TH day of APRIL 2015 in the English language.

For the Government of Ireland

For the Government of the Islamic Republic of Pakistan

[TRANSLATION IN FRENCH – TRADUCTION EN FRANÇAIS]

CONVENTION ENTRE LE GOUVERNEMENT DE L'IRLANDE ET LE GOUVERNEMENT DE LA RÉPUBLIQUE ISLAMIQUE DU PAKISTAN TENDANT À ÉVITER LES DOUBLES IMPOSITIONS ET À PRÉVENIR LA FRAUDE FISCALE EN MATIÈRE D'IMPÔTS SUR LE REVENU

Préambule

Le Gouvernement de l'Irlande et le Gouvernement de la République islamique du Pakistan, désireux de conclure une convention tendant à éviter les doubles impositions et à prévenir la fraude fiscale en matière d'impôts sur le revenu, ainsi que d'encourager et de renforcer les relations économiques entre les deux pays, sont convenus de ce qui suit :

CHAPITRE PREMIER. CHAMP D'APPLICATION DE LA CONVENTION

Article premier. Personnes visées

La présente Convention s'applique aux personnes qui sont des résidents d'un État contractant ou des deux États contractants.

Article 2. Impôts visés

1. La présente Convention s'applique aux impôts sur le revenu perçus pour le compte d'un État contractant, de ses subdivisions politiques ou de ses collectivités locales, quel que soit le système de perception.

2. Sont considérés comme impôts sur le revenu les impôts perçus sur le revenu total ou sur des éléments du revenu, y compris les impôts sur les gains provenant de l'aliénation de biens mobiliers ou immobiliers.

3. Les impôts actuels auxquels s'applique la Convention sont notamment :

a) Dans le cas de l'Irlande :

i) L'impôt sur le revenu ;

ii) La charge sociale universelle ;

iii) L'impôt sur les sociétés ; et

iv) L'impôt sur les gains en capital ;

(ci-après dénommés « impôt irlandais ») ;

b) Dans le cas du Pakistan : l'impôt sur le revenu ;

(ci-après dénommé « impôt pakistanais »).

4. La Convention s'applique aussi aux impôts de nature identique ou analogue qui seraient établis après la date de signature de la Convention et qui s'ajouteraient aux impôts actuels ou qui les remplaceraient. Les autorités compétentes des États contractants se communiquent les modifications significatives apportées à leurs législations fiscales respectives.

CHAPITRE II. DÉFINITIONS

Article 3. Définitions générales

1. Aux fins de la présente Convention, à moins que le contexte n'exige une interprétation différente :

a) Le terme « Irlande » comprend toute zone située en dehors des eaux territoriales de l'Irlande qui a été ou peut ultérieurement être désignée, conformément à la législation irlandaise relative à la zone économique exclusive et au plateau continental, comme une zone à l'intérieur de laquelle l'Irlande peut exercer ses droits souverains et sa juridiction conformément au droit international ;

b) Le terme « Pakistan », lorsqu'il est employé dans un sens géographique, désigne le Pakistan tel que défini dans la Constitution de la République islamique du Pakistan et comprend toute zone située en dehors des eaux territoriales du Pakistan qui, en vertu de la législation pakistanaise et conformément au droit international, est une zone à l'intérieur de laquelle le Pakistan exerce des droits souverains et sa juridiction exclusive relativement aux ressources naturelles du fond marin, du sous-sol et des eaux surjacentes ;

c) Les expressions « un État contractant » et « l'autre État contractant » désignent, selon le contexte, l'Irlande ou le Pakistan ;

d) Le terme « personne » comprend les personnes physiques, les sociétés et tous autres groupements de personnes ;

e) Le terme « société » désigne toute personne morale ou toute entité considérée comme une personne morale à des fins fiscales ;

f) Les expressions « entreprise d'un État contractant » et « entreprise de l'autre État contractant » désignent respectivement une entreprise exploitée par un résident d'un État contractant et une entreprise exploitée par un résident de l'autre État contractant ;

g) L'expression « trafic international » désigne tout transport effectué par un navire ou un aéronef exploité par une entreprise d'un État contractant, sauf lorsque le navire ou l'aéronef n'est exploité qu'entre des points situés dans l'autre État contractant ;

h) Le terme « ressortissant », s'agissant d'un État contractant, désigne :

   i) Toute personne physique possédant la nationalité ou la citoyenneté de cet État contractant ; et

   ii) Toute personne morale, société de personnes ou association constituée en vertu de la législation en vigueur dans cet État contractant ;

i) L'expression « autorité compétente » désigne :

   i) Dans le cas de l'Irlande, l'administration fiscale (Revenue Commissioners) ou son représentant autorisé ;

   ii) Dans le cas du Pakistan, le Comité fédéral des recettes publiques ou son représentant autorisé.

2. Pour l'application de la Convention à tout moment par un État contractant, toute expression ou tout terme qui n'y est pas défini a, à moins que le contexte n'exige une interprétation différente, le sens que lui attribue, à ce moment, le droit fiscal applicable de cet État, le sens attribué à cette

expression ou à ce terme par la législation fiscale de cet État prévalant sur le sens que lui attribuent les autres branches du droit de cet État.

Article 4. Résident

1. Aux fins de la présente Convention, l'expression « résident d'un État contractant » désigne toute personne qui, en vertu de la législation de cet État, y est assujettie à l'impôt en raison de son domicile, de sa résidence, de son siège de direction ou de tout autre critère de nature analogue et s'applique aussi à cet État, à ses subdivisions politiques ou à ses collectivités locales. Toutefois, cette expression ne comprend pas les personnes qui ne sont assujetties à l'impôt dans cet État que pour les revenus de sources situées dans cet État.

2. Lorsque, selon les dispositions du paragraphe 1, une personne physique est un résident des deux États contractants, son statut est déterminé comme suit :

a) Cette personne est considérée comme un résident seulement de l'État où elle dispose d'un foyer d'habitation permanent ; si elle dispose d'un foyer d'habitation permanent dans les deux États, elle est considérée comme un résident seulement de l'État avec lequel ses liens personnels et économiques sont les plus étroits (centre des intérêts vitaux) ;

b) Si l'État où elle a le centre de ses intérêts vitaux ne peut pas être déterminé, ou si elle ne dispose d'un foyer d'habitation permanent dans aucun des États, elle est considérée comme un résident seulement de l'État où elle séjourne de façon habituelle ;

c) Si elle séjourne de façon habituelle dans les deux États ou si elle ne séjourne de façon habituelle dans aucun d'eux, elle est considérée comme un résident seulement de l'État dont elle possède la nationalité ;

d) Si cette personne possède la nationalité des deux États ou si elle ne possède la nationalité d'aucun d'eux, les autorités compétentes des États contractants tranchent la question d'un commun accord.

3. Lorsque, selon les dispositions du paragraphe 1, une personne autre qu'une personne physique est un résident des deux États contractants, elle est considérée comme un résident seulement de l'État où son siège de direction effective est situé.

Article 5. Établissement stable

1. Aux fins de la présente Convention, l'expression « établissement stable » désigne une installation fixe d'affaires par l'intermédiaire de laquelle une entreprise exerce tout ou partie de son activité.

2. L'expression « établissement stable » désigne notamment :

a) Un siège de direction ;

b) Une succursale ;

c) Un bureau ;

d) Une usine ;

e) Un atelier ;

f) Un point de vente ; et

g) Une mine, un puits de pétrole ou de gaz, une carrière ou tout autre lieu lié à l'extraction de ressources naturelles.

3. L'expression « établissement stable » comprend également un chantier de construction, un projet de construction, de montage ou d'installation ou des activités de supervision en rapport avec celui-ci, mais seulement lorsque ce chantier, ce projet ou ces activités durent plus de six mois.

4. Nonobstant les dispositions précédentes du présent article, il est considéré qu'un « établissement stable » ne comprend pas :

a) L'utilisation d'installations aux seules fins de stockage, d'exposition ou de livraison de biens ou de marchandises appartenant à l'entreprise ;

b) L'exploitation d'un stock de biens ou de marchandises appartenant à l'entreprise aux seules fins de stockage, d'exposition ou de livraison ;

c) L'exploitation d'un stock de biens ou de marchandises appartenant à l'entreprise aux seules fins de transformation par une autre entreprise ;

d) L'exploitation d'une installation fixe d'affaires aux seules fins d'acheter des biens ou des marchandises ou de réunir des renseignements pour l'entreprise ;

e) L'exploitation d'une installation fixe d'affaires aux seules fins d'exercer, pour l'entreprise, toute autre activité de caractère préparatoire ou auxiliaire ;

f) L'exploitation d'une installation fixe d'affaires aux seules fins de l'exercice cumulé d'activités mentionnées aux alinéas a) à e), à condition que l'activité d'ensemble de l'installation fixe d'affaires résultant de ce cumul garde un caractère préparatoire ou auxiliaire.

5. Nonobstant les dispositions des paragraphes 1 et 2, lorsqu'une personne, autre qu'un agent jouissant d'un statut indépendant auquel s'applique le paragraphe 7, agit dans un État contractant pour le compte d'une entreprise de l'autre État contractant, cette entreprise est réputée avoir un établissement stable dans le premier État contractant à l'égard des activités que cette personne exerce pour l'entreprise si cette personne dispose dans cet État de pouvoirs qu'elle y exerce habituellement lui permettant de conclure des contrats au nom de l'entreprise, à moins que les activités de cette personne ne soient limitées à celles visées au paragraphe 4, lesquelles, si elles étaient exercées par l'intermédiaire d'une installation fixe d'affaires, ne permettraient pas de considérer cette installation fixe d'affaires comme un établissement stable selon les dispositions de ce paragraphe.

6. Nonobstant les dispositions précédentes du présent article, une société d'assurances d'un État contractant est, sauf en matière de réassurance, considérée comme ayant un établissement stable dans l'autre État contractant si elle assure contre des risques dans le territoire de cet autre État par l'intermédiaire d'une personne autre qu'un agent jouissant d'un statut indépendant auquel s'applique le paragraphe 7.

7. Une entreprise d'un État contractant n'est pas considérée comme ayant un établissement stable dans l'autre État contractant du seul fait qu'elle y exerce son activité par l'entremise d'un courtier, d'un commissionnaire général ou de tout autre agent jouissant d'un statut indépendant, à condition que ces personnes agissent dans le cadre ordinaire de leur activité. Toutefois, lorsqu'il agit totalement ou presque totalement pour le compte de cette entreprise, et si l'entreprise et l'agent sont, dans leurs relations commerciales et financières, liés par des conditions établies ou imposées différentes de celles qui auraient été établies entre des entreprises indépendantes, cet agent n'est pas considéré comme un agent indépendant au sens du présent paragraphe.

8. Le fait qu'une société qui est un résident d'un État contractant contrôle ou est contrôlée par une société qui est un résident de l'autre État contractant ou qui y exerce son activité (que ce soit par l'intermédiaire d'un établissement stable ou non) ne suffit pas, en lui-même, à faire de l'une quelconque de ces sociétés un établissement stable de l'autre.

CHAPITRE III. IMPOSITION DES REVENUS

Article 6. Revenus immobiliers

1. Les revenus qu'un résident d'un État contractant tire de biens immobiliers (y compris les revenus des exploitations agricoles ou forestières) situés dans l'autre État contractant sont imposables dans cet autre État.

2. L'expression « biens immobiliers » a le sens que lui attribue le droit de l'État contractant où les biens considérés sont situés. En tout état de cause, cette expression comprend les biens accessoires ainsi que les biens immobiliers, le cheptel et le matériel utilisé dans les exploitations agricoles et forestières, les droits auxquels s'appliquent les dispositions du droit privé concernant la propriété foncière, l'usufruit des biens immobiliers et les droits à des paiements variables ou fixes pour l'exploitation ou la concession de l'exploitation de gisements minéraux, sources et autres ressources naturelles ; les navires, bateaux et aéronefs ne sont pas considérés comme des biens immobiliers.

3. Les dispositions du paragraphe 1 s'appliquent aux revenus provenant de l'exploitation directe, de la location ou de toute autre forme d'exploitation de biens immobiliers.

4. Les dispositions des paragraphes 1 et 3 s'appliquent également aux revenus provenant des biens immobiliers d'une entreprise ainsi qu'aux revenus des biens immobiliers servant à l'exercice d'une profession indépendante.

Article 7. Bénéfices des entreprises

1. Les bénéfices d'une entreprise d'un État contractant ne sont imposables que dans cet État, sauf si l'entreprise exerce son activité dans l'autre État contractant par l'intermédiaire d'un établissement stable qui y est situé. Si l'entreprise exerce son activité d'une telle façon, ses bénéfices sont imposables dans l'autre État, mais uniquement dans la mesure où ils sont imputables à cet établissement stable.

2. Sous réserve des dispositions du paragraphe 3, lorsqu'une entreprise d'un État contractant exerce son activité dans l'autre État contractant par l'intermédiaire d'un établissement stable qui y est situé, il est imputé, dans chaque État contractant, à cet établissement stable les bénéfices qu'il aurait pu réaliser s'il avait constitué une entreprise distincte exerçant des activités identiques ou analogues dans des conditions identiques ou analogues et traitant en toute indépendance avec l'entreprise dont il constitue un établissement stable.

3. a) Pour déterminer les bénéfices d'un établissement stable, sont admises en déduction les dépenses relatives aux fins poursuivies par cet établissement stable, incluant uniquement les dépenses de direction et les frais généraux d'administration ainsi enregistrés, soit dans l'État où est situé cet établissement stable, soit ailleurs.

   b) Toutefois, aucune déduction n'est admise pour les sommes qui seraient, le cas échéant, versées (à d'autres titres que le remboursement des frais) par l'établissement stable au siège central de l'entreprise ou à l'un quelconque de ses bureaux, sous forme de redevances, honoraires ou autres paiements similaires, pour l'usage de brevets ou d'autres droits, ou sous forme de commission pour des services précis fournis ou pour une activité de direction ou, sauf dans le cas d'une entreprise bancaire, sous forme d'intérêts sur des sommes prêtées à l'établissement stable. De même, il n'est pas tenu compte, dans le calcul des bénéfices d'un établissement stable, des sommes (à d'autres titres que le remboursement des frais) portées par l'établissement stable au débit du siège central de l'entreprise ou de l'un quelconque de ses autres bureaux, sous forme de redevances, honoraires ou autres paiements similaires, pour l'usage de brevets ou d'autres droits, ou sous forme de commission pour des services précis fournis ou pour une activité de direction ou, sauf dans le cas d'une entreprise bancaire, sous forme d'intérêts sur des sommes prêtées au siège central de l'entreprise ou à l'un quelconque de ses autres bureaux.

4. S'il est d'usage, dans un État contractant, de déterminer les bénéfices imputables à un établissement stable sur la base d'une répartition des bénéfices totaux de l'entreprise entre ses diverses composantes, aucune disposition du paragraphe 2 n'empêche cet État contractant de déterminer les bénéfices imposables selon la répartition en usage ; la méthode de répartition adoptée doit cependant être telle que le résultat obtenu soit conforme aux principes énoncés dans le présent article.

5. Aucun bénéfice n'est imputé à un établissement stable du fait qu'il a simplement acheté des biens ou des marchandises pour l'entreprise.

6. Aux fins des paragraphes précédents, les bénéfices à imputer à l'établissement stable sont déterminés chaque année selon la même méthode, sauf s'il existe des motifs valables et suffisants de procéder autrement.

7. Lorsque les bénéfices comprennent des éléments de revenu ou des gains traités séparément dans d'autres articles de la présente Convention, les dispositions de ces articles ne sont pas affectées par les dispositions du présent article.

Article 8. Navigation maritime et aérienne

1. Les bénéfices d'une entreprise d'un État contractant qui proviennent de l'exploitation ou de la location, en trafic international, de navires ou d'aéronefs ne sont imposables que dans cet État.

2. Si le siège de direction effective d'une entreprise de transport maritime se trouve à bord d'un navire, il est considéré comme étant situé dans l'État contractant du port d'attache de ce navire ou, à défaut de port d'attache, dans l'État contractant dont l'exploitant du navire est un résident.

3. Les dispositions du paragraphe 1 s'appliquent également aux bénéfices provenant de la participation à un consortium, à une coentreprise ou à un organisme international d'exploitation.

Article 9. Entreprises associées

1. Lorsque :

a) Une entreprise d'un État contractant participe directement ou indirectement à la direction, au contrôle ou au capital d'une entreprise de l'autre État contractant ; ou que

b) Les mêmes personnes participent directement ou indirectement à la direction, au contrôle ou au capital d'une entreprise d'un État contractant et d'une entreprise de l'autre État contractant ;

et que, dans l'un et l'autre cas, les deux entreprises sont, dans leurs relations commerciales ou financières, liées par des conditions convenues ou imposées, qui diffèrent de celles qui seraient convenues entre des entreprises indépendantes, les bénéfices qui, sans ces conditions, auraient été réalisés par l'une des entreprises mais n'ont pu l'être du fait de ces conditions, peuvent être inclus dans les bénéfices de cette entreprise et imposés en conséquence.

2. Lorsqu'un État contractant inclut dans les bénéfices d'une entreprise de cet État, et impose en conséquence des bénéfices sur lesquels une entreprise de l'autre État contractant a été imposée dans cet autre État, et que les bénéfices ainsi inclus sont des bénéfices qui auraient été réalisés par l'entreprise du premier État si les conditions convenues entre les deux entreprises avaient été celles qui auraient été convenues entre des entreprises indépendantes, alors cet autre État procède à un ajustement approprié du montant de l'impôt qui y a été perçu sur ces bénéfices. Pour déterminer cet ajustement, il est tenu compte des autres dispositions de la Convention et, le cas échéant, les autorités compétentes des États contractants se consultent.

Article 10. Dividendes

1. Les dividendes payés par une société qui est un résident d'un État contractant à un résident de l'autre État contractant sont imposables dans cet autre État.

2. Toutefois, ces dividendes sont également imposables dans l'État contractant dont la société qui paie les dividendes est un résident et selon la législation de cet État, mais si le bénéficiaire effectif des dividendes est un résident de l'autre État contractant, l'impôt ainsi établi ne peut excéder :

a) 5 % du montant brut des dividendes si le bénéficiaire effectif est une société (autre qu'une société de personnes) qui détient directement au moins 25 % du capital de la société qui paie les dividendes ;

b) 10 % du montant brut des dividendes dans tous les autres cas.

Le présent paragraphe n'affecte pas l'imposition de la société au titre des bénéfices qui servent au paiement des dividendes.

3. Le terme « dividendes » employé dans le présent article désigne les revenus provenant d'actions, actions ou bons de jouissance, parts de mine, parts de fondateur ou autres parts bénéficiaires, à l'exception des créances, ainsi que les revenus d'autres parts sociales soumis au même régime fiscal que les revenus d'actions par la législation de l'État dont la société distributrice est résidente.

4. Les dispositions des paragraphes 1 et 2 ne s'appliquent pas lorsque le bénéficiaire effectif des dividendes, résident d'un État contractant, exerce dans l'autre État contractant dont la société qui paie les dividendes est un résident, soit une activité industrielle ou commerciale par l'intermédiaire d'un établissement stable qui y est situé, soit une profession indépendante au moyen d'une base fixe qui y est située, et que la participation génératrice des dividendes se rattache effectivement à cet établissement stable ou à cette base fixe. Dans ces cas, les dispositions de l'article 7 ou de l'article 14, suivant le cas, sont applicables.

5. Lorsqu'une société qui est un résident d'un des États contractants tire des bénéfices ou des revenus de l'autre État contractant, cet autre État ne peut percevoir aucun impôt sur les dividendes payés par la société, sauf dans la mesure où ces dividendes sont payés à un résident de cet autre État ou dans la mesure où la participation génératrice des dividendes se rattache effectivement à un établissement stable situé dans cet autre État, ni prélever aucun impôt, au titre de l'imposition des

bénéfices non distribués de la société, sur les bénéfices non distribués de la société, même si les dividendes payés ou les bénéfices non distribués consistent en tout ou en partie en bénéfices ou en revenus provenant de cet autre État.

Article 11. Intérêts

1. Les intérêts provenant d'un État contractant et payés à un résident de l'autre État contractant sont imposables dans cet autre État.

2. Toutefois, ces intérêts sont aussi imposables dans l'État contractant d'où ils proviennent et selon la législation de cet État, mais si le bénéficiaire effectif des intérêts est un résident de l'autre État contractant, l'impôt ainsi établi ne peut excéder 10 % du montant brut des intérêts.

3. Nonobstant les dispositions du paragraphe 2, les intérêts provenant d'un État contractant et payés à un résident de l'autre État contractant ne sont imposables que dans l'autre État contractant si ce destinataire est le bénéficiaire effectif de ces intérêts et que ceux-ci sont payés :

a) Dans le cas de l'Irlande :

i) À la Banque centrale d'Irlande ;

ii) À l'Agence nationale de gestion du Trésor ;

iii) Au Fonds national de réserve pour les retraites ; et

iv) À un organisme officiel ou à toute institution détenue en totalité par le Gouvernement de l'Irlande et dont il peut être convenu à tout moment entre les autorités compétentes des États contractants ; et

b) Dans le cas du Pakistan :

i) À la Banque d'État du Pakistan ; et

ii) À un organisme officiel ou à toute institution détenue en totalité par le Gouvernement du Pakistan et dont il peut être convenu à tout moment entre les autorités compétentes des États contractants.

4. Le terme « intérêts » employé dans le présent article désigne les revenus des créances de toute nature, assorties ou non de garanties hypothécaires ou d'une clause de participation aux bénéfices du débiteur, et notamment les revenus des fonds publics et des obligations d'emprunts, y compris les primes et lots attachés à ces titres. Les pénalités pour paiement tardif ne sont pas considérées comme des intérêts au sens du présent article.

5. Les dispositions des paragraphes 1 et 2 ne s'appliquent pas lorsque le bénéficiaire effectif des intérêts, résident d'un État contractant, exerce dans l'autre État contractant d'où proviennent les intérêts, soit une activité industrielle ou commerciale par l'intermédiaire d'un établissement stable qui y est situé, soit une profession indépendante au moyen d'une base fixe qui y est située, et que la créance génératrice des intérêts se rattache effectivement à cet établissement stable ou à cette base fixe. Dans ces cas, les dispositions de l'article 7 ou de l'article 14, suivant le cas, sont applicables.

6. Les intérêts sont considérés comme provenant d'un État contractant lorsque le débiteur est un résident de cet État. Toutefois, lorsque le débiteur des intérêts, qu'il soit ou non résident d'un État contractant, a dans un État contractant un établissement stable ou une base fixe pour lesquels la dette donnant lieu au paiement des intérêts a été contractée et qui supportent la charge de ces intérêts, ceux-ci sont considérés comme provenant de l'État où l'établissement stable, ou la base fixe, est situé.

7. Lorsque, en raison de relations spéciales entre le débiteur et le bénéficiaire effectif ou entre l'un et l'autre et quelque autre personne, le montant des intérêts, compte tenu de la créance pour laquelle ils sont payés, excède celui dont seraient convenus le débiteur et le bénéficiaire effectif en l'absence de pareilles relations, les dispositions du présent article ne s'appliquent qu'à ce dernier montant. Dans ce cas, la partie excédentaire des paiements reste imposable selon la législation de chaque État contractant et compte tenu des autres dispositions de la présente Convention.

Article 12. Redevances et honoraires pour services techniques

1. Les redevances ou les honoraires pour services techniques provenant d'un État contractant et payés à un résident de l'autre État contractant sont imposables dans cet autre État.

2. Toutefois, ces redevances ou honoraires pour services techniques sont aussi imposables dans l'État contractant de la source et selon la législation de cet État, mais si le bénéficiaire effectif des redevances ou des honoraires pour services techniques est un résident de l'autre État contractant, l'impôt ainsi établi ne peut excéder 10 % du montant brut des redevances ou des honoraires pour services techniques.

3. a) Le terme « redevances » employé dans le présent article désigne les rémunérations de toute nature payées pour l'usage ou la concession de l'usage d'un droit d'auteur sur une œuvre littéraire, artistique ou scientifique, y compris les films cinématographiques ou les films ou bandes utilisés pour les émissions radiophoniques ou télévisées, d'un brevet, d'une marque de fabrique ou de commerce, d'un dessin ou d'un modèle, d'un plan, d'une formule ou d'un procédé secrets et pour des informations ayant trait à une expérience acquise dans le domaine industriel, commercial ou scientifique.

b) L'expression « paiements reçus au titre de services techniques » désigne les rémunérations de toute nature perçues en contrepartie de services de gestion, techniques ou consultatifs, y compris la prestation de services de personnel technique ou autre, mais ne comprend pas les rémunérations reçues au titre des services mentionnés aux articles 14 et 15 de la présente Convention.

4. Les dispositions des paragraphes 1 et 2 ne s'appliquent pas lorsque le bénéficiaire effectif des redevances ou des honoraires pour services techniques, résident d'un État contractant, exerce dans l'autre État contractant source des redevances, soit une activité industrielle ou commerciale par l'intermédiaire d'un établissement stable qui y est situé, soit une profession indépendante à partir d'une base fixe qui y est située, et que le droit ou le bien générateur des redevances ou des honoraires pour services techniques se rattache effectivement à cet établissement stable ou à cette base fixe. Dans ces cas, les dispositions de l'article 7 ou de l'article 14, suivant le cas, sont applicables.

5. Les redevances ou les honoraires pour services techniques sont considérés comme provenant d'un État contractant lorsque le débiteur est un résident de cet État. Toutefois, lorsque le débiteur des redevances ou des honoraires pour services techniques, qu'il soit ou non résident d'un État contractant, a dans un État contractant un établissement stable ou une base fixe pour lesquels l'engagement donnant lieu au paiement des redevances ou des honoraires pour services techniques a été contracté et qui supportent la charge de ces redevances ou honoraires pour services techniques, ceux-ci sont considérés comme provenant de l'État où l'établissement stable, ou la base fixe, est situé.

6. Lorsque, en raison de relations spéciales qui existent entre le débiteur et le bénéficiaire effectif ou que l'un et l'autre entretiennent avec une tierce personne, le montant payé des redevances ou des honoraires pour services techniques, compte tenu de l'utilisation, du droit ou de l'information

pour lesquels ils sont payés, excède celui dont seraient convenus le débiteur et le bénéficiaire effectif en l'absence de pareilles relations, les dispositions du présent article ne s'appliquent qu'à ce dernier montant. Dans ce cas, la partie excédentaire des paiements reste imposable selon la législation de chaque État contractant et compte tenu des autres dispositions de la présente Convention.

Article 13. Gains en capital

1. Les gains qu'un résident d'un État contractant tire de l'aliénation de biens immobiliers visés à l'article 6 et situés dans l'autre État contractant sont imposables dans cet autre État.

2. Les gains issus de l'aliénation d'actions, autres que des actions cotées en bourse, du capital d'une société ou d'un intérêt dans une société de personnes, fiducie ou masse successorale, dont les biens consistent à titre principal, directement ou indirectement, en biens immobiliers situés dans un État contractant sont imposables dans cet État. En particulier :

a) Aucune disposition du présent paragraphe ne s'applique à une société, société de personnes, fiducie ou masse successorale autre qu'une société, société de personnes, fiducie ou masse successorale s'occupant de la gestion de biens immobiliers, dont les biens consistent à titre principal, directement ou indirectement, en biens immobiliers utilisés par lesdites société, société de personnes, fiducie ou masse successorale dans leurs activités industrielles ou commerciales ;

b) Aux fins du présent paragraphe, l'expression « à titre principal » appliqué à la propriété de biens immobiliers désigne la valeur de ces biens immobiliers supérieure à 50 % de la valeur globale de tous les actifs que possède la société, la société de personnes, la fiducie ou la masse successorale.

3. Les gains, autres que ceux visés au paragraphe 2, provenant de l'aliénation de biens mobiliers qui font partie de l'actif d'un établissement stable qu'une entreprise d'un État contractant a dans l'autre État contractant, ou de biens mobiliers qui appartiennent à une base fixe dont un résident d'un État contractant dispose dans l'autre État contractant pour l'exercice d'une profession indépendante, y compris les gains provenant de l'aliénation de cet établissement stable (seul ou avec l'ensemble de l'entreprise), sont imposables dans cet autre État.

4. . Les gains qu'une entreprise d'un État contractant tire de l'aliénation de navires ou d'aéronefs exploités en trafic international ou de biens mobiliers affectés à l'exploitation desdits navires ou aéronefs sont imposables exclusivement dans cet État.

5. Les gains provenant de l'aliénation de tous biens autres que ceux visés aux paragraphes 1 à 4 ne sont imposables que dans l'État contractant dont le cédant est un résident.

Article 14. Professions indépendantes

1. Les revenus qu'un résident d'un État contractant tire d'une profession libérale ou d'autres activités de caractère indépendant ne sont imposables que dans cet État, sauf dans les circonstances énoncées ci-après, auquel cas ces revenus sont également imposables dans l'autre État contractant :

a) Si ce résident dispose de façon habituelle, dans l'autre État contractant, d'une base fixe pour l'exercice de ses activités ; dans ce cas, seule la fraction des revenus qui est imputable à cette installation fixe est imposable dans cet autre État contractant ; ou

b) Si ce résident séjourne dans l'autre État contractant pendant une période ou plusieurs périodes d'une durée totale égale ou supérieure à 183 jours au cours de l'année fiscale concernée ; dans ce cas, seule la fraction des revenus qui est tirée des activités exercées dans cet autre État est imposable dans cet autre État.

2. L'expression « profession libérale » se rapporte notamment aux activités indépendantes d'ordre scientifique, littéraire, artistique, éducatif ou pédagogique, ainsi qu'aux activités indépendantes des médecins, avocats, ingénieurs, architectes, dentistes et comptables.

Article 15. Professions dépendantes

1. Sous réserve des dispositions des articles 14, 16, 18 et 19, les salaires, traitements et autres rémunérations similaires qu'un résident d'un État contractant reçoit au titre d'un emploi salarié ne sont imposables que dans cet État, à moins que l'emploi ne soit exercé dans l'autre État contractant. Si l'emploi y est exercé, les rémunérations reçues à ce titre sont imposables dans cet autre État.

2. Nonobstant les dispositions du paragraphe 1, les rémunérations qu'un résident d'un État contractant reçoit au titre d'un emploi salarié exercé dans l'autre État contractant ne sont imposables que dans le premier État si :

a) Le bénéficiaire séjourne dans l'autre État pendant une période ou plusieurs périodes n'excédant pas 183 jours au total au cours de toute période de 12 mois commençant ou se terminant au cours de l'exercice fiscal considéré ; et

b) Les rémunérations sont payées par un employeur ou pour le compte d'un employeur qui n'est pas résident de l'autre État ; et

c) La charge des rémunérations n'est pas supportée par un établissement stable ou une base fixe que l'employeur a dans l'autre État.

3. Nonobstant les dispositions précédentes du présent article, les rémunérations perçues au titre d'un emploi salarié exercé à bord d'un navire ou d'un aéronef exploité en trafic international par une entreprise d'un État contractant sont imposables dans cet État contractant.

Article 16. Tantièmes

Les tantièmes et les autres rétributions analogues qu'un résident d'un État contractant perçoit en sa qualité de membre du conseil d'administration d'une société qui est un résident de l'autre État contractant sont imposables dans cet autre État.

Article 17. Artistes et athlètes

1. Nonobstant les dispositions des articles 7, 14 et 15, les revenus qu'un résident d'un État contractant tire de ses activités personnelles exercées dans l'autre État contractant en tant qu'artiste du spectacle, tel qu'un artiste de théâtre, de cinéma, de la radio ou de la télévision, ou un musicien, ou en tant qu'athlète, sont imposables dans cet autre État.

2. Lorsque les revenus d'activités qu'un artiste du spectacle ou un athlète exerce personnellement et en cette qualité sont attribués, non pas à l'artiste du spectacle ou à l'athlète lui-même, mais à une autre personne, ces revenus sont, nonobstant les dispositions des articles 7, 14 et 15, imposables dans l'État contractant où les activités de l'artiste du spectacle ou de l'athlète sont exercées.

Article 18. Pensions, rentes et prestations de sécurité sociale

1. Sous réserve des dispositions du paragraphe 2 de l'article 19, les pensions et autres rémunérations analogues payées à un résident d'un État contractant au titre d'un emploi antérieur et les rentes payées à un tel résident au titre d'un emploi antérieur ne sont imposables que dans cet État.

2. Le terme « rente » désigne une somme déterminée payable périodiquement à des dates déterminées, la vie durant ou pendant une période qui est spécifiée ou peut l'être, en vertu d'une obligation d'effectuer des versements en contrepartie d'un capital suffisant intégralement versé en espèces ou en valeurs appréciables en espèces.

3. Nonobstant les dispositions du paragraphe 1, les pensions payées et autres versements effectués au titre d'une caisse publique qui fait partie du régime de sécurité sociale d'un État contractant ou de l'une de ses subdivisions politiques ou de ses collectivités locales ne sont imposables que dans cet État.

Article 19. Fonction publique

1. a) Les salaires, traitements et autres rémunérations similaires payés par un État contractant ou par l'une de ses subdivisions politiques ou collectivités locales à une personne physique, au titre de services fournis à cet État ou à cette subdivision ou collectivité locale dans l'exercice de fonctions de caractère public, ne sont imposables que dans cet État.

   b) Toutefois, ces salaires, traitements et autres rémunérations similaires ne sont imposables que dans l'autre État contractant si les services sont fournis dans cet État et si la personne physique est un résident de cet État qui :

      i) Est un ressortissant de cet État ; ou

      ii) N'est pas devenu un résident de cet État à seule fin de rendre les services en question.

2. a) Nonobstant les dispositions du paragraphe 1, les pensions et autres rémunérations similaires versées par un État contractant, une de ses subdivisions politiques ou une de ses collectivités locales, soit directement soit à partir de fonds qu'ils ont constitués, à une personne physique pour des services fournis à cet État, cette subdivision politique ou cette collectivité locale dans l'accomplissement de fonctions de caractère public ne sont imposables que dans cet État.

   b) Cependant, ces pensions et autres rémunérations similaires ne sont imposables que dans l'autre État contractant si la personne physique est un résident et un ressortissant de cet État.

3. Les dispositions des articles 14, 15, 16, 17 et 18 s'appliquent aux salaires, traitements, pensions et autres rémunérations similaires payés au titre de services fournis dans le cadre d'une activité industrielle ou commerciale exercée par un État contractant ou par l'une de ses subdivisions politiques ou collectivités locales.

Article 20. Études

Article 20. Étudiants

1. Les sommes qu'un étudiant, stagiaire ou apprenti, qui est ou qui était immédiatement avant de se rendre dans un État contractant un résident de l'autre État contractant et qui séjourne dans le premier État à seule fin d'y poursuivre ses études ou sa formation, reçoit pour couvrir ses frais d'entretien, d'études ou de formation ne sont pas imposables dans cet État, à condition qu'elles proviennent de sources situées en dehors de cet État.

2. En ce qui concerne les rémunérations provenant d'un emploi, l'étudiant, le stagiaire ou l'apprenti visé au paragraphe 1 bénéficie en outre, pendant la durée de cet enseignement ou de cette formation, des mêmes exonérations, crédits, dégrèvements ou réductions d'impôts que ceux dont bénéficient les résidents de l'État contractant qu'il visite, à condition que cet emploi soit en rapport direct avec cet enseignement ou cette formation ou qu'il soit exercé pour subvenir à ses besoins pendant la durée de cet enseignement ou de cette formation.

Article 21. Autres revenus

1. Les éléments du revenu d'un résident d'un État contractant, d'où qu'ils proviennent, qui ne sont pas traités dans les articles précédents de la présente Convention ne sont imposables que dans cet État.

2. Les dispositions du paragraphe 1 du présent article ne s'appliquent pas aux revenus autres que les revenus provenant de biens immobiliers, tels qu'ils sont définis au paragraphe 2 de l'article 6, lorsque le bénéficiaire de tels revenus, résident d'un État contractant, exerce dans l'autre État contractant, soit une activité industrielle ou commerciale par l'intermédiaire d'un établissement stable qui y est situé, soit une profession indépendante au moyen d'une base fixe qui y est située, et que le droit ou le bien générateur des revenus se rattache effectivement à cet établissement stable ou à cette base fixe. Dans ces cas, les dispositions de l'article 7 ou de l'article 14, suivant le cas, sont applicables.

3. Nonobstant les dispositions des paragraphes 1 et 2, les éléments du revenu d'un résident d'un État contractant qui ne sont pas traités dans les articles précédents de la présente Convention et qui proviennent de l'autre État contractant sont aussi imposables dans cet autre État conformément à la législation nationale.

Article 22. Activités en mer

1. Les dispositions du présent article s'appliquent nonobstant toute autre disposition de la présente Convention lorsque des activités (dénommées dans le présent article « activités pertinentes ») sont exercées en mer dans le cadre de l'exploration ou de l'exploitation du fond marin, du sous-sol et de leurs ressources naturelles situés dans un État contractant.

2. Une personne qui est un résident d'un État contractant et qui exerce des activités pertinentes dans l'autre État contractant est considérée, sous réserve du paragraphe 3 du présent article, comme exerçant des activités industrielles ou commerciales dans cet autre État par l'intermédiaire d'un établissement stable, ou d'une base fixe, qui y est situé.

3. Les activités pertinentes menées par une entreprise d'un État contractant dans l'autre État contractant pour une période ou plusieurs périodes n'excédant pas un total de 30 jours au cours de toute période de 12 mois ne sont pas considérées comme des activités industrielles ou commerciales

exercées par l'intermédiaire d'un établissement stable, ou d'une base fixe, qui y est situé. Aux fins du présent paragraphe :

a) Lorsqu'un résident d'un État contractant qui exerce des activités pertinentes dans l'autre État contractant est associé à une autre personne y exerçant des activités pertinentes similaires, la première personne est considérée comme exerçant toutes les activités de la deuxième sauf si ces activités sont exercées en même temps que ses propres activités ;

b) Une personne est réputée associée à une autre personne si l'une est directement ou indirectement contrôlée par l'autre, ou si les deux sont directement ou indirectement contrôlées par un ou plusieurs tiers.

4. Les salaires, traitements et rémunérations similaires qu'un résident d'un État contractant reçoit au titre d'un emploi salarié exercé dans le cadre d'activités pertinentes dans l'autre État contractant sont, dans la mesure où l'emploi est exercé en mer dans cet autre État, imposables dans ce dernier.

Chapitre IV. Méthodes pour éliminer les doubles impositions

Article 23. Élimination des doubles impositions

1. Sous réserve des dispositions de la législation irlandaise concernant le crédit déductible de l'impôt irlandais au titre des impôts payés dans un territoire en dehors d'Irlande (qui n'ont aucune incidence sur le principe général ici posé) :

a) L'impôt pakistanais exigible en vertu de la législation pakistanaise et conformément à la présente Convention, directement ou par voie de retenue, sur les bénéfices, les revenus ou les gains provenant de sources situées au Pakistan (à l'exception, en ce qui concerne les dividendes, de l'impôt dû sur les bénéfices qui ont servi au paiement des dividendes) est considéré comme un crédit déductible de tout impôt irlandais, calculé sur les mêmes bénéfices, revenus ou gains sur lesquels l'impôt pakistanais est calculé ;

b) Dans le cas de dividendes versés par une société qui est un résident du Pakistan à une société qui est un résident de l'Irlande et qui contrôle directement ou indirectement au moins 5 % des droits de vote de la société versant les dividendes, il est tenu compte, dans le calcul de la déduction (outre toute déduction de l'impôt pakistanais aux termes des dispositions de l'alinéa a) du présent paragraphe), de l'impôt pakistanais que la société doit payer sur les bénéfices affectés au paiement des dividendes en question.

2. Au Pakistan, les doubles impositions sont éliminées comme suit :

Sous réserve des dispositions de la législation pakistanaise concernant le crédit déductible de l'impôt pakistanais, le montant de l'impôt irlandais dû, en vertu de la législation irlandaise et conformément aux dispositions de la présente Convention, directement ou par voie de déduction, par un résident du Pakistan, à l'égard de revenus de sources situées en Irlande qui ont été assujettis à la fois à l'impôt au Pakistan et en Irlande, est considéré comme un crédit déductible de l'impôt pakistanais dû à l'égard de ces revenus, mais cette déduction ne peut excéder la fraction de l'impôt pakistanais que ces revenus représentent par rapport à l'ensemble des revenus soumis à l'impôt pakistanais.

3. Aux fins des paragraphes 1 et 2, les bénéfices, les revenus et les gains en capital d'un résident d'un État contractant et qui sont imposables dans l'autre État contractant conformément

aux dispositions de la présente Convention sont considérés comme provenant de sources situées dans cet autre État contractant.

4. Si, conformément à une disposition quelconque de la Convention, les revenus perçus par un résident d'un État contractant sont exonérés de l'impôt dans cet État, cet État peut néanmoins, aux fins du calcul du montant de l'impôt à percevoir sur le reste des revenus de ce résident, tenir compte des revenus exonérés.

CHAPITRE V. DISPOSITIONS SPÉCIALES

Article 24. Non-discrimination

1. Les ressortissants d'un État contractant ne sont soumis dans l'autre État contractant à aucune imposition ou obligation correspondante qui est autre ou plus lourde que celles auxquelles sont ou pourraient être assujettis les ressortissants de cet autre État qui se trouvent dans la même situation, notamment en matière de résidence. La présente disposition s'applique aussi, nonobstant les dispositions de l'article premier, aux personnes qui ne sont pas des résidents d'un État contractant ou des deux États contractants.

2. Les apatrides qui sont des résidents d'un État contractant ne sont soumis, dans l'autre État contractant, à aucune imposition ou obligation correspondante qui est autre ou plus lourde que celles auxquelles sont ou pourraient être assujettis les ressortissants de l'État concerné qui se trouvent dans la même situation.

3. L'imposition de l'établissement stable qu'une entreprise d'un État contractant a dans l'autre État contractant n'est pas établie dans cet autre État d'une façon moins favorable que l'imposition des entreprises de cet autre État qui exercent les mêmes activités. La présente disposition ne peut être interprétée comme obligeant un État contractant à accorder aux résidents de l'autre État contractant les déductions personnelles, abattements et réductions d'impôt en fonction de la situation ou des charges de famille qu'il accorde à ses propres résidents.

4. À moins que les dispositions du paragraphe 1 de l'article 9, du paragraphe 7 de l'article 11 ou du paragraphe 6 de l'article 12 ne soient applicables, les intérêts, redevances, honoraires pour services techniques et autres montants payés par une entreprise d'un État contractant à un résident de l'autre État contractant sont déductibles, pour la détermination des bénéfices imposables de cette entreprise, dans les mêmes conditions que s'ils avaient été versés à un résident du premier État.

5. Les entreprises d'un État contractant dont le capital est en totalité ou en partie, directement ou indirectement, détenu ou contrôlé par un ou plusieurs résidents de l'autre État contractant ne sont soumises dans le premier État à aucune imposition ou obligation correspondante, qui est autre ou plus lourde que celles auxquelles sont ou pourront être assujetties les autres entreprises similaires du premier État.

Article 25. Procédure amiable

1. Lorsqu'une personne estime que les mesures prises par un État contractant ou par les deux États contractants entraînent ou entraîneront pour elle une imposition non conforme aux dispositions de la présente Convention, elle peut, indépendamment des recours prévus par le droit interne de ces États, soumettre son cas à l'autorité compétente de l'État contractant dont elle est un résident ou, si son cas relève du paragraphe 1 de l'article 24, à celle de l'État contractant dont elle possède la

nationalité. Le cas doit être soumis dans les trois ans qui suivent la première notification de la mesure qui entraîne une imposition non conforme aux dispositions de la Convention.

2. L'autorité compétente s'efforce, si la réclamation lui paraît fondée et si elle n'est pas elle-même en mesure d'y apporter une solution satisfaisante, de résoudre le cas par voie d'accord amiable avec l'autorité compétente de l'autre État contractant, en vue d'éviter une imposition non conforme à la Convention. L'accord conclu est appliqué nonobstant les délais prévus par la législation interne de l'État contractant.

3. Les autorités compétentes des États contractants s'efforcent, par voie d'accord amiable, de résoudre les difficultés ou de dissiper les doutes auxquels peuvent donner lieu l'interprétation ou l'application de la Convention. Elles peuvent aussi se concerter en vue d'éliminer les doubles impositions dans les cas non prévus par la Convention.

4. Les autorités compétentes des États contractants peuvent communiquer directement entre elles, y compris au sein d'une commission mixte composée de ces autorités ou de leurs représentants, en vue de parvenir à un accord au sens des paragraphes précédents.

Article 26. Échange de renseignements

1. Les autorités compétentes des États contractants échangent les renseignements vraisemblablement pertinents pour appliquer les dispositions de la présente Convention ou celles de la législation interne relative aux impôts visés par la présente Convention et perçus pour le compte des États contractants, de leurs subdivisions politiques ou de leurs collectivités locales dans la mesure où l'imposition qu'elle prévoit n'est pas contraire à la Convention. L'échange de renseignements n'est pas restreint par les dispositions de l'article premier.

2. Les renseignements reçus par un État contractant au titre du paragraphe 1 sont tenus secrets de la même manière que les renseignements obtenus en application de la législation interne de cet État et ne sont communiqués qu'aux personnes ou autorités (y compris les tribunaux et organes administratifs) concernées par l'établissement ou le recouvrement des impôts visés au paragraphe 1, par les procédures ou poursuites concernant ces impôts, par les décisions sur les recours relatifs à ces impôts, ou par le contrôle de ce qui précède. Ces personnes ou autorités n'utilisent ces renseignements qu'à ces fins. Elles peuvent révéler ces renseignements au cours d'audiences publiques de tribunaux ou dans des jugements.

3. Les dispositions des paragraphes 1 et 2 ne peuvent en aucun cas être interprétées comme imposant à un État contractant l'obligation :

a) De prendre des mesures administratives dérogeant à sa législation et à sa pratique administrative ou à celles de l'autre État contractant ;

b) De fournir des renseignements qui ne pourraient être obtenus sur la base de sa propre législation ou dans le cadre de sa pratique administrative normale ou de celles de l'autre État contractant ;

c) De fournir des renseignements qui révéleraient un secret commercial, industriel, professionnel ou un procédé commercial, ou des renseignements dont la communication serait contraire à l'ordre public.

4. Si des renseignements sont demandés par un État contractant conformément au présent article, l'autre État contractant utilise ses mesures de collecte de renseignements pour obtenir les renseignements demandés, quand bien même il n'aurait pas besoin de ces renseignements à ses propres fins fiscales. L'obligation contenue dans la phrase précédente est soumise aux limitations

prévues au paragraphe 3, mais ces limitations ne peuvent en aucun cas être interprétées comme permettant à un État contractant de refuser de communiquer des renseignements uniquement parce qu'il ne détient aucun intérêt national dans de tels renseignements.

5. Les dispositions du paragraphe 3 ne doivent en aucun cas être interprétées comme autorisant un État contractant à refuser de fournir des renseignements pour la seule raison que les renseignements sont tenus par une banque, une autre institution financière, un mandataire ou une personne agissant en qualité d'agent ou à titre fiduciaire ou parce que cela concerne les intérêts fonciers d'une personne.

Article 27. Membres des missions diplomatiques et des postes consulaires

Aucune disposition de la présente Convention ne porte atteinte aux privilèges fiscaux dont bénéficient les membres des missions diplomatiques ou des postes consulaires en vertu soit des règles générales du droit international, soit des dispositions d'accords particuliers.

CHAPITRE VI. DISPOSITIONS FINALES

Article 28. Entrée en vigueur

1. Chacun des États contractants notifie à l'autre l'accomplissement des procédures requises par leur législation pour l'entrée en vigueur de la présente Convention.

2. La présente Convention entre en vigueur à la date de réception de la dernière de ces notifications et est applicable :

a) Dans le cas de l'Irlande :

i) En ce qui concerne l'impôt sur le revenu, la charge sociale universelle et l'impôt sur les gains en capital, pour tout exercice d'imposition commençant à partir du 1er janvier de l'année civile suivant la date à laquelle la présente Convention entre en vigueur ;

ii) En ce qui concerne l'impôt sur les sociétés, pour tout exercice financier commençant à partir du 1er janvier de l'année civile suivant la date à laquelle la présente Convention entre en vigueur ;

b) Dans le cas du Pakistan :

i) En ce qui concerne les impôts retenus à la source, aux montants versés ou crédités à partir du 1er juillet suivant la date à laquelle la présente Convention entre en vigueur ; et

ii) En ce qui concerne les autres impôts, aux années d'imposition commençant à partir du 1er juillet suivant la date à laquelle la présente Convention entre en vigueur.

3. La Convention entre le Gouvernement de l'Irlande et le Gouvernement de la République islamique du Pakistan tendant à éviter la double imposition et à prévenir l'évasion fiscale en matière d'impôts sur le revenu, signée à Paris le 13 avril 1973 (ci-après dénommée « la Convention de 1973 ») cesse de produire ses effets aux dates auxquelles la présente Convention entre en vigueur conformément au paragraphe 2 du présent article.

4. Nonobstant le paragraphe 3, dans le cas où une disposition de la Convention de 1973 aurait accordé une exonération d'impôt supérieure à celle qui est due en vertu de la présente Convention, ladite disposition continue à produire ses effets pour :

a) Une période de 12 mois ; et

b) Sous réserve du paragraphe 5, dans le cas des paragraphes 1 et 2 de l'article XV de la Convention de 1973, pour une période de cinq ans ;

à compter de la date à laquelle les dispositions de la présente Convention auraient autrement pris effet conformément aux dispositions du paragraphe 2 du présent article.

5. Aux fins de l'application du sous-alinéa i) de l'alinéa b) du paragraphe 2 de l'article XV de la Convention de 1973, les dispositions des clauses (126D), (126E) et (133) de la première partie de la deuxième annexe de l'ordonnance de 2001 relative à l'impôt sur le revenu s'appliquent à la place des dispositions énumérées dans cet alinéa.

Article 29. Dénonciation

1. La présente Convention demeure en vigueur tant qu'elle n'a pas été dénoncée par un État contractant. Chaque État contractant peut dénoncer la Convention par la voie diplomatique au moyen d'une notification de dénonciation au moins six mois avant la fin de toute année civile après un délai de cinq ans suivant l'année au cours de laquelle la Convention est entrée en vigueur.

Dans ce cas, la Convention cesse d'être applicable :

a) Dans le cas de l'Irlande :

i) En ce qui concerne l'impôt sur le revenu, la charge sociale universelle et l'impôt sur les gains en capital, pour tout exercice d'imposition commençant à partir du 1er janvier suivant la date d'expiration de la période spécifiée dans la notification de dénonciation ;

ii) En ce qui concerne l'impôt sur les sociétés, pour tout exercice financier commençant à partir du 1er janvier suivant la date d'expiration de la période spécifiée dans la notification de dénonciation ;

b) Dans le cas du Pakistan :

i) En ce qui concerne les impôts retenus à la source, aux montants imposables à partir du 1er janvier de l'année civile suivant celle au cours de laquelle la notification de dénonciation est donnée ; et

ii) En ce qui concerne les autres impôts, à l'année d'imposition commençant à partir du 1er juillet de l'année civile suivant celle au cours de laquelle la notification de dénonciation est donnée.

EN FOI DE QUOI, les soussignés, à ce dûment autorisés, ont signé la présente Convention.

FAIT à Dublin, le 16 avril 2015, en deux exemplaires en langue anglaise.

Pour le Gouvernement de l'Irlande :

[SIMON HARRIS]

Pour le Gouvernement de la République islamique du Pakistan :

[SYED RIZWAN AHMED]

PROTOCOLE

Lors de la signature de la présente Convention entre le Gouvernement de l'Irlande et le Gouvernement de la République islamique du Pakistan tendant à éviter les doubles impositions et à prévenir la fraude fiscale en matière d'impôts sur le revenu, les soussignés sont convenus des dispositions suivantes, qui font partie intégrante de la présente Convention :

1. En ce qui concerne les fonds de retraite agréés en Irlande :

Il est entendu que, compte tenu de l'exonération d'impôt accordée pour les cotisations ou primes versées au titre de régimes de retraite, de contrats de rente de retraite ou d'autres produits de retraite, et de l'exonération d'impôt des revenus et gains revenant à un fonds (dénommé dans le présent paragraphe « fonds de pension ») créé par ces cotisations ou primes, les distributions d'un fonds de pension agréé en Irlande qui a été créé par le transfert de droits accumulés ou d'actifs d'un fonds de pension ne sont imposables qu'en Irlande, nonobstant toute disposition de la présente Convention.

2. En ce qui concerne l'article 4 :

Il est entendu qu'un Fonds commun contractuel (Common Contractual Fund - CCF) créé en Irlande ne peut être considéré comme un résident de l'Irlande et doit être traité comme fiscalement transparent aux fins de l'octroi des avantages découlant d'un traité fiscal.

3. En ce qui concerne le paragraphe 5 de l'article 13 :

Lorsque :

a) Une personne physique domiciliée en Irlande cesse d'être un résident en Irlande ;

b) Cède des biens acquis avant le premier jour de l'année civile au cours de laquelle elle a cessé de résider en Irlande, comme mentionné à l'alinéa a) ci-dessus ; et

c) Redevient ensuite un résident de l'Irlande dans les cinq ans qui suivent la cessation de cette résidence ;

les dispositions du paragraphe 5 n'affectent pas le droit de l'Irlande d'imposer la personne physique selon sa législation en fonction de cette cession, mais le montant de l'impôt prélevé ne peut excéder le montant de l'impôt qui serait prélevé sur le montant de tout gain provenant d'une cession réputée par la personne physique de ce bien à la valeur marchande le jour précédant immédiatement le premier jour de l'année civile au cours de laquelle elle a cessé d'être un résident de l'Irlande, comme mentionné à l'alinéa a) ci-dessus.

Toutefois, si, après la date de signature de la présente Convention, la législation pakistanaise est modifiée de façon à inclure un impôt sur les gains en capital, le Pakistan peut informer l'autorité compétente irlandaise de cette évolution et, si le Pakistan en fait la demande, l'Irlande entame immédiatement des négociations pour examiner la pertinence, à la lumière de cette évolution, des dispositions du paragraphe précédent en vue de les modifier ou de les abroger le cas échéant.

FAIT à Dublin, le 16 avril 2015, en deux exemplaires en langue anglaise.

Pour le Gouvernement de l'Irlande :
[SIMON HARRIS]

Pour le Gouvernement de la République islamique du Pakistan :
[SYED RIZWAN AHMED]

No. 54754

Ireland
and
Canada

Audiovisual Co-Production Treaty between the Government of Ireland and the Government of Canada. Ottawa, 4 February 2016

Entry into force: *1 July 2016, in accordance with article 15*

Authentic texts: *English and French*

Registration with the Secretariat of the United Nations: *Ireland, 1 November 2017*

Irlande
et
Canada

Traité de co-production audiovisuelle entre le Gouvernement de l'Irlande et le Gouvernement du Canada. Ottawa, 4 février 2016

Entrée en vigueur : *1er juillet 2016, conformément à l'article 15*

Textes authentiques : *anglais et français*

Enregistrement au Secrétariat de l'Organisation des Nations Unies : *Irlande, 1er novembre 2017*

[TEXT IN ENGLISH – TEXTE EN ANGLAIS]

AUDIOVISUAL CO-PRODUCTION TREATY

BETWEEN

THE GOVERNMENT OF IRELAND

AND

THE GOVERNMENT OF CANADA

THE GOVERNMENT OF IRELAND AND THE GOVERNMENT OF CANADA (the "Parties"),

RECOGNISING that quality audiovisual treaty co-productions contribute to the vitality of the audiovisual industries of the Parties and to the development of their economic and cultural exchanges;

APPRECIATING that cultural diversity is nurtured by constant exchanges and interaction between cultures and that it is strengthened by the free flow of ideas;

CONSIDERING that, in pursuit of international cooperation, the UNESCO *Convention on the Protection and Promotion of the Diversity of Cultural Expressions*, done at Paris on 20 October, 2005, encourages audiovisual co-production treaties as a means of promoting international cooperation;

AGREEING that these exchanges may enhance the relations between the Parties;

RECOGNISING that these objectives may be achieved by granting, insofar as possible, domestic benefits to qualified audiovisual treaty co-productions;

HAVE AGREED as follows:

ARTICLE 1

Definitions

For the purpose of this Treaty:

(a) "audiovisual" means a film, television, and/or video work on any production support known or not yet known for any distribution platform intended for viewing;

(b) "competent authority" means for each Party, the authority which has the overall responsibility for the implementation of this Treaty;

(c) "administrative authority" means for each Party, the designated authority which administers this Treaty;

(d) "national" means a natural or legal person as defined by the law of the respective States and which, under that law, has the right to benefit from the application of this Treaty;

in the case of Ireland, "national" also includes:

(i) a national of a Member State of the European Union; or

(ii) a national of another Contracting Party to the *Agreement on the European Economic Area* of 2 May, 1992;

and "Irish", in this context, shall mean any one or more of the same;

(e) "producer" means a national managing the production of a work;

(f) "third-State" means a State which has a co-production treaty or memorandum of understanding with at least one of the Parties;

(g) "non-party" means a State which does not have a co-production treaty or memorandum of understanding with either Party;

(h) "work" means an audiovisual work to be subsequently recognised as an audiovisual treaty co-production by each Party and includes every version of that work;

(i) "Canadian elements" means expenditures made in Canada by the Canadian producer or expenditures on Canadian creative and technical personnel made in another State or States by the Canadian producer, in the course of the production of a work;

(j) "Irish elements" means expenditures made in Ireland by the Irish producer or expenditures on Irish creative and technical personnel made in another State or States by the Irish producer, in the course of the production of a work.

ARTICLE 2

General Conditions

1. Each Party shall consider every work as if it were its own production in establishing whether that work is entitled to the same benefits as that Party's own audiovisual industry.

2. Each Party shall grant the benefits referred to in paragraph 1 to the producers of a work who are its own nationals.

3. Each Party shall strive to achieve overall balance of the financing of works co-produced over a period of five years.

4. Each Party shall ensure that its producer fulfills, at a minimum, the requirements set out in articles 3 to 5 for a work to be considered eligible for the benefits of this Treaty.

5. The provisions relevant to the administration of this Treaty will be set out in the Annex.

ARTICLE 3

Participating Producers

1. To be eligible under this Treaty, a work shall be jointly produced by producers of both Parties.

2. In addition to producers of Canada and Ireland, third-State producers may also participate in a work.

ARTICLE 4

Proportionality

1. The share of work expenditures spent on Canadian elements shall be in reasonable proportion to the Canadian financial participation.

2. The share of work expenditures spent on Irish elements shall be in reasonable proportion to the Irish financial participation.

3. The Parties, through the mutual written consent of their administrative authorities, may recommend exemptions from paragraphs 1 and 2, notably for storyline and creative purposes.

ARTICLE 5

Nationality of Participants

1. Every participant in a work shall be a national of one of the Parties save as otherwise specifically provided in the Annex to this Treaty.

2. The Parties, through the mutual written consent of their administrative authorities, may in addition to the provisions of the Annex to this Treaty recommend exemptions from paragraph 1, notably to allow third-State nationals or non-party nationals to participate in a work for storyline, creative, or production purposes.

ARTICLE 6

Temporary Entry and Residence

Subject to their respective laws and regulations, each Party shall facilitate the following:

(a) the temporary entry into and residence in their respective territories of the creative and technical personnel engaged by the producer of the other Party for the purpose of the work;

(b) the temporary entry and re-export of any equipment necessary for the purpose of the work.

ARTICLE 7

Copyright and Revenues

The Parties, through their administrative authorities, shall ensure that the sharing of copyright and revenues is, in principle, proportional to their producer's financial contribution, and no lesser than the minimum financial contribution identified in the Annex.

ARTICLE 8

Distribution

1. Each Party, through its administrative authority, shall ensure that its producer demonstrates the existence of a distribution or broadcasting commitment for the work in the territories of each Party and, if third-State producers are involved in the work, in the territory of each of their respective States.

2. The Parties, through the mutual written consent of their administrative authorities, may accept an alternative distribution commitment in lieu of the commitment described in paragraph 1.

ARTICLE 9

Material Changes

Each Party shall ensure that its producer promptly advises its administrative authority of any material change to a work that may affect its qualification for benefits under this Treaty.

ARTICLE 10

Communication

1. Each Party, through its competent authority, shall promptly notify the other of any amendment or judicial interpretation of domestic law that may affect benefits available under this Treaty.

2. Each Party, through its administrative authority, shall collect and share statistical information on the performance, distribution or exhibition, on its territory, of the work receiving benefits under this Treaty.

ARTICLE 11

Annex

1. The Annex to this Treaty is for administrative purposes and is not legally binding.

2. The Annex may be modified by the Parties, through the mutual written consent of their competent authorities, provided that these modifications do not conflict with this Treaty.

ARTICLE 12

Meetings and Amendments

1. Meetings will be held as needed between representatives of the competent authority of each Party to discuss and review the terms of this Treaty.

2. The Parties may amend this Treaty by mutual written consent. Each Party shall notify the other Party in writing of the completion of the domestic procedures required for the entry into force of the amendments. The amendments shall enter into force on the first day of the first month following the date of the second of these notifications.

ARTICLE 13

Transitional Provisions

1. A Party shall not discontinue benefits granted for a work for a period of two years following termination of this Treaty, solely due to that termination.

2. This Treaty replaces the *Agreement on Film and Video Relations between the Government of Canada and the Government of Ireland*, done at Dublin on 4 April 1989 (the "1989 Agreement"). A Party may continue to confer benefits pursuant to the 1989 Agreement in relation to a work which qualified for benefits under that earlier treaty, provided that:

(a) the producer of the work, which qualified under the 1989 Agreement, notifies each administrative authority, in writing, that it elects to continue receiving such benefits under that earlier treaty; and

(b) the election is made within six months of the date of the entry into force of this Treaty.

ARTICLE 14

Settlement of Disputes

The Parties shall endeavor to resolve, by mutual consent, any dispute regarding the interpretation or application of this Treaty. They shall do so through consultations.

ARTICLE 15

Entry into Force

1. Each Party shall notify the other Party in writing of the completion of its internal procedures required for the entry into force of this Treaty. This Treaty shall enter into force on the first day of the first month following the date of the second notification of the completion of the procedures required for the entry into force.

2. This Treaty shall remain in force for a period of five years from the date of entry into force.

3. This Treaty shall renew automatically at the end of five years from the date of entry into force and at the end of every subsequent five-year period.

4. A Party wishing to terminate this Treaty shall give written notice of termination to the other Party at least six months before the end of the fifth year following entry into force or, if this Treaty is renewed, at least six months before the end of any subsequent five-year period.

IN WITNESS WHEREOF, the undersigned, being duly authorised by their respective Government, have signed this Treaty.

DONE at Ottawa on the 4th day of February 2016, in duplicate, in the English and French languages, each version being equally authentic.

FOR THE GOVERNMENT OF IRELAND	**FOR THE GOVERNMENT OF CANADA**

[TEXT IN FRENCH – TEXTE EN FRANÇAIS]

TRAITÉ DE CO-PRODUCTION AUDIOVISUELLE

ENTRE

LE GOUVERNEMENT DE L'IRLANDE

ET

LE GOUVERNEMENT DU CANADA

LE GOUVERNEMENT DE L'IRLANDE ET LE GOUVERNEMENT DU CANADA (les « Parties »),

RECONNAISSANT que les co-productions audiovisuelles de qualité qui sont régies par un traité favorisent la vitalité des industries audiovisuelles des Parties ainsi que le développement de leurs échanges économiques et culturels;

CONSCIENTS que la diversité culturelle se nourrit d'interactions et d'échanges constants entre les cultures et qu'elle est renforcée par la libre circulation des idées;

CONSIDÉRANT qu'aux fins de la coopération internationale, la *Convention sur la protection et la promotion de la diversité des expressions culturelles* de l'UNESCO, faite à Paris le 20 octobre 2005, encourage la conclusion de traités de co-production audiovisuelle comme moyen de promouvoir la coopération internationale;

CONVENANT que de tels échanges peuvent améliorer les relations entre les Parties;

RECONNAISSANT que les objectifs précités peuvent être atteints par l'octroi, dans la mesure du possible, d'avantages accordés à l'échelle nationale aux co-productions audiovisuelles admissibles qui sont régies par un traité;

SONT CONVENUS de ce qui suit :

ARTICLE PREMIER

Définitions

Aux fins du présent Traité :

a) « audiovisuel » désigne une œuvre cinématographique, télévisuelle et/ou vidéo sur tout support de production existant ou futur, destinée à n'importe quelle plate-forme de distribution à des fins de visionnement;

b) « autorité compétente » désigne, pour chaque Partie, l'autorité chargée de la responsabilité globale de la mise en œuvre du présent Traité;

c) « autorité administrative » désigne, pour chaque Partie, l'autorité désignée qui administre le présent Traité;

d) « ressortissant » désigne toute personne physique ou morale répondant à la définition donnée par le droit respectif des États et qui, en vertu dudit droit, peut bénéficier de l'application du présent Traité;

dans le cas de l'Irlande, « ressortissant » désigne également :

i) un ressortissant d'un État membre de l'Union européenne; ou

ii) un ressortissant d'une autre partie contractante de l'*Accord sur l'Espace économique européen* du 2 mai 1992;

et « irlandais », appliqué dans ce contexte, signifiera ces mêmes personnes;

e) « producteur » désigne un ressortissant qui dirige la production d'une œuvre;

f) « État tiers » désigne un État auquel au moins une des Parties est liée par un traité ou un protocole d'entente en matière de co-production;

g) « non-partie » désigne un État auquel aucune des Parties n'est liée par un traité ou un protocole d'entente en matière de co-production;

h) « œuvre » désigne une œuvre audiovisuelle, y compris toute version de celle-ci, qui est ultérieurement reconnue par chaque Partie comme étant une co-production audiovisuelle régie par un traité;

i) « éléments canadiens » désigne les dépenses faites au Canada par le producteur canadien, ou les dépenses relatives au personnel créatif et technique canadien faites par le producteur canadien dans d'autres États au cours de la production d'une œuvre;

j) « éléments irlandais » désigne les dépenses faites en Irlande par le producteur irlandais, ou les dépenses relatives au personnel créatif et technique irlandais faites par le producteur irlandais dans d'autres États au cours de la production d'une œuvre.

ARTICLE 2

Dispositions générales

1. Chaque Partie traite toute œuvre comme sa propre production lorsqu'il s'agit de déterminer si cette œuvre peut bénéficier des mêmes avantages que ceux offerts à sa propre industrie audiovisuelle.

2. Chaque Partie confère les avantages mentionnés au paragraphe 1 aux producteurs d'une œuvre qui sont ses propres ressortissants.

3. Chaque Partie s'efforce d'atteindre un équilibre global du financement des œuvres co-produites sur une période de cinq années.

4. Chaque Partie veille à ce que son producteur remplisse au minimum les exigences des articles 3 à 5 pour qu'une œuvre puisse être considérée admissible aux avantages prévus par le présent Traité.

5. Les dispositions concernant l'administration du présent Traité seront énoncées dans l'annexe.

ARTICLE 3

Producteurs participants

1. Pour être admissible au titre du présent Traité, l'œuvre doit être produite conjointement par des producteurs des deux Parties.

2. En plus des producteurs du Canada et de l'Irlande, des producteurs d'États tiers peuvent aussi participer à l'œuvre.

ARTICLE 4

Proportionnalité

1. La part des dépenses relatives à l'œuvre qui est consacrée aux éléments canadiens est raisonnablement proportionnelle à la participation financière canadienne.

2. La part des dépenses relatives à l'œuvre qui est consacrée aux éléments irlandais est raisonnablement proportionnelle à la participation financière irlandaise.

3. Les Parties peuvent, moyennant le consentement mutuel écrit de leurs autorités administratives, recommander des exemptions aux paragraphes 1 et 2, notamment aux fins du scénario et du processus créatif.

ARTICLE 5

Nationalité des participants

1. Chaque participant à l'œuvre est un ressortissant de l'une des Parties, sauf disposition contraire expresse de l'annexe du présent Traité.

2. Les Parties peuvent, moyennant le consentement mutuel écrit de leurs autorités administratives et en complément des dispositions de l'annexe du présent Traité, recommander des exemptions au paragraphe 1, notamment afin de permettre aux ressortissants d'États tiers ou de non-parties de participer à une œuvre aux fins du scénario, du processus créatif ou de la production.

ARTICLE 6

Entrée et séjour temporaires

Sous réserve de ses lois et règlements, chaque Partie facilite ce qui suit :

a) l'entrée et le séjour temporaires sur son territoire du personnel créatif et technique engagé par le producteur de l'autre Partie aux fins de la réalisation de l'œuvre;

b) l'entrée temporaire et la réexportation de tout matériel nécessaire à la réalisation de l'œuvre.

ARTICLE 7

Droits d'auteur et recettes

Les Parties veillent, par l'intermédiaire de leurs autorités administratives, à ce que la répartition des droits d'auteur et des recettes soit, en principe, proportionnelle à la contribution financière de leur producteur respectif, et à ce qu'elle ne soit pas inférieure à la contribution financière minimale prévue à l'annexe.

ARTICLE 8

Distribution

1. Chaque Partie veille, par l'intermédiaire de son autorité administrative, à ce que son producteur démontre qu'il détient un engagement de distribution ou de diffusion de l'œuvre sur les territoires de chacune des Parties et, lorsque des producteurs d'États tiers participent à l'œuvre, sur les territoires de chacun de leurs États respectifs.

2. Les Parties peuvent, moyennant le consentement mutuel écrit de leurs autorités administratives, accepter un engagement de distribution autre que celui décrit au paragraphe 1.

ARTICLE 9

Changements importants

Chaque Partie veille à ce que son producteur avise rapidement son autorité administrative de tout changement important apporté à l'œuvre pouvant influer sur l'admissibilité de celle-ci aux avantages prévus par le présent Traité.

ARTICLE 10

Communication

1. Chaque Partie informe rapidement, par l'intermédiaire de son autorité compétente, l'autre Partie de toute modification ou interprétation judiciaire apportée au droit interne pouvant influer sur les avantages prévus par le présent Traité.

2. Chaque Partie veille, par l'intermédiaire de son autorité administrative, à recueillir et à échanger des informations statistiques sur le rendement, la distribution ou la présentation, sur son territoire, de l'œuvre bénéficiant des avantages prévus par le présent Traité.

ARTICLE 11

Annexe

1. L'annexe du présent Traité sert à des fins administratives et n'est pas juridiquement contraignante.

2. Les Parties peuvent, moyennant le consentement mutuel écrit de leurs autorités compétentes, modifier l'annexe, pourvu que les modifications ne contreviennent pas au présent Traité.

ARTICLE 12

Réunions et amendements

1. Des réunions seront tenues, au besoin, entre les représentants de l'autorité compétente de chaque Partie afin de discuter des dispositions du présent Traité et d'examiner celles-ci.

2. Le présent Traité peut être amendé sur consentement mutuel écrit des Parties. Chaque Partie notifie l'autre Partie, par écrit, de l'accomplissement de ses procédures internes nécessaires à l'entrée en vigueur des amendements. Les amendements entrent en vigueur le premier jour du premier mois suivant la date de la deuxième de ces notifications.

ARTICLE 13

Dispositions transitoires

1. Pendant une période de deux ans suivant l'extinction du présent Traité, une Partie ne peut mettre un terme à l'octroi des avantages accordés à une œuvre uniquement en raison de cette extinction.

2. Le présent Traité remplace l'*Accord sur les relations cinématographiques et audiovisuelles entre le gouvernement du Canada et le gouvernement de l'Irlande*, fait à Dublin le 4 avril 1989 (l'« Accord de 1989 »). Une Partie peut continuer d'accorder les avantages conférés par l'Accord de 1989 à une œuvre admise aux avantages de ce dernier, sous réserve de ce qui suit :

a) le producteur de l'œuvre admise aux avantages de l'Accord de 1989 avise par écrit chacune des autorités administratives qu'il choisit de continuer de profiter des avantages prévus en vertu de ce traité antérieur;

b) le choix précité est fait dans les six mois suivant la date d'entrée en vigueur du présent Traité.

ARTICLE 14

Règlement des différends

Les Parties s'efforcent de régler au moyen de consultations et sur consentement mutuel tout différend concernant l'interprétation ou l'application du présent Traité.

ARTICLE 15

Entrée en vigueur

1. Chaque Partie notifie par écrit à l'autre Partie l'accomplissement de ses procédures internes nécessaires à l'entrée en vigueur du présent Traité. Le présent Traité entre en vigueur le premier jour du premier mois suivant la date de la deuxième de ces notifications.

2. Le présent Traité demeure en vigueur pendant une période de cinq ans suivant la date de son entrée en vigueur.

3. Le présent Traité est reconduit automatiquement à l'expiration de la période de cinq ans suivant son entrée en vigueur, et à la fin de chaque période de cinq ans subséquente.

4. La Partie qui souhaite mettre fin au présent Traité transmet un avis de dénonciation à l'autre Partie au moins six mois avant l'expiration de la période de cinq ans suivant la date d'entrée en vigueur du présent Traité, ou, si celui-ci est reconduit, au moins six mois avant l'expiration de toute période de cinq ans subséquente.

EN FOI DE QUOI les soussignés, dûment autorisés par leur gouvernement respectif, ont signé le présent Traité.

FAIT en double exemplaire à Ottawa, ce 4e jour de février 2016, en langues française et anglaise, chaque version faisant également foi.

POUR LE GOUVERNEMENT DE L'IRLANDE	**POUR LE GOUVERNEMENT DU CANADA**

No. 54755

Multilateral

Convention (No. 188) concerning work in the fishing sector (with annexes). Geneva, 14 June 2007

Entry into force: *16 November 2017*

Authentic texts: *English and French*

Registration with the Secretariat of the United Nations: *International Labour Organisation, 16 November 2017*

Multilatéral

Convention (n° 188) concernant le travail dans le secteur de la pêche (avec annexes). Genève, 14 juin 2007

Entrée en vigueur : *16 novembre 2017*

Textes authentiques : *anglais et français*

Enregistrement au Secrétariat de l'Organisation des Nations Unies : *Organisation internationale du Travail, 16 novembre 2017*

Participant	Ratification
Angola	11 Oct 2016
Argentina	15 Sept 2011
Bosnia and Herzegovina	4 Feb 2010
Congo	14 May 2014
Estonia	3 May 2016
France	28 Oct 2015
Lithuania	16 Nov 2016
Morocco	16 May 2013
Norway	8 Jan 2016
South Africa	20 Jun 2013

Participant	Ratification
Afrique du Sud	20 juin 2013
Angola	11 oct. 2016
Argentine	15 sept. 2011
Bosnie-Herzégovine	4 févr. 2010
Congo	14 mai 2014
Estonie	3 mai 2016
France	28 oct. 2015
Lituanie	16 nov. 2016
Maroc	16 mai 2013
Norvège	8 janv. 2016

[TEXT IN ENGLISH – TEXTE EN ANGLAIS]

Convention 188

CONVENTION CONCERNING WORK IN THE FISHING SECTOR

The General Conference of the International Labour Organization,

Having been convened at Geneva by the Governing Body of the International Labour Office, and having met in its ninety-sixth Session on 30 May 2007, and

Recognizing that globalization has a profound impact on the fishing sector, and

Noting the ILO Declaration on Fundamental Principles and Rights at Work, 1998, and

Taking into consideration the fundamental rights to be found in the following international labour Conventions: the Forced Labour Convention, 1930 (No. 29), the Freedom of Association and Protection of the Right to Organise Convention, 1948 (No. 87), the Right to Organise and Collective Bargaining Convention, 1949 (No. 98), the Equal Remuneration Convention, 1951 (No. 100), the Abolition of Forced Labour Convention, 1957 (No. 105), the Discrimination (Employment and Occupation) Convention, 1958 (No. 111), the Minimum Age Convention, 1973 (No. 138), and the Worst Forms of Child Labour Convention, 1999 (No. 182), and

Noting the relevant instruments of the International Labour Organization, in particular the Occupational Safety and Health Convention (No. 155) and Recommendation (No. 164), 1981, and the Occupational Health Services Convention (No. 161) and Recommendation (No. 171), 1985, and

Noting, in addition, the Social Security (Minimum Standards) Convention, 1952 (No. 102), and considering that the provisions of Article 77 of that Convention should not be an obstacle to protection extended by Members to fishers under social security schemes, and

Recognizing that the International Labour Organization considers fishing as a hazardous occupation when compared to other occupations, and

Noting also Article 1, paragraph 3, of the Seafarers' Identity Documents Convention (Revised), 2003 (No. 185), and

Mindful of the core mandate of the Organization, which is to promote decent conditions of work, and

Mindful of the need to protect and promote the rights of fishers in this regard, and .

Recalling the United Nations Convention on the Law of the Sea, 1982, and

Taking into account the need to revise the following international Conventions adopted by the International Labour Conference specifically concerning the fishing sector, namely the Minimum Age (Fishermen) Convention, 1959 (No. 112), the Medical Examination (Fishermen) Convention, 1959 (No. 113), the Fishermen's Articles of Agreement Convention, 1959 (No. 114), and the Accommodation of Crews (Fishermen) Convention, 1966 (No. 126), to bring them up to date and to reach a greater number of the world's fishers, particularly those working on board smaller vessels, and

Noting that the objective of this Convention is to ensure that fishers have decent conditions of work on board fishing vessels with regard to minimum requirements for work on board; conditions of service; accommodation and food; occupational safety and health protection; medical care and social security, and

Having decided upon the adoption of certain proposals with regard to work in the fishing sector, which is the fourth item on the agenda of the session, and

Having determined that these proposals shall take the form of an international Convention;

adopts this fourteenth day of June of the year two thousand and seven the following Convention, which may be cited as the Work in Fishing Convention, 2007.

PART I. DEFINITIONS AND SCOPE

DEFINITIONS

Article 1

For the purposes of the Convention:

(a) "commercial fishing" means all fishing operations, including fishing operations on rivers, lakes or canals, with the exception of subsistence fishing and recreational fishing;

(b) "competent authority" means the minister, government department or other authority having power to issue and enforce regulations, orders or other instructions having the force of law in respect of the subject matter of the provision concerned;

(c) "consultation" means consultation by the competent authority with the representative organizations of employers and workers concerned, and in particular the representative organizations of fishing vessel owners and fishers, where they exist;

(d) "fishing vessel owner" means the owner of the fishing vessel or any other organization or person, such as the manager, agent or bareboat charterer, who has assumed the responsibility for the operation of the vessel from the owner and who, on assuming such responsibility, has agreed to take over the duties and responsibilities imposed on fishing vessel owners in accordance with the Convention, regardless of whether any other organization or person fulfils certain of the duties or responsibilities on behalf of the fishing vessel owner;

(e) "fisher" means every person employed or engaged in any capacity or carrying out an occupation on board any fishing vessel, including persons working on board who are paid on the basis of a share of the catch but excluding pilots, naval personnel, other persons in the permanent service of a government, shore-based persons carrying out work aboard a fishing vessel and fisheries observers;

(f) "fisher's work agreement" means a contract of employment, articles of agreement or other similar arrangements, or any other contract governing a fisher's living and working conditions on board a vessel;

(g) "fishing vessel" or "vessel" means any ship or boat, of any nature whatsoever, irrespective of the form of ownership, used or intended to be used for the purpose of commercial fishing;

(h) "gross tonnage" means the gross tonnage calculated in accordance with the tonnage measurement regulations contained in Annex I to the International Convention on Tonnage Measurement of Ships, 1969, or any instrument amending or replacing it;

(i) "length" (L) shall be taken as 96 per cent of the total length on a waterline at 85 per cent of the least moulded depth measured from the keel line, or as the length from the foreside of the stem to the axis of the rudder stock on that waterline, if that be greater. In vessels designed with rake of keel, the waterline on which this length is measured shall be parallel to the designed waterline;

(j) "length overall" (LOA) shall be taken as the distance in a straight line parallel to the designed waterline between the foremost point of the bow and the aftermost point of the stern;

(k) "recruitment and placement service" means any person, company, institution, agency or other organization, in the public or the private sector, which is engaged in recruiting fishers on behalf of, or placing fishers with, fishing vessel owners;

(l) "skipper" means the fisher having command of a fishing vessel.

SCOPE

Article 2

1. Except as otherwise provided herein, this Convention applies to all fishers and all fishing vessels engaged in commercial fishing operations.

2. In the event of doubt as to whether a vessel is engaged in commercial fishing, the question shall be determined by the competent authority after consultation.

3. Any Member, after consultation, may extend, in whole or in part, to fishers working on smaller vessels the protection provided in this Convention for fishers working on vessels of 24 metres in length and over.

Article 3

1. Where the application of the Convention raises special problems of a substantial nature in the light of the particular conditions of service of the fishers or of the fishing vessels' operations concerned, a Member may, after consultation, exclude from the requirements of this Convention, or from certain of its provisions:

(a) fishing vessels engaged in fishing operations in rivers, lakes or canals;

(b) limited categories of fishers or fishing vessels.

2. In case of exclusions under the preceding paragraph, and where practicable, the competent authority shall take measures, as appropriate, to extend progressively the requirements under this Convention to the categories of fishers and fishing vessels concerned.

3. Each Member which ratifies this Convention shall:

(a) in its first report on the application of this Convention submitted under article 22 of the Constitution of the International Labour Organisation:

   (i) list any categories of fishers or fishing vessels excluded under paragraph 1;

   (ii) give the reasons for any such exclusions, stating the respective positions of the representative organizations of employers and workers concerned, in particular the representative organizations of fishing vessel owners and fishers, where they exist; and

   (iii) describe any measures taken to provide equivalent protection to the excluded categories; and

(b) in subsequent reports on the application of the Convention, describe any measures taken in accordance with paragraph 2.

Article 4

1. Where it is not immediately possible for a Member to implement all of the measures provided for in this Convention owing to special problems of a substantial nature in the light of insufficiently developed infrastructure or institutions, the Member may, in accordance with a plan drawn up in consultation, progressively implement all or some of the following provisions:

(a) Article 10, paragraph 1;

(b) Article 10, paragraph 3, in so far as it applies to vessels remaining at sea for more than three days;

(c) Article 15;

(d) Article 20;

(e) Article 33; and

(f) Article 38.

2. Paragraph 1 does not apply to fishing vessels which:

(a) are 24 metres in length and over; or

(b) remain at sea for more than seven days; or

(c) normally navigate at a distance exceeding 200 nautical miles from the coastline of the flag State or navigate beyond the outer edge of its continental shelf, whichever distance from the coastline is greater; or

(d) are subject to port State control as provided for in Article 43 of this Convention, except where port State control arises through a situation of force majeure,

nor to fishers working on such vessels.

3. Each Member which avails itself of the possibility afforded in paragraph 1 shall:

(a) in its first report on the application of this Convention submitted under article 22 of the Constitution of the International Labour Organisation:

  (i) indicate the provisions of the Convention to be progressively implemented;

  (ii) explain the reasons and state the respective positions of representative organizations of employers and workers concerned, and in particular the representative organizations of fishing vessel owners and fishers, where they exist; and

  (iii) describe the plan for progressive implementation; and

(b) in subsequent reports on the application of this Convention, describe measures taken with a view to giving effect to all of the provisions of the Convention.

Article 5

1. For the purpose of this Convention, the competent authority, after consultation, may decide to use length overall (LOA) in place of length (L) as the basis for measurement, in accordance with the equivalence set out in Annex I. In addition, for the purpose of the paragraphs specified in Annex III of this Convention, the competent authority, after consultation, may decide to use gross tonnage in place of length (L) or length overall (LOA) as the basis for measurement in accordance with the equivalence set out in Annex III.

2. In the reports submitted under article 22 of the Constitution, the Member shall communicate the reasons for the decision taken under this Article and any comments arising from the consultation.

PART II. GENERAL PRINCIPLES

IMPLEMENTATION

Article 6

1. Each Member shall implement and enforce laws, regulations or other measures that it has adopted to fulfil its commitments under this Convention with respect to fishers and fishing vessels under its jurisdiction. Other measures may include collective agreements, court decisions, arbitration awards, or other means consistent with national law and practice.

2. Nothing in this Convention shall affect any law, award or custom, or any agreement between fishing vessel owners and fishers, which ensures more favourable conditions than those provided for in this Convention.

COMPETENT AUTHORITY AND COORDINATION

Article 7

Each Member shall:

(a) designate the competent authority or authorities; and

(b) establish mechanisms for coordination among relevant authorities for the fishing sector at the national and local levels, as appropriate, and define their functions and responsibilities, taking into account their complementarities and national conditions and practice.

RESPONSIBILITIES OF FISHING VESSEL OWNERS, SKIPPERS AND FISHERS

Article 8

1. The fishing vessel owner has the overall responsibility to ensure that the skipper is provided with the necessary resources and facilities to comply with the obligations of this Convention.

2. The skipper has the responsibility for the safety of the fishers on board and the safe operation of the vessel, including but not limited to the following areas:

(a) providing such supervision as will ensure that, as far as possible, fishers perform their work in the best conditions of safety and health;

(b) managing the fishers in a manner which respects safety and health, including prevention of fatigue;

(c) facilitating on-board occupational safety and health awareness training; and

(d) ensuring compliance with safety of navigation, watchkeeping and associated good seamanship standards.

3. The skipper shall not be constrained by the fishing vessel owner from taking any decision which, in the professional judgement of the skipper, is necessary for the safety of the vessel and its safe navigation and safe operation, or the safety of the fishers on board.

4. Fishers shall comply with the lawful orders of the skipper and applicable safety and health measures.

PART III. MINIMUM REQUIREMENTS FOR WORK ON BOARD FISHING VESSELS

MINIMUM AGE

Article 9

1. The minimum age for work on board a fishing vessel shall be 16 years. However, the competent authority may authorize a minimum age of 15 for persons who are no longer subject to compulsory schooling as provided by national legislation, and who are engaged in vocational training in fishing.

2. The competent authority, in accordance with national laws and practice, may authorize persons of the age of 15 to perform light work during school holidays. In such cases, it shall determine, after consultation, the kinds of work permitted and shall prescribe the conditions in which such work shall be undertaken and the periods of rest required.

3. The minimum age for assignment to activities on board fishing vessels, which by their nature or the circumstances in which they are carried out are likely to jeopardize the health, safety or morals of young persons, shall not be less than 18 years.

4. The types of activities to which paragraph 3 of this Article applies shall be determined by national laws or regulations, or by the competent authority, after consultation, taking into account the risks concerned and the applicable international standards.

5. The performance of the activities referred to in paragraph 3 of this Article as from the age of 16 may be authorized by national laws or regulations, or by decision of the competent authority, after consultation, on condition that the health, safety and morals of the young persons concerned are fully protected and that the young persons concerned have received adequate specific instruction or vocational training and have completed basic pre-sea safety training.

6. The engagement of fishers under the age of 18 for work at night shall be prohibited. For the purpose of this Article, "night" shall be defined in accordance with national law and practice. It shall cover a period of at least nine hours starting no later than midnight and ending no earlier than 5 a.m. An exception to strict compliance with the night work restriction may be made by the competent authority when:

(a) the effective training of the fishers concerned, in accordance with established programmes and schedules, would be impaired; or

(b) the specific nature of the duty or a recognized training programme requires that fishers covered by the exception perform duties at night and the authority determines, after consultation, that the work will not have a detrimental impact on their health or well-being.

7. Nothing in this Article shall affect any obligations assumed by the Member arising from the ratification of any other international labour Convention.

MEDICAL EXAMINATION

Article 10

1. No fishers shall work on board a fishing vessel without a valid medical certificate attesting to fitness to perform their duties.

2. The competent authority, after consultation, may grant exemptions from the application of paragraph 1 of this Article, taking into account the safety and health of fishers, size of the vessel, availability of medical assistance and evacuation, duration of the voyage, area of operation, and type of fishing operation.

3. The exemptions in paragraph 2 of this Article shall not apply to a fisher working on a fishing vessel of 24 metres in length and over or which normally remains at sea for more than three days. In urgent cases, the competent authority may permit a fisher to work on such a vessel for a period of a limited and specified duration until a medical certificate can be obtained, provided that the fisher is in possession of an expired medical certificate of a recent date.

Article 11

Each Member shall adopt laws, regulations or other measures providing for:

(a) the nature of medical examinations;

(b) the form and content of medical certificates;

(c) the issue of a medical certificate by a duly qualified medical practitioner or, in the case of a certificate solely concerning eyesight, by a person recognized by the competent authority as qualified to issue such a certificate; these persons shall enjoy full independence in exercising their professional judgement;

(d) the frequency of medical examinations and the period of validity of medical certificates;

(e) the right to a further examination by a second independent medical practitioner in the event that a person has been refused a certificate or has had limitations imposed on the work he or she may perform; and

(f) other relevant requirements.

Article 12

In addition to the requirements set out in Article 10 and Article 11, on a fishing vessel of 24 metres in length and over, or on a vessel which normally remains at sea for more than three days:

1. The medical certificate of a fisher shall state, at a minimum, that:

(a) the hearing and sight of the fisher concerned are satisfactory for the fisher's duties on the vessel; and

(b) the fisher is not suffering from any medical condition likely to be aggravated by service at sea or to render the fisher unfit for such service or to endanger the safety or health of other persons on board.

2. The medical certificate shall be valid for a maximum period of two years unless the fisher is under the age of 18, in which case the maximum period of validity shall be one year.

3. If the period of validity of a certificate expires in the course of a voyage, the certificate shall remain in force until the end of that voyage.

PART IV. CONDITIONS OF SERVICE

MANNING AND HOURS OF REST

Article 13

Each Member shall adopt laws, regulations or other measures requiring that owners of fishing vessels flying its flag ensure that:

(a) their vessels are sufficiently and safely manned for the safe navigation and operation of the vessel and under the control of a competent skipper; and

(b) fishers are given regular periods of rest of sufficient length to ensure safety and health.

Article 14

1. In addition to the requirements set out in Article 13, the competent authority shall:

(a) for vessels of 24 metres in length and over, establish a minimum level of manning for the safe navigation of the vessel, specifying the number and the qualifications of the fishers required;

(b) for fishing vessels regardless of size remaining at sea for more than three days, after consultation and for the purpose of limiting fatigue, establish the minimum hours of rest to be provided to fishers. Minimum hours of rest shall not be less than:

(i) ten hours in any 24-hour period; and

(ii) 77 hours in any seven-day period.

2. The competent authority may permit, for limited and specified reasons, temporary exceptions to the limits established in paragraph 1(b) of this Article. However, in such circumstances, it shall require that fishers shall receive compensatory periods of rest as soon as practicable.

3. The competent authority, after consultation, may establish alternative requirements to those in paragraphs 1 and 2 of this Article. However, such alternative requirements shall be substantially equivalent and shall not jeopardize the safety and health of the fishers.

4. Nothing in this Article shall be deemed to impair the right of the skipper of a vessel to require a fisher to perform any hours of work necessary for the immediate safety of the vessel, the persons on board or the catch, or for the purpose of giving assistance to other boats or ships or persons in distress at sea. Accordingly, the skipper may suspend the schedule of hours of rest and require a fisher to perform any hours of work necessary until the

normal situation has been restored. As soon as practicable after the normal situation has been restored, the skipper shall ensure that any fishers who have performed work in a scheduled rest period are provided with an adequate period of rest.

CREW LIST

Article 15

Every fishing vessel shall carry a crew list, a copy of which shall be provided to authorized persons ashore prior to departure of the vessel, or communicated ashore immediately after departure of the vessel. The competent authority shall determine to whom and when such information shall be provided and for what purpose or purposes.

FISHER'S WORK AGREEMENT

Article 16

Each Member shall adopt laws, regulations or other measures:

(a) requiring that fishers working on vessels flying its flag have the protection of a fisher's work agreement that is comprehensible to them and is consistent with the provisions of this Convention; and

(b) specifying the minimum particulars to be included in fishers' work agreements in accordance with the provisions contained in Annex II.

Article 17

Each Member shall adopt laws, regulations or other measures regarding:

(a) procedures for ensuring that a fisher has an opportunity to review and seek advice on the terms of the fisher's work agreement before it is concluded;

(b) where applicable, the maintenance of records concerning the fisher's work under such an agreement; and

(c) the means of settling disputes in connection with a fisher's work agreement.

Article 18

The fisher's work agreement, a copy of which shall be provided to the fisher, shall be carried on board and be available to the fisher and, in accordance with national law and practice, to other concerned parties on request.

Article 19

Articles 16 to 18 and Annex II do not apply to a fishing vessel owner who is also single-handedly operating the vessel.

Article 20

It shall be the responsibility of the fishing vessel owner to ensure that each fisher has a written fisher's work agreement signed by both the fisher and the fishing vessel owner or by an authorized representative of the fishing vessel owner (or, where fishers are not employed or engaged by the fishing vessel owner, the fishing vessel owner shall have evidence of contractual or similar arrangements) providing decent work and living conditions on board the vessel as required by this Convention.

REPATRIATION

Article 21

1. Members shall ensure that fishers on a fishing vessel that flies their flag and that enters a foreign port are entitled to repatriation in the event that the fisher's work agreement has expired or has been terminated for justified reasons by the fisher or by the fishing vessel owner, or the fisher is no longer able to carry out the duties required under the work agreement or cannot be expected to carry them out in the specific circumstances. This also applies to fishers from that vessel who are transferred for the same reasons from the vessel to the foreign port.

2. The cost of the repatriation referred to in paragraph 1 of this Article shall be borne by the fishing vessel owner, except where the fisher has been found, in accordance with national laws, regulations or other measures, to be in serious default of his or her work agreement obligations.

3. Members shall prescribe, by means of laws, regulations or other measures, the precise circumstances entitling a fisher covered by paragraph 1 of this Article to repatriation, the maximum duration of service periods on board following which a fisher is entitled to repatriation, and the destinations to which fishers may be repatriated.

4. If a fishing vessel owner fails to provide for the repatriation referred to in this Article, the Member whose flag the vessel flies shall arrange for the repatriation of the fisher concerned and shall be entitled to recover the cost from the fishing vessel owner.

5. National laws and regulations shall not prejudice any right of the fishing vessel owner to recover the cost of repatriation under third party contractual agreements.

RECRUITMENT AND PLACEMENT

Article 22

Recruitment and placement of fishers

1. Each Member that operates a public service providing recruitment and placement for fishers shall ensure that the service forms part of, or is coordinated with, a public employment service for all workers and employers.

2. Any private service providing recruitment and placement for fishers which operates in the territory of a Member shall do so in conformity with a standardized system of licensing or certification or other form of regulation, which shall be established, maintained or modified only after consultation.

3. Each Member shall, by means of laws, regulations or other measures:

(a) prohibit recruitment and placement services from using means, mechanisms or lists intended to prevent or deter fishers from engaging for work;

(b) require that no fees or other charges for recruitment or placement of fishers be borne directly or indirectly, in whole or in part, by the fisher; and

(c) determine the conditions under which any licence, certificate or similar authorization of a private recruitment or placement service may be suspended or withdrawn in case of violation of relevant laws or regulations; and specify the conditions under which private recruitment and placement services can operate.

Private employment agencies

4. A Member which has ratified the Private Employment Agencies Convention, 1997 (No. 181), may allocate certain responsibilities under this Convention to private employment agencies that provide the services referred to in paragraph 1(b) of Article 1 of that Convention. The respective responsibilities of any such private employment agencies and of the fishing vessel owners, who shall be the "user enterprise" for the purpose of that Convention, shall be determined and allocated, as provided for in Article 12 of that Convention. Such a Member shall adopt laws, regulations or other measures to ensure that no allocation of the respective responsibilities or obligations to the private emloyment agencies providing the service and to the "user enterprise" pursuant to this Convention shall preclude the fisher from asserting a right to a lien arising against the fishing vessel.

5. Notwithstanding the provisions of paragraph 4, the fishing vessel owner shall be liable in the event that the private employment agency

defaults on its obligations to a fisher for whom, in the context of the Private Employment Agencies Convention, 1997 (No. 181), the fishing vessel owner is the "user enterprise".

6. Nothing in this Convention shall be deemed to impose on a Member the obligation to allow the operation in its fishing sector of private employment agencies as referred to in paragraph 4 of this Article.

PAYMENT OF FISHERS

Article 23

Each Member, after consultation, shall adopt laws, regulations or other measures providing that fishers who are paid a wage are ensured a monthly or other regular payment.

Article 24

Each Member shall require that all fishers working on board fishing vessels shall be given a means to transmit all or part of their payments received, including advances, to their families at no cost.

PART V. ACCOMMODATION AND FOOD

Article 25

Each Member shall adopt laws, regulations or other measures for fishing vessels that fly its flag with respect to accommodation, food and potable water on board.

Article 26

Each Member shall adopt laws, regulations or other measures requiring that accommodation on board fishing vessels that fly its flag shall be of sufficient size and quality and appropriately equipped for the service of the vessel and the length of time fishers live on board. In particular, such measures shall address, as appropriate, the following issues:

(a) approval of plans for the construction or modification of fishing vessels in respect of accommodation;

(b) maintenance of accommodation and galley spaces with due regard to hygiene and overall safe, healthy and comfortable conditions;

(c) ventilation, heating, cooling and lighting;

(d) mitigation of excessive noise and vibration;

(e) location, size, construction materials, furnishing and equipping of sleeping rooms, mess rooms and other accommodation spaces;

(f) sanitary facilities, including toilets and washing facilities, and supply of sufficient hot and cold water; and

(g) procedures for responding to complaints concerning accommodation that does not meet the requirements of this Convention.

Article 27

Each Member shall adopt laws, regulations or other measures requiring that:

(a) the food carried and served on board be of a sufficient nutritional value, quality and quantity;

(b) potable water be of sufficient quality and quantity; and

(c) the food and water shall be provided by the fishing vessel owner at no cost to the fisher. However, in accordance with national laws and regulations, the cost can be recovered as an operational cost if the collective agreement governing a share system or a fisher's work agreement so provides.

Article 28

1. The laws, regulations or other measures to be adopted by the Member in accordance with Articles 25 to 27 shall give full effect to Annex III concerning fishing vessel accommodation. Annex III may be amended in the manner provided for in Article 45.

2. A Member which is not in a position to implement the provisions of Annex III may, after consultation, adopt provisions in its laws and regulations or other measures which are substantially equivalent to the provisions set out in Annex III, with the exception of provisions related to Article 27.

PART VI. MEDICAL CARE, HEALTH PROTECTION AND SOCIAL SECURITY

MEDICAL CARE

Article 29

Each Member shall adopt laws, regulations or other measures requiring that:

(a) fishing vessels carry appropriate medical equipment and medical supplies for the service of the vessel, taking into account the number of fishers on board, the area of operation and the length of the voyage;

(b) fishing vessels have at least one fisher on board who is qualified or trained in first aid and other forms of medical care and who has the necessary knowledge to use the medical equipment and supplies for the vessel concerned, taking into account the number of fishers on board, the area of operation and the length of the voyage;

(c) medical equipment and supplies carried on board be accompanied by instructions or other information in a language and format understood by the fisher or fishers referred to in subparagraph (b);

(d) fishing vessels be equipped for radio or satellite communication with persons or services ashore that can provide medical advice, taking into account the area of operation and the length of the voyage; and

(e) fishers have the right to medical treatment ashore and the right to be taken ashore in a timely manner for treatment in the event of serious injury or illness.

Article 30

For fishing vessels of 24 metres in length and over, taking into account the number of fishers on board, the area of operation and the duration of the voyage, each Member shall adopt laws, regulations or other measures requiring that:

(a) the competent authority prescribe the medical equipment and medical supplies to be carried on board;

(b) the medical equipment and medical supplies carried on board be properly maintained and inspected at regular intervals established by the competent authority by responsible persons designated or approved by the competent authority;

(c) the vessels carry a medical guide adopted or approved by the competent authority, or the latest edition of the *International Medical Guide for Ships*;

(d) the vessels have access to a prearranged system of medical advice to vessels at sea by radio or satellite communication, including specialist advice, which shall be available at all times;

(e) the vessels carry on board a list of radio or satellite stations through which medical advice can be obtained; and

(f) to the extent consistent with the Member's national law and practice, medical care while the fisher is on board or landed in a foreign port be provided free of charge to the fisher.

OCCUPATIONAL SAFETY AND HEALTH
AND ACCIDENT PREVENTION

Article 31

Each Member shall adopt laws, regulations or other measures concerning:

(a) the prevention of occupational accidents, occupational diseases and work-related risks on board fishing vessels, including risk evaluation and management, training and on-board instruction of fishers;

(b) training for fishers in the handling of types of fishing gear they will use and in the knowledge of the fishing operations in which they will be engaged;

(c) the obligations of fishing vessel owners, fishers and others concerned, due account being taken of the safety and health of fishers under the age of 18;

(d) the reporting and investigation of accidents on board fishing vessels flying its flag; and

(e) the setting up of joint committees on occupational safety and health or, after consultation, of other appropriate bodies.

Article 32

1. The requirements of this Article shall apply to fishing vessels of 24 metres in length and over normally remaining at sea for more than three days and, after consultation, to other vessels, taking into account the number of fishers on board, the area of operation, and the duration of the voyage.

2. The competent authority shall:

(a) after consultation, require that the fishing vessel owner, in accordance with national laws, regulations, collective bargaining agreements and practice, establish on-board procedures for the prevention of occupational accidents, injuries and diseases, taking into account the specific hazards and risks on the fishing vessel concerned; and

(b) require that fishing vessel owners, skippers, fishers and other relevant persons be provided with sufficient and suitable guidance, training material, or other appropriate information on how to evaluate and manage risks to safety and health on board fishing vessels.

3. Fishing vessel owners shall:

(a) ensure that every fisher on board is provided with appropriate personal protective clothing and equipment;

(b) ensure that every fisher on board has received basic safety training approved by the competent authority; the competent authority may grant written exemptions from this requirement for fishers who have demonstrated equivalent knowledge and experience; and

(c) ensure that fishers are sufficiently and reasonably familiarized with equipment and its methods of operation, including relevant safety measures, prior to using the equipment or participating in the operations concerned.

Article 33

Risk evaluation in relation to fishing shall be conducted, as appropriate, with the participation of fishers or their representatives.

SOCIAL SECURITY

Article 34

Each Member shall ensure that fishers ordinarily resident in its territory, and their dependants to the extent provided in national law, are entitled to benefit from social security protection under conditions no less favourable than those applicable to other workers, including employed and self-employed persons, ordinarily resident in its territory.

Article 35

Each Member shall undertake to take steps, according to national circumstances, to achieve progressively comprehensive social security protection for all fishers who are ordinarily resident in its territory.

Article 36

Members shall cooperate through bilateral or multilateral agreements or other arrangements, in accordance with national laws, regulations or practice:

(a) to achieve progressively comprehensive social security protection for fishers, taking into account the principle of equality of treatment irrespective of nationality; and

(b) to ensure the maintenance of social security rights which have been acquired or are in the course of acquisition by all fishers regardless of residence.

Article 37

Notwithstanding the attribution of responsibilities in Articles 34, 35 and 36, Members may determine, through bilateral and multilateral agreements and through provisions adopted in the framework of regional economic integration organizations, other rules concerning the social security legislation to which fishers are subject.

PROTECTION IN THE CASE OF WORK-RELATED SICKNESS, INJURY OR DEATH

Article 38

1. Each Member shall take measures to provide fishers with protection, in accordance with national laws, regulations or practice, for work-related sickness, injury or death.

2. In the event of injury due to occupational accident or disease, the fisher shall have access to:

(a) appropriate medical care; and

(b) the corresponding compensation in accordance with national laws and regulations.

3. Taking into account the characteristics within the fishing sector, the protection referred to in paragraph 1 of this Article may be ensured through:

(a) a system for fishing vessel owners' liability; or

(b) compulsory insurance, workers' compensation or other schemes.

Article 39

1. In the absence of national provisions for fishers, each Member shall adopt laws, regulations or other measures to ensure that fishing vessel owners are responsible for the provision to fishers on vessels flying its flag, of health protection and medical care while employed or engaged or working on a vessel at sea or in a foreign port. Such laws, regulations or other measures shall ensure that fishing vessel owners are responsible for defraying the expenses of medical care, including related material assistance and support, during medical treatment in a foreign country, until the fisher has been repatriated.

2. National laws or regulations may permit the exclusion of the liability of the fishing vessel owner if the injury occurred otherwise than in the service of the vessel or the sickness or infirmity was concealed during engagement, or the injury or sickness was due to wilful misconduct of the fisher.

PART VII. COMPLIANCE AND ENFORCEMENT

Article 40

Each Member shall effectively exercise its jurisdiction and control over vessels that fly its flag by establishing a system for ensuring compliance with the requirements of this Convention including, as appropriate, inspections, reporting, monitoring, complaint procedures, appropriate penalties and corrective measures, in accordance with national laws or regulations.

Article 41

1. Members shall require that fishing vessels remaining at sea for more than three days, which:

(a) are 24 metres in length and over; or

(b) normally navigate at a distance exceeding 200 nautical miles from the coastline of the flag State or navigate beyond the outer edge of its continental shelf, whichever distance from the coastline is greater,

carry a valid document issued by the competent authority stating that the vessel has been inspected by the competent authority or on its behalf, for compliance with the provisions of this Convention concerning living and working conditions.

2. The period of validity of such document may coincide with the period of validity of a national or an international fishing vessel safety certificate, but in no case shall such period of validity exceed five years.

Article 42

1. The competent authority shall appoint a sufficient number of qualified inspectors to fulfil its responsibilities under Article 41.

2. In establishing an effective system for the inspection of living and working conditions on board fishing vessels, a Member, where appropriate, may authorize public institutions or other organizations that it recognizes as competent and independent to carry out inspections and issue documents. In all cases, the Member shall remain fully responsible for the inspection and issuance of the related documents concerning the living and working conditions of the fishers on fishing vessels that fly its flag.

Article 43

1. A Member which receives a complaint or obtains evidence that a fishing vessel that flies its flag does not conform to the requirements of this Convention shall take the steps necessary to investigate the matter and ensure that action is taken to remedy any deficiencies found.

2. If a Member, in whose port a fishing vessel calls in the normal course of its business or for operational reasons, receives a complaint or obtains evidence that such vessel does not conform to the requirements of this Convention, it may prepare a report addressed to the government of the flag State of the vessel, with a copy to the Director-General of the International Labour Office, and may take measures necessary to rectify any conditions on board which are clearly hazardous to safety or health.

3. In taking the measures referred to in paragraph 2 of this Article, the Member shall notify forthwith the nearest representative of the flag State and, if possible, shall have such representative present. The Member shall not unreasonably detain or delay the vessel.

4. For the purpose of this Article, the complaint may be submitted by a fisher, a professional body, an association, a trade union or, generally, any

person with an interest in the safety of the vessel, including an interest in safety or health hazards to the fishers on board.

5. This Article does not apply to complaints which a Member considers to be manifestly unfounded.

Article 44

Each Member shall apply this Convention in such a way as to ensure that the fishing vessels flying the flag of any State that has not ratified this Convention do not receive more favourable treatment than fishing vessels that fly the flag of any Member that has ratified it.

PART VIII. AMENDMENT OF ANNEXES I, II AND III

Article 45

1. Subject to the relevant provisions of this Convention, the International Labour Conference may amend Annexes I, II and III. The Governing Body of the International Labour Office may place an item on the agenda of the Conference regarding proposals for such amendments established by a tripartite meeting of experts. The decision to adopt the proposals shall require a majority of two-thirds of the votes cast by the delegates present at the Conference, including at least half the Members that have ratified this Convention.

2. Any amendment adopted in accordance with paragraph 1 of this Article shall enter into force six months after the date of its adoption for any Member that has ratified this Convention, unless such Member has given written notice to the Director-General of the International Labour Office that it shall not enter into force for that Member, or shall only enter into force at a later date upon subsequent written notification.

PART IX. FINAL PROVISIONS

Article 46

This Convention revises the Minimum Age (Fishermen) Convention, 1959 (No. 112), the Medical Examination (Fishermen) Convention, 1959 (No. 113), the Fishermen's Articles of Agreement Convention, 1959 (No. 114), and the Accommodation of Crews (Fishermen) Convention, 1966 (No. 126).

Article 47

The formal ratifications of this Convention shall be communicated to the Director-General of the International Labour Office for registration.

Article 48

1. This Convention shall be binding only upon those Members of the International Labour Organization whose ratifications have been registered with the Director-General of the International Labour Office.

2. It shall come into force 12 months after the date on which the ratifications of ten Members, eight of which are coastal States, have been registered with the Director-General.

3. Thereafter, this Convention shall come into force for any Member 12 months after the date on which its ratification is registered.

Article 49

1. A Member which has ratified this Convention may denounce it after the expiration of ten years from the date on which the Convention first comes into force, by an act communicated to the Director-General of the International Labour Office for registration. Such denunciation shall not take effect until one year after the date on which it is registered.

2. Each Member which has ratified this Convention and which does not, within the year following the expiration of the period of ten years mentioned in the preceding paragraph, exercise the right of denunciation provided for in this Article, will be bound for another period of ten years and, thereafter, may denounce this Convention within the first year of each new period of ten years under the terms provided for in this Article.

Article 50

1. The Director-General of the International Labour Office shall notify all Members of the International Labour Organization of the registration of all ratifications, declarations and denunciations that have been communicated by the Members of the Organization.

2. When notifying the Members of the Organization of the registration of the last of the ratifications required to bring the Convention into force, the Director-General shall draw the attention of the Members of the Organization to the date upon which the Convention will come into force.

Article 51

The Director-General of the International Labour Office shall communicate to the Secretary-General of the United Nations for registration in accordance with Article 102 of the Charter of the United Nations full particulars of all ratifications, declarations and denunciations registered by the Director-General.

Article 52

At such times as it may consider necessary, the Governing Body of the International Labour Office shall present to the General Conference a report on the working of this Convention and shall examine the desirability of placing on the agenda of the Conference the question of its revision in whole or in part, taking into account also the provisions of Article 45.

Article 53

1. Should the Conference adopt a new Convention revising this Convention, then, unless the new Convention otherwise provides:

(a) the ratification by a Member of the new revising Convention shall *ipso jure* involve the immediate denunciation of this Convention, notwithstanding the provisions of Article 49 above, if and when the new revising Convention shall have come into force;

(b) as from the date when the new revising Convention comes into force this Convention shall cease to be open to ratification by the Members.

2. This Convention shall in any case remain in force in its actual form and content for those Members which have ratified it but have not ratified the revising Convention.

Article 54

The English and French versions of the text of this Convention are equally authoritative.

ANNEX I

EQUIVALENCE IN MEASUREMENT

For the purpose of this Convention, where the competent authority, after consultation, decides to use length overall (LOA) rather than length (L) as the basis of measurement:

(a) a length overall (LOA) of 16.5 metres shall be considered equivalent to a length (L) of 15 metres;

(b) a length overall (LOA) of 26.5 metres shall be considered equivalent to a length (L) of 24 metres;

(c) a length overall (LOA) of 50 metres shall be considered equivalent to a length (L) of 45 metres.

ANNEX II

FISHER'S WORK AGREEMENT

The fisher's work agreement shall contain the following particulars, except in so far as the inclusion of one or more of them is rendered unnecessary by the fact that the matter is regulated in another manner by national laws or regulations, or a collective bargaining agreement where applicable:

(a) the fisher's family name and other names, date of birth or age, and birthplace;

(b) the place at which and date on which the agreement was concluded;

(c) the name of the fishing vessel or vessels and the registration number of the vessel or vessels on board which the fisher undertakes to work;

(d) the name of the employer, or fishing vessel owner, or other party to the agreement with the fisher;

(e) the voyage or voyages to be undertaken, if this can be determined at the time of making the agreement;

(f) the capacity in which the fisher is to be employed or engaged;

(g) if possible, the place at which and date on which the fisher is required to report on board for service;

(h) the provisions to be supplied to the fisher, unless some alternative system is provided for by national law or regulation;

(i) the amount of wages, or the amount of the share and the method of calculating such share if remuneration is to be on a share basis, or the amount of the wage and share and the method of calculating the latter if remuneration is to be on a combined basis, and any agreed minimum wage;

(j) the termination of the agreement and the conditions thereof, namely:

(i) if the agreement has been made for a definite period, the date fixed for its expiry;

(ii) if the agreement has been made for a voyage, the port of destination and the time which has to expire after arrival before the fisher shall be discharged;

(iii) if the agreement has been made for an indefinite period, the conditions which shall entitle either party to rescind it, as well as the required period of notice for rescission, provided that such period shall not be less for the employer, or fishing vessel owner or other party to the agreement with the fisher;

(k) the protection that will cover the fisher in the event of sickness, injury or death in connection with service;

(l) the amount of paid annual leave or the formula used for calculating leave, where applicable;

(m) the health and social security coverage and benefits to be provided to the fisher by the employer, fishing vessel owner, or other party or parties to the fisher's work agreement, as applicable;

(n) the fisher's entitlement to repatriation;

(o) a reference to the collective bargaining agreement, where applicable;

(p) the minimum periods of rest, in accordance with national laws, regulations or other measures; and

(q) any other particulars which national law or regulation may require.

ANNEX III

FISHING VESSEL ACCOMMODATION

General provisions

1. For the purposes of this Annex:

(a) "new fishing vessel" means a vessel for which:

   (i) the building or major conversion contract has been placed on or after the date of the entry into force of the Convention for the Member concerned; or

   (ii) the building or major conversion contract has been placed before the date of the entry into force of the Convention for the Member concerned, and which is delivered three years or more after that date; or

   (iii) in the absence of a building contract, on or after the date of the entry into force of the Convention for the Member concerned:

   – the keel is laid, or

   – construction identifiable with a specific vessel begins, or

   – assembly has commenced comprising at least 50 tonnes or 1 per cent of the estimated mass of all structural material, whichever is less;

(b) "existing vessel" means a vessel that is not a new fishing vessel.

2. The following shall apply to all new, decked fishing vessels, subject to any exclusions provided for in accordance with Article 3 of the Convention. The competent authority may, after consultation, also apply the requirements of this Annex to existing vessels, when and in so far as it determines that this is reasonable and practicable.

3. The competent authority, after consultation, may permit variations to the provisions of this Annex for fishing vessels normally remaining at sea for less than 24 hours where the fishers do not live on board the vessel in port. In the case of such vessels, the competent authority shall ensure that the fishers concerned have adequate facilities for resting, eating and sanitation purposes.

4. Any variations made by a Member under paragraph 3 of this Annex shall be reported to the International Labour Office under article 22 of the Constitution of the International Labour Organisation.

5. The requirements for vessels of 24 metres in length and over may be applied to vessels between 15 and 24 metres in length where the competent authority determines, after consultation, that this is reasonable and practicable.

6. Fishers working on board feeder vessels which do not have appropriate accommodation and sanitary facilities shall be provided with such accommodation and facilities on board the mother vessel.

7. Members may extend the requirements of this Annex regarding noise and vibration, ventilation, heating and air conditioning, and lighting to enclosed working spaces and spaces used for storage if, after consultation, such application is considered appropriate and will not have a negative influence on the function of the process or working conditions or the quality of the catches.

8. The use of gross tonnage as referred to in Article 5 of the Convention is limited to the following specified paragraphs of this Annex: 14, 37, 38, 41, 43, 46, 49, 53, 55, 61, 64, 65 and 67. For these purposes, where the competent authority, after consultation, decides to use gross tonnage (gt) as the basis of measurement:

(a) a gross tonnage of 75 gt shall be considered equivalent to a length (L) of 15 metres or a length overall (LOA) of 16.5 metres;

(b) a gross tonnage of 300 gt shall be considered equivalent to a length (L) of 24 metres or a length overall (LOA) of 26.5 metres;

(c) a gross tonnage of 950 gt shall be considered equivalent to a length (L) of 45 metres or a length overall (LOA) of 50 metres.

Planning and control

9. The competent authority shall satisfy itself that, on every occasion when a vessel is newly constructed or the crew accommodation of a vessel has been reconstructed, such vessel complies with the requirements of this Annex. The competent authority shall, to the extent practicable, require compliance with this Annex when the crew accommodation of a vessel is substantially altered and, for a vessel that changes the flag it flies to the flag of the Member, require compliance with those requirements of this Annex that are applicable in accordance with paragraph 2 of this Annex.

10. For the occasions noted in paragraph 9 of this Annex, for vessels of 24 metres in length and over, detailed plans and information concerning accommodation shall be required to be submitted for approval to the competent authority, or an entity authorized by it.

11. For vessels of 24 metres in length and over, on every occasion when the crew accommodation of the fishing vessel has been reconstructed or

substantially altered, the competent authority shall inspect the accommodation for compliance with the requirements of the Convention, and when the vessel changes the flag it flies to the flag of the Member, for compliance with those requirements of this Annex that are applicable in accordance with paragraph 2 of this Annex. The competent authority may carry out additional inspections of crew accommodation at its discretion.

12. When a vessel changes flag, any alternative requirements which the competent authority of the Member whose flag the ship was formerly flying may have adopted in accordance with paragraphs 15, 39, 47 or 62 of this Annex cease to apply to the vessel.

Design and construction

Headroom

13. There shall be adequate headroom in all accommodation spaces. For spaces where fishers are expected to stand for prolonged periods, the minimum headroom shall be prescribed by the competent authority.

14. For vessels of 24 metres in length and over, the minimum permitted headroom in all accommodation where full and free movement is necessary shall not be less than 200 centimetres.

15. Notwithstanding the provisions of paragraph 14, the competent authority may, after consultation, decide that the minimum permitted headroom shall not be less than 190 centimetres in any space – or part of any space – in such accommodation, where it is satisfied that this is reasonable and will not result in discomfort to the fishers.

Openings into and between accommodation spaces

16. There shall be no direct openings into sleeping rooms from fish rooms and machinery spaces, except for the purpose of emergency escape. Where reasonable and practicable, direct openings from galleys, storerooms, drying rooms or communal sanitary areas shall be avoided unless expressly provided otherwise.

17. For vessels of 24 metres in length and over, there shall be no direct openings, except for the purpose of emergency escape, into sleeping rooms from fish rooms and machinery spaces or from galleys, storerooms, drying rooms or communal sanitary areas; that part of the bulkhead separating such places from sleeping rooms and external bulkheads shall be efficiently constructed of steel or another approved material and shall be watertight and gas-tight. This provision does not exclude the possibility of sanitary areas being shared between two cabins.

Insulation

18. Accommodation spaces shall be adequately insulated; the materials used to construct internal bulkheads, panelling and sheeting, and floors and joinings shall be suitable for the purpose and shall be conducive to ensuring a healthy environment. Sufficient drainage shall be provided in all accommodation spaces.

Other

19. All practicable measures shall be taken to protect fishing vessels' crew accommodation against flies and other insects, particularly when vessels are operating in mosquito-infested areas.

20. Emergency escapes from all crew accommodation spaces shall be provided as necessary.

Noise and vibration

21. The competent authority shall take measures to limit excessive noise and vibration in accommodation spaces and, as far as practicable, in accordance with relevant international standards.

22. For vessels of 24 metres in length and over, the competent authority shall adopt standards for noise and vibration in accommodation spaces which shall ensure adequate protection to fishers from the effects of such noise and vibration, including the effects of noise- and vibration-induced fatigue.

Ventilation

23. Accommodation spaces shall be ventilated, taking into account climatic conditions. The system of ventilation shall supply air in a satisfactory condition whenever fishers are on board.

24. Ventilation arrangements or other measures shall be such as to protect non-smokers from tobacco smoke.

25. Vessels of 24 metres in length and over shall be equipped with a system of ventilation for accommodation, which shall be controlled so as to maintain the air in a satisfactory condition and to ensure sufficiency of air movement in all weather conditions and climates. Ventilation systems shall be in operation at all times when fishers are on board.

Heating and air conditioning

26. Accommodation spaces shall be adequately heated, taking into account climatic conditions.

27. For vessels of 24 metres in length and over, adequate heat shall be provided, through an appropriate heating system, except in fishing vessels operating exclusively in tropical climates. The system of heating shall provide heat in all conditions, as necessary, and shall be in operation when fishers are living or working on board, and when conditions so require.

28. For vessels of 24 metres in length and over, with the exception of those regularly engaged in areas where temperate climatic conditions do not require it, air conditioning shall be provided in accommodation spaces, the bridge, the radio room and any centralized machinery control room.

Lighting

29. All accommodation spaces shall be provided with adequate light.

30. Wherever practicable, accommodation spaces shall be lit with natural light in addition to artificial light. Where sleeping spaces have natural light, a means of blocking the light shall be provided.

31. Adequate reading light shall be provided for every berth in addition to the normal lighting of the sleeping room.

32. Emergency lighting shall be provided in sleeping rooms.

33. Where a vessel is not fitted with emergency lighting in mess rooms, passageways, and any other spaces that are or may be used for emergency escape, permanent night lighting shall be provided in such spaces.

34. For vessels of 24 metres in length and over, lighting in accommodation spaces shall meet a standard established by the competent authority. In any part of the accommodation space available for free movement, the minimum standard for such lighting shall be such as to permit a person with normal vision to read an ordinary printed newspaper on a clear day.

Sleeping rooms

General

35. Where the design, dimensions or purpose of the vessel allow, the sleeping accommodation shall be located so as to minimize the effects of motion and acceleration but shall in no case be located forward of the collision bulkhead.

Floor area

36. The number of persons per sleeping room and the floor area per person, excluding space occupied by berths and lockers, shall be such as to provide adequate space and comfort for the fishers on board, taking into account the service of the vessel.

37. For vessels of 24 metres in length and over but which are less than 45 metres in length, the floor area per person of sleeping rooms, excluding space occupied by berths and lockers, shall not be less than 1.5 square metres.

38. For vessels of 45 metres in length and over, the floor area per person of sleeping rooms, excluding space occupied by berths and lockers, shall not be less than 2 square metres.

39. Notwithstanding the provisions of paragraphs 37 and 38, the competent authority may, after consultation, decide that the minimum permitted floor area per person of sleeping rooms, excluding space occupied by berths and lockers, shall not be less than 1.0 and 1.5 square metres respectively, where the competent authority is satisfied that this is reasonable and will not result in discomfort to the fishers.

Persons per sleeping room

40. To the extent not expressly provided otherwise, the number of persons allowed to occupy each sleeping room shall not be more than six.

41. For vessels of 24 metres in length and over, the number of persons allowed to occupy each sleeping room shall not be more than four. The competent authority may permit exceptions to this requirement in particular cases if the size, type or intended service of the vessel makes the requirement unreasonable or impracticable.

42. To the extent not expressly provided otherwise, a separate sleeping room or sleeping rooms shall be provided for officers, wherever practicable.

43. For vessels of 24 metres in length and over, sleeping rooms for officers shall be for one person wherever possible and in no case shall the sleeping room contain more than two berths. The competent authority may permit exceptions to the requirements of this paragraph in particular cases if the size, type or intended service of the vessel makes the requirements unreasonable or impracticable.

Other

44. The maximum number of persons to be accommodated in any sleeping room shall be legibly and indelibly marked in a place in the room where it can be conveniently seen.

45. Individual berths of appropriate dimensions shall be provided. Mattresses shall be of a suitable material.

46. For vessels of 24 metres in length and over, the minimum inside dimensions of the berths shall not be less than 198 by 80 centimetres.

47. Notwithstanding the provisions of paragraph 46, the competent authority may, after consultation, decide that the minimum inside dimensions of the berths shall not be less than 190 by 70 centimetres, where it is satisfied that this is reasonable and will not result in discomfort to the fishers.

48. Sleeping rooms shall be so planned and equipped as to ensure reasonable comfort for the occupants and to facilitate tidiness. Equipment provided shall include berths, individual lockers sufficient for clothing and other personal effects, and a suitable writing surface.

49. For vessels of 24 metres in length and over, a desk suitable for writing, with a chair, shall be provided.

50. Sleeping accommodation shall be situated or equipped, as practicable, so as to provide appropriate levels of privacy for men and for women.

Mess rooms

51. Mess rooms shall be as close as possible to the galley, but in no case shall be located forward of the collision bulkhead.

52. Vessels shall be provided with mess-room accommodation suitable for their service. To the extent not expressly provided otherwise, mess-room accommodation shall be separate from sleeping quarters, where practicable.

53. For vessels of 24 metres in length and over, mess-room accommodation shall be separate from sleeping quarters.

54. The dimensions and equipment of each mess room shall be sufficient for the number of persons likely to use it at any one time.

55. For vessels of 24 metres in length and over, a refrigerator of sufficient capacity and facilities for making hot and cold drinks shall be available and accessible to fishers at all times.

Tubs or showers, toilets and washbasins

56. Sanitary facilities, which include toilets, washbasins, and tubs or showers, shall be provided for all persons on board, as appropriate for the service of the vessel. These facilities shall meet at least minimum standards of health and hygiene and reasonable standards of quality.

57. The sanitary accommodation shall be such as to eliminate contamination of other spaces as far as practicable. The sanitary facilities shall allow for reasonable privacy.

58. Cold fresh water and hot fresh water shall be available to all fishers and other persons on board, in sufficient quantities to allow for proper hygiene. The competent authority may establish, after consultation, the minimum amount of water to be provided.

59. Where sanitary facilities are provided, they shall be fitted with ventilation to the open air, independent of any other part of the accommodation.

60. All surfaces in sanitary accommodation shall be such as to facilitate easy and effective cleaning. Floors shall have a non-slip deck covering.

61. On vessels of 24 metres in length and over, for all fishers who do not occupy rooms to which sanitary facilities are attached, there shall be provided at least one tub or shower or both, one toilet, and one washbasin for every four persons or fewer.

62. Notwithstanding the provisions of paragraph 61, the competent authority may, after consultation, decide that there shall be provided at least one tub or shower or both and one washbasin for every six persons or fewer, and at least one toilet for every eight persons or fewer, where the competent authority is satisfied that this is reasonable and will not result in discomfort to the fishers.

Laundry facilities

63. Amenities for washing and drying clothes shall be provided as necessary, taking into account the service of the vessel, to the extent not expressly provided otherwise.

64. For vessels of 24 metres in length and over, adequate facilities for washing, drying and ironing clothes shall be provided.

65. For vessels of 45 metres in length and over, adequate facilities for washing, drying and ironing clothes shall be provided in a compartment separate from sleeping rooms, mess rooms and toilets, and shall be adequately ventilated, heated and equipped with lines or other means for drying clothes.

Facilities for sick and injured fishers

66. Whenever necessary, a cabin shall be made available for a fisher who suffers illness or injury.

67. For vessels of 45 metres in length and over, there shall be a separate sick bay. The space shall be properly equipped and shall be maintained in a hygienic state.

Other facilities

68. A place for hanging foul-weather gear and other personal protective equipment shall be provided outside of, but convenient to, sleeping rooms.

Bedding, mess utensils and miscellaneous provisions

69. Appropriate eating utensils, and bedding and other linen shall be provided to all fishers on board. However, the cost of the linen can be recovered as an operational cost if the collective agreement or the fisher's work agreement so provides.

Recreational facilities

70. For vessels of 24 metres in length and over, appropriate recreational facilities, amenities and services shall be provided for all fishers on board. Where appropriate, mess rooms may be used for recreational activities.

Communication facilities

71. All fishers on board shall be given reasonable access to communication facilities, to the extent practicable, at a reasonable cost and not exceeding the full cost to the fishing vessel owner.

Galley and food storage facilities

72. Cooking equipment shall be provided on board. To the extent not expressly provided otherwise, this equipment shall be fitted, where practicable, in a separate galley.

73. The galley, or cooking area where a separate galley is not provided, shall be of adequate size for the purpose, well lit and ventilated, and properly equipped and maintained.

74. For vessels of 24 metres in length and over, there shall be a separate galley.

75. The containers of butane or propane gas used for cooking purposes in a galley shall be kept on the open deck and in a shelter which is designed to protect them from external heat sources and external impact.

76. A suitable place for provisions of adequate capacity shall be provided which can be kept dry, cool and well ventilated in order to avoid deterioration of the stores and, to the extent not expressly provided otherwise, refrigerators or other low-temperature storage shall be used, where possible.

77. For vessels of 24 metres in length and over, a provisions storeroom and refrigerator and other low-temperature storage shall be used.

Food and potable water

78. Food and potable water shall be sufficient, having regard to the number of fishers, and the duration and nature of the voyage. In addition, they shall be suitable in respect of nutritional value, quality, quantity and variety, having regard as well to the fishers' religious requirements and cultural practices in relation to food.

79. The competent authority may establish requirements for the minimum standards and quantity of food and water to be carried on board.

Clean and habitable conditions

80. Accommodation shall be maintained in a clean and habitable condition and shall be kept free of goods and stores which are not the personal property of the occupants or for their safety or rescue.

81. Galley and food storage facilities shall be maintained in a hygienic condition.

82. Waste shall be kept in closed, well-sealed containers and removed from food-handling areas whenever necessary.

Inspections by the skipper or under the authority of the skipper

83. For vessels of 24 metres in length and over, the competent authority shall require frequent inspections to be carried out, by or under the authority of the skipper, to ensure that:

(a) accommodation is clean, decently habitable and safe, and is maintained in a good state of repair;

(b) food and water supplies are sufficient; and

(c) galley and food storage spaces and equipment are hygienic and in a proper state of repair.

The results of such inspections, and the actions taken to address any deficiencies found, shall be recorded and available for review.

Variations

84. The competent authority, after consultation, may permit derogations from the provisions in this Annex to take into account, without discrimination, the interests of fishers having differing and distinctive religious and social practices, on condition that such derogations do not result in overall conditions less favourable than those which would result from the application of this Annex.

The foregoing is the authentic text of the Convention duly adopted by the General Conference of the International Labour Organization during its Ninety-sixth Session which was held at Geneva and declared closed the fifteenth day of June 2007.

IN FAITH WHEREOF we have appended our signatures this fifteenth day of June 2007.

[TEXT IN FRENCH – TEXTE EN FRANÇAIS]

Convention 188

CONVENTION CONCERNANT LE TRAVAIL DANS LE SECTEUR DE LA PÊCHE

La Conférence générale de l'Organisation internationale du Travail,

Convoquée à Genève par le Conseil d'administration du Bureau international du Travail, et s'y étant réunie le 30 mai 2007, en sa quatre-vingt-seizième session;

Reconnaissant que la mondialisation a un impact profond sur le secteur de la pêche;

Notant la Déclaration de l'OIT relative aux principes et droits fondamentaux au travail, 1998;

Tenant compte des droits fondamentaux énoncés dans les conventions internationales du travail suivantes: la convention (nº 29) sur le travail forcé, 1930, la convention (nº 87) sur la liberté syndicale et la protection du droit syndical, 1948, la convention (nº 98) sur le droit d'organisation et de négociation collective, 1949, la convention (nº 100) sur l'égalité de rémunération, 1951, la convention (nº 105) sur l'abolition du travail forcé, 1957, la convention (nº 111) concernant la discrimination (emploi et profession), 1958, la convention (nº 138) sur l'âge minimum, 1973, et la convention (nº 182) sur les pires formes de travail des enfants, 1999;

Notant les instruments pertinents de l'Organisation internationale du Travail, en particulier la convention (nº 155) et la recommandation (nº 164) sur la sécurité et la santé des travailleurs, 1981, ainsi que la convention (nº 161) et la recommandation (nº 171) sur les services de santé au travail, 1985;

Notant en outre la convention (nº 102) concernant la sécurité sociale (norme minimum), 1952, et considérant que les dispositions de l'article 77 de ladite convention ne devraient pas faire obstacle à la protection offerte aux pêcheurs par les Membres dans le cadre des systèmes de sécurité sociale;

Reconnaissant que l'Organisation internationale du Travail considère la pêche comme une activité dangereuse par rapport à d'autres;

Notant également le paragraphe 3 de l'article 1 de la convention (nº 185) sur les pièces d'identité des gens de mer (révisée), 2003;

Consciente que l'Organisation a pour mandat fondamental de promouvoir des conditions de travail décentes;

Consciente de la nécessité de protéger et de promouvoir les droits des pêcheurs en la matière;

Rappelant la Convention des Nations Unies sur le droit de la mer, 1982;

Tenant compte de la nécessité de réviser les conventions internationales suivantes adoptées par la Conférence internationale du Travail concernant spécifiquement le secteur de la pêche, à savoir la convention (n° 112) sur l'âge minimum (pêcheurs), 1959, la convention (n° 113) sur l'examen médical des pêcheurs, 1959, la convention (n° 114) sur le contrat d'engagement des pêcheurs, 1959, et la convention (n° 126) sur le logement à bord des bateaux de pêche, 1966, afin de mettre à jour ces instruments et d'atteindre un plus grand nombre de pêcheurs dans le monde, en particulier ceux travaillant à bord de navires plus petits;

Notant que l'objectif de la présente convention est d'assurer que les pêcheurs bénéficient de conditions décentes pour travailler à bord des navires de pêche en ce qui concerne les conditions minimales requises pour le travail à bord, les conditions de service, le logement et l'alimentation, la protection de la sécurité et de la santé au travail, les soins médicaux et la sécurité sociale;

Après avoir décidé d'adopter diverses propositions relatives au travail dans le secteur de la pêche, question qui constitue le quatrième point à l'ordre du jour de la session;

Après avoir décidé que ces propositions prendraient la forme d'une convention internationale,

adopte, ce quatorzième jour de juin deux mille sept, la convention ci-après, qui sera dénommée Convention sur le travail dans la pêche, 2007.

PARTIE I. DÉFINITIONS ET CHAMP D'APPLICATION

DÉFINITIONS

Article 1

Aux fins de la présente convention:

a) les termes «pêche commerciale» désignent toutes les opérations de pêche, y compris les opérations de pêche dans les cours d'eau, les lacs ou les canaux, à l'exception de la pêche de subsistance et de la pêche de loisir;

b) les termes «autorité compétente» désignent le ministre, le service gouvernemental ou toute autre autorité habilités à édicter et à faire respecter les règlements, arrêtés ou autres instructions ayant force obligatoire dans le domaine visé par la disposition de la convention;

c) le terme «consultation» désigne la consultation par l'autorité compétente des organisations représentatives d'employeurs et de travailleurs intéressées, et en particulier les organisations représentatives d'armateurs à la pêche et de pêcheurs, s'il en existe;

d) les termes «armateur à la pêche» désignent le propriétaire du navire ou toute autre entité ou personne, telle que le gérant, l'agent ou l'affréteur coque nue, à laquelle le propriétaire a confié la responsabilité de l'exploitation du navire et qui, en assumant cette responsabilité, a accepté de se charger des tâches et obligations incombant aux armateurs à la pêche aux termes de la présente convention, indépendamment du fait que d'autres entités ou personnes s'acquittent en son nom de certaines de ces tâches ou responsabilités;

e) le terme «pêcheur» désigne toute personne employée ou engagée à quelque titre que ce soit ou exerçant une activité professionnelle à bord d'un navire de pêche, y compris les personnes travaillant à bord qui sont rémunérées à la part, mais à l'exclusion des pilotes, des équipages de la flotte de guerre, des autres personnes au service permanent du gouvernement, des personnes basées à terre chargées d'effectuer des travaux à bord d'un navire de pêche et des observateurs des pêches;

f) les termes «accord d'engagement du pêcheur» désignent le contrat d'emploi, le contrat d'engagement ou autre accord similaire ainsi que tout autre contrat régissant les conditions de vie et de travail du pêcheur à bord du navire;

g) les termes «navire de pêche» ou «navire» désignent tout bateau ou embarcation, quelles qu'en soient la nature et la forme de propriété, affecté ou destiné à être affecté à la pêche commerciale;

h) les termes «jauge brute» désignent le tonnage brut d'un navire évalué conformément aux dispositions de l'annexe I à la Convention internationale de 1969 sur le jaugeage des navires ou de tout instrument l'amendant ou la remplaçant;

i) le terme «longueur» (L) désigne 96 pour cent de la longueur totale à la flottaison située à une distance de la ligne de quille égale à 85 pour cent du creux minimal sur quille, ou encore à la distance entre la face avant de l'étrave et l'axe de la mèche du gouvernail à cette flottaison, si cette valeur est supérieure. Pour les navires conçus pour naviguer avec une quille inclinée, la flottaison servant à mesurer cette longueur doit être parallèle à la flottaison en charge prévue;

j) les termes «longueur hors tout» (LHT) désignent la distance mesurée en ligne droite parallèlement à la flottaison en charge prévue de l'extrémité avant de la proue à l'extrémité arrière de la poupe;

k) les termes «service de recrutement et de placement» désignent toute personne, société, institution, agence ou autre organisation du secteur public ou privé exerçant des activités relatives au recrutement de pêcheurs pour le compte, ou au placement de pêcheurs auprès, d'armateurs à la pêche;

l) le terme «patron» désigne le pêcheur chargé du commandement d'un navire de pêche.

CHAMP D'APPLICATION

Article 2

1. Sauf disposition contraire de la présente convention, celle-ci s'applique à tous les pêcheurs et à tous les navires de pêche engagés dans des opérations de pêche commerciale.

2. En cas de doute sur l'affectation d'un navire à la pêche commerciale, il appartient à l'autorité compétente de déterminer son type d'affectation après consultation.

3. Tout Membre peut, après consultation, étendre totalement ou en partie la protection prévue par la convention pour les pêcheurs travaillant sur des navires d'une longueur égale ou supérieure à 24 mètres à ceux travaillant sur des navires plus petits.

Article 3

1. Lorsque l'application de la convention soulève des problèmes particuliers d'une importance significative compte tenu des conditions spécifiques de service des pêcheurs ou des opérations des navires de pêche considérés, un Membre peut, après consultation, exclure des prescriptions de la présente convention, ou de certaines de ses dispositions:

a) les navires de pêche engagés dans des opérations de pêche sur les cours d'eau, les lacs ou les canaux;

b) des catégories limitées de pêcheurs ou de navires de pêche.

2. En cas d'exclusion visée au paragraphe précédent, et lorsque cela est réalisable, l'autorité compétente prend, si besoin est, des mesures pour étendre progressivement les prescriptions prévues par la présente convention aux catégories de pêcheurs ou de navires de pêche concernées.

3. Tout Membre qui ratifie la présente convention doit:

a) dans son premier rapport sur l'application de la convention présenté en vertu de l'article 22 de la Constitution de l'Organisation internationale du Travail:

   i) indiquer les catégories de pêcheurs ou de navires de pêche qui sont exclues en application du paragraphe 1;

   ii) donner les motifs de ces exclusions en exposant les positions respectives des organisations représentatives d'employeurs et de travailleurs intéressées, en particulier des organisations représentatives d'armateurs à la pêche et de pêcheurs, s'il en existe;

   iii) décrire toute mesure prise pour octroyer une protection équivalente aux catégories exclues;

b) dans ses rapports ultérieurs sur l'application de la convention, décrire toute mesure prise conformément au paragraphe 2.

Article 4

1. Lorsqu'il n'est pas immédiatement possible pour un Membre de mettre en œuvre l'ensemble des mesures prévues par la présente convention en raison de problèmes particuliers d'une importance significative compte tenu des infrastructures ou institutions insuffisamment développées, le Membre peut, conformément à un plan établi en consultation, mettre en œuvre progressivement tout ou partie des dispositions suivantes:

a) article 10, paragraphe 1;

b) article 10, paragraphe 3, dans la mesure où il s'applique aux navires passant plus de trois jours en mer;

c) article 15;

d) article 20;

e) article 33;

f) article 38.

2. Le paragraphe 1 ne s'applique pas aux navires de pêche:

a) d'une longueur égale ou supérieure à 24 mètres; ou

b) passant plus de sept jours en mer; ou

c) naviguant habituellement à plus de 200 milles nautiques de la côte de l'Etat du pavillon ou au-delà du rebord externe du plateau continental, si celui-ci est plus éloigné de la côte; ou

d) soumis au contrôle de l'Etat du port tel que prévu à l'article 43 de la convention, sauf lorsque le contrôle par l'Etat du port découle d'un cas de force majeure,

ni aux pêcheurs qui travaillent sur ces navires.

3. Tout Membre qui se prévaut de la possibilité prévue au paragraphe 1 doit:

a) dans son premier rapport sur l'application de la convention présenté en vertu de l'article 22 de la Constitution de l'Organisation internationale du Travail:

i) indiquer les dispositions de la convention devant être mises en œuvre progressivement;

ii) en préciser les motifs et exposer les positions respectives des organisations représentatives d'employeurs et de travailleurs intéressées, en particulier des organisations représentatives d'armateurs à la pêche et de pêcheurs, s'il en existe;

iii) décrire le plan de mise en œuvre progressive;

b) dans ses rapports ultérieurs sur l'application de la convention, décrire les mesures prises en vue de donner effet à l'ensemble des dispositions de la convention.

Article 5

1. Aux fins de la présente convention, l'autorité compétente peut, après consultation, décider d'utiliser la longueur hors tout (LHT) à la place de la longueur (L) comme critère de mesure, conformément à l'équivalence établie à l'annexe I. En outre, aux fins des paragraphes spécifiés à l'annexe III de la présente convention, l'autorité compétente peut, après consultation, décider d'utiliser la jauge brute à la place de la longueur (L) ou de la longueur hors tout (LHT) comme critère de mesure, conformément à l'équivalence établie à l'annexe III.

2. Dans les rapports présentés en vertu de l'article 22 de la Constitution, le Membre communiquera les raisons de la décision prise en vertu du présent article et les observations faites lors de la consultation.

PARTIE II. PRINCIPES GÉNÉRAUX

MISE EN ŒUVRE

Article 6

1. Tout Membre doit mettre en œuvre et faire respecter les lois, règlements ou autres mesures qu'il a adoptés afin de s'acquitter de ses obligations aux termes de la présente convention en ce qui concerne les pêcheurs et les navires de pêche relevant de sa compétence. Les autres mesures peuvent comprendre des conventions collectives, des décisions judiciaires, des sentences arbitrales et autres moyens conformes à la législation et à la pratique nationales.

2. Aucune des dispositions de la présente convention n'affecte les lois, sentences, coutumes ou accords entre armateurs à la pêche et pêcheurs qui assurent des conditions plus favorables que celles prévues par la convention.

AUTORITÉ COMPÉTENTE ET COORDINATION

Article 7

Tout Membre doit:

a) désigner l'autorité compétente ou les autorités compétentes;

b) établir des mécanismes de coordination entre les autorités concernées pour le secteur de la pêche aux niveaux national et local, selon le cas, et définir leurs fonctions et responsabilités en tenant compte de leur complémentarité ainsi que des conditions et de la pratique nationales.

RESPONSABILITÉS DES ARMATEURS À LA PÊCHE, DES PATRONS ET DES PÊCHEURS

Article 8

1. L'armateur à la pêche a la responsabilité globale de veiller à ce que le patron dispose des ressources et moyens nécessaires pour s'acquitter des obligations de la présente convention.

2. La responsabilité de la sécurité des pêcheurs à bord et du fonctionnement sûr du navire incombe au patron, notamment, mais non exclusivement, dans les domaines suivants:

a) la supervision, qui doit être exercée de façon à ce que les pêcheurs puissent, dans la mesure du possible, exécuter leur travail dans les meilleures conditions de sécurité et de santé;

b) l'organisation du travail des pêcheurs, qui doit respecter la sécurité et la santé, y compris la prévention de la fatigue;

c) la mise à disposition à bord d'une formation de sensibilisation à la sécurité et à la santé au travail;

d) le respect des normes de sécurité de la navigation et de veille et des bonnes pratiques maritimes y relatives.

3. L'armateur à la pêche ne doit pas entraver la liberté du patron de prendre toute décision qui, de l'avis professionnel de ce dernier, est nécessaire pour la sécurité du navire, de sa navigation ou de son exploitation, ou pour la sécurité des pêcheurs qui sont à bord.

4. Les pêcheurs doivent respecter les ordres légaux du patron et les mesures de sécurité et de santé applicables.

PARTIE III. CONDITIONS MINIMALES REQUISES POUR LE TRAVAIL À BORD DES NAVIRES DE PÊCHE

ÂGE MINIMUM

Article 9

1. L'âge minimum pour le travail à bord d'un navire de pêche est de 16 ans. Toutefois, l'autorité compétente peut autoriser un âge minimum de 15 ans pour les personnes qui ne sont plus soumises à l'obligation de scolarité imposée par la législation nationale et suivent une formation professionnelle en matière de pêche.

2. L'autorité compétente peut, conformément à la législation et à la pratique nationales, autoriser des personnes âgées de 15 ans à exécuter des travaux légers lors des vacances scolaires. Dans ces cas, elle déterminera, après consultation, les types de travail autorisés et prescrira les conditions dans lesquelles ce travail sera entrepris et les périodes de repos requises.

3. L'âge minimum d'affectation à des activités à bord d'un navire de pêche qui, par leur nature ou les conditions dans lesquelles elles s'exercent, sont susceptibles de compromettre la santé, la sécurité ou la moralité des jeunes gens ne doit pas être inférieur à 18 ans.

4. Les types d'activités visés au paragraphe 3 du présent article sont déterminés par la législation nationale ou l'autorité compétente, après consultation, en tenant compte des risques qu'ils comportent et des normes internationales applicables.

5. L'exécution des activités visées au paragraphe 3 du présent article dès l'âge de 16 ans peut être autorisée par la législation nationale ou par une décision de l'autorité compétente, après consultation, à condition que la santé, la sécurité et la moralité des jeunes gens soient pleinement garanties, qu'ils aient reçu une instruction ou une formation professionnelle spécifiques et adéquates et qu'ils aient suivi une formation de base aux questions de sécurité préalable à l'embarquement.

6. Il est interdit d'engager un pêcheur de moins de 18 ans pour un travail de nuit. Aux fins du présent article, le terme «nuit» est défini conformément à la législation et à la pratique nationales. Il couvre une période de neuf heures consécutives au moins, commençant au plus tard à minuit et se terminant au plus tôt à 5 heures du matin. Une dérogation à la stricte observation de la restriction concernant le travail de nuit peut être décidée par l'autorité compétente quand:

a) la formation effective des pêcheurs concernés dans le cadre de programmes et plans d'études établis pourrait en être compromise; ou

b) la nature particulière de la tâche ou un programme de formation agréé exige que les pêcheurs visés par la dérogation travaillent la nuit et l'autorité décide, après consultation, que ce travail ne portera pas préjudice à leur santé ou à leur bien-être.

7. Aucune des dispositions du présent article n'a d'incidence sur les obligations souscrites par le Membre en vertu de la ratification d'autres conventions internationales du travail.

EXAMEN MÉDICAL

Article 10

1. Aucun pêcheur ne doit travailler à bord d'un navire de pêche sans disposer d'un certificat médical valide attestant de son aptitude à exécuter ses tâches.

2. L'autorité compétente peut, après consultation, octroyer des dérogations à l'application du paragraphe 1 du présent article, compte tenu de la sécurité et de la santé des pêcheurs, de la taille du navire, de la disponibilité de l'assistance médicale et des moyens d'évacuation, de la durée du voyage, de la zone d'opération et du type d'activité de pêche.

3. Les dérogations visées au paragraphe 2 du présent article ne s'appliqueront pas à un pêcheur travaillant sur un navire de pêche d'une longueur égale ou supérieure à 24 mètres ou qui passe normalement plus de trois jours en mer. Dans les cas urgents, l'autorité compétente peut autoriser un pêcheur à travailler sur un tel navire pour une période d'une durée limitée et spécifiée en attendant qu'il puisse obtenir un certificat médical, sous réserve que ce pêcheur soit en possession d'un certificat médical expiré depuis peu.

Article 11

Tout Membre doit adopter des lois, règlements ou autres mesures concernant:

a) la nature des examens médicaux;

b) la forme et le contenu des certificats médicaux;

c) la délivrance du certificat médical par du personnel médical dûment qualifié ou, dans le cas d'un certificat concernant seulement la vue, par une personne habilitée par l'autorité compétente à délivrer un tel certificat; ces personnes doivent jouir d'une totale indépendance lorsqu'elles exercent leur jugement professionnel;

d) la fréquence des examens médicaux et la durée de validité des certificats médicaux;

e) le droit pour une personne d'être réexaminée par du personnel médical indépendant différent au cas où elle se verrait refuser un certificat ou imposer des limitations au travail qu'elle peut effectuer;

f) les autres conditions requises.

Article 12

Outre les prescriptions énoncées aux articles 10 et 11, sur un navire de pêche d'une longueur égale ou supérieure à 24 mètres ou passant normalement plus de trois jours en mer:

1. Le certificat médical du pêcheur doit au minimum indiquer:

a) que l'ouïe et la vue de l'intéressé sont satisfaisantes compte tenu de ses tâches sur le navire; et

b) que l'intéressé n'a aucun problème médical de nature à être aggravé par le service en mer ou à le rendre inapte à ce service ou à mettre en danger la sécurité ou la santé d'autres personnes à bord.

2. Le certificat médical est valide pendant deux ans au maximum à moins que le pêcheur soit âgé de moins de 18 ans, auquel cas la durée maximale de validité est d'un an.

3. Si la période de validité du certificat expire au cours d'un voyage, le certificat reste valide jusqu'à la fin du voyage.

PARTIE IV. CONDITIONS DE SERVICE

ÉQUIPAGE ET DURÉE DU REPOS

Article 13

Tout Membre doit adopter des lois, règlements ou autres mesures prévoyant que les armateurs de navires de pêche battant son pavillon veillent à ce que:

a) leurs navires soient dotés d'effectifs suffisants en nombre et en qualité pour assurer la sécurité de navigation et de fonctionnement du navire sous le contrôle d'un patron compétent;

b) soient octroyées aux pêcheurs des périodes de repos régulières d'une durée suffisante pour préserver leur sécurité et leur santé.

Article 14

1. Outre les prescriptions énoncées à l'article 13, l'autorité compétente doit:

a) pour les navires d'une longueur égale ou supérieure à 24 mètres, fixer l'effectif minimal propre à garantir la sécurité de navigation du navire et préciser le nombre de pêcheurs requis et les qualifications qu'ils doivent posséder;

b) pour les navires de pêche passant plus de trois jours en mer, quelle que soit leur taille, fixer, après consultation et en vue de limiter la fatigue, une durée minimum de repos pour les pêcheurs. Cette durée ne doit pas être inférieure à:

i) dix heures par période de 24 heures;

ii) 77 heures par période de sept jours.

2. L'autorité compétente peut, pour des raisons limitées et précises, autoriser qu'il soit dérogé temporairement aux durées de repos fixées à l'alinéa *b)* du paragraphe 1 du présent article. Dans ces cas, elle doit toutefois exiger que des périodes de repos compensatoires soient accordées aux pêcheurs dès que possible.

3. L'autorité compétente peut, après consultation, établir des prescriptions remplaçant celles fixées aux paragraphes 1 et 2 du présent article. Toutefois, lesdites prescriptions doivent être équivalentes dans l'ensemble et ne pas mettre en danger la sécurité et la santé des pêcheurs.

4. Aucune des dispositions du présent article n'affecte le droit du patron d'un navire d'exiger d'un pêcheur les heures de travail nécessaires pour assurer la sécurité immédiate du navire, des personnes à bord ou des captures ou pour porter secours à d'autres embarcations ou aux personnes en détresse en mer. Le cas échéant, le patron peut suspendre les horaires normaux de repos et exiger qu'un pêcheur accomplisse les heures de travail

nécessaires jusqu'au retour à une situation normale. Dès que cela est réalisable après le retour à une situation normale, le patron doit faire en sorte que tout pêcheur ayant effectué un travail alors qu'il était en période de repos selon l'horaire normal bénéficie d'une période de repos adéquate.

LISTE D'ÉQUIPAGE

Article 15

Tout navire de pêche doit avoir à bord une liste d'équipage, dont un exemplaire est fourni aux personnes autorisées à terre avant le départ du navire ou communiqué à terre immédiatement après. L'autorité compétente doit déterminer à qui, à quel moment et à quelles fins cette information doit être fournie.

ACCORD D'ENGAGEMENT DU PÊCHEUR

Article 16

Tout Membre doit adopter des lois, règlements ou autres mesures:

a) prévoyant que les pêcheurs travaillant à bord des navires battant son pavillon soient protégés par un accord d'engagement qui soit conforme aux dispositions de la présente convention et qui leur soit compréhensible;

b) indiquant les mentions minimales à inclure dans les accords d'engagement des pêcheurs, conformément aux dispositions de l'annexe II.

Article 17

Tout Membre doit adopter des lois, règlements ou autres mesures concernant:

a) les procédures garantissant que le pêcheur a la possibilité d'examiner les clauses de son accord d'engagement et de demander conseil à ce sujet avant de le conclure;

b) s'il y a lieu, la tenue des états de service du pêcheur dans le cadre de cet accord;

c) les moyens de régler les différends relatifs à l'accord d'engagement du pêcheur.

Article 18

L'accord d'engagement du pêcheur, dont un exemplaire lui est remis, est disponible à bord, à la disposition du pêcheur et, conformément à la législation et à la pratique nationales, de toute autre partie concernée qui en fait la demande.

Article 19

Les articles 16 à 18 et l'annexe II ne s'appliquent pas au propriétaire de navire qui exploite celui-ci seul.

Article 20

Il incombe à l'armateur à la pêche de veiller à ce que chaque pêcheur soit en possession d'un accord d'engagement de pêcheur écrit, signé à la fois par le pêcheur et l'armateur à la pêche, ou par un représentant autorisé de celui-ci (ou, lorsque le pêcheur n'est pas employé ou engagé par l'armateur à la pêche, l'armateur à la pêche doit avoir une preuve d'un arrangement contractuel ou équivalent), prévoyant des conditions de vie et de travail décentes à bord du navire, conformément aux dispositions de la présente convention.

RAPATRIEMENT

Article 21

1. Les Membres doivent veiller à ce que les pêcheurs à bord d'un navire de pêche battant leur pavillon et qui entre dans un port étranger aient le droit d'être rapatriés lorsque l'accord d'engagement du pêcheur a expiré, ou lorsque le pêcheur ou l'armateur à la pêche y a mis fin pour des raisons justifiées, ou lorsque le pêcheur n'est plus en mesure de s'acquitter des tâches qui lui incombent en vertu de l'accord d'engagement ou qu'on ne peut attendre de lui qu'il les exécute compte tenu des circonstances. La présente disposition s'applique également aux pêcheurs de ce navire qui sont transférés pour les mêmes raisons du navire vers un port étranger.

2. Les frais du rapatriement visé au paragraphe 1 du présent article doivent être pris en charge par l'armateur à la pêche, sauf si le pêcheur a été reconnu, conformément à la législation nationale ou à d'autres dispositions applicables, coupable d'un manquement grave aux obligations de son accord d'engagement.

3. Les Membres doivent déterminer, par voie de législation ou autre, les circonstances précises donnant droit à un rapatriement, la durée maximale des périodes d'embarquement au terme desquelles les pêcheurs visés au paragraphe 1 du présent article ont droit au rapatriement, et les destinations vers lesquelles ils peuvent être rapatriés.

4. Si l'armateur à la pêche omet de pourvoir au rapatriement visé au présent article, le Membre dont le navire bat pavillon doit organiser le rapatriement du pêcheur concerné et a le droit de recouvrer les frais auprès de l'armateur à la pêche.

5. La législation nationale ne doit pas faire obstacle au droit de l'armateur à la pêche de recouvrer le coût du rapatriement au titre d'arrangements contractuels avec des tiers.

RECRUTEMENT ET PLACEMENT

Article 22

Recrutement et placement des pêcheurs

1. Tout Membre qui a mis en place un service public de recrutement et de placement de pêcheurs doit s'assurer que ce service fait partie du service public de l'emploi ouvert à l'ensemble des travailleurs et des employeurs ou qu'il agit en coordination avec celui-ci.

2. Les services privés de recrutement et de placement de pêcheurs qui sont établis sur le territoire d'un Membre doivent exercer leur activité en vertu d'un système de licence ou d'agrément normalisé ou d'une autre forme de réglementation, lesquels ne seront établis, maintenus ou modifiés qu'après consultation.

3. Tout Membre doit, par voie de législation ou autres mesures:

a) interdire aux services de recrutement et de placement d'avoir recours à des moyens, mécanismes ou listes visant à empêcher ou à dissuader les pêcheurs d'obtenir un engagement;

b) interdire que des honoraires ou autres frais soient supportés par les pêcheurs, directement ou indirectement, en tout ou en partie, pour le recrutement ou le placement;

c) fixer les conditions dans lesquelles une licence, un agrément ou toute autre autorisation d'un service privé de recrutement et de placement peuvent être suspendus ou retirés en cas d'infraction à la législation pertinente et préciser les conditions dans lesquelles lesdits services privés peuvent exercer leurs activités.

Agences d'emploi privées

4. Tout Membre qui a ratifié la convention (n° 181) sur les agences d'emploi privées, 1997, peut confier certaines des responsabilités découlant de la présente convention à des agences d'emploi privées qui fournissent les services visés à l'alinéa *b)* du paragraphe 1 de l'article 1 de la convention précitée. Les responsabilités respectives de ces agences d'emploi privées et des armateurs à la pêche, qui sont les «entreprises utilisatrices» au sens de ladite convention, sont déterminées et réparties conformément à l'article 12 de cette même convention. Un tel Membre doit adopter des lois, des règlements ou d'autres mesures pour faire en sorte que l'attribution des responsabilités ou obligations respectives des agences d'emploi privées prestataires du service et de l'«entreprise utilisatrice» conformément à la présente convention n'empêche pas le pêcheur de faire valoir un droit de privilège sur un navire de pêche.

5. Nonobstant les dispositions du paragraphe 4, l'armateur à la pêche est responsable si l'agence d'emploi privée manque aux obligations qui lui

incombent à l'égard du pêcheur pour lequel, dans le cadre de la convention (n° 181) sur les agences d'emploi privées, 1997, l'armateur à la pêche est l'«entreprise utilisatrice».

6. Aucune des dispositions de la présente convention ne saurait être interprétée comme imposant à un Membre l'obligation d'autoriser dans son secteur de pêche le recours à des agences d'emploi privées telles que visées au paragraphe 4 du présent article.

PAIEMENT DES PÊCHEURS

Article 23

Tout Membre adopte, après consultation, une législation ou d'autres mesures prescrivant que les pêcheurs qui perçoivent un salaire seront payés mensuellement ou à d'autres intervalles réguliers.

Article 24

Tout Membre doit exiger que tous les pêcheurs travaillant à bord de navires de pêche aient les moyens de faire parvenir à leur famille et sans frais tout ou partie des paiements reçus, y compris les avances.

PARTIE V. LOGEMENT ET ALIMENTATION

Article 25

Tout Membre doit adopter une législation ou d'autres mesures relatives au logement, à la nourriture et à l'eau potable à bord des navires de pêche battant son pavillon.

Article 26

Tout Membre doit adopter une législation ou d'autres mesures prévoyant que le logement à bord des navires de pêche battant son pavillon sera d'une qualité et d'une taille suffisantes et qu'il sera équipé de façon adaptée au service du navire et à la durée du séjour des pêcheurs à bord. En particulier, ces mesures règlent, selon le cas, les questions suivantes:

a) approbation des plans de construction ou de modification des navires de pêche en ce qui concerne le logement;

b) maintien du logement et de la cuisine dans des conditions générales d'hygiène, de sécurité, de santé et de confort;

c) ventilation, chauffage, refroidissement et éclairage;

d) réduction des bruits et vibrations excessifs;

e) emplacement, taille, matériaux de construction, ameublement et équipement des cabines, réfectoires et autres espaces de logement;

f) installations sanitaires, comprenant des toilettes et des moyens de lavage, et fourniture d'eau chaude et froide en quantité suffisante;

g) procédures d'examen des plaintes concernant des conditions de logement qui ne satisfont pas aux prescriptions de la présente convention.

Article 27

Tout Membre doit adopter une législation ou d'autres mesures prévoyant que:

a) la nourriture transportée et servie à bord doit être d'une valeur nutritionnelle, d'une qualité et d'une quantité suffisantes;

b) l'eau potable doit être d'une qualité et d'une quantité suffisantes;

c) la nourriture et l'eau potable doivent être fournies par l'armateur à la pêche sans frais pour le pêcheur. Toutefois, conformément à la législation nationale, les frais peuvent être recouvrés sous forme de coûts d'exploitation pour autant qu'une convention collective régissant un système de rémunération à la part ou que l'accord d'engagement du pêcheur le prévoie.

Article 28

1. La législation ou les autres mesures adoptées par le Membre conformément aux articles 25 à 27 doivent donner pleinement effet à l'annexe III concernant le logement à bord des navires de pêche. L'annexe III peut être amendée de la façon prévue à l'article 45.

2. Un Membre qui n'est pas en mesure d'appliquer les dispositions de l'annexe III peut, après consultation, adopter dans sa législation des dispositions ou d'autres mesures équivalentes dans l'ensemble aux dispositions énoncées à l'annexe III, à l'exception des dispositions se rapportant à l'article 27.

PARTIE VI. SOINS MÉDICAUX, PROTECTION DE LA SANTÉ ET SÉCURITÉ SOCIALE

SOINS MÉDICAUX

Article 29

Tout Membre doit adopter une législation ou d'autres mesures prévoyant que:

a) les navires de pêche soient dotés de fournitures et d'un matériel médicaux adaptés au service du navire, compte tenu du nombre de pêcheurs à bord, de la zone d'opération et de la durée du voyage;

b) les navires de pêche aient à leur bord au moins un pêcheur qualifié ou formé pour donner les premiers secours et autres formes de soins médicaux, qui sache utiliser les fournitures et le matériel médicaux dont est doté le navire, compte tenu du nombre de pêcheurs à bord, de la zone d'opération et de la durée du voyage;

c) les fournitures et le matériel médicaux présents à bord soient accompagnés d'instructions ou d'autres informations dans une langue et une présentation compréhensibles au pêcheur ou aux pêcheurs visés à l'alinéa *b)*;

d) les navires de pêche soient équipés d'un système de communication par radio ou par satellite avec des personnes ou services à terre pouvant fournir des consultations médicales, compte tenu de la zone d'opération et de la durée du voyage;

e) les pêcheurs aient le droit de bénéficier d'un traitement médical à terre et d'être débarqués à cet effet en temps voulu en cas de lésion ou de maladie graves.

Article 30

Pour les navires de pêche d'une longueur égale ou supérieure à 24 mètres, compte tenu du nombre de pêcheurs à bord, de la zone d'opération et de la durée du voyage, tout Membre doit adopter une législation ou d'autres mesures prévoyant que:

a) l'autorité compétente prescrive le matériel médical et les fournitures médicales devant être disponibles à bord;

b) le matériel médical et les fournitures médicales disponibles à bord soient entretenus de façon adéquate et inspectés à des intervalles réguliers, fixés par l'autorité compétente, par des responsables désignés ou agréés par celle-ci;

c) les navires soient pourvus d'un guide médical de bord adopté ou approuvé par l'autorité compétente ou de l'édition la plus récente du *Guide médical international de bord*;

d) les navires en mer aient accès à un dispositif organisé de consultations médicales par radio ou par satellite, y compris à des conseils de spécialistes, à toute heure du jour ou de la nuit;

e) les navires conservent à bord une liste de stations de radio ou de satellite par l'intermédiaire desquelles des consultations médicales peuvent être obtenues;

f) dans une mesure conforme à la législation et à la pratique du Membre, les soins médicaux dispensés au pêcheur lorsqu'il est à bord ou débarqué dans un port étranger lui soient fournis gratuitement.

SÉCURITÉ ET SANTÉ AU TRAVAIL ET PRÉVENTION DES ACCIDENTS DU TRAVAIL

Article 31

Tout Membre doit adopter une législation ou d'autres mesures concernant:

a) la prévention des accidents du travail, des maladies professionnelles et des risques liés au travail à bord des navires, notamment l'évaluation et la gestion des risques, la formation des pêcheurs et l'instruction à bord;

b) la formation des pêcheurs à l'utilisation des engins de pêche dont ils se serviront et à la connaissance des opérations de pêche qu'ils auront à effectuer;

c) les obligations des armateurs à la pêche, des pêcheurs et autres personnes intéressées, compte dûment tenu de la sécurité et de la santé des pêcheurs âgés de moins de 18 ans;

d) la déclaration des accidents survenant à bord des navires de pêche battant son pavillon et la réalisation d'enquêtes sur ces accidents;

e) la constitution de comités paritaires de sécurité et de santé au travail ou, après consultation, d'autres organismes qualifiés.

Article 32

1. Les prescriptions du présent article s'appliquent aux navires d'une longueur égale ou supérieure à 24 mètres passant habituellement plus de trois jours en mer et, après consultation, à d'autres navires, compte tenu du nombre de pêcheurs à bord, de la zone d'opération et de la durée du voyage.

2. L'autorité compétente doit:

a) après consultation, faire obligation à l'armateur à la pêche d'établir, conformément à la législation, aux conventions collectives et à la pratique nationales, des procédures à bord visant à prévenir les accidents du travail et les lésions et maladies professionnelles, compte tenu des dangers et risques spécifiques du navire de pêche concerné;

b) exiger que les armateurs à la pêche, les patrons, les pêcheurs et les autres personnes concernées reçoivent suffisamment de directives et de matériel de formation appropriés ainsi que toute autre information pertinente sur la manière d'évaluer et de gérer les risques en matière de sécurité et de santé à bord des navires de pêche.

3. Les armateurs à la pêche doivent:

a) veiller à ce que tous les pêcheurs à bord reçoivent des vêtements et équipements de protection individuelle appropriés;

b) veiller à ce que tous les pêcheurs à bord aient reçu une formation de base en matière de sécurité, approuvée par l'autorité compétente; cette dernière peut cependant accorder une dérogation écrite dans le cas des pêcheurs qui démontrent qu'ils possèdent des connaissances et une expérience équivalentes;

c) veiller à ce que les pêcheurs soient suffisamment et convenablement familiarisés avec l'équipement et son utilisation, y compris avec les mesures de sécurité s'y rapportant, avant d'utiliser cet équipement ou de participer aux opérations concernées.

Article 33

L'évaluation des risques concernant la pêche est effectuée, selon le cas, avec la participation de pêcheurs ou de leurs représentants.

SÉCURITÉ SOCIALE

Article 34

Tout Membre veille à ce que les pêcheurs résidant habituellement sur son territoire et, dans la mesure prévue par la législation nationale, les personnes à leur charge bénéficient de la sécurité sociale à des conditions non moins favorables que celles qui s'appliquent aux autres travailleurs, y compris les personnes salariées ou indépendantes, résidant habituellement sur son territoire.

Article 35

Tout Membre s'engage à prendre des mesures, en fonction de la situation nationale, pour assurer progressivement une protection complète de sécurité sociale à tous les pêcheurs résidant habituellement sur son territoire.

Article 36

Les Membres doivent coopérer, dans le cadre d'accords bilatéraux ou multilatéraux ou d'autres arrangements, en conformité avec la législation ou la pratique nationales, en vue:

a) d'assurer progressivement une protection complète de sécurité sociale aux pêcheurs, sans considération de nationalité, en tenant compte du principe d'égalité de traitement;

b) de garantir le maintien des droits en matière de sécurité sociale acquis ou en cours d'acquisition par tous les pêcheurs, indépendamment de leur lieu de résidence.

Article 37

Nonobstant l'attribution des responsabilités prévues aux articles 34, 35 et 36, les Membres peuvent établir, par des accords bilatéraux ou multilatéraux ou par des dispositions adoptées dans le cadre d'organisations régionales d'intégration économique, d'autres règles relatives à la législation en matière de sécurité sociale applicable aux pêcheurs.

PROTECTION EN CAS DE MALADIE,
LÉSION OU DÉCÈS LIÉS AU TRAVAIL

Article 38

1. Tout Membre prend des mesures en vue d'assurer aux pêcheurs une protection, conformément à la législation et à la pratique nationales, en cas de maladie, de lésion ou de décès liés au travail.

2. En cas de lésion provoquée par un accident du travail ou une maladie professionnelle, le pêcheur doit:

a) avoir accès à des soins médicaux appropriés;

b) bénéficier d'une indemnisation correspondante conformément à la législation nationale.

3. Compte tenu des caractéristiques du secteur de la pêche, la protection visée au paragraphe 1 du présent article pourra être assurée:

a) soit par un régime reposant sur la responsabilité de l'armateur à la pêche;

b) soit par un régime d'assurance obligatoire d'indemnisation des travailleurs ou d'autres régimes.

Article 39

1. En l'absence de dispositions nationales applicables aux pêcheurs, tout Membre adopte une législation ou d'autres mesures visant à garantir que les armateurs à la pêche assurent la protection de la santé et les soins médicaux des pêcheurs lorsque ces derniers sont employés ou engagés ou travaillent à bord d'un navire battant son pavillon, en mer ou dans un port étranger. Cette législation ou ces autres mesures doivent garantir que les armateurs à la pêche acquittent les frais des soins médicaux, y compris l'aide et le soutien matériels correspondants pendant la durée des traitements médicaux dispensés à l'étranger jusqu'au rapatriement du pêcheur.

2. La législation nationale peut prévoir de décharger l'armateur à la pêche de sa responsabilité dans le cas où l'accident n'est pas survenu au service du navire de pêche ou si la maladie ou l'infirmité a été dissimulée lors de l'engagement ou si l'accident ou la maladie est imputable à une faute intentionnelle du pêcheur.

PARTIE VII. RESPECT ET APPLICATION

Article 40

Tout Membre exerce effectivement sa juridiction et son contrôle sur les navires battant son pavillon en se dotant d'un système propre à garantir le respect des prescriptions de la présente convention, notamment en prévoyant, s'il y a lieu, la conduite d'inspections, l'établissement de rapports, une procédure de règlement des plaintes, un suivi et la mise en œuvre de sanctions et mesures correctives appropriées conformément à la législation nationale.

Article 41

1. Les Membres doivent exiger que les navires de pêche qui passent plus de trois jours en mer et qui:

a) ont une longueur égale ou supérieure à 24 mètres, ou

b) naviguent habituellement à plus de 200 milles nautiques de la côte de l'Etat du pavillon ou au-delà du rebord externe du plateau continental, si celui-ci est plus éloigné,

aient à bord un document valide délivré par l'autorité compétente, indiquant qu'ils ont été inspectés par l'autorité compétente ou en son nom, en vue de déterminer leur conformité avec les dispositions de la présente convention concernant les conditions de vie et de travail à bord.

2. La durée de validité de ce document peut coïncider avec celle d'un certificat national ou international de sécurité des navires de pêche mais ne dépasse en aucun cas cinq ans.

Article 42

1. L'autorité compétente désigne des inspecteurs qualifiés en nombre suffisant pour assumer les responsabilités qui lui incombent en vertu de l'article 41.

2. Aux fins de l'instauration d'un système efficace d'inspection des conditions de vie et de travail à bord des navires de pêche, un Membre peut, s'il y a lieu, autoriser des institutions publiques ou d'autres organismes dont il reconnaît la compétence et l'indépendance à réaliser des inspections et à délivrer des certificats. Dans tous les cas, le Membre demeure entièrement responsable de l'inspection et de la délivrance des certificats correspondants relatifs aux conditions de vie et de travail des pêcheurs à bord des navires battant son pavillon.

Article 43

1. Si un Membre reçoit une plainte ou acquiert la preuve qu'un navire battant son pavillon ne se conforme pas aux prescriptions de la convention, il prend les dispositions nécessaires pour enquêter et s'assurer que des mesures sont prises pour remédier aux manquements constatés.

2. Si un Membre dans le port duquel un navire de pêche fait escale dans le cours normal de son activité ou pour une raison inhérente à son exploitation reçoit une plainte ou acquiert la preuve que ce navire de pêche n'est pas conforme aux prescriptions de la présente convention, il peut adresser un rapport au gouvernement de l'Etat du pavillon, avec copie au Directeur général du Bureau international du Travail, et prendre les mesures nécessaires pour redresser toute situation à bord qui constitue manifestement un danger pour la sécurité ou la santé.

3. S'il prend les mesures mentionnées au paragraphe 2 du présent article, le Membre doit en informer immédiatement le plus proche représentant de l'Etat du pavillon et demander à celui-ci d'être présent si possible. Il ne doit pas retenir ou retarder indûment le navire.

4. Aux fins du présent article, une plainte peut être soumise par un pêcheur, un organisme professionnel, une association, un syndicat ou, de

manière générale, toute personne ayant un intérêt à la sécurité du navire, y compris en ce qui concerne les risques relatifs à la sécurité ou à la santé des pêcheurs à bord.

5. Cet article ne s'applique pas aux plaintes qu'un Membre considère manifestement infondées.

Article 44

Tout Membre appliquera la présente convention de manière à garantir que les navires de pêche battant pavillon de tout Etat qui n'a pas ratifié la convention ne bénéficient pas d'un traitement plus favorable que celui accordé aux navires battant pavillon de tout Membre qui l'a ratifiée.

PARTIE VIII. AMENDEMENTS DES ANNEXES I, II ET III

Article 45

1. Sous réserve des dispositions pertinentes de la présente convention, la Conférence internationale du Travail peut amender les annexes I, II et III. Le Conseil d'administration du Bureau international du Travail peut inscrire à l'ordre du jour de la Conférence une question concernant des propositions d'amendements établies par une réunion tripartite d'experts. La majorité des deux tiers des voix des délégués présents à la Conférence, comprenant au moins la moitié des Membres ayant ratifié cette convention, est requise pour l'adoption d'amendements.

2. Tout amendement adopté conformément au paragraphe 1 du présent article entre en vigueur six mois après la date de son adoption pour tout Membre ayant ratifié la présente convention, à moins que le Membre en question n'ait adressé au Directeur général du Bureau international du Travail une notification écrite précisant que cet amendement n'entrera pas en vigueur à son égard ou n'entrera en vigueur qu'ultérieurement à la suite d'une nouvelle notification.

PARTIE IX. DISPOSITIONS FINALES

Article 46

La présente convention révise la convention (n° 112) sur l'âge minimum (pêcheurs), 1959, la convention (n° 113) sur l'examen médical des pêcheurs, 1959, la convention (n° 114) sur le contrat d'engagement des pêcheurs, 1959, et la convention (n° 126) sur le logement à bord des bateaux de pêche, 1966.

Article 47

Les ratifications formelles de la présente convention sont communiquées au Directeur général du Bureau international du Travail aux fins d'enregistrement.

Article 48

1. La présente convention ne lie que les Membres de l'Organisation internationale du Travail dont la ratification a été enregistrée par le Directeur général du Bureau international du Travail.

2. Elle entre en vigueur 12 mois après que les ratifications de dix Membres comprenant huit Etats côtiers ont été enregistrées par le Directeur général.

3. Par la suite, la convention entre en vigueur pour chaque Membre 12 mois après la date de l'enregistrement de sa ratification.

Article 49

1. Tout Membre ayant ratifié la présente convention peut la dénoncer à l'expiration d'une période de dix années après la date de la mise en vigueur initiale de la convention, par un acte communiqué au Directeur général du Bureau international du Travail aux fins d'enregistrement. La dénonciation prend effet une année après avoir été enregistrée.

2. Tout Membre ayant ratifié la présente convention qui, dans l'année après l'expiration de la période de dix années mentionnée au paragraphe précédent, ne se prévaut pas de la faculté de dénonciation prévue par le présent article sera lié pour une nouvelle période de dix années et, par la suite, pourra dénoncer la présente convention dans la première année de chaque nouvelle période de dix années dans les conditions prévues au présent article.

Article 50

1. Le Directeur général du Bureau international du Travail notifiera à tous les Membres de l'Organisation internationale du Travail l'enregistrement de toutes les ratifications, déclarations, et dénonciations qui lui seront communiquées par les Membres de l'Organisation.

2. En notifiant aux Membres de l'Organisation l'enregistrement de la dernière ratification nécessaire à l'entrée en vigueur de la présente convention, le Directeur général appelle l'attention des Membres de l'Organisation sur la date à laquelle la convention entrera en vigueur.

Article 51

Le Directeur général du Bureau international du Travail communique au Secrétaire général des Nations Unies, aux fins d'enregistrement, conformément à l'article 102 de la Charte des Nations Unies, des renseignements complets au sujet de toutes ratifications, déclarations et dénonciations enregistrées par le Directeur général.

Article 52

Chaque fois qu'il le juge nécessaire, le Conseil d'administration du Bureau international du Travail présente à la Conférence générale un rapport sur l'application de la présente convention et examine s'il y a lieu d'inscrire à l'ordre du jour de la Conférence la question de sa révision totale ou partielle, prenant également en considération les dispositions de l'article 45.

Article 53

1. Au cas où la Conférence adopte une nouvelle convention portant révision de la présente convention, et à moins que la nouvelle convention n'en dispose autrement:

a) la ratification par un Membre de la nouvelle convention portant révision entraîne de plein droit, nonobstant les dispositions de l'article 49 ci-dessus, la dénonciation immédiate de la présente convention, sous réserve que la nouvelle convention portant révision soit entrée en vigueur ;

b) à partir de la date de l'entrée en vigueur de la nouvelle convention portant révision, la présente convention cesse d'être ouverte à la ratification des Membres.

2. La présente convention demeure en tout cas en vigueur dans sa forme et teneur pour les Membres qui l'auraient ratifiée et qui ne ratifieraient pas la convention portant révision.

Article 54

Les versions française et anglaise de la présente convention font également foi.

ANNEXE I

EQUIVALENCE POUR LE MESURAGE

Aux fins de la présente convention, lorsque l'autorité compétente, après consultation, décide d'utiliser la longueur hors tout (LHT) comme critère de mesure plutôt que la longueur (L):

a) une longueur hors tout (LHT) de 16,5 mètres sera considérée comme équivalente à une longueur (L) de 15 mètres;

b) une longueur hors tout (LHT) de 26,5 mètres sera considérée comme équivalente à une longueur (L) de 24 mètres;

c) une longueur hors tout (LHT) de 50 mètres sera considérée comme équivalente à une longueur (L) de 45 mètres.

ANNEXE II

ACCORD D'ENGAGEMENT DU PÊCHEUR

L'accord d'engagement du pêcheur devra comporter les mentions suivantes, sauf dans les cas où l'inclusion de l'une de ces mentions ou de certaines d'entre elles est inutile, la question étant déjà réglée d'une autre manière par la législation nationale ou, le cas échéant, par une convention collective:

a) les nom et prénoms du pêcheur, la date de naissance ou l'âge, ainsi que le lieu de naissance;

b) le lieu et la date de la conclusion de l'accord;

c) la désignation du ou des navires de pêche et le numéro d'immatriculation du ou des navires de pêche à bord duquel ou desquels le pêcheur s'engage à travailler;

d) le nom de l'employeur ou de l'armateur à la pêche ou autre partie à l'accord;

e) le voyage ou les voyages à entreprendre, s'ils peuvent être déterminés au moment de l'engagement;

f) la fonction pour laquelle le pêcheur doit être employé ou engagé;

g) si possible, la date à laquelle et le lieu où le pêcheur sera tenu de se présenter à bord pour le commencement de son service;

h) les vivres à allouer au pêcheur, sauf si la législation nationale prévoit un système différent;

i) le montant du salaire du pêcheur ou, s'il est rémunéré à la part, le pourcentage de sa part et le mode de calcul de celle-ci, ou encore, si un système mixte de rémunération est appliqué, le montant du salaire, le pourcentage de sa part et le mode de calcul de celle-ci, ainsi que tout salaire minimum convenu;

j) l'échéance de l'accord et les conditions y relatives, soit:

- i) si l'accord a été conclu pour une durée déterminée, la date fixée pour son expiration;
- ii) si l'accord a été conclu au voyage, le port de destination convenu pour la fin de l'accord et l'indication du délai à l'expiration duquel le pêcheur sera libéré après l'arrivée à cette destination;
- iii) si l'accord a été conclu pour une durée indéterminée, les conditions dans lesquelles chaque partie pourra dénoncer l'accord ainsi que le délai de préavis requis, lequel n'est pas plus court pour l'employeur, l'armateur à la pêche ou autre partie que pour le pêcheur;

k) la protection en cas de maladie, de lésion ou de décès du pêcheur lié à son service;

l) le congé payé annuel ou la formule utilisée pour le calculer, le cas échéant;

m) les prestations en matière de protection de la santé et de sécurité sociale qui doivent être assurées au pêcheur par l'employeur, l'armateur à la pêche ou autre partie à l'accord d'engagement du pêcheur, selon le cas;

n) le droit du pêcheur à un rapatriement;

o) la référence à la convention collective, le cas échéant;

p) les périodes minimales de repos conformément à la législation nationale ou autres mesures;

q) toutes autres mentions que la législation nationale peut exiger.

Annexe III

Logement à bord des navires de pêche

Dispositions générales

1. Aux fins de la présente annexe:

a) les termes «navire de pêche neuf» désignent un navire pour lequel:

i) le contrat de construction ou de transformation importante a été passé à la date d'entrée en vigueur de la convention pour le Membre concerné ou après cette date; ou

ii) le contrat de construction ou de transformation importante a été passé avant la date d'entrée en vigueur de la convention pour le Membre concerné, et qui est livré trois ans ou plus après cette date; ou

iii) en l'absence d'un contrat de construction, à la date d'entrée en vigueur de la convention pour le Membre concerné ou après cette date:

– la quille est posée; ou

– une construction permettant d'identifier un navire particulier a commencé; ou

– le montage a commencé, employant au moins 50 tonnes ou 1 pour cent de la masse estimée de tous les matériaux de structure, si cette dernière valeur est inférieure;

b) les termes «navire existant» désignent un navire qui n'est pas un navire de pêche neuf.

2. Les dispositions suivantes s'appliquent à tous les nouveaux navires de pêche pontés, sauf exclusions autorisées aux termes de l'article 3 de la convention. L'autorité compétente peut également, après consultation, appliquer les prescriptions de la présente annexe aux navires existants, dès lors que et dans la mesure où elle décide que cela est raisonnable et réalisable.

3. L'autorité compétente peut, après consultation, autoriser des dérogations aux dispositions de la présente annexe pour des navires de pêche ne restant normalement en mer que pour des durées inférieures à 24 heures si les pêcheurs ne vivent pas à bord du navire lorsqu'il est au port. Dans le cas de tels navires, l'autorité compétente doit veiller à ce que les pêcheurs concernés aient à leur disposition des installations adéquates pour leurs repos, alimentation et hygiène.

4. Toute dérogation faite par un Membre en vertu du paragraphe 3 de la présente annexe doit être communiquée au Bureau international du Travail conformément à l'article 22 de la Constitution de l'Organisation internationale du Travail.

5. Les prescriptions valables pour les navires d'une longueur égale ou supérieure à 24 mètres peuvent s'appliquer aux navires d'une longueur comprise entre 15 et 24 mètres si l'autorité compétente décide, après consultation, que cela est raisonnable et réalisable.

6. Les pêcheurs travaillant à bord de navires nourrices dépourvus de logements et d'installations sanitaires appropriés pourront utiliser ceux du navire mère.

7. Les Membres peuvent étendre les dispositions de la présente annexe relatives au bruit et aux vibrations, à la ventilation, au chauffage et à la climatisation, à l'éclairage aux lieux de travail clos et aux espaces servant à l'entreposage si, après consultation, cette extension est considérée appropriée et n'influe pas négativement sur les conditions de travail ou sur le traitement ou la qualité des captures.

8. L'utilisation de la jauge brute visée à l'article 5 de la convention est limitée aux paragraphes de la présente annexe spécifiés ci-après: 14, 37, 38, 41, 43, 46, 49, 53, 55, 61, 64, 65 et 67. A ces fins, lorsque l'autorité compétente, après consultation, décide d'utiliser la jauge brute comme critère de mesure:

a) une jauge brute de 75 sera considérée comme équivalente à une longueur (L) de 15 mètres, ou à une longueur hors tout (LHT) de 16,5 mètres;

b) une jauge brute de 300 sera considérée comme équivalente à une longueur (L) de 24 mètres, ou à une longueur hors tout (LHT) de 26,5 mètres;

c) une jauge brute de 950 sera considérée comme équivalente à une longueur (L) de 45 mètres, ou à une longueur hors tout (LHT) de 50 mètres.

Planification et contrôle

9. L'autorité compétente doit vérifier que, chaque fois qu'un navire vient d'être construit, ou que le logement de l'équipage à bord du navire a été refait à neuf, ledit navire est conforme aux prescriptions de la présente annexe. L'autorité compétente doit, dans la mesure du possible, exiger qu'un navire dont le logement de l'équipage a été substantiellement modifié soit conforme aux prescriptions de la présente annexe et qu'un navire qui remplace son pavillon par le pavillon du Membre soit conforme aux prescriptions de la présente annexe applicables conformément au paragraphe 2 de ladite annexe.

10. Dans les situations visées au paragraphe 9 de la présente annexe, pour les navires d'une longueur égale ou supérieure à 24 mètres, l'autorité compétente doit demander que les plans détaillés du logement de l'équipage et des informations à son sujet soient soumis pour approbation à l'autorité compétente ou à une entité qu'elle a habilitée à cette fin.

11. Pour les navires d'une longueur égale ou supérieure à 24 mètres, l'autorité compétente doit contrôler, chaque fois que le logement de

l'équipage a été refait à neuf ou substantiellement modifié, que celui-ci est conforme aux prescriptions de la convention, et lorsque le navire remplace son pavillon par le pavillon du Membre, contrôler qu'il est conforme aux prescriptions de la présente annexe applicables conformément au paragraphe 2 de ladite annexe. L'autorité compétente peut réaliser, lorsqu'elle le juge opportun, des inspections complémentaires du logement de l'équipage.

12. Lorsqu'un navire change de pavillon, toute prescription que l'autorité compétente du Membre dont le navire battait précédemment pavillon peut avoir adoptée conformément aux dispositions des paragraphes 15, 39, 47 ou 62 de la présente annexe cesse de s'appliquer au navire.

Conception et construction

Hauteur sous barrot

13. Tous les logements doivent avoir une hauteur sous barrot adéquate. L'autorité compétente doit prescrire la hauteur sous barrot minimale des locaux où les pêcheurs doivent se tenir debout pendant de longues périodes.

14. Sur les navires d'une longueur égale ou supérieure à 24 mètres, la hauteur sous barrot minimale autorisée dans tous les logements où les pêcheurs doivent pouvoir jouir d'une entière liberté de mouvement ne doit pas être inférieure à 200 centimètres.

15. Nonobstant les dispositions du paragraphe 14, l'autorité compétente peut, après consultation, décider que la hauteur sous barrot minimale autorisée ne doit pas être inférieure à 190 centimètres dans tout logement, ou partie de logement, où elle s'est assurée que cela est raisonnable et ne causera pas d'inconfort aux pêcheurs.

Ouvertures donnant sur les locaux d'habitation et entre eux

16. Les ouvertures directes entre les postes de couchage et les cales à poissons et salles des machines doivent être proscrites, sauf lorsqu'il s'agit d'issues de secours. Dans la mesure où cela est raisonnable et réalisable, les ouvertures directes entre les postes de couchage et les cuisines, cambuses, séchoirs ou installations sanitaires communes doivent être évitées, à moins qu'il n'en soit expressément disposé autrement.

17. Sur les navires d'une longueur égale ou supérieure à 24 mètres, il ne doit y avoir aucune ouverture reliant directement les postes de couchage aux cales à poissons, salles des machines, cuisines, cambuses, séchoirs ou installations sanitaires communes, sauf lorsqu'il s'agit d'issues de secours; la partie de la cloison séparant ces locaux des postes de couchage et des cloisons externes doit être convenablement construite en acier ou autre matériau homologué et être étanche à l'eau et aux gaz. La présente disposition n'exclut pas la possibilité d'un partage d'installations sanitaires entre deux cabines.

Isolation

18. L'isolation du logement de l'équipage doit être adéquate; les matériaux employés pour construire les cloisons, les panneaux et les vaigrages intérieurs, ainsi que les revêtements de sol et les joints doivent être adaptés à leur emploi et de nature à garantir un environnement sain. Des dispositifs d'écoulement des eaux suffisants doivent être prévus dans tous les logements.

Autres

19. Tous les moyens possibles doivent être mis en œuvre pour empêcher que les mouches et autres insectes ne pénètrent dans les locaux d'habitation de l'équipage des navires de pêche, en particulier lorsque ceux-ci opèrent dans des zones infestées de moustiques.

20. Tous les logements d'équipage doivent être dotés des issues de secours nécessaires.

Bruits et vibrations

21. L'autorité compétente doit prendre des mesures pour réduire les bruits et vibrations excessifs dans les locaux d'habitation, si possible en conformité avec les normes internationales pertinentes.

22. Sur les navires d'une longueur égale ou supérieure à 24 mètres, l'autorité compétente doit adopter des normes réglementant les niveaux de bruit et de vibrations dans les locaux d'habitation de manière à protéger adéquatement les pêcheurs des effets nocifs de ces bruits et vibrations, notamment de la fatigue qu'ils induisent.

Ventilation

23. Les locaux d'habitation doivent être ventilés en fonction des conditions climatiques. Le système de ventilation doit permettre une aération satisfaisante des locaux lorsque les pêcheurs sont à bord.

24. Le système de ventilation doit être conçu ou d'autres mesures doivent être prises de manière à protéger les non-fumeurs de la fumée de tabac.

25. Les navires d'une longueur égale ou supérieure à 24 mètres doivent être équipés d'un système de ventilation réglable des locaux d'habitation, de façon à maintenir l'air dans des conditions satisfaisantes et à en assurer une circulation suffisante par tous les temps et sous tous les climats. Les systèmes de ventilation doivent fonctionner en permanence lorsque les pêcheurs sont à bord.

Chauffage et climatisation

26. Les locaux d'habitation doivent être chauffés de manière adéquate en fonction des conditions climatiques.

27. Sur les navires d'une longueur égale ou supérieure à 24 mètres, un chauffage adéquat fourni par un système de chauffage approprié doit être prévu sauf sur les navires de pêche opérant exclusivement en zone tropicale. Le système de chauffage doit fournir de la chaleur dans toutes les conditions, suivant les besoins, et fonctionner lorsque les pêcheurs séjournent ou travaillent à bord et que les conditions l'exigent.

28. Sur les navires d'une longueur égale ou supérieure à 24 mètres, à l'exception de ceux opérant dans des zones où les conditions climatiques tempérées ne l'exigent pas, les locaux d'habitation, la passerelle, les salles de radio et toute salle de contrôle des machines centralisée doivent être équipés d'un système de climatisation.

Eclairage

29. Tous les locaux d'habitation doivent bénéficier d'un éclairage adéquat.

30. Dans la mesure du possible, les locaux d'habitation doivent, outre un éclairage artificiel, être éclairés par la lumière naturelle. Lorsque les postes de couchage sont éclairés par la lumière naturelle, un moyen de l'occulter doit être prévu.

31. Chaque couchette doit être dotée d'un éclairage de chevet en complément de l'éclairage normal du poste de couchage.

32. Les postes de couchage doivent être équipés d'un éclairage de secours.

33. Si à bord d'un navire les réfectoires, les coursives et les locaux qui sont ou peuvent être traversés comme issues de secours ne sont pas équipés d'un éclairage de secours, un éclairage permanent doit y être prévu pendant la nuit.

34. Sur les navires d'une longueur égale ou supérieure à 24 mètres, les locaux d'habitation doivent être éclairés conformément à une norme établie par l'autorité compétente. En tous points du local d'habitation où l'on peut circuler librement, la norme minimale de cet éclairage doit être telle qu'une personne dotée d'une acuité visuelle normale puisse lire, par temps clair, un journal imprimé ordinaire.

Postes de couchage

Dispositions générales

35. Lorsque la conception, les dimensions ou l'usage même du navire le permettent, les postes de couchage doivent être situés de telle manière que les mouvements et l'accélération du navire soient ressentis le moins possible mais ils ne doivent être situés en aucun cas en avant de la cloison d'abordage.

Superficie au sol

36. Le nombre de personnes par poste de couchage ainsi que la superficie au sol par personne, déduction faite de la superficie occupée par les couchettes et les armoires, doivent permettre aux pêcheurs de disposer de suffisamment d'espace et de confort à bord, compte tenu de l'utilisation du navire.

37. Sur les navires d'une longueur égale ou supérieure à 24 mètres, mais inférieure à 45 mètres, la superficie au sol par occupant d'un poste de couchage, déduction faite de la superficie occupée par les couchettes et les armoires, ne doit pas être inférieure à 1,5 mètre carré.

38. Sur les navires d'une longueur égale ou supérieure à 45 mètres, la superficie au sol par occupant d'un poste de couchage, déduction faite de la superficie occupée par les couchettes et les armoires, ne doit pas être inférieure à 2 mètres carrés.

39. Nonobstant les dispositions des paragraphes 37 et 38, l'autorité compétente peut, après consultation, décider que la superficie au sol minimale autorisée par occupant d'un poste de couchage, déduction faite de la superficie occupée par les couchettes et les armoires, ne doit pas être inférieure à 1,0 et 1,5 mètre carré respectivement, si elle s'est assurée que cela est raisonnable et ne causera pas d'inconfort aux pêcheurs.

Nombre de personnes par poste de couchage

40. Dans la mesure où il n'en est pas expressément disposé autrement, le nombre de personnes autorisées à occuper un poste de couchage ne doit pas être supérieur à six.

41. Sur les navires d'une longueur égale ou supérieure à 24 mètres, le nombre de personnes autorisées à occuper un poste de couchage ne doit pas être supérieur à quatre. L'autorité compétente peut accorder des dérogations à cette prescription dans certains cas si la taille et le type du navire ou son utilisation la rendent déraisonnable ou irréalisable.

42. Dans la mesure où il n'en est pas expressément disposé autrement, une ou plusieurs cabines séparées doivent être réservées aux officiers, lorsque cela est possible.

43. Sur les navires d'une longueur égale ou supérieure à 24 mètres, les postes de couchage réservés aux officiers doivent accueillir une seule personne dans la mesure du possible et ne doivent en aucun cas contenir plus de deux couchettes. L'autorité compétente peut accorder des dérogations aux prescriptions de ce paragraphe dans certains cas si la taille et le type du navire ou son utilisation les rendent déraisonnables ou irréalisables.

Autres

44. Le nombre maximal de personnes autorisées à occuper un poste de couchage doit être inscrit de manière lisible et indélébile à un endroit où il peut se lire facilement.

45. Des couchettes individuelles de dimensions suffisantes doivent être prévues. Les matelas doivent être d'un matériau adéquat.

46. Sur les navires d'une longueur égale ou supérieure à 24 mètres, les dimensions internes minimales des couchettes ne doivent pas être inférieures à 198 centimètres sur 80 centimètres.

47. Nonobstant les dispositions du paragraphe 46, l'autorité compétente peut, après consultation, décider que les dimensions internes minimales des couchettes ne doivent pas être inférieures à 190 centimètres par 70 centimètres, si elle s'est assurée que cela est raisonnable et ne causera pas d'inconfort aux pêcheurs.

48. Les postes de couchage doivent être conçus et équipés de manière à garantir aux occupants un confort raisonnable et à faciliter leur maintien en ordre. Les équipements fournis doivent comprendre des couchettes, des armoires individuelles suffisamment grandes pour contenir des vêtements et autres effets personnels et une surface plane adéquate où il est possible d'écrire.

49. Sur les navires d'une longueur égale ou supérieure à 24 mètres, un bureau pour écrire et une chaise adaptés doivent être fournis.

50. Les postes de couchage doivent, dans la mesure du possible, être situés ou équipés de telle manière que tant les hommes que les femmes puissent convenablement préserver leur intimité.

Réfectoires

51. Les réfectoires doivent être aussi proches que possible de la cuisine, mais en aucun cas en avant de la cloison d'abordage.

52. Les navires doivent posséder un réfectoire adapté à leur utilisation. Le local du réfectoire doit être si possible à l'écart des postes de couchage, dans la mesure où il n'en est pas expressément disposé autrement.

53. Sur les navires d'une longueur égale ou supérieure à 24 mètres, le réfectoire doit être séparé des postes de couchage.

54. Les dimensions et l'aménagement de chaque réfectoire doivent être suffisants pour qu'il puisse accueillir le nombre de personnes susceptibles de l'utiliser en même temps.

55. Sur les navires d'une longueur égale ou supérieure à 24 mètres, les pêcheurs doivent à tout moment avoir accès à un réfrigérateur d'un volume suffisant et avoir la possibilité de se préparer des boissons chaudes ou froides.

Baignoires ou douches, toilettes et lavabos

56. Des installations sanitaires appropriées à l'utilisation du navire, qui comprennent des toilettes, lavabos, baignoires ou douches, doivent être prévues pour toutes les personnes à bord. Ces installations doivent correspondre aux normes minimales en matière de santé et d'hygiène et offrir un niveau de qualité raisonnable.

57. Les installations sanitaires doivent être conçues de manière à éliminer dans la mesure où cela est réalisable la contamination d'autres locaux. Les installations sanitaires doivent préserver un degré d'intimité raisonnable.

58. Tous les pêcheurs et toute autre personne à bord doivent avoir accès à de l'eau douce froide et chaude en quantité suffisante pour assurer une hygiène convenable. L'autorité compétente peut déterminer, après consultation, le volume d'eau minimal nécessaire.

59. Lorsque des installations sanitaires sont prévues, elles doivent être ventilées vers l'extérieur et situées à l'écart de tout local d'habitation.

60. Toutes les surfaces des installations sanitaires doivent être faciles à nettoyer correctement. Les sols doivent être recouverts d'un revêtement antidérapant.

61. Sur les navires d'une longueur égale ou supérieure à 24 mètres, tous les pêcheurs n'occupant pas un poste doté d'installations sanitaires doivent avoir accès au moins à une baignoire ou une douche, ou les deux, une toilette et un lavabo pour quatre personnes ou moins.

62. Nonobstant les dispositions du paragraphe 61, l'autorité compétente peut, après consultation, décider de prévoir au moins une baignoire ou une douche, ou les deux, et un lavabo pour six personnes ou moins, et au moins une toilette pour huit personnes ou moins, si elle s'est assurée que cela est raisonnable et ne causera pas d'inconfort aux pêcheurs.

Buanderies

63. Dans la mesure où il n'en est pas expressément disposé autrement, des installations appropriées pour le lavage et le séchage des vêtements doivent être prévues selon les besoins, en tenant compte des conditions d'utilisation du navire.

64. Sur les navires d'une longueur égale ou supérieure à 24 mètres, des installations adéquates pour le lavage, le séchage et le repassage des vêtements doivent être prévues.

65. Sur les navires d'une longueur égale ou supérieure à 45 mètres, ces installations doivent être adéquates et situées dans des locaux séparés des postes de couchage, des réfectoires et des toilettes qui soient suffisamment ventilés, chauffés et pourvus de cordes à linge ou autres moyens de séchage.

Installations pour les pêcheurs malades ou blessés

66. Chaque fois que nécessaire, une cabine doit être mise à la disposition d'un pêcheur blessé ou malade.

67. Sur les navires d'une longueur égale ou supérieure à 45 mètres, une infirmerie séparée doit être prévue. Ce local doit être correctement équipé et maintenu dans un état hygiénique.

Autres installations

68. Un endroit approprié à l'extérieur des postes de couchage et aisément accessible à partir de ces derniers doit être prévu pour pendre les vêtements de gros temps et autre équipement de protection personnel.

Literie, vaisselle et couverts et fournitures diverses

69. Tous les pêcheurs à bord doivent avoir à leur disposition de la vaisselle, du linge de lit et autres linges appropriés. Toutefois, les frais de linge peuvent être recouvrés sous forme de coûts d'exploitation pour autant qu'une convention collective ou que l'accord d'engagement du pêcheur le prévoie.

Installations de loisirs

70. A bord des navires d'une longueur égale ou supérieure à 24 mètres, tous les pêcheurs doivent avoir accès à des installations, des équipements et des services de loisirs. Le cas échéant, les réfectoires peuvent être utilisés comme installations de loisirs.

Installations de communications

71. Dans la mesure du possible, tous les pêcheurs à bord du navire doivent avoir raisonnablement accès à des équipements pour effectuer leurs communications à un coût raisonnable n'excédant pas le coût total facturé à l'armateur à la pêche.

Cuisine et cambuse

72. Des équipements doivent être prévus pour la préparation des aliments. Dans la mesure où il n'en est pas expressément disposé autrement, ces équipements sont installés, si possible, dans une cuisine séparée.

73. La cuisine, ou coin cuisine lorsqu'il n'existe pas de cuisine séparée, doit être d'une dimension adéquate, être bien éclairée et ventilée et être correctement équipée et entretenue.

74. Les navires d'une longueur égale ou supérieure à 24 mètres doivent être équipés d'une cuisine séparée.

75. Les bouteilles de gaz butane ou propane utilisé à des fins de cuisine doivent être placées sur le pont découvert, dans un lieu abrité conçu pour les protéger contre les sources extérieures de chaleur et les chocs.

76. Un emplacement adéquat pour les provisions, d'un volume suffisant, doit être prévu et pouvoir être maintenu sec, frais et bien aéré pour éviter que les provisions ne se gâtent. Dans la mesure où il n'en est pas expressément disposé autrement, des réfrigérateurs ou autres moyens de stockage à basse température sont si possible utilisés.

77. Pour les navires d'une longueur égale ou supérieure à 24 mètres, une cambuse et un réfrigérateur ou autre local d'entreposage à basse température doivent être utilisés.

Nourriture et eau potable

78. L'avitaillement doit être suffisant compte tenu du nombre de pêcheurs à bord ainsi que de la durée et de la nature du voyage. Il doit être en outre d'une valeur nutritionnelle, d'une qualité, d'une quantité et d'une variété satisfaisantes eu égard également aux exigences de la religion des pêcheurs et à leurs habitudes culturelles en matière alimentaire.

79. L'autorité compétente peut établir des prescriptions concernant les normes minimales et la quantité de nourriture et d'eau devant être disponible à bord.

Conditions de salubrité et de propreté

80. Le logement des pêcheurs doit être maintenu dans un état de propreté et de salubrité et ne doit contenir ni bien ni marchandise qui ne soit pas la propriété personnelle des occupants ou destiné à leur sécurité ou sauvetage.

81. La cuisine et les installations d'entreposage des aliments doivent être maintenues dans des conditions hygiéniques.

82. Les déchets doivent être gardés dans des conteneurs fermés et hermétiques qui sont retirés, quand il y a lieu, des espaces de manutention des vivres.

Inspections effectuées par le patron ou sous son autorité

83. Sur les navires d'une longueur égale ou supérieure à 24 mètres, l'autorité compétente doit exiger que des inspections fréquentes soient conduites par le patron ou sous son autorité pour assurer que:

a) les logements sont propres, décemment habitables, sûrs et maintenus en bon état;

b) les provisions d'eau et de nourriture sont suffisantes;

c) la cuisine, la cambuse et les équipements servant à l'entreposage de la nourriture sont hygiéniques et bien entretenus.

Les résultats de ces inspections ainsi que les mesures prises pour remédier à tout manquement sont consignés et sont disponibles pour consultation.

Dérogations

84. L'autorité compétente peut, après consultation, permettre des dérogations aux dispositions de la présente annexe pour tenir compte, sans discrimination, des intérêts des pêcheurs ayant des pratiques religieuses et sociales différentes et particulières, sous réserve qu'il n'en résulte pas des conditions qui, dans l'ensemble, seraient moins favorables que celles qui auraient découlé de l'application de l'annexe.

Le texte qui précède est le texte authentique de la convention dûment adoptée par la Conférence générale de l'Organisation internationale du Travail dans sa quatre-vingt-seizième session qui s'est tenue à Genève et qui a été déclarée close le quinzième jour de juin 2007.

EN FOI DE QUOI ont apposé leurs signatures, ce quinzième jour de juin 2007:

The President of the Conference,
Le Président de la Conférence,

KASTRIOT SULKA

The Director-General of the International Labour Office,
Le Directeur général du Bureau international du Travail,

JUAN SOMAVIA

No. 54756

Peru
and
United Nations Educational, Scientific and Cultural Organization

Agreement between the Government of the Republic of Peru and the United Nations Educational, Scientific and Cultural Organization concerning the meeting of the Bureau of the International Coordinating Council of the Man and the Biosphere Programme (MAB) and the 28th session of the International Coordinating Council of the MAB (with annex). Paris, 4 February 2016

Entry into force: *4 February 2016 by signature, in accordance with its provisions*

Authentic text: *English*

Registration with the Secretariat of the United Nations: *Peru, 1 November 2017*

Not published in print, in accordance with article 12(2) of the General Assembly regulations to give effect to Article 102 of the Charter of the United Nations, as amended, and the publication practice of the Secretariat.

Pérou
et
Organisation des Nations Unies pour l'éducation, la science et la culture

Accord entre le Gouvernement de la République du Pérou et l'Organisation des Nations Unies pour l'éducation, la science et la culture relatif à la réunion du Bureau du Conseil international de coordination du Programme sur l'Homme et la biosphère (MAB) et la 28e session du Conseil international de coordination du MAB (avec annexe). Paris, 4 février 2016

Entrée en vigueur : *4 février 2016 par signature, conformément à ses dispositions*

Texte authentique : *anglais*

Enregistrement au Secrétariat de l'Organisation des Nations Unies : *Pérou, 1er novembre 2017*

Non disponible en version imprimée, conformément au paragraphe 2 de l'article 12 du règlement de l'Assemblée générale destiné à mettre en application l'Article 102 de la Charte des Nations Unies, tel qu'amendé, et à la pratique du Secrétariat en matière de publication.

No. 54757

Peru
and
United Nations Educational, Scientific and Cultural Organization

Agreement between the Government of the Republic of Peru and the United Nations Educational, Scientific and Cultural Organization concerning the Regional Centre for the Safeguarding of the Intangible Cultural Heritage of Latin America (CRESPIAL) in Cusco, Peru. Paris, 21 July 2014

Entry into force: *22 January 2015 by notification, in accordance with article 17*

Authentic texts: *English and Spanish*

Registration with the Secretariat of the United Nations: *Peru, 6 November 2017*

Not published in print, in accordance with article 12(2) of the General Assembly regulations to give effect to Article 102 of the Charter of the United Nations, as amended, and the publication practice of the Secretariat.

Pérou
et
Organisation des Nations Unies pour l'éducation, la science et la culture

Accord entre le Gouvernement de la République du Pérou et l'Organisation des Nations Unies pour l'éducation, la science et la culture concernant le Centre régional pour la sauvegarde du patrimoine culturel immatériel de l'Amérique latine (CRESPIAL) à Cusco (Pérou). Paris, 21 juillet 2014

Entrée en vigueur : *22 janvier 2015 par notification, conformément à l'article 17*

Textes authentiques : *anglais et espagnol*

Enregistrement au Secrétariat de l'Organisation des Nations Unies : *Pérou, 6 novembre 2017*

Non disponible en version imprimée, conformément au paragraphe 2 de l'article 12 du règlement de l'Assemblée générale destiné à mettre en application l'Article 102 de la Charte des Nations Unies, tel qu'amendé, et à la pratique du Secrétariat en matière de publication.

No. 54758

Peru and Poland

Agreement between the Government of the Republic of Peru and the Government of the Republic of Poland on gainful activity by family members dependent on a member of the staff of a diplomatic mission or consular post. Warsaw, 8 May 2017

Entry into force: *17 August 2017, in accordance with article 10*

Authentic texts: *English, Polish and Spanish*

Registration with the Secretariat of the United Nations: *Peru, 6 November 2017*

Not published in print, in accordance with article 12(2) of the General Assembly regulations to give effect to Article 102 of the Charter of the United Nations, as amended, and the publication practice of the Secretariat.

Pérou et Pologne

Accord entre le Gouvernement de la République du Pérou et le Gouvernement de la République de Pologne relatif à l'exercice d'une activité rémunérée par les membres de la famille à charge d'un membre du personnel d'une mission diplomatique ou d'un poste consulaire. Varsovie, 8 mai 2017

Entrée en vigueur : *17 août 2017, conformément à l'article 10*

Textes authentiques : *anglais, polonais et espagnol*

Enregistrement au Secrétariat de l'Organisation des Nations Unies : *Pérou, 6 novembre 2017*

Non disponible en version imprimée, conformément au paragraphe 2 de l'article 12 du règlement de l'Assemblée générale destiné à mettre en application l'Article 102 de la Charte des Nations Unies, tel qu'amendé, et à la pratique du Secrétariat en matière de publication.

No. 54759

Peru
and
European Union

Financing Agreement between the European Union and the Republic of Peru concerning the Programme to support the national drug control strategy 2012-2016 (with annexes). Lima, 20 December 2013, 15 January 2014 and 21 January 2014

Entry into force: *7 March 2014 by notification, in accordance with article 9*

Authentic text: *Spanish*

Registration with the Secretariat of the United Nations: *Peru, 6 November 2017*

Not published in print, in accordance with article 12(2) of the General Assembly regulations to give effect to Article 102 of the Charter of the United Nations, as amended, and the publication practice of the Secretariat.

Pérou
et
Union européenne

Accord de financement entre l'Union européenne et la République du Pérou concernant le Programme d'appui à la stratégie nationale de lutte contre les drogues 2012-2016 (avec annexes). Lima, 20 décembre 2013, 15 janvier 2014 et 21 janvier 2014

Entrée en vigueur : *7 mars 2014 par notification, conformément à l'article 9*

Texte authentique : *espagnol*

Enregistrement au Secrétariat de l'Organisation des Nations Unies : *Pérou, 6 novembre 2017*

Non disponible en version imprimée, conformément au paragraphe 2 de l'article 12 du règlement de l'Assemblée générale destiné à mettre en application l'Article 102 de la Charte des Nations Unies, tel qu'amendé, et à la pratique du Secrétariat en matière de publication.

No. 54760

Peru
and
United States of America

Assistance Agreement between the United States of America and the Republic of Peru (with annexes). Lima, 29 September 2008

Entry into force: *29 September 2008 by signature*

Authentic texts: *English and Spanish*

Registration with the Secretariat of the United Nations: *Peru, 6 November 2017*

Not published in print, in accordance with article 12(2) of the General Assembly regulations to give effect to Article 102 of the Charter of the United Nations, as amended, and the publication practice of the Secretariat.

Pérou
et
États-Unis d'Amérique

Accord d'assistance entre les États-Unis d'Amérique et la République du Pérou (avec annexes). Lima, 29 septembre 2008

Entrée en vigueur : *29 septembre 2008 par signature*

Textes authentiques : *anglais et espagnol*

Enregistrement au Secrétariat de l'Organisation des Nations Unies : *Pérou, 6 novembre 2017*

Non disponible en version imprimée, conformément au paragraphe 2 de l'article 12 du règlement de l'Assemblée générale destiné à mettre en application l'Article 102 de la Charte des Nations Unies, tel qu'amendé, et à la pratique du Secrétariat en matière de publication.

No. 54761

Poland
and
Latvia

Agreement between the Republic of Poland and the Republic of Latvia for the avoidance of double taxation and prevention of fiscal evasion with respect to taxes on income and on capital. Warsaw, 17 November 1993

Entry into force: *30 November 1994 by notification, in accordance with article 29*

Authentic text: *English*

Registration with the Secretariat of the United Nations: *Poland, 8 November 2017*

Pologne
et
Lettonie

Accord entre la République de Pologne et la République de Lettonie tendant à éviter les doubles impositions et à prévenir la fraude fiscale en matière d'impôts sur le revenu et sur la fortune. Varsovie, 17 novembre 1993

Entrée en vigueur : *30 novembre 1994 par notification, conformément à l'article 29*

Texte authentique : *anglais*

Enregistrement au Secrétariat de l'Organisation des Nations Unies : *Pologne, 8 novembre 2017*

[TEXT IN ENGLISH – TEXTE EN ANGLAIS]

AGREEMENT

BETWEEN

THE REPUBLIC OF POLAND

AND

THE REPUBLIC OF LATVIA

FOR THE AVOIDANCE OF DOUBLE TAXATION AND PREVENTION OF FISCAL EVASION WITH RESPECT TO TAXES ON INCOME AND ON CAPITAL

The Government of the Republic of Poland
and
the Government of the Republic of Latvia

Desiring to conclude an Agreement for the avoidance of double taxation and the prevention of fiscal evasion with respect to taxes on income and on capital,

Have agreed as follows:

ARTICLE 1

PERSONAL SCOPE

This Agreement shall apply to persons who are residents of one or both of the Contracting States.

ARTICLE 2

TAXES COVERED

1. This Agreement shall apply to taxes on income and on capital imposed on behalf of a Contracting State or of its political subdivisions or local authorities, irrespective of the manner in which they are levied.

2. There shall be regarded as taxes on income and on capital all taxes imposed on total income, on total capital, or on elements of income or of capital, including taxes on gains from the alienation of movable or immovable property, as well as taxes on capital appreciation.

3. The existing taxes to which the Agreement shall apply are in particular:

a) in Poland:
   (i) the personal income tax (podatek dochodowy od osób fizycznych);
   (ii) the corporate income tax (podatek dochodowy od osób prawnych);
   (hereinafter referred to as "Polish tax");

b) in Latvia:
(i) the profits tax (pelnas nodoklis);
(ii) the personal income tax (iedzivotaju ienakuma nodoklis);
(iii) the property tax (ipasuma nodoklis);
(hereinafter referred to as "Latvian tax").

4. The Agreement shall apply also to any identical or substantially similar taxes which are imposed after the date of signature of the Agreement in addition to, or in place of, the existing taxes. The competent authorities of the Contracting States shall notify each other of any significant changes which have been made in their respective taxation laws.

ARTICLE 3

GENERAL DEFINITIONS

1. For the purposes of this Agreement, unless the context otherwise requires:

a) the term "Poland" when used in geographical sense means the territory of the Republic of Poland, including any area beyond its territorial waters, within which under the laws of Poland and in accordance with international law, Poland may exercise its sovereign rights over the sea-bed, its subsoil and their natural resources;

b) the term "Latvia" means the Republic of Latvia and, when used in the geographical sense, means the territory of the Republic of Latvia and any other area adjacent to the territorial waters of the Republic of Latvia within which under the laws of the Republic of Latvia and in accordance with international law, the rights of Latvia may be exercised with respect to the sea-bed and its sub-soil and their natural resources;

c) the terms "a Contracting State" and " the other Contracting State" mean Poland or Latvia as the context requires;

d) the term "national" means any individual possessing the nationality of a Contracting State and any legal person, partnership or association deriving its status as such from the laws in force in a Contracting State;

e) the term "person" includes an individual, a company and any other body of persons;

f) the term "company" means any body corporate or any entity which is treated as a body corporate for tax purposes;

g) the terms "enterprise of a Contracting State" and "enterprise of the other Contracting State" mean respectively an enterprise carried on by a resident of a Contracting State and an enterprise carried on by a resident of the other Contracting State;

h) the term "international traffic" means any transport by a ship, aircraft or road transport vehicle operated by an enterprise of a Contracting State, except when the ship, aircraft or road transport vehicle is operated solely between places in the other Contracting State;

i) the term "competent authority" means:
   (i) in the case of Poland, the Minister of Finance or his authorised representative;
   (ii) in the case of Latvia, the Minister of Economic Reforms and the Head of State Finance Inspectorate or their authorised representative.

2. As regards the application of the Agreement by a Contracting State any term not defined therein shall, unless the context otherwise requires, have the meaning which it has under the law

of that State concerning the taxes to which this Agreement applies.

ARTICLE 4

RESIDENT

1. For the purposes of this Agreement, the term "resident of a Contracting State" means any person who, under the laws of that State, is liable to tax therein by reason of his domicile, residence, place of management, place of incorporation or any other criterion of a similar nature. The term also includes a Government of that State itself, its political subdivisions and local authorities and any agency or wholly owned entity of such State, political subdivision or local authority that is established under the laws in that State. The term does not include any person who is liable to tax in that State in respect only of income from sources in that State or capital situated therein.

2. Where by reason of the provisions of paragraph 1 an individual is a resident of both Contracting States, then his status shall be determined as follows:

a) he shall be deemed to be a resident of the State in which he has a permanent home available to him; if he has a permanent home available to him in both States, he shall be deemed to be a resident of the State with which his personal and economic relations are closer (centre of vital interests);

b) if the State in which he has his centre of vital interests cannot be determined, or if he has not a permanent home available to him in either State, he shall be deemed to be a resident of the State in which he has an habitual abode;

c) if he has an habitual abode in both States or in neither of them, he shall be deemed to be a resident of the State of which he is a national;

d) if the status of a resident cannot be determined according to subparagraphs a)-c), the competent authorities of the Contracting States shall settle the question by mutual agreement.

3. Where by reason of the provisions of paragraph 1 a person other than an individual is a resident of both Contracting States, then it shall be deemed to be a resident of the Contracting State under the laws of which it derives its status as such.

ARTICLE 5

PERMANENT ESTABLISHMENT

1. For the purposes of this Agreement, the term "permanent establishment" means a fixed place of business through which the business of an enterprise is wholly or partly carried on.

2. The term "permanent establishment" includes especially:
   a) a place of management;
   b) a branch;
   c) an office;
   d) a factory;
   e) a workshop, and
   f) a mine, an oil or gas well, a quarry or any other place of extraction of natural resources.

3. A building site, a construction, assembly or installation project or a supervisory or consultancy activity connected therewith constitutes a permanent establishment only if such site, project or activity lasts for a period of more than nine months.

4. Notwithstanding the preceding provisions of this Article, the term "permanent establishment" shall be deemed not to include:

a) the use of facilities solely for the purpose of storage, display or delivery of goods or merchandise belonging to the enterprise;

b) the maintenance of a stock of goods or merchandise belonging to the enterprise solely for the purpose of storage, display or delivery;

c) the maintenance of a stock of goods or merchandise belonging to the enterprise solely for the purpose of processing by another enterprise;

d) the maintenance of a fixed place of business solely for the purpose of purchasing goods or merchandise or of collecting information, for the enterprise;

e) the maintenance of a fixed place of business solely for the purpose of carrying on, for the enterprise, any other activity of a preparatory or auxiliary character;

f) the maintenance of a fixed place of business solely for any combination of activities mentioned in subparagraphs a) to e), provided that the overall activity of the fixed place of business resulting from this combination is of a preparatory or auxiliary character.

5. Notwithstanding the provisions of paragraphs 1 and 2, where a person - other than an agent of an independent status to whom paragraph 6 applies - is acting on behalf of an enterprise and has, and habitually exercises, in a Contracting State an authority to conclude contracts in the name of the enterprise, that enterprise shall be deemed to have a permanent establishment in that State in respect of any activities which that person undertakes for the enterprise, unless the activities of such person are limited to those mentioned in paragraph 4 which, if exercised through a fixed place of business, would not make this fixed place of business a permanent establishment under the provisions of that paragraph.

6. An enterprise shall not be deemed to have a permanent establishment in a Contracting State merely because it carries on business in that State through a broker, general commission agent or any other agent of an independent status, provided that such persons are acting in the ordinary course of their business. However, when the activities of such an agent are devoted wholly or almost wholly on behalf of that enterprise, he will not be considered an agent of an independent status within the meaning of this paragraph.

7. The fact that a company which is a resident of a Contracting State controls or is controlled by a company which is a resident of the other Contracting State, or which carries on business in that other State (whether through a permanent establishment or otherwise), shall not of itself constitute either company a permanent establishment of the other.

ARTICLE 6

INCOME FROM IMMOVABLE PROPERTY

1. Income derived by a resident of a Contracting State from immovable property (including income from agriculture or forestry) situated in the other Contracting State may be taxed in that other State.

2. The term "immovable property" shall have the meaning which it has under the law of the Contracting State in which the property in question is situated. The term shall in any case include property accessory to immovable property, in particular buildings, livestock and equipment used in agriculture and forestry, rights to which the provisions of general law respecting landed property apply, in particular any options or similar rights, usufruct of immovable property and rights to variable or fixed payments as consideration for the working of, or the right to work, mineral deposits, sources and other natural resources; ships, boats, aircraft and road transport vehicles shall not be regarded as immovable property.

3. The provisions of paragraph 1 shall apply to income derived from the direct use, letting, or use in any other form of immovable property, as well as income from the alienation of immovable property.

4. Where the ownership of shares or other corporate rights in a company entitles the owner of such shares or corporate rights to the enjoyment of immovable property held by the company, the income from the direct use, letting, or use in any other form of such right to enjoyment may be taxed in the Contracting State in which the immovable property is situated.

5. The provisions of paragraphs 1 and 3 shall also apply to the income from immovable property of an enterprise and to income from immovable property used for the performance of independent personal services.

ARTICLE 7

BUSINESS PROFITS

1. The profits of an enterprise of a Contracting State shall be taxable only in that State unless the enterprise carries on business in the other Contracting State through a permanent establishment situated therein. If the enterprise carries on business as aforesaid, the profits of the enterprise may be taxed in the other State but only so much of them as is attributable to:

a) that permanent establishment; or

b) sales in that other State of goods or merchandise of the same or similar kind as those sold through that permanent establishment; or

c) other business activities carried on in that other State of the same or similar kind as those effected through that permanent establishment.

2. Subject to the provisions of paragraph 3, where an enterprise of a Contracting State carries on business in the other Contracting State through a permanent establishment situated therein, there shall in each Contracting State be attributed to that permanent establishment the profits which it might be expected to make if it were a distinct and separate enterprise engaged in the same or similar activities under the same or

similar conditions and dealing wholly independently with the enterprise of which it is a permanent establishment.

3. In determining the profits of a permanent establishment, there shall be allowed as deductions expenses which are incurred for the purposes of the permanent establishment, including executive and general administrative expenses so incurred, whether in the State in which the permanent establishment is situated or elsewhere. The expenses to be allowed as deductions by a Contracting State shall include only expenses that are deductible under domestic laws of that State.

4. Insofar as it has been customary in a Contracting State to determine the profits to be attributed to a permanent establishment on the basis of an apportionment of the total profits of the enterprise to its various parts, nothing in paragraph 2 shall preclude that Contracting State from determining the profits to be taxed by such an apportionment as may be customary; the method of apportionment adopted shall, however, be such that the result shall be in accordance with the principles contained in this Article.

5. No profits shall be attributed to a permanent establishment by reason of the mere purchase by that permanent establishment of goods or merchandise for the enterprise.

6. For the purposes of the preceding paragraphs, the profits to be attributed to the permanent establishment shall be determined by the same method year by year unless there is good and sufficient reason to the contrary.

7. Where profits include items of income which are dealt with separately in other Articles of this Agreement, then the provisions of those Articles shall not be affected by the provisions of this Article.

ARTICLE 8

INTERNATIONAL TRANSPORT

1. Profits of an enterprise of a Contracting State from the operation of ships, aircraft or road transport vehicles in international traffic shall be taxable only in that State.

2. The provisions of paragraph 1 shall also apply to profits from the participation in a pool, a joint business or an international operating agency.

ARTICLE 9

ASSOCIATED ENTERPRISES

1. Where

a) an enterprise of a Contracting State participates directly or indirectly in the management, control or capital of an enterprise of the other Contracting State, or

b) the same persons participate directly or indirectly in the management, control or capital of an enterprise of a Contracting State and an enterprise of the other Contracting State,

and in either case conditions are made or imposed between the two enterprises in their commercial or financial relations which differ from those which would be made between independent enterprises, then any profits which would, but for those conditions, have accrued to one of the enterprises, but, by reason of those conditions, have not so accrued, may be included in the profits of that enterprise and taxed accordingly.

2. Where a Contracting State includes in the profits of an enterprise of that State - and taxes accordingly - profits on which an enterprise of the other Contracting State has been charged to tax in that other State and the profits so included are profits which would have accrued to the enterprise of the first-mentioned State if the conditions made between the two enterprises had been those which would have been made between independent enterprises, then that other State shall make an appropriate adjustment to the amount of the tax charged therein on those profits. In determining such adjustment, due regard shall be had to the other provisions of this Agreement and the competent authorities of the Contracting States shall if necessary consult each other.

ARTICLE 10

DIVIDENDS

1. Dividends paid by a company which is a resident of a Contracting State to a resident of the other Contracting State may be taxed in that other State.

2. However, such dividends may also be taxed in the Contracting State of which the company paying the dividends is a resident and according to the laws of that State, but if the recipient is the beneficial owner of the dividends the tax so charged shall not exceed:

a) 5 per cent of the gross amount of the dividends if the beneficial owner is a company (other than a partnership) which holds directly at least 25 per cent of the capital of the company paying the dividends;

b) 15 per cent of the gross amount of the dividends in all other cases.

The competent authorities of the Contracting States may by mutual agreement settle the mode of application of these limitations. This paragraph shall not affect the taxation of the company in respect of the profits out of which the dividends are paid.

3. The term "dividends" as used in this Article means income from shares, or other rights, not being debt-claims, participating in profits, as well as income from other corporate rights which is subjected to the same taxation treatment as income from shares by the taxation laws of the State of which the company making the distribution is a resident.

4. The provisions of paragraphs 1 and 2 shall not apply if the beneficial owner of the dividends, being a resident of a Contracting State, carries on business in the other Contracting State of which the company paying the dividends is a resident, through a permanent establishment situated therein, or performs in that other State independent personal services from a fixed base situated therein, and the holding in respect of which the dividends are paid is effectively connected with such permanent establishment or fixed base. In such case the provisions of Article 7 or Article 14, as the case may be, shall apply.

5. Where a company which is a resident of a Contracting State derives profits or income from the other Contracting State, that other State may not impose any tax on the dividends paid by the company, except insofar as such dividends are paid to a resident of that other State or insofar as the holding in respect of which the dividends are paid is effectively connected with a permanent establishment or a fixed base situated in that other State, nor subject the company's undistributed profits to a tax on the company's undistributed profits, even if the dividends paid or the undistributed profits consist wholly or partly of

profits or income arising in such other State.

ARTICLE 11

INTEREST

1. Interest arising in a Contracting State and paid to a resident of the other Contracting State may be taxed in that other State.

2. However, such interest may also be taxed in the Contracting State in which it arises and according to the laws of that State, but if the recipient is the beneficial owner of the interest the tax so charged shall not exceed 10 per cent of the gross amount of the interest. The competent authorities of the Contracting States may by mutual agreement settle the mode of application of this limitation.

3. Notwithstanding the provisions of paragraph 2, interest arising in a Contracting State, derived and beneficially owned by the Government of the other Contracting State, including political subdivisions and local authorities thereof, the Central Bank or any financial institution wholly owned by that Government, or interest derived on loans guaranteed by that Government shall be exempt from tax in the first-mentioned State.

4. The term "interest" as used in this Article means income from debt-claims of every kind, whether or not secured by mortgage, and in particular, income from government securities and income from bonds or debentures, including premiums and prizes attaching to such securities, bonds or debentures. Penalty charges for late payment shall not be regarded as interest for the purpose of this Article.

5. The provisions of paragraphs 1 and 2 shall not apply if the beneficial owner of the interest, being a resident of a Contracting State, carries on business in the other Contracting State in which the interest arises, through a permanent establishment situated therein, or performs in that other State independent personal services from a fixed base situated therein, and the debt-claim in respect of which the interest is paid is effectively connected with such permanent establishment or fixed base. In such case the provisions of Article 7 or Article 14, as the case may be, shall apply.

6. Interest shall be deemed to arise in a Contracting State when the payer is that State itself, a political subdivision, a local authority or a resident of that State. Where, however, the person paying the interest, whether he is a resident of a Contracting State or not, has in a Contracting State a permanent establishment or a fixed base in connection with which the indebtedness on which the interest is paid was incurred, and such interest is borne by such permanent establishment or fixed base, then such interest shall be deemed to arise in the State in which the permanent establishment or fixed base is situated.

7. Where, by reason of a special relationship between the payer and the beneficial owner or between both of them and some other person, the amount of the interest, having regard to the debt-claim for which it is paid, exceeds the amount which would have been agreed upon by the payer and the beneficial owner in the absence of such relationship, the provisions of this Article shall apply only to the last-mentioned amount. In such case, the excess part of the payments shall remain taxable according to the laws of each Contracting State, due regard being had to the other provisions of this Agreement.

ARTICLE 12

ROYALTIES

1. Royalties arising in a Contracting State and paid to a resident of the other Contracting State may be taxed in that other State.

2. However, the royalties referred to in paragraph 1 of this Article may also be taxed in the Contracting State in which they arise and according to the laws of that State, but if the recipient is the beneficial owner of the royalties the tax so charged shall not exceed 10 per cent of the gross amount of the royalties. The competent authorities of the Contracting States may by mutual agreement settle the mode of application of this limitation.

3. The term "royalties" as used in this Article means payments of any kind received as a consideration for the use of, or the right to use, any copyright of literary, artistic or scientific work, including cinematograph films and films or tapes for radio or television broadcasting, any patent, trade mark, design or model, plan, secret formula or process, or for the use of, or the right to use, industrial, commercial, or scientific equipment, or for information concerning industrial, commercial or scientific experience.

4. The provisions of paragraphs 1 and 2 shall not apply if the beneficial owner of the royalties, being a resident of a Contracting State, carries on business in the other Contracting State in which the royalties arise, through a permanent establishment situated therein, or performs in that other State independent personal services from a fixed base situated therein, and the right or property in respect of which the

royalties are paid is effectively connected with such permanent establishment or fixed base. In such case the provisions of Article 7 or Article 14, as the case may be, shall apply.

5. Royalties shall be deemed to arise in a Contracting State when the payer is that State itself, a political subdivision, a local authority or a resident of that State. Where, however, the person paying the royalties, whether he is a resident of a Contracting State or not, has in a Contracting State a permanent establishment or a fixed base in connection with which the liability to pay the royalties was incurred, and such royalties are borne by such permanent establishment or fixed base, then such royalties shall be deemed to arise in the State in which the permanent establishment or fixed base is situated.

6. Where, by reason of a special relationship between the payer and the beneficial owner or between both of them and some other person, the amount of the royalties, having regard to the use, right or information for which they are paid, exceeds the amount which would have been agreed upon by the payer and the beneficial owner in the absence of such relationship, the provisions of this Article shall apply only to the last-mentioned amount. In such case, the excess part of the payments shall remain taxable according to the laws of each Contracting State, due regard being had to the other provisions of this Agreement.

ARTICLE 13

CAPITAL GAINS

1. Gains derived by a resident of a Contracting State from the alienation of immovable property referred to in Article 6 and situated in the other Contracting State or shares in a company the assets of which consist mainly of such property may be taxed in that other State.

2. Gains from the alienation of movable property forming part of the business property of a permanent establishment which an enterprise of a Contracting State has in the other Contracting State or of movable property pertaining to a fixed base available to a resident of a Contracting State in the other Contracting State for the purpose of performing independent personal services, including such gains from the alienation of such permanent establishment (alone or with the whole enterprise) or of such fixed base, may be taxed in that other State.

3. Gains derived by an enterprise of a Contracting State from the alienation of ships, aircraft or road transport vehicles operated in international traffic or movable property pertaining to the operation of such ships, aircraft or road transport vehicles shall be taxable only in that State.

4. Gains from the alienation of any property other than that referred to in paragraphs 1, 2 and 3, shall be taxable only in the Contracting State of which the alienator is a resident.

ARTICLE 14

INDEPENDENT PERSONAL SERVICES

1. Income derived by an individual who is a resident of a Contracting State in respect of professional services or other activities of an independent character shall be taxable only in that State unless he has a fixed base regularly available to him in the other Contracting State for the purpose of performing his activities. If he has such a fixed base, the income may be taxed in the other Contracting State but only so much of it as is attributable to that fixed base. For this purpose, where a resident of a Contracting State stays in the other Contracting

State for a period or periods exceeding in the aggregate 183 days in any twelve-month period commencing or ending in the tax year concerned, he shall be deemed to have a fixed base regularly available to him in that other State and the income that is derived from his activities referred to above that are performed in that other State shall be attributable to that fixed base.

2. The term "professional services" includes especially independent scientific, literary, artistic, educational or teaching activities as well as the independent activities of physicians, lawyers, engineers, architects, dentists and accountants.

ARTICLE 15

DEPENDENT PERSONAL SERVICES

1. Subject to the provisions of Articles 16, 18, 19 and 21, salaries, wages and other similar remuneration derived by a resident of a Contracting State in respect of an employment shall be taxable only in that State unless the employment is exercised in the other Contracting State. If the employment is so exercised, such remuneration as is derived therefrom may be taxed in that other State.

2. Notwithstanding the provisions of paragraph 1, remuneration derived by a resident of a Contracting State in respect of an employment exercised in the other Contracting State shall be taxable only in the first-mentioned State if:

a) the recipient is present in the other State for a period or periods not exceeding in the aggregate 183 days in any twelve months period commencing or ending in the fiscal year concerned, and

b) the remuneration is paid by, or on behalf of, an employer who is not a resident of the other State, and

c) the remuneration is not borne by a permanent establishment or a fixed base which the employer has in the other State.

3. Notwithstanding the preceding provisions of this Article, remuneration derived in respect of an employment exercised aboard a ship, aircraft or road transport vehicle operated in international traffic by a resident of a Contracting State, may be taxed in that State.

ARTICLE 16

DIRECTORS' FEES

Directors' fees and other similar payments derived by a resident of a Contracting State in his capacity as a member of the board of directors or any other similar organ of a company which is a resident of the other Contracting State may be taxed in that other Contracting State.

ARTICLE 17

ARTISTES AND SPORTSMEN

1. Notwithstanding the provisions of Articles 14 and 15, income derived by a resident of a Contracting State as an entertainer, such as a theatre, motion picture, radio or television artiste, or a musician, or as a sportsman, from his personal activities

as such exercised in the other Contracting State, may be taxed in that other State.

2. Where income in respect of personal activities exercised by an entertainer or a sportsman in his capacity as such accrues not to the entertainer or sportsman himself but to another person, that income may, notwithstanding the provisions of Articles 7, 14 and 15, be taxed in the Contracting State in which the activities of the entertainer or sportsman are exercised.

3. The provisions of paragraphs 1 and 2 shall not apply to income derived from activities exercised in a Contracting State by an entertainer or a sportsman if the visit to that State is wholly or mainly supported by public funds of the other Contracting State, or a political subdivision or a local authority thereof. In such case, the income shall be taxable only in the Contracting State of which the entertainer or sportsman is a resident.

ARTICLE 18

PENSIONS

1. Subject to the provisions of paragraph 2 of Article 19, pensions and other similar remuneration paid to a resident of a Contracting State in consideration of past employment shall be taxable only in the State of which the recipient of the pension is a resident.

2. Notwithstanding the provisions of paragraph 1, and the provisions of paragraph 2 of Article 19, pensions paid and other benefits, whether periodic or lump-sum compensation, granted under the social security legislation of a Contracting State or

under any public scheme organized by a Contracting State for social welfare purposes shall be taxable only in that State.

ARTICLE 19

GOVERNMENT SERVICE

1. a) Remuneration, other than a pension, paid by a Contracting State or a political subdivision or a local authority thereof, or an agency thereof or an entity wholly owned by such State, subdivision or authority, to an individual in respect of dependent personal services rendered to that State, subdivision, authority, agency or entity shall be taxable only in that State.

   b) However, such remuneration shall be taxable only in the other Contracting State if the services are rendered in that State and the individual is a resident of that State who:
   (i) is a national of that State; or
   (ii) did not become a resident of that State solely for the purpose of rendering the services.

2. a) Any pension paid by, or out of funds created by, a Contracting State or a political subdivision or a local authority thereof, or an agency thereof or an entity wholly owned by such State, subdivision or authority, to an individual in respect of services rendered to that State, subdivision, authority, agency or entity shall be taxable only in that State.

   b) However, such pension shall be taxable only in the other Contracting State if the individual is a resident of, and a national of, that State.

3. The provisions of Articles 15, 16 and 18 shall apply to remuneration and pensions in respect of services rendered in connection with a business carried on by a Contracting State or a political subdivision or a local authority thereof, or an agency thereof or an entity wholly owned by such State, subdivision or authority.

ARTICLE 20

STUDENTS

Payments which a student, an apprentice or a trainee who is or was immediately before visiting a Contracting State a resident of the other Contracting State and who is present in the first-mentioned State solely for the purpose of his education or training receives for the purpose of his maintenance, education or training shall not be taxed in that State, provided that such payments arise from sources outside that State.

ARTICLE 21

PROFESSORS AND RESEARCHERS

1. An individual who visits a Contracting State for the purpose of teaching or carrying out research at a university, college or other recognized educational institution in that Contracting State and who is or was immediately before that visit a resident of the other Contracting State, shall be exempted from taxation in the first-mentioned Contracting State on remuneration for such teaching or research for a period not exceeding two years from the date of his first visit for that purpose.

2. The provisions of paragraph 1 of this Article shall not apply to income from research if such research is undertaken not in the public interest but primarily for the private benefit of a specific person or persons.

ARTICLE 22

OTHER INCOME

1. Items of income of a resident of a Contracting State, wherever arising, not dealt with in the foregoing Articles of this Agreement shall be taxable only in that State.

2. The provisions of paragraph 1 shall not apply to income, other than income from immovable property as defined in paragraph 2 of Article 6, if the recipient of such income, being a resident of a Contracting State, carries on business in the other Contracting State through a permanent establishment situated therein, or performs in that other State independent personal services from a fixed base situated therein, and the right or property in respect of which the income is paid is effectively connected with such permanent establishment or fixed base. In such case the provisions of Article 7 or Article 14, as the case may be, shall apply.

ARTICLE 23

CAPITAL

1. Capital represented by immovable property referred to in Article 6, owned by a resident of a Contracting State and situated in the other Contracting State, or by shares in a

company the assets of which consist mainly of such property may be taxed in that other State.

2. Capital represented by movable property forming part of the business property of a permanent establishment which an enterprise of a Contracting State has in the other Contracting State or by movable property pertaining to a fixed base available to a resident of a Contracting State in the other Contracting State for the purpose of performing independent personal services, may be taxed in that other State.

3. Capital represented by ships, aircraft or road transport vehicles operated in international traffic by an enterprise of a Contracting State, and by movable property pertaining to the operation of such ships, aircraft and road transport vehicles, shall be taxable only in that State.

4. All other elements of capital of a resident of a Contracting State shall be taxable only in that State.

ARTICLE 24

ELIMINATION OF DOUBLE TAXATION

1. In the case of a resident of Poland, double taxation shall be avoided as follows:

a) Where a resident of Poland derives income or owns capital which, in accordance with the provisions of this Agreement may be taxed in Latvia, Poland shall, subject to the provisions of subparagraph b), exempt such income or capital from tax. Poland may in calculating the amount of tax on the remaining income or capital of such resident apply the rate of tax which would have been applicable if the exempted income or capital had not been so exempted.

b) Where a resident of Poland derives items of income which in accordance with the provisions of Articles 10, 11 and 12, may be taxed in Latvia, Poland shall allow as a deduction from the tax on the income of that resident an amount equal to the income tax paid in Latvia. Such deduction shall not, however, exceed that part of the tax, as computed before the deduction is given, which is attributable to such items of income derived from Latvia.

2. In the case of a resident of Latvia, double taxation shall be avoided as follows:

a) Where a resident of Latvia derives income or owns capital which in accordance with this Agreement, may be taxed in Poland, unless a more favourable treatment is provided in its domestic law, Latvia shall allow:

(i) as a deduction from the tax on the income of that resident, an amount equal to the income tax paid thereon in Poland;

(ii) as a deduction from the tax on the capital of that resident, an amount equal to the capital tax paid thereon in Poland.

Such deduction in either case shall not, however, exceed that part of the income or capital tax in Latvia as computed before the deduction is given, which is attributable, as the case may be, to the income or the capital which may be taxed in Poland.

b) For the purpose of subparagraph a) of this paragraph, where a company that is a resident of Latvia receives a dividend from a company that is a resident of Poland in which it owns at least 10 per cent of its shares having full voting rights, the tax paid in Poland shall include not only the tax paid on the dividend, but also the tax paid on the underlying profits of the company out of which the dividend was paid.

ARTICLE 25

NON-DISCRIMINATION

1. Nationals of a Contracting State shall not be subjected in the other Contracting State to any taxation or any requirement connected therewith, which is other or more burdensome than the taxation and connected requirements to which nationals of that other State in the same circumstances, in particular with respect to residence, are or may be subjected. This provision shall, notwithstanding the provisions of Article 1, also apply to persons who are not residents of one or both of the Contracting States.

2. The taxation on a permanent establishment which an enterprise of a Contracting State has in the other Contracting State shall not be less favourably levied in that other State than the taxation levied on enterprises of that other State carrying on the same activities. This provision shall not be construed as obliging a Contracting State to grant to residents of the other Contracting State any personal allowances, reliefs and reductions for taxation purposes on account of civil status or family responsibilities which it grants to its own residents.

3. Except where the provisions of paragraph 1 of Article 9, paragraph 7 of Article 11, or paragraph 6 of Article 12, apply, interest, royalties, and other disbursements paid by an enterprise of a Contracting State to a resident of the other Contracting State shall, for the purpose of determining the taxable profits of such enterprise, be deductible under the same conditions as if they had been paid to a resident of the first-mentioned State. Similarly, any debts of an enterprise of a Contracting State to a resident of the other Contracting State shall, for the purpose of determining the taxable capital of

such enterprise, be deductible under the same conditions as if they had been contracted to a resident of the first-mentioned State.

4. Enterprises of a Contracting State, the capital of which is wholly or partly owned or controlled, directly or indirectly, by one or more residents of the other Contracting State, shall not be subjected in the first-mentioned State to any taxation or any requirement connected therewith which is other or more burdensome than the taxation and connected requirements to which other similar enterprises of that first-mentioned State are or may be subjected.

5. The provisions of this Article shall, notwithstanding the provisions of Article 2, apply to the taxes of every kind and description.

ARTICLE 26

MUTUAL AGREEMENT PROCEDURE

1. Where a person considers that the actions of one or both of the Contracting State result or will result for him in taxation not in accordance with the provisions of this Agreement, he may, irrespective of the remedies provided by the domestic law of those States, present his case to the competent authority of the Contracting State of which he is a resident or, if his case comes under paragraph 1 of Article 25, to that of the Contracting State of which he is a national. The case must be presented within three years from the first notification of the action resulting in taxation not in accordance with the provisions of the Agreement.

2. The competent authority shall endeavour, if the objection appears to it to be justified and if it is not itself able to arrive at a satisfactory solution, to resolve the case by mutual agreement with the competent authority of the other Contracting State, with a view to the avoidance of taxation which is not in accordance with the Agreement. Any agreement reached shall be implemented notwithstanding any time limits in the domestic law of the Contracting States.

3. The competent authorities of the Contracting States shall endeavour to resolve by mutual agreement any difficulties or doubts arising as to the interpretation or application of the Agreement. They may also consult together for the elimination of double taxation in cases not provided for in the Agreement.

4. The competent authorities of the Contracting States may communicate with each other directly for the purpose of reaching an agreement in the sense of the preceding paragraphs. When it seems advisable in order to reach agreement to have an oral exchange of opinions, such exchange may take place through a Commission consisting of representatives of the competent authorities of the Contracting States.

ARTICLE 27

EXCHANGE OF INFORMATION

1. The competent authorities of the Contracting States shall exchange such information as is necessary for carrying out the provisions of this Agreement or of the domestic laws of the Contracting States concerning taxes covered by the Agreement insofar as the taxation thereunder is not contrary to the Agreement. The exchange of information is not restricted by Article 1. Any information received by a Contracting State shall

be treated as secret in the same manner as information obtained under the domestic laws of that State and shall be disclosed only to persons or authorities (including courts and administrative bodies) involved in the assessment or collection of, the enforcement or prosecution in respect of, or the determination of appeals in relation to, the taxes covered by the Agreement. Such persons or authorities shall use the information only for such purposes. They may disclose the information in public court proceedings or in judicial decisions.

2. In no case shall the provisions of paragraph 1 be construed so as to impose on a Contracting State the obligation:

a) to carry out administrative measures at variance with the laws and the administrative practice of that or of the other Contracting State;

b) to supply information which is not obtainable under the laws or in the normal course of the administration of that or of the other Contracting State;

c) to supply information which would disclose any trade, business, industrial, commercial or professional secret or trade process, or information, the disclosure of which would be contrary to public policy (ordre public).

ARTICLE 28

DIPLOMATIC AGENTS AND CONSULAR OFFICERS

Nothing in this Agreement shall affect the fiscal privileges of diplomatic agents or consular officers under the general rules of international law or under the provisions of special agreements.

ARTICLE 29

ENTRY INTO FORCE

1. The Governments of the Contracting States shall notify each other that the constitutional requirements for the entry into force of this Agreement have been complied with.

2. This Agreement shall enter into force on the date of the latter of the notifications referred to in paragraph 1 and its provisions shall have effect:

a) in respect of taxes withheld at source, on income derived on or after 1st January in the calendar year next following the year in which the Agreement enters into force;

b) in respect of other taxes on income, and taxes on capital, for taxes chargeable for any taxable year beginning on or after 1st January in the calendar year next following the year in which the Agreement enters into force.

ARTICLE 30

TERMINATION

This Agreement shall remain in force until terminated by a Contracting State. Either Contracting State may terminate the Agreement, through diplomatic channels, by giving written notice of termination at least six months before the end of any calendar year. In such event, the Agreement shall cease to have effect:

a) in respect of taxes withheld at source, on income derived on or after 1st January in the calendar year next following the year in which such notice is given;

b) in respect of other taxes on income, and taxes on capital, for taxes chargeable for any tax year beginning on or after 1st January in the calendar year next following the year in which such notice is given.

IN WITNESS whereof the undersigned, being duly authorized thereto, have signed this Agreement.

DONE in duplicate at Warsaw this 17th day of November 19 93 in the English language.

For the Republic of Poland

[signature]

For the Republic of Latvia

[signature]

[TRANSLATION IN FRENCH – TRADUCTION EN FRANÇAIS]

ACCORD ENTRE LA RÉPUBLIQUE DE POLOGNE ET LA RÉPUBLIQUE DE LETTONIE TENDANT À ÉVITER LES DOUBLES IMPOSITIONS ET À PRÉVENIR LA FRAUDE FISCALE EN MATIÈRE D'IMPÔTS SUR LE REVENU ET SUR LA FORTUNE

Le Gouvernement de la République de Pologne et le Gouvernement de la République de Lettonie,

Désireux de conclure un Accord tendant à éviter les doubles impositions et à prévenir la fraude fiscale en matière d'impôts sur le revenu et sur la fortune,

Sont convenus de ce qui suit :

Article premier. Personnes visées

Le présent Accord s'applique aux personnes qui sont des résidents d'un État contractant ou des deux États contractants.

Article 2. Impôts visés

1. Le présent Accord s'applique aux impôts sur le revenu et sur la fortune prélevés pour le compte d'un État contractant, de ses subdivisions politiques ou de ses collectivités locales, quel que soit le système de perception.

2. Sont considérés comme impôts sur le revenu et sur la fortune les impôts perçus sur le revenu total, sur la fortune totale, ou sur des éléments du revenu ou de la fortune, y compris les impôts sur les gains provenant de l'aliénation de biens mobiliers ou immobiliers ainsi que les impôts sur les gains en capital.

3. Les impôts actuels auxquels s'applique le présent Accord sont notamment :

a) En Pologne :

i) L'impôt sur le revenu des personnes physiques (podatek dochodowy od osób fizycznych) ;

ii) L'impôt sur les sociétés (podatek dochodowy od osób prawnych) ;

(ci-après dénommés « impôt polonais ») ;

b) En Lettonie :

i) L'impôt sur les bénéfices (pelnas nodoklis) ;

ii) L'impôt sur le revenu des personnes physiques (iedzivotaju ienakuma nodoklis) ;

iii) L'impôt foncier (ipasuma nodoklis) ;

(ci-après dénommés « impôt letton »).

4. L'Accord s'applique également aux impôts de nature identique ou analogue qui seraient établis après la signature de l'Accord et qui s'ajouteraient aux impôts actuels ou qui les remplaceraient. Les autorités compétentes des États contractants se notifient toute modification significative apportée à leur législation fiscale respective.

Article 3. Définitions générales

1. Aux fins du présent Accord, à moins que le contexte n'exige une autre interprétation :

a) Le terme « Pologne », lorsqu'il est employé au sens géographique, désigne le territoire de la République de Pologne, y compris toute zone située au-delà de ses eaux territoriales, sur laquelle la Pologne peut exercer ses droits souverains, en vertu de sa législation et conformément au droit international à l'égard des fonds marins, de leur sous-sol et de leurs ressources naturelles ;

b) Le terme « Lettonie » désigne la République de Lettonie et, au sens géographique, il désigne le territoire de la République de Lettonie et toute zone adjacente aux eaux territoriales de la République de Lettonie à l'intérieur de laquelle, en vertu de la législation de la Lettonie et conformément au droit international, les droits de la Lettonie peuvent être exercés à l'égard des fonds marins et de leur sous-sol ainsi que de leurs ressources naturelles ;

c) Les expressions « un État contractant » et « l'autre État contractant » désignent soit la Pologne soit la Lettonie, selon le contexte ;

d) Le terme « ressortissant » désigne toute personne physique ayant la nationalité d'un État contractant et toute personne morale, société de personnes ou association constituée en conformité avec la législation en vigueur dans l'un des États contractants ;

e) Le terme « personne » comprend les personnes physiques, les sociétés et tous autres groupements de personnes ;

f) Le terme « société » désigne toute entité dotée de la personne morale ou de toute entité considérée comme une personne morale aux fins d'imposition ;

g) Les expressions « entreprise d'un État contractant » et « entreprise de l'autre État contractant » désignent respectivement une entreprise exploitée par un résident d'un État contractant et une entreprise exploitée par un résident de l'autre État contractant ;

h) L'expression « trafic international » désigne tout transport effectué par un navire, un aéronef ou un véhicule de transport routier exploité par une entreprise d'un État contractant, sauf lorsque ledit navire, aéronef ou véhicule de transport routier n'est exploité qu'entre des points situés dans l'autre État contractant ;

i) L'expression « autorité compétente » désigne :

  i) Dans le cas de la Pologne, le Ministre des finances ou son représentant autorisé ;

  ii) Dans le cas de la Lettonie, le Ministre des réformes économiques et le Chef de l'Inspection des finances de l'État ou leur représentant autorisé.

2. Pour l'application des dispositions du présent Accord par un État contractant, toute expression ou tout terme qui n'y est pas défini a, à moins que le contexte n'exige une interprétation différente, le sens que lui attribue la législation de cet État en ce qui concerne les impôts auxquels s'applique le présent Accord.

Article 4. Résident

1. Aux fins du présent Accord, l'expression « résident d'un État contractant » désigne toute personne qui, en vertu de la législation de cet État, est assujettie à l'impôt dans cet État en raison de son domicile, de sa résidence, de son siège de direction, de son lieu de constitution ou de tout autre critère de nature analogue. L'expression s'applique également à cet État lui-même, à ses subdivisions politiques et collectivités locales, ainsi qu'à tout organisme ou à toute entité entièrement détenue par cet État, cette subdivision politique ou cette collectivité locale et qui est établi en vertu des lois de cet État. Toutefois, cette expression ne comprend pas les personnes qui ne sont assujetties à l'impôt dans cet État que pour les revenus de sources situées dans cet État ou pour la fortune qui y est située.

2. Lorsque, selon les dispositions du paragraphe 1, une personne physique est résidente des deux États contractants, sa situation est réglée de la manière suivante :

a) Cette personne est considérée comme résidente de l'État où elle dispose d'un foyer d'habitation permanent ; si elle dispose d'un foyer d'habitation permanent dans les deux États, elle est considérée comme résidente de l'État avec lequel ses liens personnels et économiques sont les plus étroits (centre des intérêts vitaux) ;

b) Si l'État où cette personne a le centre de ses intérêts vitaux ne peut pas être déterminé, ou si elle ne dispose d'un foyer d'habitation permanent dans aucun des États, elle est considérée comme résidente de l'État où elle séjourne de façon habituelle ;

c) Si cette personne séjourne de façon habituelle dans les deux États ou si elle ne séjourne habituellement dans aucun d'eux, elle est considérée comme résidente de l'État dont elle possède la nationalité ;

d) Si le statut d'un résident ne peut être déterminé selon les dispositions des alinéas a) à d), les autorités compétentes des États contractants règlent la question d'un commun accord.

3. Lorsque, selon les dispositions du paragraphe 1, une personne autre qu'une personne physique est résidente des deux États contractants, elle est réputée être résidente de l'État contractant en vertu de la législation duquel elle est constituée.

Article 5. Établissement stable

1. Aux fins du présent Accord, l'expression « établissement permanent » désigne une installation fixe d'affaires par l'intermédiaire de laquelle une entreprise exerce tout ou partie de son activité.

2. L'expression « établissement stable » désigne notamment :

a) Un siège de direction ;

b) Une succursale ;

c) Un bureau ;

d) Une usine ;

e) Un atelier ; et

f) Une mine, un puits de pétrole ou de gaz, une carrière ou tout autre lieu d'extraction de ressources naturelles.

3. Un chantier de construction, un projet de montage ou d'installation ou des activités de supervision ou consultatives liées à ce projet constituent un « établissement stable », mais uniquement si ce chantier, ce projet ou ces activités ont une durée supérieure à neuf mois.

4. Nonobstant les dispositions précédentes du présent article, il est considéré que l'expression « établissement stable » ne comprend pas :

a) L'utilisation d'installations aux seules fins de stockage, d'exposition ou de livraison de biens ou de marchandises appartenant à l'entreprise ;

b) L'exploitation d'un stock de biens ou de marchandises appartenant à l'entreprise aux seules fins de stockage, d'exposition ou de livraison ;

c) L'exploitation d'un stock de biens ou de marchandises appartenant à l'entreprise aux seules fins de transformation par une autre entreprise ;

d) L'exploitation d'une installation fixe d'affaires aux seules fins d'acheter des biens ou des marchandises ou de recueillir des informations pour l'entreprise ;

e) L'exploitation d'une installation fixe d'affaires aux seules fins d'exercer, pour l'entreprise, toute autre activité de caractère préparatoire ou auxiliaire ;

f) L'exploitation d'une installation fixe d'affaires aux seules fins d'exercice cumulé d'activités mentionnées aux alinéas a) à e), à condition que l'activité d'ensemble de l'installation fixe d'affaires résultant de ce cumul ait un caractère préparatoire ou auxiliaire.

5. Nonobstant les dispositions des paragraphes 1 et 2, lorsqu'une personne (autre qu'un agent ou jouissant d'un statut indépendant auquel s'applique le paragraphe 6) agit pour le compte d'une entreprise et dispose dans un État contractant de pouvoirs qu'elle y exerce habituellement lui permettant de conclure des contrats au nom de l'entreprise, cette entreprise est considérée comme ayant un établissement stable dans cet État pour toutes les activités que cette personne exerce pour l'entreprise, à moins que les activités de cette personne ne soient limitées à celles qui sont mentionnées au paragraphe 4 et qui, si elles étaient exercées par l'intermédiaire d'une installation fixe d'affaires, ne permettraient pas de considérer cette installation comme un établissement stable selon les dispositions de ce paragraphe.

6. Une entreprise n'est pas considérée comme ayant un établissement stable dans un État contractant du seul fait qu'elle y exerce son activité par l'entremise d'un courtier, d'un commissionnaire général ou de tout autre agent jouissant d'un statut indépendant, à condition que ces personnes agissent dans le cadre ordinaire de leur activité. Toutefois, lorsqu'il agit totalement ou presque totalement pour le compte de cette entreprise, cette personne n'est pas considérée comme un agent indépendant au sens du présent paragraphe.

7. Le fait qu'une société qui est résidente d'un État contractant contrôle ou est contrôlée par une société qui est résidente de l'autre État contractant ou qui y exerce son activité (que ce soit par l'intermédiaire d'un établissement stable ou non) ne suffit pas, en lui-même, à faire de l'une quelconque de ces sociétés un établissement stable de l'autre.

Article 6. Revenus immobiliers

1. Les revenus qu'un résident d'un État contractant tire de biens immobiliers (y compris les revenus des exploitations agricoles ou forestières) situés dans l'autre État contractant sont imposables dans cet autre État.

2. L'expression « biens immobiliers » a le sens que lui attribue le droit de l'État contractant où les biens en question sont situés. Cette expression comprend dans tous les cas les biens accessoires aux biens immobiliers, en particulier les bâtiments, le cheptel et le matériel utilisé dans les exploitations agricoles et forestières, les droits auxquels s'appliquent les dispositions du droit privé concernant la propriété foncière, en particulier toutes options ou droits analogues, l'usufruit des biens immobiliers et les droits à des paiements variables ou fixes pour l'exploitation ou la concession de l'exploitation de gisements minéraux, sources ou autres ressources naturelles. Les navires, bateaux, aéronefs et véhicules de transport routier ne sont pas considérés comme des biens immobiliers.

3. Les dispositions du paragraphe 1 s'appliquent aux revenus provenant de l'exploitation directe, de la location ou de toute autre forme d'exploitation de biens immobiliers, ainsi qu'aux revenus provenant de l'aliénation de tels biens.

4. Lorsque la propriété d'actions ou d'autres parts sociales d'une société donne au propriétaire de ces actions ou parts sociales le droit de jouissance de biens immobiliers détenus par la société, les revenus provenant de l'exploitation directe, de la location ou de l'affermage, ainsi que de toute autre forme d'exploitation de tels droits de jouissance sont imposables dans l'État contractant où les biens immobiliers sont situés.

5. Les dispositions des paragraphes 1 et 3 s'appliquent également aux revenus provenant des biens immobiliers d'une entreprise ainsi qu'aux revenus des biens immobiliers servant à l'exercice d'une profession indépendante.

Article 7. Bénéfices des entreprises

1. Les bénéfices d'une entreprise d'un État contractant ne sont imposables que dans cet État, à moins que l'entreprise n'exerce son activité dans l'autre État contractant par l'intermédiaire d'un établissement stable qui y est situé. Si l'entreprise exerce son activité d'une telle façon, les bénéfices de l'entreprise sont imposables dans l'autre État, mais uniquement dans la mesure où ils sont imputables :

a) Audit établissement stable ; ou

b) Aux ventes, dans cet autre État, de biens ou de marchandises identiques ou analogues à ceux qui sont vendus par l'intermédiaire de l'établissement stable ; ou

c) À d'autres activités commerciales exercées dans cet autre État, de nature identique ou analogue à celles exercées par l'intermédiaire de cet établissement stable.

2. Sous réserve des dispositions du paragraphe 3, lorsqu'une entreprise d'un État contractant exerce son activité dans l'autre État contractant par l'intermédiaire d'un établissement stable qui y est situé, il est imputé à cet établissement stable, dans chaque État contractant, les bénéfices qu'il aurait pu réaliser s'il avait constitué une entreprise distincte exerçant des activités identiques ou analogues dans des conditions identiques ou analogues et traitant en toute indépendance avec l'entreprise dont il constitue un établissement stable.

3. Pour déterminer les bénéfices d'un établissement stable, sont admises en déduction les dépenses relatives aux fins poursuivies par cet établissement stable, y compris les dépenses de direction et les frais généraux d'administration ainsi enregistrés, soit dans l'État où est situé cet établissement stable, soit ailleurs. Les dépenses admises en déduction par un État contractant sont exclusivement celles qui sont déductibles en vertu de la législation interne de cet État contractant.

4. S'il est d'usage, dans un État contractant, de déterminer les bénéfices imputables à un établissement stable sur la base d'une répartition des bénéfices totaux de l'entreprise entre ses diverses composantes, aucune disposition du paragraphe 2 n'empêche cet État contractant de déterminer les bénéfices imposables selon la répartition en usage ; la méthode de répartition adoptée doit cependant être telle que le résultat obtenu soit conforme aux principes contenus dans le présent article.

5. Aucun bénéfice n'est imputé à un établissement stable du seul fait qu'il a acheté des biens ou des marchandises pour l'entreprise.

6. Aux fins des paragraphes précédents, les bénéfices à imputer à l'établissement stable sont déterminés selon la même méthode chaque année, à moins qu'il n'existe des raisons valables et suffisantes de procéder autrement.

7. Lorsque les bénéfices comprennent des éléments de revenu qui sont traités séparément dans d'autres articles du présent Accord, les dispositions de ces articles ne sont pas affectées par les dispositions du présent article.

Article 8. Transport international

1. Les bénéfices qu'une entreprise d'un État contractant tire de l'exploitation, en trafic international, de navires, d'aéronefs ou de véhicules routiers automobiles ne sont imposables que dans cet État.

2. Les dispositions du paragraphe 1 s'appliquent également aux bénéfices provenant de la participation à un consortium, à une coentreprise ou à un organisme international d'exploitation.

Article 9. Entreprises associées

1. Lorsque :

a) Une entreprise d'un État contractant participe directement ou indirectement à la direction, au contrôle ou au capital d'une entreprise de l'autre État contractant ; ou que

b) Les mêmes personnes participent directement ou indirectement à la direction, au contrôle ou au capital d'une entreprise d'un État contractant et d'une entreprise de l'autre État contractant ;

et que, dans l'un et l'autre cas, les deux entreprises sont, dans leurs relations commerciales ou financières, liées par des conditions convenues ou imposées, qui diffèrent de celles qui seraient convenues entre des entreprises indépendantes, les bénéfices qui, sans ces conditions, auraient été réalisés par l'une des entreprises, mais n'ont pu l'être en fait à cause de ces conditions, peuvent être inclus dans les bénéfices de cette entreprise et imposés en conséquence.

2. Lorsqu'un État contractant inclut dans les bénéfices d'une entreprise de cet État, et impose en conséquence des bénéfices sur lesquels une entreprise de l'autre État contractant a été imposée dans cet autre État et que les bénéfices ainsi inclus sont des bénéfices qui auraient été réalisés par l'entreprise du premier État si les conditions convenues entre les deux entreprises avaient été celles qui auraient été convenues entre des entreprises indépendantes, alors cet autre État procède à un ajustement approprié du montant de l'impôt qui y a été perçu sur ces bénéfices. Pour déterminer cet ajustement, il est tenu compte des autres dispositions du présent Accord et, si nécessaire, les autorités compétentes des États contractants se consultent.

Article 10. Dividendes

1. Les dividendes payés par une société qui est résidente d'un État contractant à une personne résidente de l'autre État contractant sont imposables dans cet autre État.

2. Toutefois, ces dividendes sont aussi imposables dans l'État contractant dont la société distributrice est résidente et selon la législation de cet État, mais si la personne qui reçoit les dividendes en est le bénéficiaire effectif, l'impôt ainsi établi ne peut excéder :

a) 5 % du montant brut des dividendes si le bénéficiaire effectif est une société (autre qu'une société de personnes) qui détient directement au moins 25 % du capital de la société qui paie les dividendes ;

b) 15 % du montant brut des dividendes, dans tous les autres cas.

Les autorités compétentes des États contractants peuvent régler d'un commun accord les modalités d'application de ces limitations. Le présent paragraphe n'affecte pas l'imposition de la société au titre des bénéfices qui servent au versement des dividendes.

3. Le terme « dividendes » employé dans le présent article désigne les revenus provenant d'actions ou autres parts bénéficiaires, à l'exception des créances, ainsi que les revenus d'autres parts sociales soumis au même régime fiscal que les revenus d'actions par la législation fiscale de l'État dont la société distributrice est une résidente.

4. Les dispositions des paragraphes 1 et 2 ne s'appliquent pas lorsque le bénéficiaire effectif des dividendes, résident d'un État contractant, exerce dans l'autre État contractant dont la société qui paie les dividendes est résidente soit une activité industrielle ou commerciale par l'intermédiaire d'un établissement stable qui y est situé, soit une profession indépendante au moyen d'une base fixe qui y est située, et que la participation génératrice des dividendes s'y rattache effectivement. Dans ce cas, les dispositions de l'article 7 ou de l'article 14, selon le cas, s'appliquent.

5. Lorsqu'une société qui est résidente d'un État contractant tire des bénéfices ou des revenus de l'autre État contractant, cet autre État ne peut percevoir aucun impôt sur les dividendes payés par la société, sauf dans la mesure où ces dividendes sont payés à un résident de cet autre État ou dans la mesure où la participation génératrice des dividendes se rattache effectivement à un établissement stable ou à une base fixe situés dans cet autre État, ni prélever aucun impôt, au titre de l'imposition des bénéfices non distribués, sur les bénéfices non distribués de la société, même si les dividendes versés ou les bénéfices non distribués consistent en tout ou partie en bénéfices ou revenus provenant de cet autre État.

Article 11. Intérêts

1. Les intérêts provenant d'un État contractant et payés à un résident de l'autre État contractant sont imposables dans cet autre État.

2. Toutefois, ces intérêts sont aussi imposables dans l'État contractant d'où ils proviennent, et selon la législation de cet État, mais si la personne qui reçoit les intérêts en est le bénéficiaire effectif, l'impôt ainsi établi ne peut excéder 10 % du montant brut des intérêts. Les autorités compétentes des États contractants peuvent régler d'un commun accord les modalités d'application de cette limitation.

3. Nonobstant les dispositions du paragraphe 2 du présent article, les intérêts produits dans un État contractant et qui sont perçus par le Gouvernement de l'autre État contractant, y compris ses subdivisions politiques et collectivités locales, sa Banque centrale (nationale) ou toute institution

financière entièrement détenue par ce Gouvernement, qui en est également le bénéficiaire effectif, ou les intérêts provenant de prêts garantis par ce Gouvernement, sont exonérés d'impôt dans le premier État.

4. Le terme « intérêts » employé dans le présent article désigne les revenus des créances de toute nature, assorties ou non de garanties hypothécaires, et notamment les revenus des fonds publics et des obligations d'emprunts, y compris les primes et lots attachés à ces titres. Les pénalités pour retard de paiement ne sont pas considérées comme des intérêts au sens du présent article.

5. Les dispositions des paragraphes 1 et 2 ne s'appliquent pas lorsque le bénéficiaire effectif des intérêts, résident d'un État contractant, exerce dans l'autre État contractant d'où proviennent les intérêts, soit une activité industrielle ou commerciale par l'intermédiaire d'un établissement stable qui y est situé, soit une profession indépendante au moyen d'une base fixe qui y est située, et que la créance génératrice des intérêts s'y rattache effectivement. Dans ce cas, les dispositions de l'article 7 ou de l'article 14, selon le cas, s'appliquent.

6. Les intérêts sont considérés comme provenant d'un État contractant lorsque le débiteur est cet État lui-même ou une subdivision politique, une collectivité locale ou un résident de cet État. Toutefois, lorsque le débiteur des intérêts, qu'il soit ou non résident d'un État contractant, a dans un État contractant un établissement stable ou une base fixe pour lesquels la dette donnant lieu au paiement des intérêts a été contractée et qui supportent la charge de ces intérêts, ceux-ci sont considérés comme provenant de l'État où l'établissement stable, ou la base fixe, est situé.

7. Lorsque, en raison de relations spéciales existant entre le débiteur et le bénéficiaire effectif ou que l'un et l'autre entretiennent avec de tierces personnes, le montant des intérêts, compte tenu de la créance pour laquelle ils sont payés, excède celui dont seraient convenus le débiteur et le bénéficiaire effectif en l'absence de pareilles relations, les dispositions du présent article ne s'appliquent qu'à ce dernier montant. Dans ce cas, la partie excédentaire des versements reste imposable selon la législation de chaque État contractant et compte tenu des autres dispositions du présent Accord.

Article 12. Redevances

1. Les redevances générées dans un État contractant et payées à un résident de l'autre État contractant sont imposables dans cet autre État.

2. Toutefois, les redevances visées au paragraphe 1 du présent article sont aussi imposables dans l'État contractant de la source et selon la législation de cet État, mais si la personne qui les reçoit est le bénéficiaire effectif des redevances, l'impôt ainsi établi ne peut excéder 10 % du montant brut des redevances. Les autorités compétentes des États contractants peuvent régler d'un commun accord les modalités d'application de cette limitation.

3. Le terme « redevances » employé dans le présent article désigne les rémunérations de toute nature payées pour l'usage ou la concession de l'usage de droits d'auteur sur une œuvre littéraire, artistique ou scientifique (y compris les films cinématographiques ainsi que les œuvres cinématographiques ou les films ou bandes utilisés pour des émissions radiophoniques ou télévisées), d'un brevet, d'une marque de fabrique ou de commerce, d'un dessin ou d'un modèle, d'un plan, d'une formule ou d'un procédé secrets, ainsi que pour l'usage ou la concession de l'usage d'un équipement industriel, commercial ou scientifique ou pour des informations ayant trait à une expérience acquise dans le domaine industriel, commercial ou scientifique.

4. Les dispositions des paragraphes 1 et 2 ne s'appliquent pas lorsque le bénéficiaire effectif des redevances, résident d'un État contractant, exerce dans l'autre État contractant source des redevances, soit une activité industrielle ou commerciale par l'intermédiaire d'un établissement stable qui y est situé, soit une profession indépendante au moyen d'une base fixe qui y est située, et que le droit ou le bien générateur des redevances s'y rattache effectivement. Dans ce cas, les dispositions de l'article 7 ou de l'article 14, selon le cas, s'appliquent.

5. Les redevances sont réputées avoir été générées dans un État contractant lorsque le débiteur est cet État, ou une subdivision politique, une collectivité locale ou un résident de cet État. Toutefois, lorsque le débiteur des redevances, qu'il soit ou non résident d'un État contractant, a dans un État contractant un établissement stable ou une base fixe pour lesquels l'engagement donnant lieu au paiement des redevances a été contracté et qui supportent ces redevances, celles-ci sont considérées comme provenant de l'État contractant où l'établissement stable ou la base fixe sont situés.

6. Lorsque, en raison de relations spéciales existant entre le débiteur et le bénéficiaire effectif ou que l'un et l'autre entretiennent avec de tierces personnes, le montant des redevances, compte tenu de la prestation pour laquelle elles sont payées, excède celui dont seraient convenus le débiteur et le bénéficiaire effectif en l'absence de pareilles relations, les dispositions du présent article ne s'appliquent qu'à ce dernier montant. Dans ce cas, la partie excédentaire des versements reste imposable selon la législation de chaque État contractant et compte tenu des autres dispositions du présent Accord.

Article 13. Gains en capital

1. Les gains qu'un résident d'un État contractant tire de l'aliénation de biens immobiliers visés à l'article 6 et situés dans l'autre État contractant, ou de parts d'une société dont l'actif est principalement constitué de tels biens, sont imposables dans cet autre État.

2. Les gains issus de l'aliénation de biens meubles qui font partie de l'actif d'un établissement stable qu'une entreprise d'un État contractant a dans l'autre État contractant, ou de biens meubles qui appartiennent à une base fixe dont un résident d'un État contractant dispose dans l'autre État contractant pour l'exercice d'une profession indépendante, y compris de tels gains dégagés par l'aliénation de cet établissement stable (seul ou avec l'ensemble de l'entreprise) ou de cette base fixe, sont imposables dans cet autre État.

3. Les gains qu'une entreprise d'un État contractant tire de l'aliénation de navires, d'aéronefs ou de véhicules de transport routier exploités en trafic international, ou de biens mobiliers affectés à l'exploitation de ces navires, aéronefs ou véhicules de transport routier, ne sont imposables que dans cet État.

4. Les gains provenant de l'aliénation de tous biens autres que ceux visés aux paragraphes 1, 2 et 3, ne sont imposables que dans l'État contractant dont le cédant est un résident.

Article 14. Professions indépendantes

1. Les revenus qu'une personne physique qui est résidente d'un État contractant tire d'une profession libérale ou d'autres activités de caractère indépendant ne sont imposables que dans cet État, à moins qu'elle ne dispose de façon habituelle dans l'autre État contractant d'une base fixe pour l'exercice de ses activités. Si elle dispose d'une telle base, les revenus sont imposables dans l'autre État contractant, mais uniquement dans la mesure où ils sont imputables à ladite base fixe. À cette fin, lorsqu'un résident d'un État contractant séjourne dans l'autre État contractant pendant une

période ou des périodes excédant au total 183 jours au cours de toute période de 12 mois commençant ou se terminant au cours de l'année fiscale considérée, il est considéré comme disposant régulièrement d'une base fixe dans cet autre État et les revenus qui proviennent de ses activités visées ci-dessus et qui sont exercées dans cet autre État sont imputables à cette base fixe.

2. L'expression « profession libérale » comprend notamment les activités indépendantes d'ordre scientifique, littéraire, artistique, éducatif ou pédagogique ainsi que les activités indépendantes des médecins, avocats, ingénieurs, architectes, dentistes et comptables.

Article 15. Professions dépendantes

1. Sous réserve des dispositions des articles 16, 18, 19 et 21, les salaires, traitements et autres rémunérations similaires qu'un résident d'un État contractant reçoit au titre d'un emploi salarié ne sont imposables que dans cet État, à moins que l'emploi ne soit exercé dans l'autre État contractant. Dans ce cas, les rémunérations reçues à ce titre sont imposables dans cet autre État.

2. Nonobstant les dispositions du paragraphe 1, les rémunérations qu'un résident d'un État contractant reçoit au titre d'un emploi salarié exercé dans l'autre État contractant ne sont imposables que dans le premier État si :

a) Le bénéficiaire séjourne dans l'autre État pendant une période ou des périodes n'excédant pas au total 183 jours au cours de toute période de 12 mois commençant ou se terminant durant l'année fiscale considérée ; et

b) Les rémunérations sont payées par un employeur, ou pour le compte d'un employeur, qui n'est pas un résident de l'autre État ; et

c) La charge des rémunérations n'est pas supportée par un établissement stable ou une base fixe que l'employeur a dans l'autre État.

3. Nonobstant les dispositions précédentes du présent article, les rémunérations perçues au titre d'un emploi salarié exercé à bord d'un navire, d'un aéronef ou d'un véhicule routier exploité en trafic international par un résident d'un État contractant sont imposables dans cet État.

Article 16. Tantièmes

Les tantièmes et autres rétributions similaires qu'un résident d'un État contractant reçoit en sa qualité de membre du conseil d'administration ou de tout autre organisme analogue d'une société qui est résidente de l'autre État contractant ne sont imposables que dans cet autre État contractant.

Article 17. Artistes et athlètes

1. Nonobstant les dispositions des articles 14 et 15, les revenus qu'un résident d'un État contractant tire de ses activités personnelles exercées dans l'autre État contractant en tant qu'artiste du spectacle (artiste de théâtre, de cinéma, de radio ou de télévision, musicien) ou en tant qu'athlète sont imposables dans cet autre État.

2. Lorsque les revenus d'activités qu'un artiste du spectacle ou qu'un athlète exerce personnellement et en cette qualité sont attribués, non pas à l'artiste du spectacle ou à l'athlète lui-même, mais à une autre personne, ces revenus sont, nonobstant les dispositions des articles 7, 14 et 15, imposables dans l'État contractant où sont exercées les activités de l'artiste du spectacle ou de l'athlète.

3. Les dispositions des paragraphes 1 et 2 ne s'appliquent pas aux revenus provenant d'activités exercées dans un État contractant par un artiste du spectacle ou un athlète si la visite dans cet État est entièrement ou principalement financée par des fonds publics de l'autre État contractant ou de l'une de ses subdivisions politiques ou collectivités locales. Dans ce cas, les revenus ne sont imposables que dans l'État contractant dont l'artiste du spectacle ou l'athlète est un résident.

Article 18. Pensions

1. Sous réserve des dispositions du paragraphe 2 de l'article 19, les pensions et autres rémunérations similaires payées à un résident d'un État contractant au titre d'un emploi antérieur ne sont imposables que dans l'État contractant d'où elles proviennent.

2. Nonobstant les dispositions du paragraphe 1, et les dispositions du paragraphe 2 de l'article 19, les pensions payées et autres prestations, qu'elles soient périodiques ou forfaitaires, accordées au titre de la législation en matière de sécurité sociale d'un État contractant ou en vertu de tout mécanisme public mis en place par un État contractant à des fins de sécurité sociale, ne sont imposables que dans cet État.

Article 19. Fonction publique

1. a) Les rémunérations, autres que les pensions, payées par un État contractant ou par l'une de ses subdivisions politiques ou collectivités locales, l'un de ses organismes ou par une entité intégralement détenue par cet État, cette subdivision ou cette collectivité, à une personne physique au titre de services fournis à cet État ou à cette subdivision, cette collectivité, cet organisme ou cette entité, ne sont imposables que dans cet État.

b) Toutefois, ces rémunérations ne sont imposables que dans l'autre État contractant si les services sont fournis dans cet État et si la personne physique est un résident de cet État qui :

i) Possède la nationalité de cet État ; ou

ii) N'est pas devenu résident de cet État aux seules fins d'exécuter les services en question.

2. a) Les pensions payées par un État contractant ou par l'une de ses subdivisions politiques, l'une de ses collectivités locales ou l'un de ses organismes ou par une entité intégralement détenue par cet État, soit directement soit par prélèvement sur des fonds qu'ils ont constitués, à une personne physique, au titre de services fournis à cet État, à cette subdivision, à cette collectivité, à cet organisme ou à cette entité, ne sont imposables que dans cet État.

b) Toutefois, ces pensions ne sont imposables que dans l'autre État contractant si la personne physique est résidente de cet État et en possède la nationalité.

3. Les dispositions des articles 15, 16 et 18 s'appliquent aux rémunérations et aux pensions payées au titre de services fournis dans le cadre d'une activité lucrative exercée par un État contractant ou par une de ses subdivisions politiques, collectivités locales ou organismes ou par une entité intégralement détenue par cet État, cette subdivision ou collectivité.

Article 20. Étudiants

Les paiements qu'un étudiant, un apprenti, ou un stagiaire qui est ou était, immédiatement avant de se rendre dans un État contractant, un résident de l'autre État contractant et qui séjourne dans le premier État à seule fin d'y poursuivre ses études ou sa formation, reçoit pour son entretien, son éducation ou sa formation, ne sont pas imposables dans cet État, à condition que ces paiements proviennent de sources situées en dehors de cet État.

Article 21. Professeurs et chercheurs

1. Une personne physique qui se rend dans un État contractant aux fins d'y mener des activités d'enseignement ou de recherche dans une université ou une autre institution d'éducation reconnue dans cet État contractant et qui est, ou qui était immédiatement avant ce séjour, résidente de l'autre État contractant, est exonérée de l'impôt dans le premier État contractant sur les revenus qu'elle tire de ses activités d'enseignement ou de recherche durant une période n'excédant pas deux ans à compter de la date de sa première arrivée.

2. Les dispositions du paragraphe 1 ne s'appliquent pas aux revenus d'activités de recherche si ces activités sont entreprises, non pas dans l'intérêt public, mais essentiellement dans l'intérêt particulier d'une ou de plusieurs personnes spécifiques.

Article 22. Autres revenus

1. Les éléments du revenu d'un résident d'un État contractant, d'où qu'ils proviennent, qui ne sont pas traités dans les articles précédents du présent Accord ne sont imposables que dans cet État.

2. Les dispositions du paragraphe 1 ne s'appliquent pas aux revenus, autres que les revenus provenant de biens immobiliers tels que définis au paragraphe 2 de l'article 6, lorsque le bénéficiaire de ces revenus, résident d'un État contractant, exerce dans l'autre État contractant soit une activité industrielle ou commerciale par l'intermédiaire d'un établissement stable qui y est situé, soit une profession indépendante au moyen d'une base fixe qui y est située, et que le droit ou le bien générateur des revenus s'y rattache effectivement. Dans ce cas, les dispositions de l'article 7 ou de l'article 14, selon le cas, s'appliquent.

Article 23. Fortune

1. La fortune constituée par des biens immobiliers visés à l'article 6, que possède un résident d'un État contractant et qui sont situés dans l'autre État contractant, est imposable dans cet autre État.

2. La fortune constituée par des biens mobiliers qui font partie de l'actif d'un établissement stable qu'une entreprise d'un État contractant a dans l'autre État contractant, ou par des biens mobiliers qui appartiennent à une base fixe dont un résident d'un État contractant dispose dans l'autre État contractant pour l'exercice d'une profession indépendante, est imposable dans cet autre État.

3. La fortune constituée par des navires, des aéronefs ou des véhicules routiers exploités en trafic international par une entreprise d'un État contractant, et par des biens mobiliers consacrés à l'exploitation de ces navires, aéronefs et véhicules routiers, n'est imposable que dans cet État.

4. Les autres éléments de la fortune d'un résident d'un État contractant ne sont imposables que dans cet État.

Article 24. Élimination des doubles impositions

1. Dans le cas d'un résident de la Pologne, les doubles impositions sont évitées comme suit :
   a) Lorsqu'un résident de Pologne reçoit des revenus ou possède de la fortune qui, conformément aux dispositions du présent Accord, sont imposables en Lettonie, la Pologne exempte ces revenus ou cette fortune de l'impôt, sous réserve des dispositions de l'alinéa b) du présent paragraphe. La Pologne peut, pour calculer le montant de l'impôt sur le reste des revenus ou de la fortune de ce résident, appliquer le taux d'imposition qui aurait été applicable si les revenus ou la fortune exonérés n'avaient pas été ainsi exonérés ;
   b) Lorsqu'un résident de la Pologne tire des éléments de revenu qui, en vertu des dispositions des articles 10, 11 et 12, sont imposables en Lettonie, la Pologne autorise, en déduction fiscale sur l'impôt sur les revenus de ce résident, un montant égal à l'impôt payé en Lettonie. Toutefois, cette déduction ne saurait excéder la partie de l'impôt calculé avant déduction qui correspond aux éléments du revenu provenant de Lettonie.
2. Dans le cas d'un résident de la Lettonie, les doubles impositions sont évitées comme suit :
   a) Lorsqu'un résident de Lettonie tire un revenu ou possède de la fortune qui, conformément au présent Accord, est imposable en Pologne, à moins qu'un traitement plus favorable ne soit prévu par la législation nationale, la Lettonie permet :
      i) De déduire de l'impôt sur le revenu de ce résident un montant égal à l'impôt sur le revenu payé en Pologne ;
      ii) De déduire de l'impôt sur la fortune de ce résident un montant égal à l'impôt sur la fortune payé en Pologne ;

      Dans un cas comme dans l'autre, cette déduction ne peut toutefois dépasser la partie du montant de l'impôt sur le revenu ou sur la fortune en Lettonie, tel que calculé avant que la déduction ne soit accordée, qui est imputable, selon le cas, au revenu ou à la fortune imposable en Pologne ;
   b) Aux fins des dispositions de l'alinéa a) du présent paragraphe, lorsqu'une société résidente de Lettonie reçoit des dividendes d'une société qui est résidente de Pologne, dans laquelle elle possède au moins 10 % des parts avec les pleins droits de vote, l'impôt payé en Pologne inclut non seulement l'impôt payé sur les dividendes, mais aussi l'impôt payé sur les bénéfices intrinsèques de la société qui servent au paiement des dividendes.

Article 25. Non-discrimination

1. Les ressortissants d'un État contractant ne sont soumis, dans l'autre État contractant, à aucune imposition ou obligation correspondante qui est autre ou plus lourde que celles auxquelles sont ou peuvent être assujettis les ressortissants de cet autre État qui se trouvent dans la même situation, notamment au regard de la résidence. La présente disposition s'applique aussi, nonobstant

les dispositions de l'article premier, aux personnes qui ne sont pas résidentes d'un État contractant ou des deux États contractants.

2. L'imposition d'un établissement stable qu'une entreprise d'un État contractant a dans l'autre État contractant n'est pas établie dans cet autre État d'une façon moins favorable que l'imposition des entreprises de cet autre État qui exercent la même activité. La présente disposition ne peut être interprétée comme obligeant un État contractant à accorder aux résidents de l'autre État contractant les déductions personnelles, abattements et réductions d'impôt en fonction de la situation ou des charges de famille qu'il accorde à ses propres résidents et résidentes.

3. À moins que les dispositions du paragraphe 1 de l'article 9, du paragraphe 7 de l'article 11 ou du paragraphe 6 de l'article 12 ne soient applicables, les intérêts, redevances et autres montants payés par une entreprise d'un État contractant à un résident de l'autre État contractant sont déductibles, pour la détermination des bénéfices imposables de cette entreprise, dans les mêmes conditions que s'ils avaient été payés à un résident du premier État. De même, les dettes d'une entreprise d'un État contractant envers un résident de l'autre État contractant sont déductibles, pour la détermination de la fortune imposable de cette entreprise, dans les mêmes conditions que si elles avaient été contractées envers un résident du premier État.

4. Les entreprises d'un État contractant dont le capital est en totalité ou en partie, directement ou indirectement, détenu ou contrôlé par un ou plusieurs résidents de l'autre État contractant, ne sont soumises dans le premier État à aucune imposition ou obligation correspondante qui est autre ou plus lourde que celles auxquelles sont ou pourront être assujetties les autres entreprises similaires de ce premier État.

5. Les dispositions du présent article s'appliquent, nonobstant les dispositions de l'article 2, aux impôts de toute nature ou dénomination.

Article 26. Procédure amiable

1. Lorsqu'une personne estime que les mesures prises par un État contractant ou par les deux États contractants entraînent ou entraîneront pour elle une imposition non conforme aux dispositions du présent Accord, elle peut, indépendamment des recours prévus par le droit interne de ces États, présenter son cas à l'autorité compétente de l'État contractant dont elle est résidente ou, si sa situation relève du paragraphe 1 de l'article 25, à celle de l'État contractant dont elle possède la nationalité. Le cas doit être présenté dans un délai de trois ans à compter de la première notification de la mesure entraînant une imposition non conforme aux dispositions de l'Accord.

2. L'autorité compétente s'efforce, si la requête lui paraît fondée et si elle n'est pas elle-même en mesure d'y apporter une solution satisfaisante, de résoudre le cas par voie d'accord amiable avec l'autorité compétente de l'autre État contractant, en vue d'éviter une imposition non conforme à l'Accord. Tout accord conclu sera mis en œuvre indépendamment des délais prévus par le droit interne des États contractants.

3. Les autorités compétentes des États contractants s'efforcent, par voie d'accord amiable, de résoudre les difficultés ou de dissiper les doutes auxquels peuvent donner lieu l'interprétation ou l'application de l'Accord. Elles peuvent également se concerter en vue d'éliminer les doubles impositions dans les cas non prévus par le présent Accord.

4. Les autorités compétentes des États contractants peuvent communiquer directement entre elles en vue de parvenir à un accord au sens des paragraphes précédents. S'il semble souhaitable, pour parvenir à un tel accord, qu'un échange verbal d'opinions ait lieu, celui-ci peut se dérouler par l'intermédiaire d'une commission composée de représentants des autorités compétentes des États contractants.

Article 27. Échange de renseignements

1. Les autorités compétentes des États contractants échangent les renseignements nécessaires pour appliquer les dispositions du présent Accord ou celles du droit interne des États contractants concernant les impôts visés par l'Accord, dans la mesure où l'imposition prévue n'est pas incompatible avec l'Accord. L'échange de renseignements n'est pas restreint par les dispositions de l'article premier. Les renseignements reçus par un État contractant sont tenus secrets de la même manière que les renseignements obtenus en vertu de la législation interne de cet État, et ne sont communiqués qu'aux personnes ou autorités (y compris les tribunaux et organes administratifs) concernées par l'établissement ou le recouvrement des impôts, par les procédures ou poursuites concernant ces impôts ou par les décisions sur les recours relatifs à ces impôts. Ces personnes ou autorités n'utilisent les renseignements qu'à ces fins. Elles peuvent divulguer les renseignements dans des procédures judiciaires publiques ou dans des décisions judiciaires.

2. En aucun cas les dispositions du paragraphe 1 ne peuvent être interprétées comme imposant à un État contractant l'obligation :

a) De prendre des mesures administratives dérogeant à sa propre législation et à sa pratique administrative ou à celles de l'autre État contractant ;

b) De fournir des renseignements qui ne pourraient être obtenus en vertu de sa législation ou dans le cadre de sa pratique administrative normale ou de celles de l'autre État contractant ;

c) De fournir des renseignements qui révéleraient un secret commercial, industriel, professionnel ou un procédé commercial, ou des renseignements dont la communication serait contraire à l'ordre public.

Article 28. Agents diplomatiques et consulaires

Rien dans le présent Accord ne porte atteinte aux privilèges fiscaux dont bénéficient les membres des missions diplomatiques ou des postes consulaires en vertu des règles générales du droit international ou des dispositions d'accords particuliers.

Article 29. Entrée en vigueur

1. Les Gouvernements des États contractants s'informent mutuellement de l'accomplissement des formalités constitutionnelles requises pour l'entrée en vigueur du présent Accord.

2. Le présent Accord entre en vigueur à la date de la dernière des notifications visées au paragraphe 1, et ses dispositions sont applicables :

a) En ce qui concerne les impôts retenus à la source, aux revenus perçus à partir du 1er janvier de l'année civile qui suit celle au cours de laquelle l'Accord entre en vigueur ;

b) En ce qui concerne les autres impôts sur le revenu et les impôts sur la fortune, aux impôts exigibles pour tout exercice fiscal commençant le 1er janvier de l'année civile qui suit celle au cours de laquelle l'Accord entre en vigueur, ou après cette date.

Article 30. Dénonciation

Le présent Accord demeure en vigueur tant qu'il n'a pas été dénoncé par un État contractant. Chaque État contractant peut dénoncer l'Accord par voie diplomatique avec une notification écrite envoyée au moins six mois avant la fin de chaque année civile. Dans ce cas, l'Accord cesse de produire ses effets :

a) En ce qui concerne les impôts retenus à la source, sur les revenus perçus à partir du 1er janvier de l'année civile qui suit celle au cours de laquelle cette notification est donnée ;

b) En ce qui concerne les autres impôts sur le revenu et sur la fortune, pour les impôts exigibles pour tout exercice fiscal commençant le 1er janvier de l'année civile suivant celle au cours de laquelle la notification est donnée, ou après cette date.

EN FOI DE QUOI, les soussignés, à ce dûment autorisés, ont signé le présent Accord.

FAIT à Varsovie, le 17 novembre 1993, en deux exemplaires en langue anglaise.

Pour la République de Pologne :
[MAREK BOROWSKI]

Pour la République de Lettonie :
[OJĀRS KEHRIS]

No. 54762

Poland
and
Egypt

Agreement between the Government of the Republic of Poland and the Government of the Arab Republic of Egypt for the avoidance of double taxation and the prevention of fiscal evasion with respect to taxes on income and on capital. Warsaw, 24 June 1996

Entry into force: *16 July 2001 by the exchange of the instruments of ratification, in accordance with article 29(2)*

Authentic text: *English*

Registration with the Secretariat of the United Nations: *Poland, 8 November 2017*

Pologne
et
Égypte

Accord entre le Gouvernement de la République de Pologne et le Gouvernement de la République arabe d'Égypte tendant à éviter les doubles impositions et à prévenir la fraude fiscale en matière d'impôts sur le revenu et sur la fortune. Varsovie, 24 juin 1996

Entrée en vigueur : *16 juillet 2001 par l'échange des instruments de ratification, conformément au paragraphe 2 de l'article 29*

Texte authentique : *anglais*

Enregistrement au Secrétariat de l'Organisation des Nations Unies : *Pologne, 8 novembre 2017*

[TEXT IN ENGLISH – TEXTE EN ANGLAIS]

AGREEMENT

between

THE GOVERNMENT OF THE REPUBLIC OF POLAND

and

THE GOVERNMENT OF THE ARAB REPUBLIC OF EGYPT

for the avoidance of double taxation and the prevention of fiscal evasion with respect to taxes on income and on capital

The Government of the Republic of Poland and the Government of the Arab Republic of Egypt desiring to conclude an Agreement for the avoidance of double taxation and the prevention of fiscal evasion with respect to taxes on income and capital

HAVE AGREED AS FOLLOWS:

Article 1

PERSONAL SCOPE

This Agreement shall apply to persons who are residents of one or both of the Contracting States.

Article 2

TAXES COVERED

1. This Agreement shall apply to taxes on income and on capital imposed on behalf of a Contracting State or of its political subdivisions or local authorities, irrespective of the manner in which they are levied.

2. There shall be regarded as taxes on income and on capital all taxes imposed on total income, on total capital, or on elements of income or elements of capital, including taxes on gains from the alienation of movable or immovable property, taxes on the total amounts of wages or salaries paid by enterprises, as well as taxes on capital appreciation.

3. The existing taxes to which the Agreement shall apply are in particular:

a) in the case of the Republic of Poland:

i) the personal income tax;
ii) the corporate income tax;

(hereinafter referred to as "Polish Tax")

b) in the case of the Arab Republic of Egypt:

i) the tax on income derived from immovable property (including the agriculture land tax, the building tax)
ii) the unified tax on income of individuals;
iii) the tax on corporation profits;

iv) the development duty tax;
v) supplementary taxes imposed as percentage of taxes mentioned above or otherwise;

(hereinafter referred to as "Egyptian Tax");

4. The Agreement shall apply also to any identical or substantially similar taxes which are imposed by either Contracting State after the date of signature of the Agreement in addition to, or in place of, the existing taxes. The competent authorities of the Contracting States shall notify each other of significant changes which have been made in their respective taxation laws.

Article 3

GENERAL DEFINITIONS

1. For the purposes of this Agreement, unless the context otherwise requires:

a) the term "the Republic of Poland " when used in the geographical sense means the territory of the Republic of Poland, including any area beyond its territorial waters, within which under the laws of Poland and in accordance with international law, Poland may exercise its sovereign rights over the sea bed, its subsoil and their natural resources;

b) the term "Egypt" means the Republic of Egypt and when used in a geographical sense, the term "Egypt" includes:

i) the territorial seas thereof, and

ii) the seabed and subsoil of the submarine areas adjacent to the coast thereof, but beyond the territorial sea, over which Egypt exercises sovereign rights, in accordance with international law for the purpose of exploration or exploitation of the natural resources of such areas but only to the extent that the personal property or activity to which the agreement is being applied is connected with such exploration or exploitation.

c) the terms " a Contracting State" and "the other Contracting State" mean Poland or Egypt as the context requires;

d) the term "person" includes an individual, a company and any other body of persons;

e) the term "company" means any body corporate or any entity which is treated as a body corporate for tax purposes;

f) the terms "enterprise of a Contracting State" and "enterprise of the other Contracting State" mean respectively an enterprise carried on by a resident of a Contracting State and an enterprise carried on by a resident of the other Contracting State;

g) the term "national" means all individuals possessing the nationality of a Contracting State and all legal persons, partnerships and associations deriving their status as such from the law in force in a Contracting State;

h) the term "international traffic" means any transport by a ships or aircraft operated by an enterprise which has its head office in a Contracting State, except when the ships or aircraft are operated solely between places situated in the territory of the other Contracting State.

i) the term "competent authority" means:

i) in the case of Poland the Ministry of Finance or his authorized representative;

ii) in the case of Egypt, the Minister of Finance or his authorized representative.

2. As regards the application of this Agreement by a Contracting State, any term not defined therein shall, unless the context otherwise requires, have the meaning which it has under the laws of that State concerning the taxes to which the Agreement applies.

Article 4

RESIDENT

1. For the purposes of this Agreement, the term "resident of a Contracting State" means a person who, under the laws of that State, is liable to tax therein by reason of his domicile, residence, place of management or any other criterion of a similar nature.

2. Where by a reason of the provisions of paragraph 1, an individual is a resident of both Contracting States, then his status shall be determined as follows:

a) he shall be deemed to be a resident of the State in which he has a permanent home available to him; if he has a permanent home available to him in both States, he shall be deemed to be a resident of the State in which he has his center of vital interests;

b) if the State in which he has his center of vital interests cannot be determined, or if he has not a permanent home available to him in either Contracting State, he shall be deemed to be a resident of the State in which he has an habitual abode;

c) if he has an habitual abode in both States or in neither of them, he shall be deemed to be a resident of the State of which he is a national;

d) if he is a national of both States or of neither of them, the competent authorities of the Contracting States shall settle the question by a mutual agreement.

3. Where by reason of the provisions of paragraph 1, a person other than an individual is a resident of both Contracting States, then it shall be deemed to be a resident of the State in which its place of effective management is situated.

Article 5

PERMANENT ESTABLISHMENT

1. For the purposes of this Agreement, the term " permanent establishment" means a fixed place of business through which the business of an enterprise is wholly or partly carried on:

2. The term "permanent establishment" includes especially:

a) a place of management;

b) a branch;

c) an office;

d) a factory;

e) a workshop, and

f) a mine, an oil or gas well, a quarry or any other place of extraction of natural resources,

g) a farm or a plantation,

h) premises and warehouses used as sales outlets.

3. The term "permanent establishment" likewise encompasses:

a) A building site or construction or assembly project or installation project or supervisory activities in connection therewith, but only if such site, project or activities continues for a period of more than six months, within 12 months period;

b) The furnishing of services, including consultancy services, , by an enterprise to through employees other personnel, but only where activities of that nature continue (for the same or a connected project) within the country for a period or periods aggregating more than six months within any 12 months period.

4. Notwithstanding the preceding provisions of this article the term "permanent establishment" shall be deemed not to include:

a) the use of facilities solely for the purpose of storage or display of goods or merchandise belonging to the enterprise;

b) the maintenance of a stock of goods or merchandise belonging to the enterprise solely for the purpose of storage or display;

c) the maintenance of a stock of goods or merchandise belonging to the enterprise solely for the purpose of processing by another enterprises;

d) the maintenance of a fixed place of business solely for the purpose of purchasing goods or merchandise or of collecting information, for the enterprise;

e) the maintenance of a fixed place of business solely for the purpose of carrying on, for the enterprise, any other activity of a preparatory or auxiliary character;

f) the maintenance of a fixed place of business solely for any combination of activities mentioned in subparagraphs a) to e), provided that the overall activity of the fixed place of business resulting from this combination is of a preparatory or auxiliary character.

5. Notwithstanding the provisions of paragraphs 1 and 2, where a person - other than an agent of an independent status to whom the paragraph 7 applies - is acting in a Contracting State on behalf of an enterprise of the other Contracting State, that enterprise shall be deemed to have a permanent establishment in the first-mentioned Contracting State in respect of any activities which that person undertakes for the enterprise, if such a person has and habitually exercises in that State an authority to conclude contracts in the name of the enterprise, unless the activities of such person are limited to those mentioned in paragraph 4 which, if exercised through a fixed place of business would not make this fixed place of business a permanent establishment under the provisions of that paragraph.

6. Notwithstanding the preceding provisions of this Article an insurance enterprise of a Contracting State shall-except in regard to reinsurance-be deemed to have a permanent establishment in the other Contracting State if it collects premiums in the territory of that

other State or insures risks situated therein through a person other than an agent of an independent status to whom paragraph 7 applies.

7 An enterprise of a Contracting State shall not be deemed to have a permanent establishment in the other Contracting State merely because it carries on business in that other State through a broker, general commission agent or any other agent of an independent status, provided that such persons are acting in the ordinary course of their business. However, when the activities of such an agent are devoted wholly or almost wholly on behalf of that enterprise, he will not be considered an agent of an independent status within the meaning of this paragraph.

8. The fact that a company which is a resident of a Contracting State controls or is controlled by a company which is a resident of the other Contracting State, or which carries on business in that other State (whether through a permanent establishment or otherwise), shall not of itself constitute either company a permanent establishment of the other.

Article 6

INCOME FROM IMMOVABLE PROPERTY

1. Income derived by a resident of a Contracting State from immovable property (including income from agriculture) situated in the other Contracting State, may be taxed in that other State.

2. The term "immovable property" shall have the meaning which it has under the law of the Contracting State in which the property in question is situated. The term shall in any case include property accessory to immovable property, livestock and equipment used in agriculture, rights to which the provisions of general law respecting landed property apply, usufruct of immovable property and rights to variable or fixed payments as consideration for the working of, or the right to work, mineral deposits, sources and other natural resources; ships and aircraft shall not be regarded as immovable property.

3. The provisions of paragraph 1 shall apply to income derived from the direct use, letting, or use in any other form of immovable property.

4. The provisions of paragraphs 1 and 3 of this Article, shall also apply to the income from immovable property of an enterprise and to income from immovable property used for the performance of independent personal services.

Article 7

BUSINESS PROFITS

1. The profits of an enterprise of a Contracting State shall be taxable only in that State unless the enterprise carries on business in the other Contracting State through a permanent establishment situated therein. If the enterprise carries on business as aforesaid the profits of the enterprise may be taxed in the other State but only so much of them as is attributable to that permanent establishment.

2. Subject to the provisions of paragraph 3 of this Article, where an enterprise of a Contracting State carries on business in the other Contracting State through a permanent establishment situated therein, there shall in each Contracting State be attributed to that permanent establishment the profits which it might be expected to make if it were a distinct and separate enterprise, engaged in the same or similar activities under the same or similar conditions and dealing wholly independently with the enterprise of which it is a permanent establishment.

3. In determining the profits of a permanent establishment, there shall be allowed as deductions expenses which are incurred for the purposes of the business activity of the permanent establishment, including executive and general administrative expenses so incurred, whether in the State in which the permanent establishment is situated or elsewhere.

4. Insofar as it has been customary in a Contracting State to determine the profits to be attributed to a permanent establishment on the basis of an apportionment of the total profits of

the enterprise to its various parts, nothing in paragraph 2 shall preclude that Contracting State from determining the profits to be taxed by such an apportionment as may be customary. The method of apportionment adopted shall, however be such that the result shall be in accordance with the principles contained in this Article.

5. For the purposes of the preceding paragraphs, the profits to be attributed to the permanent establishment shall be determined by the same method year by year, unless there is a good sufficient reason to the contrary.

6. Where profits include items of income which are dealt with separately in other Articles of this Agreement, then the provisions of those Articles shall not be affected by the provisions of this Article.

Article 8

INTERNATIONAL TRANSPORT

1. Profits from the operation of ships or aircraft in international traffic, shall be taxable only in the Contracting State in which the place of effective management of the enterprise is situated.

2. If the place of effective management of a shipping enterprise is aboard a ship then it shall be deemed to be situated in the Contracting State in which the home harbour of the ship is situated or if there is no such home harbour, in the Contracting State of which the operator of the ship is a resident.

3. The provisions of paragraph 1 shall also apply to profits from the participation in a pool, a joint business or an international operating agency.

Article 9

ASSOCIATED ENTERPRISES

1. Where:

a) an enterprise of a Contracting State participates directly or indirectly in the management, control or capital of an enterprise of the other Contracting State, or

b) the same persons participate directly or indirectly in the management, control or capital of an enterprise of a Contracting State and an enterprise of the other Contracting State,

and in either case conditions are made or imposed between the two enterprises in their commercial or financial relations which differ from those which would be made between independent enterprises, then any profits which would, but for those conditions, have accrued to one of the enterprises, but, by reason of those conditions, have not accrued, may be included in the profits of that enterprise and taxed accordingly.

2. Where a Contracting State includes in the profits of an enterprise of that State - and taxes accordingly - profits on which an enterprise of the other Contracting State has been charged to tax in that other State and the profits so included are profits which would have accrued to the enterprise of the first-mentioned State if the conditions made between the two enterprises had been those which would have been made between independent enterprises, then that other State shall make an appropriate adjustment to the amount of the tax charged therein on those profits. In determining such adjustment, due regard shall be had to the other provisions of this Agreement.

3. A Contracting State shall not change the profits of an enterprise in the circumstances referred to in paragraph 1 after the expire of the time limits provided in its national laws and, in any case, after five years from the end of the year in which the profits which would be subject to such change would have accrued to an enterprise of that State.

4. The provisions of paragraphs 2 and 3 shall not apply in the case of fraud, willful default or neglect.

Article 10

DIVIDENDS

1. Dividends paid by a company which is a resident of a Contracting State to a resident of the other Contracting State may be taxed in that other State.

2. However, such dividends may also be taxed in the Contracting State of which the company paying the dividends is a resident, and according to the laws of that State, but if the recipient, is the beneficial owner of the dividends the tax so charged shall not exceed 12 per cent of the gross amount of the dividends.This paragraph shall not affect the taxation of the company in respect of the profits out of which the dividends are paid.

3. The term "dividends" as used in this Article, means income from shares, mining shares, founders shares or other rights, not being debt-claims, participating in profits, as well as income from other corporate rights which is subjected to the same taxation treatment as income from shares by the laws of the State of which the company making the distribution is a resident.

4. The provisions of paragraphs 1 and 2 shall not apply if the beneficial owner of the dividends, being a resident of a Contracting State, carries on business in the other Contracting State of which the company paying the dividends is a resident, through a permanent establishment situated therein, or performs in that other State independent personal services from a fixed base situated therein, and the holding in respect of which the dividends are paid is effectively connected with such permanent establishment or fixed base. In such case the provisions of Article 7 or 14 shall apply.

5. Where a company which is a resident of a Contracting State derives profits or income from the other Contracting State, that other State may not impose any tax on the dividends paid by the company, except insofar as such dividends are paid to a resident of

that other State or insofar as the holding in respect of which the dividends are paid is effectively connected with a permanent establishment or a fixed base situated in that other State, nor subject the company's undistributed profits to a tax on the company's undistributed profits, even if the dividends paid or the undistributed profits consist wholly or partly of profits or income arising in such other State.

Article 11

INTEREST

1. Interest arising in a Contracting State and paid to a resident of the other Contracting State may be taxed in that other State.

2. However, such interest may also be taxed in the Contracting State in which it arises and according to the laws of that State, but if the recipient is the beneficial owner of the interest the tax so charged shall not exceed 12 per cent of the gross amount of the interest.

3. Notwithstanding the provisions of paragraph 2, interest arising in a Contracting State and derived by the Government of other Contracting State including local authorities thereof and the Central Bank shall be exempt from tax in the first mentioned State.

4. The term "interest" as used in this Article means income from debt-claims of every kind, whether or not secured by mortgage and whether or not carrying a right to participate in the debtor's profits, and in particular, income from government securities and income from bonds or debentures, including premiums and prizes attaching to such securities, bonds and debentures.

5. The provisions of paragraphs 1 and 2 shall not apply if the beneficial owner of the interest, being a resident of a Contracting State, carries on business in the other Contracting State in which the interest arises, through a permanent establishment situated therein or performs in that other State an independent personal services from a fixed base situated therein, and the debt-claim in respect of which

the interest is paid is effectively connected with such permanent establishment or fixed base. In such case the provisions of Article 7 or 14, as the case may be, shall apply.

6. Interest shall be deemed to arise in a Contracting State when the payer is that State itself, a political subdivision, a local authority or a resident of that State. Where however, the person paying the interest, whether he is a resident of a Contracting State or not, has in a Contracting State a permanent establishment or a fixed base in connection with which the indebtedness on which the interest is paid was incurred, and such interest is borne by such permanent establishment or fixed base, then such interest shall be deemed to arise in the State in which the permanent establishment or fixed base is situated.

7. Where, by a reason of a special relationship between the payer and the beneficial owner or between both of them and some other person, the amount of the interest, having regard to the debt-claim for which it is paid, exceeds the amount which would have been agreed upon by the payer and the beneficial owner in the absence of such relationship, the provisions of this article shall apply only to the last-mentioned amount. In such case, the excess part of the payments shall remain taxable according to the laws of each Contracting State, due regard being had to the other provisions of this Agreement.

Article 12

ROYALTIES

1. Royalties arising in a Contracting State and paid to a resident of the other Contracting State may be taxed in that other State.

2. However, such royalties may also be taxed in the Contracting State in which they arise, and according to the laws of that State, but if the recipient is the beneficial owner of the royalties the tax so charged shall not exceed 12 per cent of the gross amount of the royalties.

3. The term " royalties" as used in this article means payments of any kind as a consideration for the use of, or the right

to use, any copyright of literary, artistic or scientific work including cinematography films, and films or tapes used for radio and television broadcasting, any patent, trade mark, design or model, plan, secret formula or process, or for the use of, or the right to use, industrial, commercial, or scientific equipment or for information concerning industrial, commercial or scientific experience.

4. The provisions of paragraphs 1 and 2 shall not apply if the beneficial owner of the royalties, being a resident of a Contracting State, carries on business in the other Contracting State in which the royalties arise, through a permanent establishment situated therein, or performs in that other State independent personal services from a fixed base situated therein, and the right or property in respect of which the royalties are paid is effectively connected with such permanent establishment or fixed base. In such case the provisions of Article 7 or Article 14, as the case may be, shall apply.

5. Royalties shall be deemed to arise in a Contracting State when the payer is that State itself, a political subdivision, a local authority or a resident of that State. Where, however, the person paying the royalties, whether he is a resident of a Contracting State or not, has in a Contracting State a permanent establishment or a fixed base in connection with which the liability to pay the royalties was incurred and such royalties are borne by such permanent establishment or fixed base, then such royalties shall be deemed to arise in the State in which the permanent establishment or fixed base is situated.

6. Where, by reason of a special relationship between the payer and the beneficial owner or between both of them and some other person, the amount of the royalties, having regard to the use, right or information for which they are paid, exceeds the amount which would have been agreed upon by the payer and the beneficial owner in the absence of such relationship, the provisions of this article shall apply only to the last-mentioned amount. In such case, the excess part of the payments shall remain taxable according to the laws of each Contracting State, due regard being had to the other provisions of this Agreement.

Article 13

CAPITAL GAINS

1. Gains derived by a resident of a Contracting State from the alienation of immovable property referred to in Article 6 and situated in the other Contracting State may be taxed in that other State.

2. Gains from the alienation of movable property forming part of the business property of a permanent establishment which an enterprise of a Contracting State has in the other Contracting State or of movable property pertaining to a fixed base available to a resident of a Contracting State in the other Contracting State for the purpose of performing independent personal services, including such gains from the alienation of such a permanent establishment (alone or with the whole enterprise) or of such fixed base, may be taxed in the other State.

3. Gains from the alienation of ships or aircraft operated in international traffic, or movable property pertaining to the operation of such ships or aircraft, shall be taxable only in the Contracting State in which the place of effective management of the enterprise is situated.

4. Gains from the alienation of shares of the capital stock of a company the property of which consists directly or indirectly principally of immovable property situated in a Contracting State may be taxed in that State.

5. Gains from the alienation of any property other than that referred to in preceding paragraphs may be taxed only in the Contracting State where the income arises.

Article 14

INDEPENDENT PERSONAL SERVICES

1. Income derived by a resident of a Contracting State in respect of professional services or other activities of an independent character shall be taxable only in that State, except the following

circumstances, when such income may also be taxed in the other Contracting State:

a) if he has a fixed base regularly available to him in the other Contracting State for the purpose of performing his activities, in that case, only so much of the income as is attributable to that fixed base, may be taxed in that other Contracting State;

b) if his stay in the other Contracting State is for a period or periods amounting to or exceeding to the aggregate 183 days within a 12-months period, in that case, only so much of the income as is derived from his activities performed in that other Contracting State may be taxed in the other State.

2. The term " professional services" includes especially independent scientific, literary, artistic, educational or teaching activities, as well as the independent activities of physicians, lawyers, engineers, architects, dentists and accountants.

Article 15

DEPENDENT PERSONAL SERVICES

1. Subject to the provisions of Articles 16, 19, 20 and 21 of this Agreement, salaries, wages and other similar remuneration derived by a resident of a Contracting State in respect of an employment, shall be taxable only in that State, unless the employment is exercised in the other Contracting State. If the employment is so exercised, such remuneration as is derived therefrom may be taxed in that other State.

2. Notwithstanding the provisions of paragraph 1, remuneration derived by a resident of a Contracting State in respect of an employment exercised in the other Contracting State, shall be taxable only in the first-mentioned State if:

a) the recipient is present in the other Contracting State for a period or periods not exceeding in the aggregate 183 days within a twelve months period, and

b) the remuneration is paid by, or on behalf of, an employer who is not a resident of the other State, and

c) the remuneration is not borne by a permanent establishment or fixed base which the employer has in the other State.

3. Notwithstanding the preceding provisions of this Article, remuneration derived in respect of an employment exercised aboard a ship or aircraft operated in international traffic, may be taxed in the Contracting State in which the place of effective management of the enterprise is situated.

Article 16

DIRECTORS' FEES

1. Directors' fees and other similar payments derived by a resident of a Contracting State in his capacity as a member of the board of directors or any other similar organ of a company which is a resident of the other Contracting State, may be taxed in that other State.

2. Salaries, wages and other similar remuneration derived by a resident of a Contracting State in his capacity as an official in a top level managerial position of a company which is a resident of the other Contracting State may be taxed in that other State.

Article 17

ARTISTS AND SPORTSMEN

1. Notwithstanding the provisions of Articles 14 and 15, income derived by a resident of a Contracting State as an entertainer, such as a theater, motion picture, radio or television artist, or a musician, or as a sportsman from his personal activities

as such exercised in the other Contracting State, may be taxed in that other State.

2. Where income in respect of personal activities exercised by an entertainer or a sportsman in his capacity as such accrues not to the entertainer or sportsman himself but to another person, that income may, notwithstanding the provisions of Article 7, 14 and 15, be taxed in the Contracting State in which the activities of the entertainer or the sportsman are exercised, if that person is directly or indirectly controlled by the entertainer or sportsman.

Article 18

PENSIONS

1. Subject to the provisions of paragraph 2 of Article 19, pensions and other similar remuneration paid to a resident of a Contracting State in consideration of past employment, shall be taxable only in that State.

2.Notwithstanding the provisions of paragraph 1, pensions paid and other payments made under a public scheme which is part of the social security system of a Contracting State or a political subdivision or a local authority thereof shall be taxable only in that State.

Article 19

GOVERNMENT SERVICE

1. a) Remuneration, other than a pension, paid by a Contracting State or a political subdivision or a local authority thereof to an individual in respect of services rendered to that State or subdivision or local authority shall be taxable only in that State.

b) However, such remuneration shall be taxable only in the other Contracting State if the services are rendered in that State and the individual is a resident of that State who:

(i) is a national of that State; or

(ii) did not become a resident of that State solely for the purpose of rendering the services.

2. The provisions of Articles 15, 16 and 18 shall apply to remuneration and pensions in respect of services rendered in connection with a business carried on by a Contracting State or political subdivision or a local authority thereof.

Article 20

STUDENTS

1. Payments which a student or a business apprentice who is or was immediately before visiting Contracting State a resident of the other Contracting State and who is present in the first-mentioned State solely for the purpose of his education or training receives for the purpose of his maintenance, education or training shall not be taxed in that State, provided that such payments arise from sources outside that State.

2. Income derived by a university student or a post graduate apprentice in respect of activities exercised in the Contracting State in which he is present solely for the purpose of his education or training, shall not be taxable in that State, unless it exceeds the amount reasonably necessary for maintenance, education or training of a student or apprentice.

Article 21

PROFESSORS AND RESEARCHERS

1. An individual who visits one of the Contracting State for the purpose of teaching or engaging in research at university, collage or other recognized educational institution in that Contracting State, and who was immediately before that visit a resident of the other Contracting State, shall be exempt from tax by the first-mentioned Contracting State on remuneration for such teaching or research for period not exceeding one year from the date he first visit that State for such purpose.

2. This Article shall only apply to income from research, if such research is undertaken by the individual in the public interest, and not primarily for the benefit of some other private person or persons.

Article 22

OTHER INCOME

1. Subject to the provisions of paragraph 2, items of income of a resident of a Contracting State, wherever arising, not dealt with in the foregoing Articles of this Agreement, shall be taxable only in that State.

2. The provisions of paragraph 1 shall not apply to income, other than income from immovable property as defined in paragraph 2 of Article 6, if the recipient of such income, being a resident of a Contracting State, carries on business in the other Contracting State through a permanent establishment situated therein, or performs in that other State independent personal services from a fixed base situated therein, and the right or property in respect of which the income is paid is effectively connected with such permanent establishment or fixed base. In such case, the provisions of Article 7 or Article 14, as the case may be, shall apply.

3. However, if such income is derived by a resident of a Contracting State from sources in the other Contracting State, such income may also be taxed in the State in which it arises, and according to the law of that State.

Article 23

CAPITAL

1. Capital represented by immovable property referred to in Article 6, owned by a resident of a Contracting State and situated in the other Contracting State, may be taxed in that other State.

2. Capital represented by movable property forming part of the business property of a permanent establishment which an enterprise of a Contracting State has in the other Contracting State

or by movable property pertaining to a fixed base available to a resident of a Contracting State in the other Contracting State for the purpose of performing independent personal services, may be taxed in that other State.

3. Capital represented by ships or aircraft operated in international traffic and by movable property pertaining to the operation of such ships or aircraft, shall be taxable only in the Contracting State in which the place of effective management of the enterprise is situated.

4. All other elements of capital of a resident of a Contracting State, shall be taxable only in that State in which the capital is located.

Article 24

ELIMINATION OF DOUBLE TAXATION

1. Where a resident of Contracting State derives income or owns capital which, in accordance with the provisions of this Agreement may be taxed in the other Contracting State, the first-mentioned State shall allow as a deduction from the tax on the income or on the capital of that resident as amount equal to that income tax or to the capital tax paid in that other State. Such deduction shall not, however, exceed that part of the income tax or capital tax, as computed before the deduction is given, which is attributable, as the case may be, to the income or the capital which may be taxed in that other State.

2 Where, in accordance with any provision of this Agreement income derived or capital owned by a resident of a Contracting State is exempt from tax in that State, such State may nevertheless, in calculating the amount of tax on the remaining income or capital of such resident, take into account the exempted income or capital.

3. For the purposes of the deduction from the tax on income or on capital in a Contracting State, the tax paid in the other Contracting State shall be deemed to include the tax which is otherwise payable in that other Contracting State, but has been reduced or waived by that Contracting State under its legal provisions for tax incentives.

Article 25

NON-DISCRIMINATION

1. Nationals of a Contracting State shall not be subjected in the other Contracting State to any taxation or any requirement connected therewith, which is other or more burdensome than the taxation and connected requirements to which nationals of that other State in the same circumstances are or may be subjected.

2. The taxation on a permanent establishment which an enterprise of a Contracting State has in the other Contracting State, shall not be less favorably levied in that other State than the taxation levied on enterprises of that other State carrying on the same activities. This provision shall not be construed as obliging a Contracting State to grant to residents of the other Contracting State any personal allowances, reliefs and reductions for taxation purposes on account of civil status of family responsibilities which it grants to its own residents.

3. Except where the provisions of Article 9, paragraph 7 of Article 11, or paragraph 6 of Article 12, apply, interest, royalties and other disbursements paid by an enterprise of a Contracting State to a resident of the other Contracting State shall, for the purpose of determining the taxable profits of such enterprise, be deductible under the same conditions as if they had been paid to a resident of the first-mentioned State. Similarly, any debts of an enterprise of a Contracting State to a resident of the other Contracting State shall, for the purpose of determining the taxable capital of such enterprise, be deductible under the same conditions as if they had been contracted to a resident of the first-mentioned State.

4. Enterprises of a Contracting State, the capital of which is wholly or partly owned or controlled, directly or indirectly, by one or more residents of the other Contracting State, shall not be subjected in the first-mentioned State to any taxation or any requirement connected therewith which is more burdensome than the taxation and connected requirements to which other similar enterprises of the first-mentioned State are or may be subjected.

5. The provisions of this Article shall, notwithstanding the provisions of Article 2, apply to taxes of every kind and description.

Article 26

MUTUAL AGREEMENT PROCEDURE

1. Where a person considers that the actions of one or both of the Contracting States result or will result for him in taxation not in accordance with the provisions of this Agreement, he may, irrespective of the remedies provided by the domestic law of those States, present his case to the Competent authority of the Contracting State of which he is a resident, or if his case comes under paragraph 1 of Article 24, to that Contracting State of which he is a national. The case must be presented within three years from the first notification of the action resulting in taxation not in accordance with the provisions of the Agreement.

2. The competent authority shall endeavor, if the objection appears to it to be justified and if it is not itself able to arrive at a satisfactory solution, to resolve the case by mutual agreement with the competent authority of the other Contracting State, with a view to the avoidance of taxation which is not in accordance with this Agreement.

3. The competent authorities of the Contracting States shall endevour to resolve by mutual agreement any difficulties or doubts arising as to the interpretation or application of the Agreement. They may also consult together for the elimination of double taxation in cases not provided for in the Agreement.

4. A Contracting State shall not after the expiry of the time limits provided in its national laws and, in any case, after five years from the end of taxable period in which the income connected has accrued, increase the tax base of a resident of either of the Contracting States by including therein items of income which have also been charged to tax in the other Contracting State. This paragraph shall not apply in the case of fraud, willful default or neglect.

Article 27

EXCHANGE OF INFORMATION

1. The competent authorities of the Contracting States shall exchange such information as is necessary for carrying out the provisions of this Agreement or of the domestic laws of the Contracting State concerning taxes covered by the Agreement insofar as the taxation thereunder is not contrary to the Agreement, in particular for the prevention of fraud or evasion of such taxes. The exchange of information is not restricted by Article 1. Any information received by a Contracting State shall be treated as secret in the same manner as information obtained under the domestic laws of that State. However, if the information is originally regarded as secret in the transmitting State it shall be disclosed only to persons or authorities including courts and administrative bodies involved in the assessment or collection of, the enforcement or prosecution in respect of or the determination of appeals in relation to, the taxes which are the subject of the Agreement. Such persons or authorities shall use the information only for such purposes but may disclose the information in public court proceedings or in judicial decisions.

2. In no case shall the provisions of paragraph 1 be construed so as to impose on a Contracting State the obligation:

a) to carry out administrative measures at variance with the laws and administrative practice of that or of the other Contracting State;

b) to supply information which is not obtainable under the laws or in the normal course of the administration of that or of the other Contracting State;

c) to supply information which would disclose any trade, business, industrial, commercial or professional secret or trade process, or information, the disclosure of which would be contrary to public policy (ordre public).

Article 28

MEMBERS OF DIPLOMATIC OR CONSULAR MISSIONS

Nothing in this Agreement shall affect the fiscal privileges of members of diplomatic or consular missions under the general rules in international law or under the provisions of special agreements.

Article 29

ENTRY INTO FORCE

1. This Agreement shall be ratified and the instruments of ratification shall be exchanged at....Cairo...........................

2. The Agreement shall enter into force upon the exchange of instruments of ratification and its provisions shall have effect for the first time:

a) in respect of tax withheld at the source on amounts paid or credited on or after the first day of January in the calendar year following that in which the exchange of instruments of the ratification takes place; and

b) in respect of other taxes for taxation years beginning on or after the first day of January in the calendar year following that in which the exchange of instruments of the ratification takes place.

Article 30

TERMINATION

1. This Agreement shall continue to be in effect indefinitely but either Contracting State may, on or before June 30 in any calendar year after the years of the exchange of instruments of ratification, give to the other Contracting State notice of termination

in writing through diplomatic channels, in such event , the Agreement shall cease to have effect:

a) in respect of tax withheld at the source on amounts paid or credited on or after the first day of January in the calendar year following that in which the notice is given; and

b) in respect of other taxes for taxation years beginning on or after the first day of January in the calendar year following that in which the notice is given.

IN WITNESS WHEREOF the undersigned, duly authorized to that effect, have signed this Agreement,

Done in duplicate at...Warsaw....... in the English language. on June 24th, 1996.

For the Government of	**For the Government of**
the Republic of Poland	**the Arab Republic of Egypt**
[signature]	M. Elghareeb

[TRANSLATION IN FRENCH – TRADUCTION EN FRANÇAIS]

ACCORD ENTRE LE GOUVERNEMENT DE LA RÉPUBLIQUE DE POLOGNE ET LE GOUVERNEMENT DE LA RÉPUBLIQUE ARABE D'ÉGYPTE TENDANT À ÉVITER LES DOUBLES IMPOSITIONS ET À PRÉVENIR LA FRAUDE FISCALE EN MATIÈRE D'IMPÔTS SUR LE REVENU ET SUR LA FORTUNE

Le Gouvernement de la République de Pologne et le Gouvernement de la République arabe d'Égypte, désireux de conclure un Accord tendant à éviter les doubles impositions et à prévenir la fraude fiscale en matière d'impôts sur le revenu et sur la fortune,

Sont convenus de ce qui suit :

Article premier. Personnes visées

Le présent Accord s'applique aux personnes qui sont des résidents d'un État contractant ou des deux États contractants.

Article 2. Impôts visés

1. Le présent Accord s'applique aux impôts sur le revenu et sur la fortune perçus pour le compte d'un État contractant, de ses subdivisions politiques ou de ses collectivités locales, quel que soit le système de perception.

2. Sont considérés comme impôts sur le revenu et sur la fortune les impôts perçus sur le revenu total, sur la fortune totale, ou sur des éléments du revenu ou de la fortune, y compris les impôts sur les gains provenant de l'aliénation de biens mobiliers ou immobiliers, sur le montant global des salaires payés par les entreprises, ainsi que les impôts sur les gains en capital.

3. Les impôts actuels auxquels s'applique l'Accord sont notamment :

   a) Dans le cas de la République de Pologne :

      i) L'impôt sur le revenu des personnes physiques ;

      ii) L'impôt sur les bénéfices des sociétés ;

      (ci-après dénommés « impôt polonais ») ;

   b) Dans le cas de la République arabe d'Égypte :

      i) L'impôt sur le revenu des biens immobiliers (y compris la taxe sur les terres agricoles et la taxe sur les constructions) ;

      ii) L'impôt unifié sur le revenu des personnes physiques ;

      iii) L'impôt sur les bénéfices des sociétés ;

      iv) La taxe sur les droits d'aménagement ;

      v) Les impôts supplémentaires imposés en pourcentage des impôts mentionnés ci-dessus, ou d'une autre façon ;

      (ci-après dénommés « impôt égyptien »).

4. L'Accord s'applique également aux impôts identiques ou analogues qui seraient établis par l'un ou l'autre des États contractants après la date de signature de l'Accord, et qui s'ajouteraient aux impôts actuels ou qui les remplaceraient. Les autorités compétentes des États contractants se communiquent les modifications significatives apportées à leur législation fiscale respective.

Article 3. Définitions générales

1. Aux fins du présent Accord, à moins que le contexte n'exige une interprétation différente :
   a) Le terme « Pologne », lorsqu'il est employé dans un sens géographique, désigne le territoire de la République de Pologne, y compris toute zone située au-delà de ses eaux territoriales dans laquelle, en vertu de la législation polonaise et conformément au droit international, la Pologne peut exercer ses droits souverains sur le fond marin, son sous-sol et leurs ressources naturelles ;
   b) Le terme « Égypte » désigne la République d'Égypte et, lorsqu'il est utilisé dans un sens géographique, ce terme inclut :
      i) Ses mers territoriales ; et
      ii) Le fond marin et le sous-sol des zones sous-marines adjacentes à ses côtes, mais situées au-delà de la mer territoriale, sur lesquels l'Égypte exerce ses droits souverains, conformément au droit international, aux fins de l'exploration et de l'exploitation des ressources naturelles de ces zones, mais seulement dans la mesure où les biens ou activités auxquels le présent Accord s'applique sont liés à cette exploration ou cette exploitation ;
   c) Les expressions « un État contractant » et « l'autre État contractant » désignent, suivant le contexte, la Pologne ou l'Égypte ;
   d) Le terme « personne » comprend les personnes physiques, les sociétés et tout autre groupement de personnes ;
   e) Le terme « société » désigne toute personne morale ou toute entité qui est considérée comme une personne morale aux fins d'imposition ;
   f) Les expressions « entreprise d'un État contractant » et « entreprise de l'autre État contractant » désignent, respectivement, une entreprise exploitée par un résident d'un État contractant et une entreprise exploitée par un résident de l'autre État contractant ;
   g) Le terme « ressortissant » désigne toute personne physique possédant la nationalité d'un État contractant et toute personne morale, société de personnes ou association constituée en vertu de la législation en vigueur dans un État contractant ;
   h) L'expression « trafic international » désigne tout transport effectué par un navire ou aéronef exploité par une entreprise ayant son siège dans un État contractant, sauf lorsque le navire ou l'aéronef est exploité uniquement entre des points situés dans l'autre État contractant ;
   i) L'expression « autorité compétente » désigne :
      i) Dans le cas de la Pologne, le Ministère des finances ou son représentant autorisé ;
      ii) Dans le cas de l'Égypte, le Ministre des finances ou son représentant autorisé ;

2. Pour l'application du présent Accord par un État contractant, toute expression ou tout terme qui n'y est pas défini a, à moins que le contexte n'exige une interprétation différente, le sens que lui attribue la législation fiscale de cet État concernant les impôts auxquels s'applique l'Accord.

Article 4. Résident

1. Aux fins du présent Accord, l'expression « résident d'un État contractant » désigne toute personne qui, en vertu de la législation de cet État, est assujettie à l'impôt dans cet État en raison de son domicile, de sa résidence, de son siège de direction ou de tout autre critère de nature analogue.

2. Lorsque, selon les dispositions du paragraphe 1, une personne physique est un résident des deux États contractants, sa situation est déterminée de la manière suivante :

a) Cette personne est considérée comme un résident de l'État où elle dispose d'un foyer d'habitation permanent ; si elle dispose d'un foyer d'habitation permanent dans les deux États, elle est considérée comme un résident de l'État dans lequel se trouve le centre de ses intérêts vitaux ;

b) Si l'État où se trouve le centre des intérêts vitaux de cette personne ne peut pas être déterminé, ou si elle ne dispose d'un foyer d'habitation permanent dans aucun des États contractants, elle est considérée comme un résident de l'État où elle séjourne de façon habituelle ;

c) Si cette personne séjourne de façon habituelle dans les deux États ou si elle ne séjourne de façon habituelle dans aucun d'eux, elle est considérée comme un résident de l'État dont elle possède la nationalité ;

d) Si cette personne possède la nationalité des deux États ou si elle ne possède la nationalité d'aucun d'eux, les autorités compétentes des États contractants tranchent la question d'un commun accord.

3. Lorsque, selon les dispositions du paragraphe 1, une personne autre qu'une personne physique est un résident des deux États contractants, elle est considérée comme un résident de l'État où son siège de direction effective est situé.

Article 5. Établissement stable

1. Aux fins du présent Accord, l'expression « établissement stable » désigne une installation fixe d'affaires par l'intermédiaire de laquelle une entreprise exerce tout ou partie de son activité.

2. L'expression « établissement stable » désigne notamment :

a) Un siège de direction ;

b) Une succursale ;

c) Un bureau ;

d) Une usine ;

e) Un atelier ; et

f) Une mine, un puits de pétrole ou de gaz, une carrière ou tout autre lieu d'extraction de ressources naturelles ;

g) Une exploitation agricole ou une plantation ;

h) Des locaux et entrepôts utilisés comme points de vente.

3. L'expression « établissement stable » désigne également :

a) Un chantier, un projet de construction, de montage ou d'installation ou des activités de supervision qui y sont liées, mais seulement lorsque ce chantier, ce projet ou ces activités se poursuivent pendant plus de six mois au cours de toute période de 12 mois ;

b) La fourniture, par une entreprise, de services, y compris de services de consultants, par l'intermédiaire d'employés ou autre personnel, mais seulement lorsque des activités de cette nature se poursuivent (pour le même projet ou un projet connexe) dans le pays pendant une période ou des périodes totalisant plus de six mois au cours de toute période de 12 mois.

4. Nonobstant les dispositions précédentes du présent article, il est considéré que l'expression « établissement stable » ne comprend pas :

a) L'utilisation d'installations aux seules fins de stockage ou d'exposition de biens ou de marchandises appartenant à l'entreprise ;

b) L'exploitation d'un stock de biens ou de marchandises appartenant à l'entreprise aux seules fins de stockage ou d'exposition ;

c) L'exploitation d'un stock de biens ou de marchandises appartenant à l'entreprise aux seules fins de transformation par une autre entreprise ;

d) L'exploitation d'une installation fixe d'affaires aux seules fins d'acheter des biens ou des marchandises, ou pour réunir des informations, pour l'entreprise ;

e) L'exploitation d'une installation fixe d'affaires aux seules fins d'exercer, pour l'entreprise, toute autre activité de caractère préparatoire ou auxiliaire ;

f) L'exploitation d'une installation fixe d'affaires aux seules fins de l'exercice cumulé d'activités mentionnées aux alinéas a) à e), à condition que l'activité d'ensemble de l'installation résultant de ce cumul garde un caractère préparatoire ou auxiliaire.

5. Nonobstant les dispositions des paragraphes 1 et 2 si une personne, autre qu'un agent jouissant d'un statut indépendant auquel s'applique le paragraphe 7, agit dans un État contractant pour le compte d'une entreprise de l'autre État contractant, celle-ci est réputée avoir un établissement stable dans le premier État contractant à l'égard des activités que cette personne exerce pour l'entreprise, si cette personne dispose de pouvoirs qu'elle y exerce habituellement lui permettant de conclure des contrats au nom de l'entreprise, à moins que les activités de cette personne ne soient limitées à celles mentionnées au paragraphe 4 et qui, si elles étaient exercées par l'intermédiaire d'une installation fixe d'affaires, ne permettraient pas de considérer cette installation comme un établissement stable selon les dispositions de ce paragraphe.

6. Nonobstant les dispositions précédentes du présent article, une société d'assurances d'un État contractant est, sauf en matière de réassurance, considérée comme ayant un établissement stable dans l'autre État contractant si elle perçoit des primes sur le territoire de cet autre État ou si elle y assure contre des risques par l'intermédiaire d'une personne autre qu'un agent jouissant d'un statut indépendant auquel s'applique le paragraphe 7.

7. Une entreprise d'un État contractant n'est pas réputée avoir un établissement stable dans l'autre État contractant du seul fait qu'elle y exerce une activité par l'entremise d'un courtier, d'un commissionnaire général ou de tout autre intermédiaire jouissant d'un statut indépendant, à condition que ces personnes agissent dans le cadre ordinaire de leurs activités. Toutefois, lorsqu'il agit totalement ou presque totalement pour le compte de cette entreprise, il n'est pas considéré comme un agent jouissant d'un statut indépendant au sens du présent paragraphe.

8. Le fait qu'une société qui est un résident d'un État contractant contrôle ou est contrôlée par une société qui est un résident de l'autre État contractant ou qui y exerce son activité (que ce soit par l'intermédiaire d'un établissement stable ou non) ne suffit pas, en lui-même, à faire de l'une quelconque de ces sociétés un établissement stable de l'autre.

Article 6. Revenus immobiliers

1. Les revenus qu'un résident d'un État contractant tire de biens immobiliers (y compris les revenus des exploitations agricoles) situés dans l'autre État contractant, sont imposables dans cet autre État.

2. L'expression « biens immobiliers » a le sens que lui attribue le droit de l'État contractant où les biens en question sont situés. En tout état de cause, cette expression inclut les biens accessoires aux biens immobiliers, le cheptel et le matériel utilisé dans les exploitations agricoles, les droits auxquels s'appliquent les dispositions du droit privé concernant la propriété foncière, l'usufruit des biens immobiliers et les droits à des paiements variables ou fixes pour l'usage ou de la concession de l'usage de gisements minéraux, sources et autres sources ; les navires et aéronefs ne sont pas considérés comme des biens immobiliers.

3. Les dispositions du paragraphe 1 s'appliquent aux revenus provenant de l'exploitation directe, de la location ou de l'affermage, ou de toute autre forme d'exploitation des biens immobiliers.

4. Les dispositions des paragraphes 1 et 3 du présent article s'appliquent également aux revenus provenant des biens immobiliers d'une entreprise et à ceux provenant des biens immobiliers servant à l'exercice d'une profession indépendante.

Article 7. Bénéfices des entreprises

1. Les bénéfices d'une entreprise d'un État contractant ne sont imposables que dans cet État, à moins que l'entreprise n'exerce son activité dans l'autre État contractant par l'intermédiaire d'un établissement stable qui y est situé. Si l'entreprise exerce son activité d'une telle façon, les bénéfices de cette entreprise sont imposables dans l'autre État, mais uniquement dans la mesure où ils sont imputables à cet établissement stable.

2. Sous réserve des dispositions du paragraphe 3 du présent article, lorsqu'une entreprise d'un État contractant exerce une activité dans l'autre État contractant par l'intermédiaire d'un établissement stable qui y est situé, il est imputé audit établissement stable, dans chaque État contractant, les bénéfices qu'il aurait pu réaliser s'il avait constitué une entreprise distincte exerçant des activités identiques ou analogues dans des conditions identiques ou analogues et traitant en toute indépendance avec l'entreprise dont il constitue un établissement stable.

3. Pour déterminer les bénéfices d'un établissement stable, sont admises en déduction les dépenses relatives aux fins poursuivies par cet établissement stable, y compris les dépenses de direction et les frais généraux d'administration ainsi enregistrés, soit dans l'État où est situé cet établissement stable, soit ailleurs.

4. S'il est d'usage, dans un État contractant, de déterminer les bénéfices imputables à un établissement stable sur la base d'une répartition des bénéfices totaux de l'entreprise entre ses diverses composantes, rien dans les dispositions du paragraphe 2 n'empêche cet État contractant de déterminer les bénéfices imposables selon la répartition en usage. La méthode de répartition adoptée doit cependant être telle que le résultat obtenu soit conforme aux principes énoncés dans le présent article.

5. Aux fins des paragraphes précédents, les bénéfices à imputer à l'établissement stable sont déterminés chaque année selon la même méthode, à moins qu'il n'existe des motifs valables et suffisants de procéder autrement.

6. Lorsque les bénéfices comprennent des éléments de revenu qui sont traités séparément dans d'autres articles du présent Accord, les dispositions de ces articles ne sont pas affectées par les dispositions du présent article.

Article 8. Transport international

1. Les bénéfices provenant de l'exploitation en trafic international de navires ou d'aéronefs ne sont imposables que dans l'État contractant où le siège de direction effective de l'entreprise est situé.

2. Si le siège de direction effective d'une compagnie maritime se trouve à bord d'un navire, il est considéré comme étant situé dans l'État contractant du port d'attache de ce navire ou, à défaut de port d'attache, dans l'État contractant dont l'exploitant du navire est un résident.

3. Les dispositions du paragraphe 1 s'appliquent également aux bénéfices provenant de la participation à un consortium, à une coentreprise ou à un organisme international d'exploitation.

Article 9. Entreprises associées

1. Lorsque :

a) Une entreprise d'un État contractant participe directement ou indirectement à la direction, au contrôle ou au capital d'une entreprise de l'autre État contractant ; ou que

b) Les mêmes personnes participent directement ou indirectement à la direction, au contrôle ou au capital d'une entreprise d'un État contractant et d'une entreprise de l'autre État contractant ;

et que, dans l'un ou l'autre cas, les deux entreprises sont liées, dans leurs relations commerciales ou financières, par des conditions convenues ou imposées qui diffèrent de celles qui seraient convenues entre des entreprises indépendantes, les bénéfices qui, sans ces conditions, auraient été réalisés par l'une des entreprises, mais n'ont pu l'être à cause de ces conditions, peuvent être inclus dans les bénéfices de cette entreprise et imposés en conséquence.

2. Lorsqu'un État contractant inclut dans les bénéfices d'une entreprise de cet État (et impose en conséquence) des bénéfices sur lesquels une entreprise de l'autre État contractant a été imposée dans cet autre État et que les bénéfices ainsi inclus auraient été réalisés par l'entreprise du premier État si les conditions convenues entre les deux entreprises avaient été celles qui auraient été convenues entre des entreprises indépendantes, cet autre État procède à un ajustement approprié du montant de l'impôt perçu sur ces bénéfices. Pour déterminer cet ajustement, il est tenu compte des autres dispositions du présent Accord.

3. Un État contractant ne modifie pas les bénéfices d'une entreprise dans les cas visés au paragraphe 1 après l'expiration des délais prévus par son droit interne et, en aucun cas, après l'expiration de cinq ans à compter de la fin de l'année au cours de laquelle les bénéfices qui feraient l'objet d'une telle modification auraient été réalisés par une entreprise de cet État.

4. Les dispositions des paragraphes 2 et 3 ne s'appliquent pas en cas de fraude, d'omission volontaire ou de négligence.

Article 10. Dividendes

1. Les dividendes payés par une société qui est un résident d'un État contractant à un résident de l'autre État contractant sont imposables dans cet autre État.

2. Toutefois, ces dividendes sont également imposables dans l'État contractant dont la société qui paie les dividendes est un résident, selon la législation de cet État, mais si la personne qui reçoit les dividendes en est le bénéficiaire effectif, l'impôt ainsi établi ne peut excéder 12 % du montant brut des dividendes. Le présent paragraphe n'affecte pas l'imposition de la société au titre des bénéfices qui servent au paiement des dividendes.

3. Le terme « dividendes » tel qu'employé dans le présent article désigne les revenus provenant d'actions, y compris de parts de mines, parts de fondateurs ou autres parts bénéficiaires, à l'exception des créances, ainsi que les revenus d'autres parts sociales soumis au même régime fiscal que les revenus d'actions par la législation de l'État dont la société distributrice est un résident.

4. Les dispositions des paragraphes 1 et 2 ne s'appliquent pas lorsque le bénéficiaire effectif des dividendes, résident d'un État contractant, exerce dans l'autre État contractant dont la société qui paie les dividendes est un résident, soit une activité industrielle ou commerciale par l'intermédiaire d'un établissement stable qui y est situé, soit une profession indépendante au moyen d'une base fixe qui y est située, et que la participation génératrice des dividendes s'y rattache effectivement. Dans ce cas, les dispositions de l'article 7 ou de l'article 14 sont applicables.

5. Lorsqu'une société qui est un résident d'un État contractant tire des bénéfices ou des revenus de l'autre État contractant, cet autre État ne peut percevoir aucun impôt sur les dividendes payés par la société, sauf dans la mesure où ces dividendes sont payés à un résident de cet autre État ou dans la mesure où la participation génératrice des dividendes se rattache effectivement à un établissement stable ou à une base fixe situés dans cet autre État, ni prélever aucun impôt, au titre de l'imposition des bénéfices non distribués, sur les bénéfices non distribués de la société, même si les dividendes payés ou les bénéfices non distribués consistent en tout ou partie en bénéfices ou revenus provenant de cet autre État.

Article 11. Intérêts

1. Les intérêts provenant d'un État contractant et payés à un résident de l'autre État contractant sont imposables dans cet autre État.

2. Toutefois, ces intérêts sont également imposables dans l'État contractant d'où ils proviennent et selon la législation de cet État, mais si la personne qui reçoit les intérêts en est le bénéficiaire effectif, l'impôt ainsi établi ne peut excéder 12 % du montant brut des intérêts.

3. Nonobstant les dispositions du paragraphe 2, les intérêts provenant d'un État contractant obtenus par le Gouvernement de l'autre État contractant, y compris ses collectivités locales et la Banque centrale, sont exemptés d'impôt dans le premier État.

4. Le terme « intérêts » tel qu'employé dans le présent article désigne les revenus des créances de toute nature, assorties ou non de garanties hypothécaires ou d'une clause de participation aux bénéfices du débiteur, et notamment les revenus des fonds publics et des obligations d'emprunts, y compris les primes et lots attachés à ces titres.

5. Les dispositions des paragraphes 1 et 2 ne s'appliquent pas lorsque le bénéficiaire effectif des intérêts, résident d'un État contractant, exerce dans l'autre État contractant d'où proviennent les intérêts, soit une activité industrielle ou commerciale par l'intermédiaire d'un établissement stable

qui y est situé, soit une profession indépendante au moyen d'une base fixe qui y est située, et que la créance génératrice des intérêts se rattache effectivement à cet établissement stable ou à cette base fixe. Dans ce cas, les dispositions de l'article 7 ou de l'article 14, suivant le cas, sont applicables.

6. Les intérêts sont réputés provenir d'un État contractant lorsque le débiteur est cet État, une subdivision politique, une collectivité locale ou un résident de cet État. Toutefois, lorsque le débiteur des intérêts, qu'il soit ou non résident d'un État contractant, a dans un État contractant un établissement stable ou une base fixe pour lesquels la dette donnant lieu au paiement des intérêts a été contractée et qui supportent la charge de ces intérêts, ceux-ci sont considérés comme provenant de l'État où l'établissement stable, ou la base fixe, est situé.

7. Lorsque, en raison de relations spéciales existant entre le débiteur et le bénéficiaire effectif ou que l'un et l'autre entretiennent avec de tierces personnes, le montant des intérêts, compte tenu de la créance pour laquelle ils sont payés, excède celui dont seraient convenus le débiteur et le bénéficiaire effectif en l'absence de pareilles relations, les dispositions du présent article ne s'appliquent qu'à ce dernier montant. Dans ce cas, la partie excédentaire des paiements reste imposable selon la législation de chaque État contractant et compte tenu des autres dispositions du présent Accord.

Article 12. Redevances

1. Les redevances générées dans un État contractant et payées à un résident de l'autre État contractant sont imposables dans cet autre État.

2. Toutefois, ces redevances sont également imposables dans l'État contractant de la source et selon la législation de cet État, mais si la personne qui reçoit les redevances en est le bénéficiaire effectif, l'impôt ainsi établi ne peut excéder 12 % du montant brut des redevances.

3. Le terme « redevances » tel qu'employé dans le présent article désigne les rémunérations de toute nature payées pour l'usage ou la concession de l'usage d'un droit d'auteur sur une œuvre littéraire, artistique ou scientifique, y compris les films cinématographiques, ou les films ou bandes utilisés pour les émissions radiophoniques ou télévisées, d'un brevet, d'une marque de fabrique ou de commerce, d'un dessin ou d'un modèle, d'un plan, d'une formule ou d'un procédé secrets, ainsi que pour l'usage ou la concession de l'usage d'un équipement industriel, commercial ou scientifique et pour des informations ayant trait à une expérience acquise dans le domaine industriel, commercial ou scientifique.

4. Les dispositions des paragraphes 1 et 2 ne s'appliquent pas lorsque le bénéficiaire effectif des redevances, résident d'un État contractant, exerce dans l'autre État contractant source des redevances soit une activité industrielle et commerciale par l'intermédiaire d'un établissement stable qui y est situé, soit une profession indépendante au moyen d'une base fixe qui y est située, et que le droit ou le bien générateur des redevances s'y rattache effectivement. Dans ce cas, les dispositions de l'article 7 ou de l'article 14, suivant le cas, sont applicables.

5. Les redevances sont considérées comme provenant d'un État contractant lorsque le débiteur est cet État, une subdivision politique, une collectivité locale, ou un résident de cet État. Toutefois, lorsque le débiteur des redevances, qu'il soit résident ou non d'un État contractant, a dans un État contractant un établissement stable ou une base fixe pour lesquels l'engagement donnant lieu au paiement des redevances a été contracté et qui supportent la charge de ces redevances, celles-ci sont considérées comme provenant de l'État contractant où l'établissement stable, ou la base fixe, est situé.

6. Lorsque, en raison de relations spéciales existant entre le débiteur et le bénéficiaire effectif ou que l'un et l'autre entretiennent avec de tierces personnes, le montant des redevances, compte tenu de la prestation pour laquelle elles sont payées, excède celui dont seraient convenus le débiteur et le bénéficiaire effectif en l'absence de pareilles relations, les dispositions du présent article ne s'appliquent qu'à ce dernier montant. Dans ce cas, la partie excédentaire des paiements reste imposable selon la législation de chaque État contractant, compte tenu des autres dispositions du présent Accord.

Article 13. Gains en capital

1. Les gains qu'un résident d'un État contractant tire de l'aliénation de biens immobiliers visés à l'article 6 et situés dans l'autre État contractant sont imposables dans cet autre État.

2. Les gains provenant de l'aliénation de biens meubles faisant partie de l'actif d'un établissement stable qu'une entreprise d'un État contractant a dans l'autre État contractant, ou de biens meubles appartenant à une base fixe dont un résident d'un État contractant dispose dans l'autre État contractant pour l'exercice d'une profession indépendante, y compris de tels gains provenant de l'aliénation de cet établissement stable (seul ou avec l'ensemble de l'entreprise) ou de cette base fixe, sont imposables dans cet autre État.

3. Les gains provenant de l'aliénation de navires ou d'aéronefs exploités en trafic international ou de biens meubles affectés à l'exploitation de ces navires ou aéronefs ne sont imposables que dans l'État contractant où le siège de direction effective de l'entreprise est situé.

4. Les gains provenant de l'aliénation d'actions du capital d'une société qui tire sa valeur ou la plus grande partie de sa valeur, directement ou indirectement, de biens immobiliers situés dans un État contractant, sont imposables dans cet État.

5. Les gains provenant de l'aliénation de tous biens autres que ceux visés aux paragraphes précédents ne sont imposables que dans l'État contractant d'où proviennent les revenus.

Article 14. Professions indépendantes

1. Les revenus qu'un résident d'un État contractant tire d'une profession libérale ou d'autres activités de caractère indépendant ne sont imposables que dans cet État, sauf dans les circonstances suivantes, dans lesquelles ces revenus sont également imposables dans l'autre État contractant :

a) Si ce résident dispose de façon habituelle, dans l'autre État contractant, d'une base fixe pour l'exercice de ces activités, dans ce cas, seule la fraction des revenus imputable à ladite base fixe est imposable dans l'autre État contractant ;

b) Si son séjour dans l'autre État contractant s'étend sur une période ou plusieurs périodes d'une durée totale égale ou supérieure à 183 jours au cours de toute période de 12 mois, dans ce cas, seule la fraction des revenus provenant des activités exercées dans cet autre État contractant est imposable dans cet autre État.

2. L'expression « profession libérale » comprend notamment les activités indépendantes d'ordre scientifique, littéraire, artistique, éducatif ou pédagogique, ainsi que les activités indépendantes des médecins, avocats, ingénieurs, architectes, dentistes et comptables.

Article 15. Professions dépendantes

1. Sous réserve des dispositions des articles 16, 19, 20 et 21 du présent Accord, les salaires, traitements et autres rémunérations similaires qu'un résident d'un État contractant reçoit au titre d'un emploi salarié ne sont imposables que dans cet État, à moins que l'emploi ne soit exercé dans l'autre État contractant. Si l'emploi y est exercé, les rémunérations reçues à ce titre sont imposables dans cet autre État.

2. Nonobstant les dispositions du paragraphe 1, les rémunérations qu'un résident d'un État contractant reçoit au titre d'un emploi salarié exercé dans l'autre État contractant ne sont imposables que dans le premier État si :

a) Le bénéficiaire séjourne dans l'autre État contractant pendant une période ou des périodes n'excédant pas un total de 183 jours au cours de toute période de 12 mois ; et

b) Les rémunérations sont payées par un employeur, ou pour le compte d'un employeur, qui n'est pas un résident de l'autre État ; et

c) La charge des rémunérations n'est pas supportée par un établissement stable ou une base fixe que l'employeur a dans l'autre État.

3. Nonobstant les dispositions précédentes du présent article, les rémunérations reçues au titre d'un emploi salarié exercé à bord d'un navire ou d'un aéronef exploité en trafic international sont imposables dans l'État contractant où le siège de direction effective de l'entreprise est situé.

Article 16. Tantièmes

1. Les tantièmes et autres rémunérations similaires qu'un résident d'un État contractant reçoit en sa qualité de membre du conseil d'administration ou de tout autre organe analogue d'une société qui est un résident de l'autre État contractant sont imposables dans cet autre État.

2. Les salaires, traitements et autres rémunérations analogues qu'un résident d'un État contractant reçoit en sa qualité de dirigeant occupant un poste de direction de haut niveau dans une société qui est un résident de l'autre État contractant sont imposables dans cet autre État.

Article 17. Artistes et sportifs

1. Nonobstant les dispositions des articles 14 et 15, les revenus qu'un résident d'un État contractant tire de ses activités personnelles exercées dans l'autre État contractant en tant qu'artiste du spectacle, tel qu'un artiste de théâtre, de cinéma, de la radio ou de la télévision, ou un musicien, ou en tant que sportif, sont imposables dans cet autre État.

2. Lorsque les revenus d'activités qu'un artiste du spectacle ou un sportif exerce personnellement et en cette qualité sont attribués, non pas à l'artiste du spectacle ou au sportif lui-même, mais à une autre personne, ces revenus sont, nonobstant les dispositions des articles 7, 14 et 15, imposables dans l'État contractant où les activités de l'artiste du spectacle ou du sportif sont exercées, dans le cas où cette personne est contrôlée directement ou indirectement par l'artiste du spectacle ou le sportif.

Article 18. Pensions

1. Sous réserve des dispositions du paragraphe 2 de l'article 19, les pensions et autres rémunérations similaires payées à un résident d'un État contractant au titre d'un emploi antérieur, ne sont imposables que dans cet État.

2. Nonobstant les dispositions du paragraphe 1, les pensions payées et autres versements effectués au titre d'une caisse publique faisant partie du régime de sécurité sociale d'un État contractant ou de l'une de ses subdivisions politiques ou de ses collectivités locales ne sont imposables que dans cet État.

Article 19. Fonction publique

1. a) Les rémunérations, autres que les pensions, payées par un État contractant ou l'une de ses subdivisions politiques ou collectivités locales à une personne physique, au titre de services fournis à cet État ou à cette subdivision ou collectivité, ne sont imposables que dans cet État.

   b) Toutefois, ces rémunérations ne sont imposables que dans l'autre État contractant si les services sont fournis dans cet État et si la personne physique est un résident de cet État qui :

      i) Possède la nationalité de cet État ; ou

      ii) N'est pas devenu un résident de cet État aux seules fins de fournir ces services.

2. Les dispositions des articles 15, 16 et 18 s'appliquent aux rémunérations et aux pensions payées au titre de services fournis dans le cadre d'une activité industrielle ou commerciale exercée par un État contractant ou par l'une de ses subdivisions politiques ou collectivités locales.

Article 20. Étudiants

1. Les sommes qu'un étudiant ou un apprenti qui est ou qui était, immédiatement avant de se rendre dans un État contractant, un résident de l'autre État contractant, et qui séjourne dans le premier État à seule fin d'y poursuivre ses études ou sa formation, reçoit afin d'assurer son entretien, son éducation ou sa formation ne sont pas imposables dans cet État, à condition qu'elles proviennent de sources situées en dehors de cet État.

2. Les revenus qu'un étudiant ou un stagiaire tire d'activités exercées dans un État contractant dans lequel il séjourne aux seules fins de ses études ou de sa formation ne sont pas imposables dans cet État, sauf s'ils excèdent la somme nécessaire à son entretien, son éducation ou sa formation.

Article 21. Professeurs et chercheurs

1. Une personne physique qui se rend dans un État contractant pour y mener des activités d'enseignement ou de recherche dans une université, une faculté ou d'autres établissements d'enseignement reconnus dans cet État contractant et qui est, ou était immédiatement avant cette visite, un résident de l'autre État contractant, est exonérée d'impôt dans le premier État contractant sur les rémunérations versées au titre de ces activités d'enseignement ou de recherche pendant une période n'excédant pas un an à compter de la date de sa première visite dans cet État à cette fin.

2. Les dispositions du présent article ne s'appliquent aux revenus provenant d'activités de recherche que si ces activités sont menées par une personne physique dans l'intérêt public et non essentiellement dans l'intérêt particulier d'une personne ou de plusieurs personnes privées.

Article 22. Autres revenus

1. Sous réserve des dispositions du paragraphe 2, les éléments du revenu d'un résident d'un État contractant, d'où qu'ils proviennent, qui ne sont pas traités dans les articles précédents du présent Accord, ne sont imposables que dans cet État.

2. Les dispositions du paragraphe 1 ne s'appliquent pas aux revenus autres que les revenus provenant de biens immobiliers, tels que définis au paragraphe 2 de l'article 6, lorsque le bénéficiaire de ces revenus, résident d'un État contractant, exerce dans l'autre État contractant soit une activité industrielle ou commerciale par l'intermédiaire d'un établissement stable qui y est situé, soit une profession indépendante au moyen d'une base fixe qui y est située, et que le droit ou le bien générateur des revenus s'y rattache effectivement. Dans ce cas, les dispositions de l'article 7 ou de l'article 14, suivant le cas, sont applicables.

3. Toutefois, si ces revenus perçus par un résident d'un État contractant proviennent de sources situées dans l'autre État contractant, ils sont également imposables dans l'État d'où ils proviennent et selon la législation de cet État.

Article 23. Fortune

1. La fortune constituée par des biens immobiliers visés à l'article 6, que possède un résident d'un État contractant et qui sont situés dans l'autre État contractant, est imposable dans cet autre État.

2. La fortune constituée par des biens mobiliers faisant partie de l'actif d'un établissement stable qu'une entreprise d'un État contractant a dans l'autre État contractant, ou par des biens mobiliers appartenant à une base fixe dont un résident d'un État contractant dispose dans l'autre État contractant pour l'exercice d'une profession indépendante, est imposable dans cet autre État.

3. La fortune constituée par des navires ou des aéronefs exploités en trafic international et des biens mobiliers affectés à l'exploitation de ces navires ou aéronefs n'est imposable que dans l'État contractant où est situé le siège de direction effective de l'entreprise.

4. Tous les autres éléments de la fortune d'un résident d'un État contractant ne sont imposables que dans l'État où cette fortune est située.

Article 24. Élimination des doubles impositions

1. Lorsqu'un résident d'un État contractant perçoit des revenus ou possède une fortune qui, conformément aux dispositions des articles du présent Accord, sont imposables dans l'autre État contractant, le premier État accorde une déduction, sur l'impôt qu'il perçoit sur les revenus ou sur la fortune de ce résident, d'un montant égal à l'impôt sur les revenus ou sur la fortune payé dans cet autre État. Cette déduction ne peut toutefois excéder la fraction de l'impôt sur le revenu ou sur la fortune, calculé avant déduction, correspondant, selon le cas, aux revenus ou à la fortune imposable dans cet autre État.

2. Lorsque, conformément à une disposition quelconque du présent Accord, les revenus qu'un résident d'un État contractant reçoit ou la fortune qu'il possède sont exempts d'impôt dans cet État, cet État peut néanmoins, pour calculer le montant de l'impôt sur le reste des revenus ou de la fortune de ce résident, tenir compte des revenus ou de la fortune exemptés.

3. Aux fins de déduction de l'impôt sur les revenus ou sur la fortune dans un État contractant, l'impôt payé dans l'autre État contractant est réputé inclure l'impôt qui aurait été dû dans cet autre État contractant, mais qui a été réduit ou levé par cet État contractant en vertu de ses dispositions législatives en matière d'incitations fiscales.

Article 25. Non-discrimination

1. Les ressortissants d'un État contractant ne sont soumis, dans l'autre État contractant, à aucune imposition ou obligation correspondante qui est autre ou plus lourde que celles auxquelles sont ou pourraient être assujettis les ressortissants de cet autre État qui se trouvent dans la même situation.

2. L'imposition d'un établissement stable qu'une entreprise d'un État contractant a dans l'autre État contractant n'est pas établie dans cet autre État d'une façon moins favorable que l'imposition des entreprises de cet autre État qui exercent la même activité. La présente disposition ne peut être interprétée comme obligeant un État contractant à accorder aux résidents de l'autre État contractant les déductions personnelles, abattements et réductions d'impôt en fonction de la situation ou des charges de famille qu'il accorde à ses propres résidents.

3. À moins que les dispositions de l'article 9, du paragraphe 7 de l'article 11, ou du paragraphe 6 de l'article 12 ne soient applicables, les intérêts, redevances et autres montants payés par une entreprise d'un État contractant à un résident de l'autre État contractant sont déductibles, pour la détermination des bénéfices imposables de cette entreprise, dans les mêmes conditions que s'ils avaient été payés à un résident du premier État. De même, les dettes d'une entreprise d'un État contractant envers un résident de l'autre État contractant sont déductibles, pour la détermination de la fortune imposable de cette entreprise, dans les mêmes conditions que si elles avaient été contractées envers un résident du premier État.

4. Les entreprises d'un État contractant dont le capital est en tout ou en partie détenu ou contrôlé, directement ou indirectement, par un ou plusieurs résidents de l'autre État contractant, ne sont assujetties, dans le premier État, à aucune imposition ou obligation correspondante qui est plus lourde que celles auxquelles sont ou pourraient être assujetties d'autres entreprises similaires du premier État.

5. Les dispositions du présent article s'appliquent, nonobstant les dispositions de l'article 2, aux impôts de toute nature ou dénomination.

Article 26. Procédure amiable

1. Lorsqu'une personne estime que les mesures prises par un État contractant ou par les deux États contractants entraînent ou entraîneront pour elle une imposition non conforme aux dispositions du présent Accord elle peut, indépendamment des recours prévus par le droit interne de ces États, soumettre son cas à l'autorité compétente de l'État contractant dont elle est un résident ou, si son cas relève du paragraphe 1 de l'article 24, à celle de l'État contractant dont elle possède la nationalité. Le cas doit être présenté dans un délai de trois ans à compter de la première notification de la mesure ayant entraîné une imposition non conforme aux dispositions de l'Accord.

2. L'autorité compétente s'efforce, si la réclamation lui paraît fondée et si elle n'est pas elle-même en mesure d'y apporter une solution satisfaisante, de résoudre le cas par voie d'accord amiable avec l'autorité compétente de l'autre État contractant, en vue d'éviter une imposition non conforme au présent Accord.

3. Les autorités compétentes des États contractants s'efforcent, par voie d'accord amiable, de résoudre les difficultés ou de dissiper les doutes auxquels peuvent donner lieu l'interprétation ou l'application de l'Accord. Elles peuvent également se concerter en vue d'éliminer les doubles impositions dans les cas non prévus par le présent Accord.

4. Un État contractant ne peut augmenter la base imposable d'un résident de l'un ou l'autre État contractant, en y incluant des éléments de revenu qui ont aussi été imposés dans l'autre État contractant, après l'expiration des délais prévus par son droit interne et, en aucun cas, après l'expiration de cinq ans à compter de la fin de la période imposable au cours de laquelle les revenus en cause ont été réalisés. Le présent paragraphe ne s'applique pas en cas de fraude, d'omission volontaire ou de négligence.

Article 27. Échange de renseignements

1. Les autorités compétentes des États contractants échangent les renseignements nécessaires pour appliquer les dispositions du présent Accord ou celles du droit interne des États contractants relatif aux impôts visés par le présent Accord, dans la mesure où l'imposition prévue par ce droit n'est pas contraire aux dispositions de l'Accord, en particulier afin de prévenir la fraude et l'évasion fiscale dans le cas de ces impôts. L'échange de renseignements n'est pas restreint par les dispositions de l'article premier. Les renseignements reçus par un État contractant sont tenus secrets de la même manière que les renseignements obtenus en application du droit interne de cet État. Toutefois, si ces renseignements sont initialement considérés comme secrets dans l'État qui les transmet, ils ne sont communiqués qu'aux personnes ou autorités, y compris les tribunaux et organes administratifs, concernées par l'établissement ou le recouvrement des impôts visés par le présent Accord, par les procédures ou poursuites s'y rapportant ou par les décisions sur les recours relatifs à ces impôts. Ces personnes ou autorités n'utilisent ces renseignements qu'à ces fins, mais elles peuvent en faire état au cours d'audiences publiques de tribunaux ou dans des jugements.

2. En aucun cas les dispositions du paragraphe 1 ne peuvent être interprétées comme imposant à un État contractant l'obligation :

a) De prendre des mesures administratives dérogeant à sa législation et à sa pratique administrative ou à celles de l'autre État contractant ;

b) De fournir des renseignements qui ne pourraient être obtenus sur la base de sa législation ou dans le cadre de sa pratique administrative normale ou de celles de l'autre État contractant ;

c) De fournir des renseignements qui révéleraient un secret commercial, industriel, professionnel ou un procédé commercial ou des renseignements dont la communication serait contraire à l'ordre public.

Article 28. Membres des missions diplomatiques ou consulaires

Les dispositions du présent Accord ne portent pas atteinte aux privilèges fiscaux dont bénéficient les membres des missions diplomatiques ou consulaires en vertu des règles générales du droit international ou des dispositions d'accords particuliers.

Article 29. Entrée en vigueur

1. Le présent Accord est ratifié, et les instruments de ratification sont échangés au Caire.

2. L'Accord entre en vigueur dès l'échange des instruments de ratification et ses dispositions s'appliquent :

a) Concernant l'impôt retenu à la source, sur les montants payés ou crédités à partir du 1er janvier de l'année civile qui suit celle de l'échange des instruments de ratification ; et

b) Concernant les autres impôts, pour toute année d'imposition commençant à partir du 1er janvier de l'année civile qui suit celle de l'échange des instruments de ratification.

Article 30. Dénonciation

1. Le présent Accord reste en vigueur pour une durée indéterminée, mais chacun des États contractants peut, jusqu'au 30 juin inclus de toute année civile postérieure à l'année de l'échange des instruments de ratification, donner, par la voie diplomatique une notification écrite de dénonciation à l'autre État contractant et, dans ce cas, l'Accord cesse d'être applicable :

a) Concernant l'impôt retenu à la source, à l'égard des montants payés ou crédités à partir du 1er janvier de l'année civile qui suit celle au cours de laquelle la notification de dénonciation est donnée ; et

b) Concernant les autres impôts, pour toute année d'imposition commençant à partir du 1er janvier de l'année civile qui suit celle au cours de laquelle la notification de dénonciation est donnée.

EN FOI DE QUOI, les soussignés, à ce dûment autorisés, ont signé le présent Accord.

FAIT à Varsovie, le 24 juin 1996, en double exemplaire en langue anglaise.

Pour le Gouvernement de la République de Pologne :

[SIGNÉ]

Pour le Gouvernement de la République arabe d'Égypte :

[SIGNÉ]